An Introduction to Islam in the 21st Century

An Introduction to

ISLAM
IN THE 21ST CENTURY

Edited by

Aminah Beverly McCloud,
Scott W. Hibbard,
and Laith Saud

A John Wiley & Sons, Ltd., Publication

This edition first published 2013
© 2013 Blackwell Publishing Ltd

Blackwell Publishing was acquired by John Wiley & Sons in February 2007. Blackwell's publishing program has been merged with Wiley's global Scientific, Technical, and Medical business to form Wiley-Blackwell.

Registered Office
John Wiley & Sons, Ltd, The Atrium, Southern Gate, Chichester, West Sussex, PO19 8SQ, UK

Editorial Offices
350 Main Street, Malden, MA 02148-5020, USA
9600 Garsington Road, Oxford, OX4 2DQ, UK
The Atrium, Southern Gate, Chichester, West Sussex, PO19 8SQ, UK

For details of our global editorial offices, for customer services, and for information about how to apply for permission to reuse the copyright material in this book please see our website at www.wiley.com/wiley-blackwell.

The right of Aminah Beverly McCloud, Scott W. Hibbard, and Laith Saud to be identified as the authors of the editorial material in this work has been asserted in accordance with the UK Copyright, Designs and Patents Act 1988.

Library of Congress Cataloging-in-Publication Data

An introduction to islam in the 21st century / edited by Aminah Beverly McCloud,
Scott W. Hibbard, and Laith Saud.
      pages   cm
   Includes bibliographical references and index.
   ISBN 978-1-4051-9361-0 (hardback) – ISBN 978-1-4051-9360-3
(pbk) – ISBN 978-1-118-27392-0 (epdf) – ISBN 978-1-118-27391-3
(epub) – ISBN 978-1-118-27390-6 (emobi) – ISBN 978-1-118-27389-0
(coursesmart) – ISBN 978-1-118-27388-3 (desktop)   1. Islam.   2. Islam–21st century.
I. McCloud, Aminah Beverly, 1948–   II. Hibbard, Scott W., 1962–
III. Saud, Laith.
   BP161.3.I58 2013
   297.09′05–dc23

                                        2012042925

A catalogue record for this book is available from the British Library.

Cover image: Courtyard of Masjed-e-Jomeh Mosque, Isfahan. © Damon Lynch / Salam Stock
Cover design by Simon Levy Associates

Set in 11/13pt Dante by SPi Publisher Services, Pondicherry, India

1   2013

Brief Contents

Contents

Notes on Contributors

Scott W. Hibbard is an Associate Professor in the Department of Political Science at DePaul University, Chicago, where he teaches courses on Middle East politics, American foreign policy, and religion and politics. He received his PhD from Johns Hopkins University in 2005 and holds advanced degrees from the London School of Economics and Political Science (MSc Political Theory, 1989), and from Georgetown University (MA Liberal Studies, 1988). Hibbard also taught at the American University in Cairo, as part of a Fulbright Award, during the 2009–1010 academic year. Hibbard is the author of *Religious Politics and Secular States: Egypt, India and the United States* (2010) and co-author (with David Little) of *Islamic Activism and US Foreign Policy* (1997).

John Tofik Karam teaches in the Latin American and Latino Studies Program at DePaul University, Chicago. He studies Arab cultural practices and social networks as a window to understanding national and hemispheric orders. Revealing how Arabness reflects and shapes the neoliberal turn in Brazil, his first book, *Another Arabesque*, won awards from the Arab American National Museum (AANM) and the Brazilian Studies Association (BRASA). Karam is now working on his second book, *Redrawing US–South American Geopolitics: Arabs, the Tri-Border, and the Rise of Brazil*. Focusing on the 50-year history of Muslim Lebanese and Palestinians at a South American trinational border, this book maps how their diaspora has helped define Brazil's emergence as a hemispheric power in relation to Argentina, Paraguay, and the US, in a novel redrawing US–South American relations.

Saeed A. Khan teaches Islamic and Middle East history, politics and culture in the Department of Classical and Modern Languages, Literatures and Cultures at Wayne State University, Detroit, where he is also Fellow at the Center for the Study of Citizenship. His area of research is the identity politics of Muslim diaspora communities in the US, UK, and Europe. Publications include contributions in the volumes *Muslim Youth: Challenges, Opportunities and Expectations* (edited by Mohammad Seddon and Fauzia Ahmad, 2012); *Defining and Re-Defining*

Diaspora: From Theory to Reality (edited by Marianne David and Javier Muñoz-Basols, 2011); *Negotiating Boundaries? Identities, Sexualities, Diversities* (edited by Clare Beckett, Owen Heathcote, and Marie Macey 2007); the *Encyclopedia of Islam in the United States* (edited by Jocelyn Cesari, 2007); and the *Encyclopedia of Women and Islamic Culture* (edited by Suad Joseph, 2007). He is also on the Editorial Board of the *Journal of Islamic Law and Culture*.

Maria Louw is Associate Professor in Anthropology at the Department of Culture and Society, Aarhus University, Denmark. She has done extensive fieldwork in Central Asia – in particular Uzbekistan and Kyrgyzstan – focusing on everyday religion and secularism, morality and politics in the context of post-Soviet social change.

Babacar Mbengue is Adjunct Professor of Islamic Studies in the Islamic World Studies Program and Religious Studies Department at DePaul University, Chicago. He also teaches international relations and Islam and politics at Loyola University Chicago's Political Science Department. Dr. Mbengue's areas of focus are Islam in Africa, West African Muslim communities in the West, and the intersection between premodern Islamic business law and contemporary Islamic finance. As a former Fulbright scholar, Dr. Mbengue is fluent in four languages: Wolof, Arabic, French, and English.

Aminah Beverly McCloud is Director of the Islamic World Studies Program and Professor of Islamic Studies in the Department of Religious Studies at DePaul University, Chicago. Since 2006 she has directed the nation's only undergraduate baccalaureate program in Islamic World Studies. During her tenure at DePaul University she founded the Islam in America Conference and established the Islam in America Archives and the Journal of Islamic Law and Culture, of which she is the current Editor in Chief. In addition to her work at the university, she is author of African American Islam (1995), Questions of Faith (1999), and Transnational Muslims in American Society (2006). She is currently working on Silks: The Textures of American Muslim Women's Lives and has also authored over thirty-five articles on topics ranging from Islamic law to Muslim women. Dr. McCloud is a Fulbright Scholar, a consultant on Muslim affairs for the courts, a regular reviewer for The Oxford Journal of Islamic Studies, an advisory board member of the Institute for Social and Policy Understanding, and a participant in the Feminist Sexual Ethics Project at Brandeis University. She has received grants for her work from the Ford Foundation, the Illinois Humanities Council, the Graham Architectural Foundation, and the Lilly Foundation. She has also worked on a number of television projects on Muslims and on task forces for the East West Institute and for the Chicago Council on Foreign Affairs relating to Islam and Muslims.

Laith Saud is Visiting Assistant Professor of Religious Studies at DePaul University, Chicago. A former contributing writer for *al-Jazeera*, Mr. Saud specializes in Islamic political thought and in the analysis of the Middle East, particularly the Arab world. He has conducted fieldwork in Egypt, interviewed members of the Muslim Brotherhood, and published articles on Islamic thought and the philosophical underpinnings of the "Arab Spring." He makes regular appearances on national and international media such as NPR and PBS.

Acknowledgments

We must dedicate this text to husbands, wives, mothers, fathers, and children who, through their support, enabled us to work diligently on it. To Frederick Thaufeer al-Deen (husband of Aminah McCloud) and especially to Tara Magner (wife of Scott Hibbard), who came to the rescue of a chapter in the eleventh hour, we thank you for your love and support of this project. To Sabah and Nasrin Saud (parents of Laith Saud), we thank you for your support and grandchild care. To a wonderful young lady who will now have more time with her dad, Yasmine Saud, thanks for sharing him with us. We must also acknowledge two extremely dedicated students, Trent Carl and Richard Reinhardt, for their tireless work on and dedication to this project. Our thanks to Blackwell editorial people – Isobel Bainton and staff – who worked diligently with us on this project. We are deeply indebted to Manuela Tecusan, our copy-editor, who lost considerable sleep assisting us in bringing this text to light. Your guidance and patience have seen us through. We hope to work with you in the future. Thank all of you.

1

Introduction

AMINAH BEVERLY MCCLOUD, SCOTT W. HIBBARD,
AND LAITH SAUD

Introduction

This text provides an introduction to Islam that begins its inquiry with the social and political realities that inform 21st-century Islamic practice. It is consciously global in perspective, and seeks to capture the diversity of Islam as it manifests in different regions and countries. The book also examines the different interpretations and debates that characterize the tradition, both yesterday and today. Like other textbooks, it addresses what are traditionally seen as the historical contexts in which Islam emerged, and the core elements of the tradition. However, the book seeks to move beyond these basic topics, and address issues that are not typically covered, such as the ideas and practices of Islam in different regions and countries, the phenomenon of militancy, Islamophobia, and the teaching of Islam in the West, among other issues.

An Introduction to Islam in the 21st Century, First Edition. Edited by Aminah Beverly McCloud,
Scott W. Hibbard, and Laith Saud.
© 2013 Blackwell Publishing Ltd. Published 2013 by Blackwell Publishing Ltd.

The central theme of this book is that the image of Islam (particularly in the West) is very different from the lived reality of over a billion adherents around the globe. While Islam is often imagined as a static and monolithic tradition, the reality is quite different. Like other world religions, it is fluid, dynamic, and characterized by enormous diversity. By examining trends in different countries and regions – Asia, Africa, the Middle East, Latin America, the United States and Europe – we hope to give a more accurate depiction of Islam as a living religion.

The authors undertook this project because they believed that there is a need for a more contemporary and holistic introduction to Islam, one that captures not simply the past but also the present. Particularly given the misinformed and often misleading characterization of the Islamic tradition that appears in the mass media (and by the ever increasing number of "experts" that have emerged since the events of 9/11), such a textbook will be an important contribution to public understanding and to university-level education. The text begins with an examination of Islamic history, the central elements of the tradition, and long-standing debates. It also highlights key patterns within Islamic history that shed light upon the origins and evolution of current movements and thought. We subsequently move on to more contemporary issues and examine a plethora of countries and thinkers in order to put those issues in context.

An Introduction to Islam in the 21st Century also addresses controversial issues directly. The text examines topics including political violence and "terrorism," anti-Western sentiments, and Islamophobia. We examine these issues as realities in the contemporary world, and we inquire why they exist and look at the underlying causes that give rise to such phenomena. In doing so, we reject the common tendency to explain such issues as simply matters of culture or tradition. Rather, we look to history, patterns of political economy, and the evolution of particular ideologies to help us understand such trends. We also seek to explore contemporary forms of globalization (economic, cultural, and political), and the nature of trans-Atlantic and trans-Pacific Muslim responses to such trends. The world is changing everywhere, not least the Muslim world. Finally, we are particularly interested in what is different, if anything, in both the understanding and the articulation of Islam in the post-9/11 environment for Muslims and non-Muslims throughout the world.

Image and Reality

The image of Islam in the West is rooted in centuries of misperceptions. The vision that emerges from the early European experience with different Muslim powers is one defined by antagonism and conflict. This is a part of what fueled the Christian Crusades between the 11th and 15th centuries, but was also apparent in later periods of European development, which was similarly informed by the opposition to an external, Turkish, or Muslim "other." Throughout this early history, the Islamic world was perceived as hostile to the Christian West, and that this political rivalry was rooted in religious differences. The characterization of

Islam by the so-called Orientalist writers of the Colonial period "essentialized" the tradition – that is, identified certain characteristics of the Islamic tradition as embodying the "essence" of the religion. This constructed essence included such things as unquestioned belief, an emphasis upon the community at the expense of the individual, and an innate inclination to oppress women. This essence was perceived to be not only definitive, but unchanging.

Such assumptions are fundamentally incorrect, but, nonetheless, continue to influence popular perceptions of Islam in the modern world. Much of the Islamophobia of the post-9/11 era has seized on these ideas, and portrays Islam (and Muslims) as hostile to Western values. This hostility is seen, moreover, as being rooted in the realm of religion and ideology. The inherent bias in this characterization of Islam is evident in any number of ways, and has frequently had the effect of subjecting Muslim citizens in the West to discrimination and abuse. The portrayal of young Arabs and Muslims in the popular media and the denigration of Islam by Western politicians and public figures all contribute to a public perception of Islam as monolithic, unchanging, and largely hostile to the Enlightenment norms which inform Western civilization.

The lived reality of Islam is quite different from this stereotype, and is as varied as humanity itself. Significant Muslim populations can be found in countries across the planet. 1.54 billion Muslims in the world live on every continent as majorities and minorities. While historically centered in the Middle East and North Africa, today the largest populations are found in Asia (see Map 1.1).

This geographical diversity reflects cultural and theological differentiation as well. The practices and beliefs that are prevalent in Indonesia or Western Africa differ in significant ways from the distinctive practices of Saudi Arabia, for example. Similarly, the internal theological debates of today reflect

Sidebar 1.1   Sources for population information

Reliable sources for population information are:

- US Census Bureau, International Data Base (December 2008);
- CIA Online World Factbook (April 2009);
- Pew Forum on Religion and Public Life (October 2009).

Sidebar 1.2   Countries with the largest Muslim populations

According to statistics produced by the Pew Research Center, the list of countries with the largest Muslim populations is as follows (*Mapping The Global Muslim Population: A Report on the Size and Distribution of* the World's Muslim Population, Washington, DC: Pew Research Center, October 2009; at http://www.pewforum.org/Mapping-the-Global-Muslim-Population.aspx, accessed September 22, 2012):

Indonesia: 203 million
Pakistan: 174 million
India: 161 million
Bangladesh: 145 million
Egypt: 79 million
Nigeria: 78 million
Iran: 74 million
Turkey: 74 million
Algeria: 34 million
Morocco: 32 million
Iraq: 30 million
Sudan: 30 million
Afghanistan: 28 million
Ethiopia: 28 million
Uzbekistan: 26 million
Saudi Arabia: 25 million
Yemen: 23 million
China: 22 million
Syria: 20 million
Russia: 16 million.

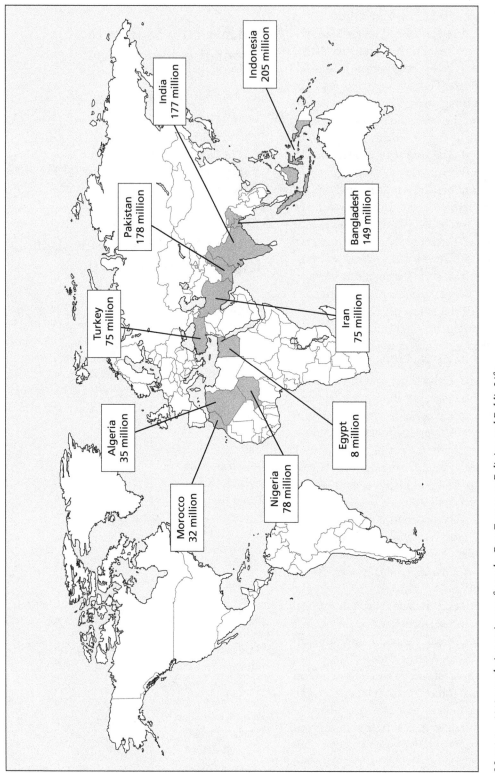

Map 1.1 2010 population estimates from the Pew Forum on Religion and Public Life.

Source: *Mapping The Global Muslim Population: A Report on the Size and Distribution of the World's Muslim Population*, Washington, DC: Pew Research Center, October 2009: 3 (at http://www.pewforum.org/Mapping-the-Global-Muslim-Population.aspx, accessed September 22, 2012).

long-standing differences within the Islamic tradition over interpretation. These debates have multiplied in the postcolonial period as different communities negotiate modernity and come to grips with a rapidly changing world. These trends have become even more relevant in the post-Cold War era, which has been characterized by a high degree of economic and political globalization. Even if there are certain principles to which all Muslims adhere – such as recognition of the underlying unity of God (in Arabic, *tawhīd*) – interpreting the meaning and implications of these principles, and applying them in a lived reality, remains a source of ongoing discussion and debate. Rather than representing a monolithic unity, then, these different approaches to understanding God's Will represent a spectrum of thought, one that is characterized by diversity, not homogeneity.

From the Muslim intellectual perspective, there are several key philosophical issues – particularly the relationship between knowledge and authority, and the related matter of defining legitimate authority – that continue to provide the structure of 21st-century conversations. In this text, clarifying these debates and discussions takes precedence over any reiteration of Islamic history which readers can find elsewhere. The following chapters expand upon these ideas.

Organization of the Text

Part I provides an overview of the basic structures and debates within Islam. It begins with a historical chapter (Chapter 2), which provides an introduction to the context in which Islam first emerged, and how the early political structures developed. This includes a brief overview of the historical eras which formed the early Islamic period; the history of the Prophet Muhammad, the rise of the early caliphates, the expansion of Islam, and subsequent dynasties. This chapter will also examine the "Gunpowder Empires," and the rise of European colonialism and its legacies.

The three chapters that follow discuss the structures, tenets, debates, and sects of the Islamic tradition with the concept of a "spectrum of belief" organized around a central belief in God. Chapter 3 will introduce the reader to fundamental elements of the Islamic worldview that have structured the discourses within the religious tradition both in the past and in the present. A key organizing belief in the Islamic tradition is *tawhīd*, the underlying unity of God and all creation. Chapter 3 examines this concept, and how it has informed all aspects of Islamic civilization. This chapter also examines the influence of the life of the Prophet Muhammad upon the evolution of the faith, and provides an overview of the basic beliefs and texts of the Islamic tradition, as well as a discussion of the five Pillars of Islam.

An issue that is central to the pedagogy (i.e. educational philosophy) of this text is that the Islamic worldview must be rendered in its full diversity and complexity. This idea is very much reflected in Chapter 4, which focuses on the evolution of Islamic doctrines, beliefs, and practices. This includes the development of Islamic law, *kalam* (dialectical theology), philosophy, ethics, and social theory. A central feature of this chapter is its elaboration on the spectrum of thought that has defined the tradition, and the tension between those who rely on tradition to guide their interpretation of the religion and those who rely on human reason to interpret Islam. It is important to remember that these aspects of the religion developed through a process of dialogue and debate; this is a community discourse and not a product of one particular religious hierarchy. These dialogues and debates, moreover, continue to this day.

In Chapter 5 we explore the fundamental features of what are commonly referred to as "Islamic sects." A number of particular "spiritual types," to use the words of Seyyed Hossein Nasr, have emerged within the tradition, which include Sunnism, Shi'ism, and the diversity therein. This chapter will examine these types via their theological and philosophical contributions to the Islamic discourse. One of the important contributions of this chapter is that it allows readers to better understand the modern implications of these debates, which are more fully discussed in subsequent chapters.

Part II examines Islam in a modern political context. This includes a discussion of the ongoing debate about the proper relationship between Islam and political authority. Although it is commonly argued that there is no distinction between religion and state in the Islamic tradition, the reality has always been otherwise. While the Prophet Muhammad embodied both religious and political authority, the relationship between the two remained unclear during the reign of the immediate successors to the Prophet. Subsequent trends in Islamic history, moreover, saw the emergence of a separation of function – and even competition – between religious authorities and their political counterparts. At issue in this ongoing competition is, on the one hand, the role of religious authorities in regulating the affairs of state, and, on the other, the danger to Islamic tradition of its overt manipulation by political leaders. An additional issue involves the reassertions of the demands for a caliphate (the single embodiment of both religious and political authority). These debates are not unique to the Islamic tradition, nor are there settled answers within Islam regarding the proper role of religion in government. Rather, in the contemporary period, the reality is defined by ongoing debates about the role of religion in the modern state.

Chapter 6 examines these issues in the context of societies that established secular political structures in the early and mid-20th century. The most influential – and extreme – example of the secular trend is Turkey, whose modern founder, Mustapha Kemal Ataturk, sought to orient a newly recreated Turkey toward Europe, not the Arab Middle East. The secular political structure in Turkey marked a sharp break from the Ottoman past. Turkey was not the only case, however. Pre-revolutionary Iran (1906–1979), Nasser's Egypt, the Arab nationalist states of Syria and Iraq, among others, were all consciously secular. At the heart of this movement was a twofold belief. On the one hand, the effort to modernize entailed a de-emphasis (or elimination) of religion, or at least its relegation to the margins of public life. These debates also have their origins in the philosophical debates of

Chapter 3, as religious structures were profoundly changed by choices made with regard to the role of religion in government. There was, however, a second feature as well: the diversity within various societies – particularly in Asia – required a greater degree of official neutrality in matters of religion. Hence, Arab Christians, South Asian Hindus, and Chinese Christians living as minorities in places such as Indonesia or India demanded a more religiously neutral political authority. This sets the stage for our later examinations.

Chapter 7 looks at states that took very different approaches to these issues, and linked religious authority to state authority in various ways. Here we review the underlying rationale – the assumption that Islam is both a religion and a state (*din wa dawla*) – and how this relationship has manifested in practice. The most well-known examples of this close affiliation of religion and state power are in Iran (which has a self-consciously theocratic political structure) and Saudi Arabia (a *sharia*-inclined state where religious officials do not actually rule). However, there are numerous other examples (and precedents), such as those found in Afghanistan, Pakistan, and Sudan (both during the 19th century Mahdist regime and under the current government). We also examine religious opposition groups that have argued for a more central role for religion in government. Sometimes religion is an opposition discourse, and sometimes it is invoked in support of the modern state. Regardless of whether religion is tied to a particular regime or to the political opposition, the arguments for a more overt role of religion in governance are similar: God is the ultimate source of sovereignty, and the Qur'an ought to provide the basis for legislation, law, and public order.

It is important to recognize that the distinction between "Islamic states" (or what we will refer to as "traditionalist states") and "secular states" is not always sharp or clearly defined. Secular governments regularly invoke religion as a basis of popular support even if they remain largely neutral in theological matters. More to the point, however, is that the debates over the proper interpretation of religion in public life, and the proper relationship between religious and state authority, are never resolved in a permanent manner, in much the same way as the underlying philosophical debates endure. These issues remain a source of continuing debate and periodically recur in the context of modern politics. Our discussion of religious and political authority and their often contentious dynamics leads us to a discussion of political violence as one means of promoting a narrow religious vision by a vocal minority. To these conversations are added the reactions, both within the Islamic community and from outside.

Chapter 8 examines the question of Muslim minorities living in the West. At issue are the various challenges associated with integrating into Western society while retaining one's cultural and religious heritage. On the one hand, there is an understandable resistance among Muslim minorities to assimilate into a largely secular culture, while on the other, there is an often visceral opposition within majority communities to tolerate in a non-discriminatory manner minority populations in their midst. This is not a new challenge, but is an enduring feature of human history. What makes the issue of Muslim minorities living in the West so unique in the 21st century is the high level of emigration that has transpired since the end of World War II. The resulting diversity within Western societies has created numerous issues for both the host populations and the migrant communities. This chapter examines these challenges in four countries with the largest Muslim communities – the United States, the United Kingdom, France, and Germany – and the different ways in which each have sought to deal with the minorities in their midst.

Part III focuses on regional examinations. The next four chapters offer a survey of Muslims in different regions and continents. These regions were selected, in large measure, by their significant history and size of Muslim populations. They were also selected to provide a glimpse into the diversity of Islam culture and traditions. Chapter 9 begins this exploration in Africa. It looks at the penetration, expansion, and assimilation of Islam on the African continent, with a particular focus on the regions south of the Sahara desert. This review sheds light on the diversity of the religious experience, the historical context and, ultimately, the emergence of powerful Muslim states. The chapter also looks at the development of important movements of Islamic reform during the colonial and postcolonial eras. This helps to shed light on both the past and present traits of Islam in Africa, often neglected in the study of Islam as a global phenomenon.

Chapter 10 looks at Islam within the countries of South Asia: India, Pakistan, Bangladesh, and Sri Lanka. Out of the roughly 1.6 billion who live on the subcontinent, nearly a third are Muslim. This gives the subcontinent one of the largest Muslim populations in the world. Like the other regions in Asia, Islam first arrived via commercial traders in the 8th century, though its influence became most pronounced in later centuries, particularly with the rise of the Mughal Empire in the 16th century. While the Mughals were eclipsed by British colonial rule in the mid-19th century, Islam has nonetheless remained a powerful cultural and political force in the region. It has given rise to a variety of political movements, and various South Asian thinkers have greatly influenced popular understandings of Islam throughout the world. The South Asian experience of Islam has also been characterized by a great deal of diversity. This is due, in part, to the historical circumstances, and the fact that India's Muslims are a minority population, while across the border, Islam is the official state religion in Pakistan. In short, Islamic thought and practice shape the lives of millions of people throughout the region, though this occurs in a variety of diverse ways.

In Chapter 11 we explore Islam in the much understudied regions of the former Soviet Republics. This area is home to more than 50 million Muslims. Scholars have previously only focused on the non-Muslim peoples, presuming that Islam had been relegated to extinction by decades of policies of eradication. This chapter provides a look at the Islamic revival present in the region.

The focus of Chapter 12 turns our attention to the experience of Islam in Indonesia and Malaysia. Indonesia is, of course, the nation with the largest Muslim population on the planet, and would be of interest for that reason alone. But it is also of interest because of its democratic governing structures, its pluralist vision of Islam, and its model of economic development. While Indonesia is not immune to the economic, political, and social pressures endemic in the region, the country has, nonetheless, navigated these challenges in an innovative manner. Similarly, in Malaysia, the diversity of the population – with numerous Hindus, ethnic Chinese Christians, and other populations – has limited the appeal (and viability) of an exclusive religious politics. The chapter subsequently looks at the politics, culture, and development of these societies and how they were shaped by – and helped to shape – Islam in the region.

In Chapter 13, we examine the Muslim histories in Latin America and the Caribbean. Though not traditionally considered a Muslim region, the history of Muslims in this area goes back over 500 years. Individuals of Moorish descent from both the Iberian Peninsula and North Africa arrived along with Spanish colonization. Though many came as slaves, they nonetheless brought with them their religion, tradition, and culture. Subsequent migrations came in later centuries, and have contributed to a distinct sensibility of the region. This chapter helps to reveal the global breadth of Islam and its indelible but often overlooked role in shaping the culture, architecture, and life in Latin America and the Caribbean.

Part IV, the final part of the textbook, examines Islam in a globalized world. Chapter 14 takes up this topic by viewing the challenges of teaching Islam in the post-9/11 West. Given the politicization of Islam and the involvement of Western governments in Iraq, Afghanistan, the Horn of Africa, and other Muslim countries, providing unbiased information on the diversity of the Islamic experience has proved contentious and difficult. A central part of the issue is the lack of qualified instructors, as well as the unevenness of knowledge. A second feature is the atmosphere in which instructors are teaching. The politicized nature of the course content and the classroom make frank and open conversations difficult at best. Chapter 14 seeks to offer a positive alternative for teaching about Islam in the 21st century. It begins by examining the "ecosystem" of the classroom – the relationship between the environment, the students, and the teachers – and how this can be reconstructed in a more open manner. Within the Islamic tradition, knowledge is produced through dialogue. Hence, a truly open educational environment encourages not just teaching, but discourse. It also demands a nuanced appreciation of Islam – by recognizing the spectrum of thought – as well as a civic (and civil) approach to the subject.

What makes the teaching of Islam particularly difficult in the contemporary context is the question of violence, terrorism, and extremism. Chapter 15 addresses these issues directly. It begins with a recognition that the connections between religion and violence can been found in all traditions. This is what Scott Appleby has referred to as the "ambivalence of the sacred," where religion serves as both a warrant for violent action and a call for peace and tolerance. While the core ethical teachings of Islam concern justice and peace, Islamist organizations such as al-Qaeda have nonetheless resorted to violence as a means of pursuing their political ends. This has contributed to a perception in the West that Islam (as a world religion) has a unique predisposition toward violence. Ironically, the moral judgment of the West with regard to the question of violence by Islamic activists is itself highly ambivalent. When the US supported the *mujahidin* (holy warriors) fighting the Soviet Union in Afghanistan during the Cold War, they were seen as heroic and led Ronald Reagan to deem them to be the "moral equivalent of America's Founding Fathers." Nonetheless, it is the memories of the 1979 Iranian Revolution, and, later, the first Gulf War, that shaped a view of Islam as hostile to the West.

The attacks of September 11, 2001 reinforced this perception. Although it is obvious that over 1 billion people did not participate in these attacks, Western commentators commonly blame the entirety of Islam for the violence. Moreover, Western governmental actions are a central part of the conflicts that plague the Middle East, South Asia, and Africa. The United States has fought two wars with Iraq, imposed sanctions on Iran and Iraq, supported autocratic regimes throughout these regions, and otherwise promoted policies that antagonize populations throughout the Muslim world. These policies – and the politics behind them – are the real source of anti-American sentiment, and have their roots in America's post-World War II foreign policies. The media depiction of 9/11 and the subsequent US invasion of Afghanistan and Iraq as part of a new trend is, thus, misleading. Rather, it is simply another chapter in a long history of Western interaction in the region. The media coverage of recent events and its anti-Islam biases, however, is somewhat new. The conscious effort of certain commentators and analysts to stigmatize Islam and Muslims has greatly influence popular media, and has contributed to the Islamophobia that has emerged in recent years. Not only is this trend troubling for minority populations, but it should be of concern to all Americans. The denigration of Muslim Americans (and of Islam) undermines such key American values as the freedom of religion, equal treatment of peoples, and the belief that we, as a people, judge others by the content of their character, not the color of their skin.

Discussion Questions

1   How and why did Islam spread to so many different areas and regions?
2   Are other religious traditions characterized by the same kind of diversity of peoples and practices? How does this shape the experience of religion by people in different regions with different cultural practices?
3   How does the discussion above fit with your presuppositions about Islam?

Part I

Overview
Islam: Image and Reality

2

The Historical Context

AMINAH BEVERLY MCCLOUD, SCOTT W. HIBBARD,
AND LAITH SAUD

An Introduction to Islam in the 21st Century, First Edition. Edited by Aminah Beverly McCloud,
Scott W. Hibbard, and Laith Saud.
© 2013 Blackwell Publishing Ltd. Published 2013 by Blackwell Publishing Ltd.

Introduction

The present chapter provides a brief overview of the historical context in which Islam emerged and evolved as a religious tradition. The chapter begins with an examination of pre-Islamic Arabia and of the social and political circumstances in which Prophet Muhammad received his message. It will then review the events and people associated with the establishment of the faith and the rise of a political order associated with the message of Islam. This early period of Islamic history was defined, first and foremost, by the Prophet's – Muhammad ibn Abdullah's – experience of Revelation and by the subsequent formation of an early community, transformed in faith by the message of the Qur'an. This was also a time that was shaped by the collapse of neighboring empires and the dramatic expansion of the young Islamic community across North Africa into the Iberian Peninsula and north and east into the Levant and Byzantine heartland. Ultimately Islam would spread into Southeastern Europe and well into Central Asia, India, Thailand, and Java.

The story of Islam is in essence a story of the effect that a profound revelation – and a new prophet – had upon the world. Although originating in the Arabian Peninsula, Islam would make its influence felt far beyond its early territorial boundaries. Central to this history is a dramatic and ongoing narrative of different communities struggling to interpret the Revelation, while synthesizing their indigenous cultures with the Islamic ethos. The result has been a diversity of religious experiences and practices that, combined, mark Islam as a world religion. Although the ethical values and worldview of the Qur'an are immutable, the particular manifestations and practices of Islam differ across regions and cultures. As Islam took root in areas outside of the Arab world, local populations made Islam their own, keeping the core teachings intact but providing Islam with the unique coloring of their own indigenous worlds. A key feature of this history, then, is the relationship between the Arab center and Muslims in other lands with respect to the control of religious interpretation and of the institutions that have come to define the tradition.

Another key feature is the relationship of Islam to politics. Many have argued that Islam is both a religion and a state (*din wa dawla*) and has never known the separation between religion and politics. History, however, reveals a much more complex – and often contentious – relationship, wherein religious knowledge (and authority) came to lie within the *ulamā* – the community of learned scholars of Islam – and political power remained with the sultan or ruler. The changing nature of these relationships is one significant aspect of the premodern history of Islam. All of this began, of course, with the Revelation of the Prophet and the political turmoil that this event generated within pre-Islamic Arabia. For the purposes of this opening historical overview, then, it is important to examine the politics surrounding the emergence of the early Islamic community and the social and political forces that helped to shape the religion's dramatic expansion. This chapter will also examine the early caliphate and the rise and fall of subsequent dynasties: the Umayyad, the Abbasid, and the so-called "gunpowder" empires. Subsequent chapters – particularly Chapters 6 and 7 – will pick up on this narrative and examine the continuing evolution of the politics and governing structures common to the Muslim world. The historical background provided here is, then, important because it helps to put the subsequent chapters into context, and also because it offers a glimpse into a fascinating – and truly momentous – period in human history.

Pre-Islamic Arabia: Culture, Commerce, and Contexts

Islam emerged in Arabia – the vast and desolate peninsula of Southwest Asia. However, to speak of Arabia without discussing the entire region to which it belongs is not to say much. Today, in the West, we refer to this region as the Middle East or the Near East. Situated at the center of the three major continents of the so-called "Old World" – what we know as Africa, Asia, and Europe – the Near East was, and in many ways remains, the nexus of civilization. The peoples of this region have been witness to many civilizations of varying climes. But, of course, the region also produced what we consider to be the "first" civilizations.

Egypt and Mesopotamia (present-day Iraq) constitute the space where the first elements considered to be essential to "civilization" emerged: law, statehood, religious doctrines and symbols, as well as arts, crafts, textile production, and other things relevant to material life. From the laws of Hammurabi in Mesopotamia to the pyramids of the Egyptian pharaohs, the peoples and rulers of these two lands sought to create permanent structures that would provide stable political and social orders. In doing so they fostered an environment that allowed for the development of an advanced culture.

It does this region little justice to summarize its long history in just a few paragraphs. However, one can say that what distinguished Mesopotamian and Egyptian life from other forms was the emergence of an "urban" life, as we may call it. That is, the peoples of these civilizations inhabited areas of concentrated settlement. They did not live as nomads, although many others still did. We call this type of lifestyle "sedentary," as opposed to the pastoral or nomadic. Moreover, the relationship between sedentary and nomadic peoples is one of the major themes in Near Eastern history up until very recent times.

Nomads or pastoralists, generally speaking, continuously moved between areas in order to feed their domesticated animals (such as sheep or camels). This type of lifestyle was not conducive to the accumulation of large amounts of surplus goods: the less you possessed, the lighter and quicker on your feet you remained.

Sidebar 2.1   Ibn Khaldun

Ibn Khaldun (d. 1406) was a 14th-century Muslim thinker from North Africa, of Berber or (more likely) Arab ancestry. Ibn Khaldun committed himself to writing a history of the successive dynasties that had ruled in the region, and in the process he "invented" sociology: he was the first thinker actually to tie cultural institutions to socio-economic conditions. At the center of his analysis was the relationship between nomadic and sedentary peoples.

Sedentary populations, on the other hand, remained in one place, which made the accumulation of surplus goods not only possible, but desirable. Thus, with time, we begin to see class distinctions emerge among urban populations. Classes were often regarded as "castes" necessary for social life. The world was made of peasants, artisans, merchants, religious scribes, and rulers; and the complementarity of their roles produced social life. It is difficult to conceive of art, textiles, or market-type trade outside of urbanized life.

Whereas sedentary peoples produced the items natural to a settled life, organizing them under the auspices of "the state," nomads were more independent of hierarchal structures. They were more egalitarian. But, more importantly for our purposes, their mobile lifestyle and excellent riding skills made them apt warriors. At times nomads needed the urban market to sell whatever excess milk, meat, or fur they may have produced. At other times they would invade the cities, which were not well equipped either culturally or temperamentally to fight off the invaders. During such periods the nomads would establish themselves as the new rulers, would strike new coins in their own names, would establish new dynasties, and would patronize new arts. In short, they would become settled and, in time, as they lost touch with their pastoral roots, a new confederation of tribes would invade them – and the process would start all over again.

Sidebar 2.2   Zoroastrianism

Zoroastrianism is an ancient religion that espoused ideas common to the Abrahamic faiths of today. Its adherents believed in good and evil, and (as a corollary) in moral accountability.

Islam was brought to the people of Arabia in the 7th century by a man named Muhammad ibn Abdullah. We will present his life in the following chapter; just now we will discuss Arabia's relation to the region during his period. At the time of Muhammad's birth Arabia was a peninsula peopled largely by nomads and located just south of two major empires characterized by a sophisticated urban life. To the northwest lay the Byzantine Empire, with its capital in Constantinople. Christian by religion and Greek in culture, this empire rivaled the Sassanian Empire to the east. The Sassanian (or Persian) Empire, in its turn, was centered around the Iranian Plateau; its capital Ctesiphon was in present-day Iraq. It had a Zoroastrian religion and was Persian in culture. In between the two lies the region known as the Fertile Crescent. Semitic peoples who spoke Aramaic and Arabic and gravitated politically toward one empire or the other largely inhabited this area. The populations of the Fertile Crescent were predominantly Christian (interspersed with some pockets of Jews); but, importantly, their interpretation of Christianity was at odds with Byzantine orthodoxy. Hence, at times they were persecuted by the state for holding heterodox views. Lastly, the Arabs of Arabia (obviously a Semitic population in terms of their linguistic heritage) were for the most part pagan, living among other Arabic-speaking Jews and Christians.

The rise of Islam must be seen against this backdrop. The Arabs were aware of monotheistic traditions; many of them even subscribed to Judaism or Christianity.

But most of them were pagans. They identified in the cosmos the irreversible flow of time, of which they had an essentially atheistic–agnostic conception. Yet within this view of time the various Arab tribes expressed fidelity to a whole host of different gods and deities, which were represented by statues and by various natural objects like the stars or the moon. The polytheistic practices of the Arabs corresponded to the tribal politics of Arabian society, wherein many tribes felt beholden only to their own divine symbols and felt at odds with other tribes. With the rise of Islam, the Arabs were able to transcend their tribal differences and formed a confederation based on a unified message and goal.

As mentioned earlier, the relationship between nomadic forms of life and settlements is one of the great themes in Near Eastern history. And in many ways the Islamic conquests exemplify this theme. With a newfound unity and the confidence of faith, the Arabs came out of the desert and conquered the settled lands of the Fertile Crescent. And, although they certainly did *not* spread their faith by the sword (in fact it is against Islamic law to compel others in matters of conscience), the establishment of the Islamic polity, what would become the seed of Islamic civilization, was done through the might and skill of Arab tribesmen. Since this is only a brief overview of the historical context, let us examine the early caliphate period and some of the major themes of the early Islamic conquests.

The Early Caliphates and the Spread of Islam

As will be discussed in greater detail in the next chapter, Prophet Muhammad received a series of revelations that would ultimately come to form the teachings of the central Islamic holy text, the Qur'an. A group of converts to the new religion formed around the Prophet and his teachings. Many of the earliest converts were Muhammad's kin or other members of his tribe, the Quraysh. His revelation, as will be discussed later, was perceived as threatening to the existing social order, and, as a result of the subsequent persecution, the early Muslim community was forced to relocate in Medina (originally Yathrib). It was there that the community was able to create an early Islamic state, or political order, with Muhammad at its head. At this point Muhammad not only acted as a prophet but, to use Montgomery Watt's (1961) words, he became a statesman. After the defeat of Muhammad's former rivals in Mecca, the Islamic community began a process of expansion that would ultimately take the message of Islam to the far corners of the world.

By the time of the Prophet's death in 632 CE, all of Arabia had heard of him. A large part of its population was paying tribute to Medina, and a substantial part was under its direct rule. More to the point, the early Muslim community had made incursions to the north against the outposts of the Byzantine Empire in the desert. It is in this context that Abu Bakr succeeded the Prophet as the head of both the religious and the political community and came to be known as the first "caliph" (*khalīfah*, "successor"). There is much to be said about how Abu Bakr succeeded Muhammad, but for now we will focus our sights on the administration of the Arabs under his rule. First, Abu Bakr, the Prophet's best friend, was concerned with the phenomenon of *riddah* ("relapse," "apostasy") and engaged in a series of Wars of Apostasy – the Ridda Wars (632–633). Some of the Arab tribes no longer felt obligated to remain united with the new Islamic polity after Muhammad's death. Abu Bakr felt that these defections were a threat to the monotheism of Islam and would pull the Arabs back into a state of ignorance. Se he chose to fight them with vigor. Once he succeeded in defeating the defecting tribes, he made other administrative decisions, which would affect the entire region.

North of Arabia lay the provinces of the two empires mentioned above, which had just spent decades at war with each other: the Byzantine Empire had just wrestled back its provinces of Syria, Palestine, and Egypt from the Persian Empire of the Sassanians. Abu Bakr sent two armies, one to Syria and the other to Iraq, but was not able to see their success; this was to be his successor's privilege. Before his death, Abu Bakr appointed Umar to succeed him as second caliph. Umar ruled from 634 to 644 CE. His tenure is known, in part, for the fact that he established institutions that greatly affected the direction of the new Islamic Empire and the religion itself, both its Sunni and Shi'i branch. Umar's first order of business was to send reinforcements to the Muslims fighting in Syria; these reinforcements met the Byzantine troups at the Yarmuk River (636 CE) in the Jordan Valley and routed them, leaving the province of Syria open to the Muslim army. The other decisive battle occurred in the same year on the Persian front, at Qadissiyya; not only did it result in a crushing defeat of the Persians, but it also marked the beginning of the decay and fall of the Sassanian Empire. It was also under Umar that Muslim forces were able to penetrate North Africa; the conquest of Egypt occurred in 640/1 CE.

A number of very important institutions were created during Umar's reign. The first of these was the *misr* (plural *amsar*), a type of military encampment or settlement built in a newly conquered province. The most important *amsar* were Fustat (the future Cairo) in Egypt and Kufa and Basra in Iraq. These areas housed the governor and the military. Each *misr* was divided into quarters that hosted different tribes – not only the fighting men, but also their women and children. *Amsar* were staging areas for further conquests.

The next notable institution related to Umar's name was that of the *diwan* ("registry"), which organized the division of spoils. In view of the large amounts of booty taken from the newly conquered lands, Umar sought to create a system whereby the state would give a monthly stipend to its members. The state also patronized notables and relatives of the Prophet. Following his example, Umar continued the practice of having the state receive one fifth of the spoils for the purpose of sustaining the poor and of providing similar services. Umar's rule was brought to an abrupt end when he was stabbed by a disgruntled Persian slave. However, before he died, Umar instituted the elective council (Shura) from which the next caliph was to be chosen. The council was made up of six members, all of whom were early converts: 'Ali ibn Abi Talib, Uthman ibn Affan, Talhah ibn Abdallah, al-Zubayr ibn Awwam, Sa'd ibn Abi Waqqas, and Abd al-Rahman ibn Awf. The last member removed himself from the ranks of potential caliphs and was given the privilege of being the "king-maker"; eventually he chose Uthman ibn Affan.

Uthman ruled from 644 to 656 CE. It was during his reign that the standardization of the Qur'an took place. The vast majority of the early Islamic conquests were completed under the caliphates of Umar and Uthman. By the end of Uthman's reign Muslims ruled over the whole of the former Sassanian Empire, had pushed the Byzantines into Anatolia, and had spread across all of North Africa (see Map 2.1). The quick and impressive defeats of the Byzantine and Sassanian Empire by the Arabs have been the subject of great historical interest. Some of this success was facilitated by the ethnic and cultural proximity between the Arabs of Arabia and those of Iraq and Syria. In addition, Muslim attitudes toward Jews and Christians played an important role. Whereas Nestorian and monophysite Christians, not to mention Jews, were subject to discrimination by the Byzantine state, Islamic doctrine was much more tolerant in this respect. So long as *dhimmi* – the people of the *dhimma*, that is, protected non-Muslim religious communities – paid their required taxes, they were free to practice their faiths freely, and, above all, the state did not interfere with their religious doctrines.

After being assassinated by disgruntled troops from the provinces, Uthman was succeeded by 'Ali, the cousin and son-in-law of Prophet Muhammad. The confrontation, and the assassination, set the stage for the first Civil War (*fitna*). 'Ali's reign as fourth caliph lasted from 656 to 661 CE, and encompassed the whole period of that civil war. 'Ali's first order of business was to try to reconcile the various contending factions. Mu'awiya ibn Abi Sufyan demanded nonetheless that the killers of his cousin Uthman be brought to justice. The tension between Mu'awiya's clan and 'Ali's clan plays an important part in early Islamic history and will be addressed at greater length in subsequent chapters. But, in short, the Umayyads represented the traditional elites of the Quraysh in Mecca, while 'Ali's clan, the Hashim, was the clan of the Prophet. It is worth noting that the Umayyads were for a long time Islam's most bitter opponents. In the meanwhile, before 'Ali could go to Syria to face Mu'awiya, he was told that two of the men from the Shura, Talha and al-Zubayr, and a widow of the Prophet, Aisha, were on their way to Basra to contest 'Ali as well. 'Ali left for Iraq and arrived in Kufa; in this way Medina lost its status as a capital for ever.

The issues of the first Civil War centered on leadership of the community: Who has the right to elect the caliph? When someone has been elected, do the people have a right to remove the caliph if he becomes corrupt – and, if so, how? The first issue was decided by the power struggles that ensued during the Civil War; but the second was never resolved. We will expand upon this topic in greater detail later, because it will enlighten us as to the foundation of the Sunni–Shi'a split within Islam. For the purpose of our basic history, though, it is sufficient to note here that a series of events ensued that saw the assassination of 'Ali, the rightful caliph, and the rise of Mu'awiya, the powerful governor of Syria, as the new caliph. From this point on the caliphate would be forever changed and turned into dynastic rule. The first of the dynasties to be mentioned is that of the Umayyads.

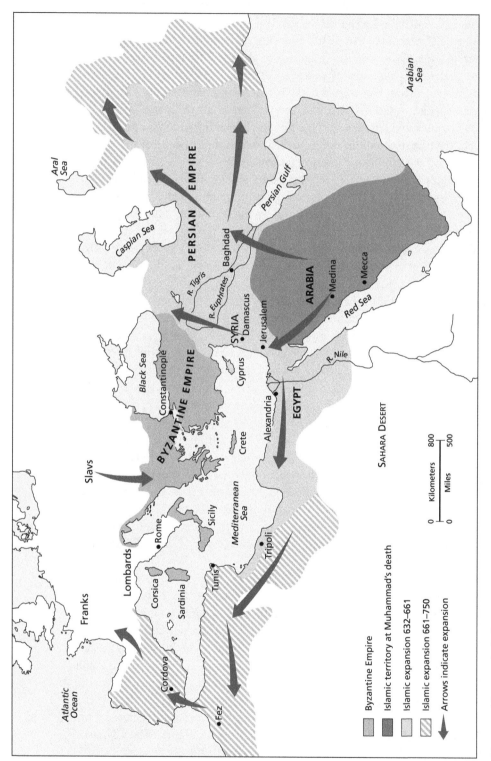

Map 2.1 The spread of Islam.

The Umayyad Dynasty

Below you will find a list of the most important members of the Umayyad Dynasty, their accomplishments, and important events that occurred during their reign. The first of these is of course Mu'awiya, who ruled from 660 to 680 CE. He was the founder of the Sufyanid branch of the dynasty, which only lasted until the death of his grandson in 683. Mu'awiya brought stability to the empire and set a number of precedents in the winter and summer campaigns against the Byzantines. He moved the capital to Damascus and re-administered the two *amsar* in Iraq, Kufa and Basra. Mu'awiya was followed by his son Yazid (r. 680–683). The most important event during Yazid's reign was the ill-fated rebellion of al-Husayn ibn 'Ali ibn Abi Talib, the Prophet's grandson. Husayn was asked by the Kufans to come to Iraq and lead their campaign against Yazid. However, as Husayn was traveling through present-day Iraq, he and his supporters were intercepted by Yazid's governor at a place called Karbala. Facing greater numbers and receiving no aid from the Kufans, Husayn and his family stood their ground, but they were defeated after a day of fighting and subsequently massacred by the superior forces. The head of the Prophet's grandson was subsequently taken to Yazid, in a show of defiance. This battle and the subsequent events became a very important incident in the history of Islam, especially for the Shi'a. The rebellion and its crushing are imbued with theological significance, which will be discussed in detail in Chapter 5.

After Yazid's death in 683, his son succeeded him as Mu'awiya II. There are some disagreements as to how long Mu'awiya II ruled, how old he was when he died, and even whether he wanted to be caliph. During his time the empire continued to see civil conflict. This civil conflict lasted for ten years (683–693). The victor of this round was another Umayyad – one from the Marwanid branch of the dynasty. His name was Abd al-Malik ibn Marwan and he ruled the empire for the next 65 years (685–705). Abd al-Malik's greatest achievements were the Arabization of the Empire's bureaucracy and the setting up of a fairly stable succession protocol. Abd al-Malik ruled that all bureaucratic correspondence should turn from the local languages of the provinces into Arabic; and, while until then Muslims had been using Byzantine coins, he began minting coins with the testament of faith on them.

The next important caliph would be Umar II (r. 717–720), the only Umayyad who earned the admiration of all the sects; and he managed to do this through his reforms. Umar II was a nephew of Abd al-Malik and, even though his reign was a short one, he was able to bring about a number of changes that have made a profound impact on Islam. He put an end to the Umayyad tradition of cursing Husayn (which had been performed in mosques since 657); and he commissioned the writing down of the first collection of hadith (the Prophet's words and actions) and sira (*al-sira*, the Prophet's biographical tradition). He also had to deal with far more conversions of non-Muslims to Islam than his predecessors. The early Islamic leaders were hesitant about advocating conversion to the non-Muslim population. Usually such populations were monotheist to begin with; Islamic leaders therefore regarded them as a part of the monotheistic tradition they had undertaken to protect. Besides, their status as protected religious communities was economically vital: the tax extolled for this protection secured the maintenance of the state. (Muslims were subject to some taxes as well.)

The next important caliph of the 8th century is Hisham ibn Abd al-Malik (r. 724–743). He was important not so much for what he himself did as for what happened under his rule – to the empire in general and, more specifically, to the Umayyad Dynasty. His reign registered a near fiscal collapse, setbacks in the conquests, and open rebellions. Discontent continued to simmer throughout the whole empire, leading eventually to the Abbasid revolution (747–750).

The Abbasid Dynasty

The Abbasid revolution started in the province of Khurasan, in eastern Iran. The success of the revolution was due in part to the ability of the Abbasid clan to tap into the widespread opposition to Umayyad rule and to unify a disparate group of peoples behind the call for a return to a more authentic application of Islam. By characterizing the Umayyids as impious – and un-Islamic – the Abbasids were able to foment dissent and revolt, which would ultimately bring the Umayyad Dynasty down. The Abbasids' ability to establish a new caliphate, however, also relied upon an element of secrecy in the proceedings: the proposed candidate for the caliphate – the one who would restore Islam to its pristine state – would be from the family of the Prophet, but the branch was not specified. This prompted many of Alid's partisans to support this movement, not realizing that they acted on behalf of the descendants of Abbas, the Prophet's uncle, and not on behalf of ʿAli's descendants. The Abbasids were thus able in 750 to administer to the Umayyads a sound defeat and to establish themselves in Iraq, where they eventually built a new capital, Baghdad, in 763.

In its heyday in the 9th century, Baghdad was able to sustain a population of more than 1 million people – with universities, hospitals, hotels, and international markets. It was in fact one of the main centers of the civilized world. Much of Islamic thought – including that involving the *sharia*, Islamic law – developed under the Abbasids. Many of the Abbasid caliphs acted as patrons of the arts and sciences. It was in Baghdad that the famous Bayt al Hikma ("House of Wisdom") was built. This institute was commissioned by the state to translate all the scientifical, mathematical, and philosophical literature it could find into Arabic, the common language (lingua franca) of the time. When these works made their way to Europe, they reacquainted Northern Europeans with the full range of the works of Plato and Aristotle and of the latter's early commentators. The many cultural achievements of the Abbasids should not be understated. This was, indeed, the flowering of Arab (and Islamic) civilization: a time that witnessed extraordinary advances in medicine, philosophy, architecture, science, and other fields. It is to this period that we owe the modern hospital, the modern university, and even the modern checkbook. In the 9th century, a member of the Islamic world could write a check in Samaraqand and cash it in Seville.

Although Abbasid rule continued until the 13th century, its power began to wane around 950, so that in the 10th and 11th centuries powerful Shi'ite dynasties started to rule large parts of the Islamic world. The Buyyids and the Fatimids were among these dynasties. The Buyyids were a family of Daylami soldiers – leaders of the Daylamite people southwest of the Caspian Sea – who were able to take over large areas of Iran in 934. Later on they invaded Baghdad and ruled there for a century, from 943 to 1055. Since the Buyyids were adherents of Imami (Twelver) Shi'ism, some of the best works of this doctrine were written during their reign. They kept the Sunni caliph, without seeking to change the Sunni character of the empire, and they allowed for the co-existence of Shi'ism and Sunnism, albeit favoring the former. Even though they held political power, the ruling members of the Abbasid Dynasty remained figureheads of the empire.

In the landscape of the regional revolts that occurred during this period of upheaval, another rebellious group that established de facto autonomy (though continuing its nominal allegiance to the Abbasids) was that of the Fatimids. The Fatimid Dynasty represented the Isma'ili branch of Shi'ism; it was centered first in North Africa (between 909 and 973), then in Egypt (between 973 and 1171). This dynasty was responsible for a number of contributions to Islamic civilization: it built the city of Cairo and the Al-Azhar University; it created several Shi'i philosophical–religious movements. During its reign there was a flowering of Jewish culture in the Mediterranean, too, until the last Fatimid ruler was removed by Salah al-Din and much of Egypt reverted to Sunnism.

The difficulty of maintaining control over an empire that stretched from Morocco to Central Asia explains in part the decline of the Abbasid caliphate. Another part of the explanation was the usurpation of authority by other Muslim factions. But it was the Mongol invasion from Central Asia and the sacking of Baghdad in 1258 that finally brought to an end this long period in Islamic history.

The Medieval Empires

Marshall Hodgson (1977) once wrote that if a Martian had landed on earth around the year 1500, he would have thought that Islam ruled the world. The Ottomans were the strongest military force on earth. The Safavids of Iran had the grandest court culture known in their day, and the Mughals oversaw the administration of the richest land on earth, India. Since much scholarship on Islamic history focuses on the classical period and on the influence that the Arab world had upon other peoples, we often forget that these empires represent the most important historical origins of our own times. Let us look not only at them, but also at their regional settings, as the "internationalism" of Islam during the period under discussion is one of Islam's main features today too. Here we are essentially following the work of Ira Lapidus (2002), whose *A History of Islamic Societies* has given us very accessible view of these regions.

Iran: The Mongol, Timurid, and Safavid Empires

The Sassanid Empire was waning (as most of them do) at the dawn of Arab Muslims' incursion in the 7th century. Overtaking their dynasty was, however, not an easy feat; it took the Muslim forces a decade to quell resistance in the major areas of Iran, and most of the Persians did not become Muslim until the 9th century. In this long process Muslims adopted Sassanid coinage and many of the Persians' administrative practices. Arabic became the official language of the court in 696, although Persian continued to be widely used as the spoken language.

From the 9th century to the 11th persistent controversies arose in which Arabs and Persians each lauded their own and denigrated each other's cultural traits. The Persians were determined to retain their distinct Persian identity. Already by the 9th century, ruling dynasties of purely Persian origin witnessed a revival of the Persian language, enriched by Arabic code-words and using the Arabic script. Another legacy of the Arab conquest was Shiʿa Islam – which, although now closely identified with Iran, originated with the Arab Muslims. The largest concentration of Muslims who sided with ʿAli in the first century (as mentioned earlier) was in southern Iraq. It was not until the 16th century, under the Safavid Dynasty, that a majority of Iranians became Shiʿa. Much more detailed light on this area of the Muslim world will be shed in later chapters.

Although the Mongol invasions affected the whole of Asia, it was perhaps in Iran that the Mongols' presence was most significant and culturally sustained. One can detect there patterns similar to those described by Ibn Khaldun in North Africa: a nomadic confederation rises to the status of dynasty, only to weaken with time and be replaced by another confederation. In Iran, both the Mongols and Timurids could be described as such dynasties. Yet the Safavids are somewhat different, insofar as they began as a Sufi order

---

Sidebar 2.3   *Shanameh*

The *Shanameh – The Book of Kings –* is a Persian epic poem written some time in the late 10th or early 11th century by Hakim Abu al-Qasim Ferdowsi. This poem traces a mythical history of Persia and the rise and fall of kings and heroes. It is an important literary piece that has shaped Persian identity in a variety of ways for centuries.

Sidebar 2.4   Crusades and Mongols

Two events to have a most devastating impact on the Muslim world were the Crusades (1096–1249) and the Mongol invasion, with its near-destruction of Baghdad in 1258. In particular, these events had two effects that the Muslim world still has to come to terms with, even to this day. The first consisted in the establishment of a military class as an elite of defenders of the faith. Unlike the first warriors of the faith, who also represented the elite, these new warriors were foreigners; they were for the most part Central Asian slaves trained in the art of war and implanted into foreign areas with which they had no affinity whatever (apart from sharing the local religion). The second effect consisted in the adoption of a defensive mentality that became a pervasive feature of Islamic civilization. Innovation was limited to warfare; everything was subordinated to the military needs of the various states.

rather than a military group. But the Mongol invasions are the event that set Iran off on its own path.

The Mongolian legacy is twofold: first, the administration and land distribution were rearranged according to Mongolian traditions and Iranian bureaucratic practices. Second, these invasions injected a new cultural vibrancy into Islam itself, since the Mongols, like so many other populations in Islam, produced an original synthesis between their own cultural traditions and the Islamic ethos.

Unlike the Arabs – who, upon conquering the region, exerted an enormous influence on its pre-existing language and religion – the Mongols let themselves be absorbed both into Islam and into Iranian court culture. Yet they brought to this culture their own unique experiences and aesthetic tastes. For example, the Chinese influence upon Iranian art, manuscript making, and pottery is evident. Artifacts of this kind are exhibited in museums throughout the world as testimonials of Il-Khanid culture. The Il-Khans, descendants of Genghis Khan, were scions of the Mongol dynasty that ruled Iran; they upheld Mongol traditions while eventually converting to Islam. With time, the territory ruled by the Il-Khanid Dynasty eventually collapsed into smaller competing states, which in turn would be conquered and centralized under Tamerlane.

Tamerlane, unlike his Mongol predecessors, was born a Muslim. His conquests are significant in that they influenced Central and South Asian Islamic culture and architecture (including the Taj Mahal) for ever after – quite apart from his being perhaps the last great nomadic conqueror. With Tamerlane, the rise of Sufi orders becomes even more of a political phenomenon. Given the relative instability of the Mongol and Timurid periods, one can see how the Sufi orders emerged as well-organized means of sustaining faith. The manner in which one would conduct his or her life during this period was in large part shaped by his or her local Sufi sheikh's interpretation of Islamic principles, doctrines, and law. Upon Tamerlane's death, his empire descended into competing states, and one of these Sufi orders would give rise to yet another new dynasty – the Safavid.

The Safavid Dynasty was founded by Shah Isma'il in 1501. Isma'il was a charismatic descendant of the Safi order's founder, Safi al-Din (d. 1334). In time, the order produced militant followers, who began to wage a concentrated campaign in northwestern Iran and southeastern Anatolia. In 1501 Isma'il, now head of the order, claimed the title of shah or king. He spent the rest of his life consolidating his power. But his most lasting contribution was the conversion, *en masse*, of Iranian inhabitants to Shi'ism. Generally speaking, Shah Abbas I (d. 1629) is considered the greatest Safavid ruler. Under him courtly life flourished and new forms of Islamic philosophy began to take shape, giving rise to Neoplatonism, which produced the works of Mir Damad and Mulla Sadra (d. 1640). Sadra's influence can still be felt throughout the Muslim world. Abbas' most important achievement, however, was the strengthening of the Iranian state. The Safavids collapsed in the 18th century, eventually giving rise to the Qajars, who would rule until the 1920s.

Anatolia: The Seljuk and Ottoman Empires

The "Turkification" of Anatolia took centuries. Turkish nomads from Central Asia and the Steppe migrated to the Near East over a period of centuries. The rocky political environment these nomads created was managed through the emergence of new states, which sought to use their power and control them. The Seljuks formed the most important of these states. Under the Seljuks there was a "re-vitalization," if you will, of Sunni Islam. They exerted patronage over Sunni thinkers and schools and challenged other interpretations of Islam. This patronage was closely linked to Seljuk views on state, power, and governance. One of the greatest figures of the Seljuk period was Nizam al-Mulk (d. 1092), the chief advisor to the Seljuk sultan. He wrote works on politics, governance, and religion and set up a state-funded system of higher education. In his view education was indispensable to governance, as it opened a way of training subjects so as to bring them in line with the vision of the state.

The Seljuks attained a high level of sophistication and power. They were to leave an indelible imprint on Islamic civilization. But the region would eventually be devastated by the Mongol invasions and, in the process, Turkic migrants in flight from the Mongol conquest in the East changed the demography of certain parts of the Near East, giving rise to a host of Turkish principalities. One of these was the Ottoman principality.

The Ottomans have a long history. In 1453 they became the undisputed rulers of the old Byzantine Empire. They were Muslims, but they ruled over a largely Christian land, many of whose inhabitants would eventually become Muslims; today Islam is as much a part of the Balkans as Orthodoxy or Catholicism is. In 1517 one of their greatest sultans, Selim I, conquered much of the Arabic-speaking world, turning the Ottomans into an international power overnight. They would continue to rule much of Eastern Europe and much of the Arab world right up until the turn of the 20th century; their empire would not collapse until after World War I. But what are the Ottomans known for?

Apart from the fact that the Ottomans were a bridge between Europe and the Islamic world, some of the most beautiful architecture in the world was produced under their patronage. The famous mosques of Sinan (d. 1588) are renowned throughout the world for their Anatolian character and splendor; there we find the expression of an Islamic–Byzantine synthesis – the mosques are modeled on the imperial majesty of the Hagia Sophia but inscribed in Arabic calligraphy and decorated with Islamic motifs, both on the outside and on the interior walls. The most famous Ottoman sultan was Suleiman the Magnificent – known in the Muslim world as al-Qanuni, "the Lawgiver." Under his reign *sharia* was reconciled with secular law (*qanun*). Developments in military tactics secured overall Ottoman dominance for some three hundred years; the Ottoman dynasty lasted roughly twice as long.

India and South Asia

By 711 India, already almost 1 millennium old, had withstood many invaders and had undergone substantial changes to its military organization and culture. The situation in 711 was different: the country faced an enemy whose culture and religion were as sophisticated and powerful as its own. In fact Islam, as a religion and body of thought, appealed to many in the Indian population, especially among the lower castes. A permanent base was established between 711 and 713 by the teenage commander Muhammad ibn al-Qasim, but not much documentation about these Muslims survives. Historians note that other major cities were conquered from this base, but the record ends in the 16th century, when a dynasty arose.

A series of invasions and other political developments led to the establishment and rule of the Mughal Dynasty in India in 1526. From the 8th to the 16th century Muslims, Mongols, and Persians had continued to fight for different parts of the Indian subcontinent. During the 13th century, with Muslim support, the Mongols had seized large parts of China and had moved on to new conquests – in Iraq, in Europe, and elsewhere. In 1526, with the help of an Islamic population comprised of Arabs, Persians, and converts from Hinduism, Mughal forces were able to capture most of northern India and subsequently imposed Islam as the religion of the government. The Mughals were themselves Muslims of Turkic origin, descended from Timur and Genghis Khan.

Conflicts arose naturally between a passionately monotheistic Islam and a much older polytheistic Hinduism, which was powerful and deeply rooted. Muslims slaughtered animals and ate their meat (except that of pigs), while Hindus were predominantly vegetarian; moreover, they venerated cows, which were

---

Sidebar 2.5   Spain: Al-Andalus

Islamic Spain, too, deserves much more attention than it can receive here. Islam was present in Spain from 711 to 1492: during all this period the country was under the rule of Arabs and Moors. For a while, the geographic area of present-day Spain and Portugal functioned as one of the most fertile territories of intellectual growth, scientific discovery, and cultural transmission in the Muslim world. Architecture, mathematics, science, and philosophy flourished there. One strong influence on this intellectual climate was the Qur'an, which is permeated by exhortations to pursue knowledge and by advice on its value. God knows everything, while human knowledge is imperfect; hence Muslims should get to know not only God's laws, but also the world God created. Shah Abbas I the Great, the greatest Safavid ruler, requires extending the frontiers of human knowledge through constant exploration and advocates advancement through research and experimentation. Such pursuits are pleasing to God.

Indeed in the Middle Ages the Muslims led the world through their pursuit of knowledge. They made discoveries in the natural world, especially about the human body; and they added to the intellectual reservoir of mankind through knowledge gleaned from cultures such as the Greek, the Persian, the Indian, and the Chinese. In the 9th century a monumental enterprise of translating the great works of classical antiquity started at the court of Harun al-Rashid. Great commentaries, systems of interpretation, and even original philosophies – such as those of Ibn Sina (Avicenna) and Ibn Rushd (Averroes) – were produced alongside strict translations of Plato, Aristotle, or Galen. The Muslims synthesized knowledge and elaborated upon it; then, in the 11th century, all this reached Spain and from there spread into Europe, thus being transmitted to the entire West. People in search of knowledge traveled to Spain to study. The libraries of Spain held almost half a million manuscripts – which was more than the number of manuscripts in all the libraries of Europe, taken together.

never to be molested, let alone slaughtered. Hindus cremated their dead; Muslims buried theirs. Religious conflicts were initially appeased with the help of the Mughals' pragmatism. Much of the mediation between communities was done through intermarriage and tolerant rule. Arab and Persian Muslims assimilated Indian culture; Indians adopted an Arabic language mixed with Persian; Islamic mysticism integrated Hindu techniques. The rule of Shah Jahan (1628–1658) saw the building of the Taj Mahal, one of the architectural wonders of the world. It was not until the reign of Aurangzeb (1658–1707) that the seeds of decline were sown for the Mughals. In a reversal of a centuries-old policy, Aurangzeb started the persecution of Hindus and unsuccessfully attempted to expand the empire, emptying resources along the way. These two moves proved disastrous for the Mughal Dynasty, and their consequences opened the way for the British to occupy India – a largely Hindu population ruled by Muslims. Much more on this history and its legacy will be discussed in a later chapter (Chapter 10 on South Asia).

European Colonialism and Its Legacy

The empires reviewed above were defeated and dismembered by various European powers in the 18th and 19th centuries. These powers had a negative effect on the Muslim world, in large measure because of the nature of their conquests. Even though one can depict the Mongols as a phenomenon of devastating effects on the Muslims, they were assimilated and Islamized just like the earlier migrants. The Europeans, on the other hand, were loath to accept the indigenous religions and civilizations of the lands they occupied. There was a tendency among European conquerors to regard the peoples of the Muslim world as an inferior race with an inferior religion. This was coupled with a conscious effort on the part of European missionaries to seek converts – both to their religion and to their civilizational values. The Muslim world reacted in much the same way as it had reacted to the Crusades: various peoples began to rely increasingly on their military elite and to see technological advances in the sciences as the only means of improving their lot.

The legacy of European colonialism has reshaped much of the world, particularly the Islamic world. On the one hand, exposure to the industrial civilization of Europe – and to the Enlightenment-derived norms that informed the West – forced societies throughout the world to re-evaluate their traditions in light of the modern era. The political boundaries of today's nation-states were also defined during this period. In the Middle East, for example, these borders were a product of the Sykes-Picot agreement, which was negotiated between the British and the French. The West aggressively solicited the support of the Arabs against the Ottomans during World War I, promising the Arabs an independent Arab nation-state in return. Nevertheless, behind closed doors, the British and French had imperial ambitions in the region. When the Ottoman Empire collapsed, Ottoman rule was replaced by British and French rule, through an international mandate system. Sir Percy Cox, a

British officer, was largely responsible for drawing up borders in the former Ottoman region. Thus, alongside historical countries like Egypt, Syria, and Iraq, completely new and unimagined states like Jordan were created. The mandate system also facilitated the eventual creation of Israel – a topic of tremendous political import. By and large – with the exception of Iran, whose revolution reinvigorated its Islamic past – the Muslim world, in the form of these states, is an amalgamation of European, Islamic, and local custom and culture, thrown together to produce for the most part an uprooted people, which has yet to come to terms with its own heritage.

Discussion Questions

1 What is the significance of the phrase "gunpowder empires"?
2 How do modern empires differ from their predecessors?
3 What is the common cycle of power in the premodern Near East?

Suggested Further Reading

Denny, Frederick (2010). An Introduction to Islam (4th ed.). Upper Saddle River, NJ: Prentice Hall.

Esposito, John (2010). *Islam: The Straight Path* (4th ed.). New York, NY: Oxford University Press.

Hodgson, Marshall (1977). *The Venture of Islam*, 3 vols. Chicago, IL: University of Chicago Press.

Hourani, Albert (1992). *A History of the Arab Peoples*. Cambridge, MA: Harvard University Press.

Lapidus, Ira (2002). *A History of Islamic Societies* (2nd ed.). New York, NY: Cambridge University Press.

Montgomery Watt, W. (1961). *Muhammad: Prophet and Statesman*. New York, NY: Oxford University Press.

Rahman, Fazlur (1979). *Islam* (2nd ed.). Chicago, IL: University of Chicago Press.

3

Religious Structures
Tawhīd

LAITH SAUD

Introduction

Of the Abrahamic faiths, Islam is the easiest to understand theologically: it has only one central concept – that of the one single creator, who is the source of the universe. Dogma is relatively absent from Islam. In Christianity the Trinity – a concept related to the nature of God – is central; in Judaism the Covenant – which pertains to the Hebrews' contract with God – is fundamental. In Christianity dogma revolves around the mystery of the Trinity; in Judaism, the idea of a covenant with God has strong implications and informs the study of the law. In Islam there is no trinity and no covenant, but only the fundamental concept of *tawhīd*: the absolute unity of the

An Introduction to Islam in the 21st Century, First Edition. Edited by Aminah Beverly McCloud, Scott W. Hibbard, and Laith Saud.
© 2013 Blackwell Publishing Ltd. Published 2013 by Blackwell Publishing Ltd.

deity. The Qur'an insists that there is only one God and that all the prophets and messengers in history – from Adam to David, from Abraham to Jesus, from Moses to Muhammad, and many others – all testified to this unity. In Islam, the unity of God constitutes the singular core – not just of a particular belief system but of a dynamic worldview. The following chapter will be devoted to explaining what this means.

Tawhīd: The Organizing Principle of Islamic Thought

What is civilization? At the very least, civilization is possible when we possess enough material security to reflect on our existence and to produce thought, culture, and social norms. In the following chapters we will explore not only what Muslims "believe" but, perhaps even more importantly, what Muslim "do" as members of an Islamic society or civilization. Much of what we "do" is celebrated in any given civilization's "thought." Thought may take the form of art, literature, philosophy, astronomy, science, medicine, music, the law, and so on. Before introducing ourselves to central Islamic texts like the Qur'an and the hadith collections, it is important to understand that they are expressions of a higher concept, that of *tawhīd*, and that all of the disciplines mentioned above, insofar as they belong to Islamic civilization, elaborate on *tawhīd*. Since this concept is so broad and so vast, rather than commanding conformity, it facilitates a wide spectrum of thought. In Islamic philosophy this spectrum ranges from rationalism and mysticism to traditionalism; in politics, from libertarianism to theocracy; in law, from literalism to constructionism. As we survey the various domains of Islamic civilization, we will touch upon the full range of these forms, while at the same time demonstrating how all this diversity is anchored in the fundamental concept of *tawhīd*. It is important to understand that in Islam the unity of God goes beyond being simply a matter of "correct belief," in other words a dogma; *tawhīd* rather constitutes the center of reality. Belief in one God is known as *monotheism*, but Islamic monotheism has a penetrating and pervasive character. The opposite of *tawhīd* is not just polytheism (belief in many gods); to deny *tawhīd* is to misunderstand reality in a fundamental way – to be ignorant of reality as given in the Islamic worldview. Before proceeding any further, let us outline the fundamental relationship between *tawhīd* and knowledge.

In 1640, roughly 1,000 years after the death of Prophet Muhammad, a Persian philosopher named Sadr al-Din Muhammad al-Shirazi, also known as Mulla Sadra, died in Basra, Iraq. Sadra was returning from his seventh pilgrimage to Mecca. This ascetic philosopher devoted his life to the study of Being, God, and the Islamic sciences. In many ways his thought represents the culmination of Islamic epistemology (theory of knowledge). Throughout Islamic history Muslim thinkers have asked themselves: What constitutes good conduct? What does it mean to live a good life? What does it mean to worship? What does it mean to know the one God? What are the implications of such knowledge? According to Mulla Sadra, all of these questions revolve around a more fundamental concept; for him there is an inextricable unity between the knower, what is to be known, and knowledge – for example, between the human being, God, and knowledge.

We can think about this unity as being analogous to the unity between the lover, the beloved, and love or the unity between the beholder, the beheld, and beauty. Imagine for a moment that you are at the Museum of Modern Art in New York City and you come across Vincent Van Gogh's *Starry Night*. The rich texture of Van Gogh's bold strokes impress you as beautiful, so you stop and behold the painting for a moment. What happens in that moment? In that moment you experience beauty and you are aware of that beauty as *you* behold the painting; furthermore, the emergence of beauty is only made possible by the relationship between you and the object of beauty. Hence, in your beholding something beautiful, three things happen: first, your state of aware-ness changes, so you change; when you have become aware of beauty, you are aware of something meaningful and valuable. Second, the painting changes from an arbitrary object into an object of beauty. Third, beauty manifests itself as a concept.

Mulla Sadra makes similar arguments about knowledge, the individual, and God. When one becomes aware of God, one changes; he/she becomes aware of him/herself as a created, finite being. He/she also becomes aware of his/her debt to his/her creator. Second, God is realized as the opposite; God is understood as the embodiment of the uncreated and infinite. Third, the relationship between created and creator, finite and infinite emerges *as knowledge*. The content of this knowledge constitutes an important part of Islamic literature and thought.

Aristotle's definition of knowledge is useful to us here; he defined knowledge as nothing less than being aware of the "cause of a fact." In Islam, knowledge is a state of awareness of the cause of creation – the creator; possessing it also means acknowledging the essence of humanity as that of a created thing. The human being is not something arbitrary, nor is he or she a fallen entity; rather the human being is a creature endowed with the purpose of being aware of the creator. As the Qur'an states: "God created all things and He is the agent on which all things depend" (39: 62). "And God created you all and whatever you do" (37: 96).

This is *tawhīd* at its most fundamental. *Tawhīd* is more than the simple assertion "there is one God": *tawhīd* testifies to the Muslim belief in the ultimate "unity of God." The Muslim idea of God is that all power, all presence, and all knowledge arise through God, which results in the continuous and unified link between creation, creator, and creativity.

As we said before, the opposite of *tawhīd* is not "multiplicity" but ignorance; and Aristotle's definition continues to be of use to us here. If knowledge is to know the "cause of a fact" and in Islam God is the cause of literally everything, then being unaware of God is ultimately to be ignorant of the world around you – including its essence and its being. And this – the unified relationship between creation, the creator, and creativity – is the organizing principle of Islamic thought and of all of the constituents of Islamic civilization we men-tioned above. What constitutes a civilization is its creativity, and what defines a Muslim is the character of his/her creative acts, be they ethical, philosophical, commercial, judicial, social, or domestic.

Introducing Basic Islamic Beliefs and Texts

It is important to remember that all the concepts that are considered "religious" in nature emerge and develop within historical contexts. Material forces – economical and political – impose themselves on societies and affect the sort of questions any given society may ask of it-self. For example, if you live in a society where there is a large disparity between those who have and those who have not, you may ask questions about the distribution of wealth. Or, if you live in a society where political leaders are corrupt, you may question the ideas that such leaders use to legitimize themselves. Sometimes remarkable, charismatic individuals who dare to ask such questions challenge the status quo through the answers they come up with. Prophet Muhammad was such a man.

Muhammad was born in an area known as the Hijaz, in western Arabia, around 570 CE. Arabia was a tribal society made up of large confederations of tribes. Muhammad belonged to Quraysh, a powerful tribe that controlled Mecca, the commercial capital of western Arabia. Mecca also housed the famous Kaaba, a shrine that served as a place of pilgrimage for tribes throughout the peninsula. The Arabs believed that the Kaaba was originally built by Abraham and his son Ishmael; in the days when Muhammad was born, however, the Kaaba was used for pagan rites and practices. Its position of dominance over Mecca made the Quraysh one of the most powerful tribes of Arabia, and it would be the Quraysh, Muhammad's fellow tribesmen, that he would eventually challenge.

Muhammad's father Abdullah died before his son's birth, and his mother Amina died while he was still a child. Orphaned by the age of six, the young Muhammad was taken in by his grandfather, Abdul-Mutalib, a well-respected member of the Quraysh. Abdul-Mutalib loved him dearly and sheltered him from the abuses of Meccan society. In a tribal culture an orphan, having no mother or father to protect him / her, is particularly exposed. In such a society an individual's prestige and social worth waxes and wanes with the fate of his tribe, and even more so with that of his or her clan – a subset within the tribe. Muhammad belonged to the clan of his grandfather, the Banu Hashim. Being raised by Abdul-Mutalib, a notable and respected figure in Mecca, implanted in young Muhammad qualities that would stand out in his adult years. Muhammad was compassionate yet confident; critical yet honest. Being an orphan, he was sensitive to the plight of the marginalized and dispossessed. At the same time Abdul-Mutalib instilled in him the confidence and dignity of social responsibility and leadership – so much so that Muhammad was known among the Meccans as "al-Amin" – the "trustworthy."

When Abdul-Mutalib passed away, Muhammad was taken in by his uncle Abi Talib, who assumed the deceased's role within the clan and raised Muhammad into adulthood, teaching him trade, tribal customs, the use of the bow and arrow, and riding – all typical skills expected of a young man in Arabian society at the time. At the age of 25 Muhammad married Khadija, a wealthy widow 15 years his senior. He had managed some of Khadija's business affairs in Syria; she noticed his integrity and his intellect and proposed marriage.

From youth into middle age, Muhammad reflected continuously on the nature of the world around him. Meccan society was dominated by an aristocratic elite. Men of wealth and power benefited from the social order of the time. The Kaaba brought pilgrims from all over the peninsula, and with them came wealth. Mecca also occupied an important place among the trade routes between India, Yemen, and the Levant, and this made several clans extremely wealthy and powerful. The scarcity of water and the need to develop ties with the powerful sedentary tribes of the towns made competition between the nomadic tribes fierce. Arab tribes were locked in incessant blood feuds with one another. In pre-Islamic Arabia social practices were based on individual interests in the consolidation of wealth; for example, since female children brought the family little hope of increased wealth, infanticide was commonly practiced on female babies. Or a man could marry a woman, take her dowry, and then divorce her without her having any recourse. Above all, paganism facilitated a fragmented social order. Certain clans claimed favors from certain gods, while individuals made requests for gold, power, and reputation from statues fashioned by their own hands.

Muhammad was deeply disturbed by the society he saw around him. The cries of female newborns being buried alive troubled him; the exploitation of orphans stirred in him the compassion cultivated by his upbringing; the continual blood feuds between fellow Arabs violated his sense of social responsibility; and, ultimately, the worship of statues, stones, or stars violated his sense of rationality. But Muhammad was not alone in having such feelings. There were in Arabian society certain figures known as *hanifs* – "freelance" monotheists – who did not invest in the paganism that surrounded them. Muhammad was a *hanif* too; he practiced seclusion and devoted himself to reflection. Each year he would spend time at the cave of Mount Hira, engaged in solitary meditation (*tahannuth*). In the 40th year of his life, during the month of Ramadan, Muhammad had a revelation.

> "Read!" A voice commanded of him.
> "What shall I read?" Muhammad replied after some resistance.
> "Read: In the name of thy Lord who created,
> Created man of a blood-clot.
> Read: And thy Lord is most generous,
> Who taught by the pen,
> Taught man that which he knew not." (Qur'an 96: 1–5)

The verses above are the first in a series of revelations that would span the next 22 years – that is, the remaining lifetime of the prophet – marking various events in his life. We can already note the Qur'an's central themes: Creator, creation, and knowledge. Islamic tradition recalls that Muhammad was terrified of this vision and fled the cave, whereupon he was confronted by the Archangel Gabriel standing astride the horizon before him. According to Islamic tradition, Gabriel assured Muhammad that he need not fear; indeed what he brought him was a message from his Lord, expressed in the verse: "The heart lied not in seeing what it saw," but rather the experience "is nothing except a revelation that is revealed" (Qur'an 53: 4).

As you may recall, we began this section by discussing the importance of the historical context in the development of beliefs and practices. Unlike other traditions, the correspondence between belief and history is a fundamental part of Islam. As Tarif Khalidi (1994: 14) points out, "among the so-called Abrahamic religions, Islam was the fastest to provide itself with a chronology." The nature of the Muslims' approach to the Qur'an is largely responsible for the Islamic attitude to history.

Muslims believe that the Qur'an was revealed in time, and hence the historical "occasions of revelation" (*asbab al-nuzul*) constitute material of study for the Muslim exegete; thus the *history* of the Qur'an is inextricably linked to the *meaning* of the Qur'an. For this reason, a more judicious and accurate pursuit of the Qur'an's history was considered to render its meaning more faithfully, and thus to approximate the Will of God more closely. In short, good history makes for good religion. Muslim exegetes have traditionally divided the Qur'an into "Meccan" Suras and "Medinese" Suras; in turn the Suras are divided into early-, middle-, and late-period revelations.

To return to what was said before, over the next 22 years Prophet Muhammad would continue to receive revelations testifying to the unity of God, the destiny of humanity, the role of prophets in the world, and the fate of civilizations. Muhammad began to challenge the Meccan elites for a more just social order and he publicly testified to the unity of God. The Qur'an is our most enduring record of his life and challenges. The Qur'an comments on his struggle against pagans – a struggle that would evolve into a war over the soul of Arabia. His call to social and spiritual reform threatened the status quo. He denounced female infanticide as a transgression of God's sovereignty over life. Muhammad decried the treatment of the dispossessed in Meccan society and called for just treatment for all persons; for example, he granted women property rights and marital protections. And, of course, he reduced paganism to superstition – and this in the very capital of Arabian paganism, Mecca. Feeling that their way of life and their source of income were threatened, members of the Meccan elite attempted to assassinate Muhammad in his sleep. But Muhammad managed to escape into the night, accompanied by his dear friend and fellow Muslim Abu Bakr. He and the other Muslims fled to Yathirb, which thereafter was known as Madinat al Nabi ("the city of the Prophet" – Medina).

The Prophet's years in Medina were spent building a community based on *tawhīd*; they were also spent at war with the Meccans, who feared that the spread of monotheism would undermine their commercial strength and social status. Eventually, after ten years of war, Muhammad returned to his hometown victorious. Upon arrival he went to the Kaaba, the noble sanctuary, and destroyed the old idols with his staff: paganism was to be wiped off the face of the peninsula. The birth of Islam was complete – but the fulfillment of its destiny had only just begun.

Rethinking Islam: The Message, the Messenger, and God

The most significant honor attributed to Prophet Muhammad is the title "messenger of God." Muhammad is not the son of God, and he is not considered a messiah in any respect; rather he is simply a man standing in a long line of people who carry the message of *tawhīd*. But what does this message entail? If God is the source of all things, what does that mean for me? Islam, unlike the other great monotheist religion, Christianity, does not develop the doctrine of a fallen man. According to Saint Augustine, the fall constitutes the human being's transition from a state of grace and bliss to a state of sin. In this kind of theology a savior is required – someone to absolve humans of their sin. In spite of common foundations, Islam diverges from Christianity in this respect; there is no original sin in Islam and, as Tilman Nagel (2000: 18) notes, "for this reason, it is not the Prophet's task to elevate man into a state of grace that never existed before, but to lay bare his original destination."

It is not insignificant that Islam does not begin with particularistic dogmas or with the fall of man. Even the many complex social and political ideas being negotiated in the Muslim world today are, in part, a reflection of Islam's different structure. In order to introduce Islamic belief and practice, let us point out what these differences between Islam and Christianity imply.

As John Esposito (2005: 68) points out, it is not correct to ask "What do Muslims believe?" – but rather "What do Muslims do?" The reason for this is directly related to the structure of Islam, which in turn should be seen in juxtaposition to the structure of Christianity. In Christianity, the fall implies humankind's need for an external savior, and this externality also implies that politics and social organizing are inherently flawed. Rather than emphasizing social behavior in pursuit of salvation, Christianity emphasizes the individual's access to salvation vis-à-vis John 3: 14, which famously states: "And God so loved the world that he gave his one and only son…"

In Islam, the absence of a "fall" means that there is no inhibition on pursuing one's own salvation, which in turn has major structural implications. First, a "not-fallen" humanity is a humanity that still lives in its original state; and this original state is characterized by being saved and by being free. Humanity does not live in sin, but in a state known as *fitrah* – the inherent disposition toward God. Yet the individual must be diligent about preserving his/her salvation or state of *fitrah*; he/she must constantly cultivate it through good works and by remaining aware of *tawhīd*. The question of course arises: How do we lose this original state? We lose it by losing sight of God and of the inextricable link between all things. By pursuing money, power, fame, beauty – or anything – as an end in and of itself, we dislodge our actions from the larger network of unity.

The pursuit of wealth or power may consume our thoughts and become the sole source of our actions. When wealth or power replaces *tawhīd* as the source of one's actions, then imbalance, inequity, and injustice are perpetrated throughout the world. Once we are in that condition, we justify such imbalances and injustices through ideas and arguments, or we preserve them through laws – all in an effort to have more, keep more, make more. The basic Islamic idea is that man-made ideas that serve such ends are "false," and by investing in them we invest in fallacy. In fact the Qur'an makes a correlation between "false ideas" and idol worship: "Do not fall in idol worship […] like those who divide their religion into sects, each party rejoicing with what they have" (30: 30–32). We might easily apply this to political or ideological partisanship as well. (Here one can already see that the structure of Islam implicates political and social thought in a different way from that of Christianity; we can add, on the other hand, that Judaism shares a great deal with Islam.)

The issue of idolatry gives us another opportunity to examine just how pervasive and penetrating the Muslim conception of monotheism is. Idolatry refers to the practice of employing man-made objects or objects found in the natural world – such as stones or stars – as "empowered" spirits, things supposed to mediate between the human individual and God. Idolatry is known as *shirk* in Islam. Muhammad – who in Muslim belief is the "seal of the prophets" – radically denounced *shirk* as superstitious and dangerous. He noted that each tribe worshipped its own god and justified its own ways on the grounds of idolatry. Even more important was the intellectual implication: Muhammad developed a sense that idolatry involved a contradiction. If a person could fashion an idol with his/her own hands, how could he/she then treat the idol as divine? This corresponds to the human tendency to deify other man-made things or ideas, like money or power. As we noted above, the Qur'an makes a correlation between false ideas, sectarianism and partisanship, and idol worship. So, if people are willing to deify a man-made object and to treat it like an idol, they display a willingness to subject themselves to a number of falsehoods, including false ideologies. So it comes about that the all-consuming pursuit of money, power, or fame is classified in Islam as a form of idolatry – *shirk*. Again, monotheism does not simply come down to saying that there is only one divinity; it involves relegating all other considerations to a place where they are understood to be "man-made."

Now we can begin to understand the role of prophets and texts in Islam. As Nagel (2000) notes, the Prophet is not a savior but simply a guide, a teacher who reminds people of the source of all things and shows them how to live in harmony with that source. Religious texts such as the Qur'an or the various hadith (prophetic sayings) have a similar function. Yet guidance is not found only in the prophets or in texts; it is also found in the universe. The Qur'an says:

> He has constrained into your service the night and the day, and the sun and the moon; and the stars too have been constrained into your service through His command. Surely there are signs here for people who make use of their reason. (Qur'an 16: 13)

To think about Islam is to think not only about personal salvation, but also about a harmonious relationship with the world and universe around you; since in Islam the world is not fallen, such a relationship is possible. This meaning is conveyed by the term "Islam" itself. In Western literature this word is often translated as "submission," connoting the notion of "submission to God's will." Yet, like many treatments of Islam in the West, this translation is incredibly misleading, and Muslims have not helped matters, for they, too, often employ the term "submission" when they translate "Islam."

The most rudimentary examination of the word "Islam" reveals the basic premise of the concept. The word is formed from the root *slm-*, which has also generated the word "peace" – peace, not submission.[1] True, the word has a connotation of "submission," but this is not its main, denotative meaning. Submission is not Islam's *raison d'être*; peace is – peace for the individual and peace for society. "Islam" means in fact "peace achieved through submission to the reality of God." And, in order for one to submit to the reality of God, one must have knowledge of that reality.

There are other terms that reinforce this meaning of "Islam": for example *taqwā*, recurrent in the Qur'an, means "God consciousness." Another word in the Islamic religious vocabulary – *ihsān* – means "the total realization of God in your daily activities."[2] Islam revolves around action, not around belief. Consider the following passage from Sayyid Qutb (1945: 09), a famous 20th-century Muslim thinker and political activist (he died in 1966):

> So Islam does not prescribe worship as the only basis of its beliefs, but rather reckons all the activities of life as constituting worship in themselves – so long as they are within the bounds of conscience, goodness and honesty. A man once passed by the Prophet, and the companions of Muhammad noticed in the man an eager intentness on his business, which caused them to say: "Oh messenger of God, if only this man would be in the path of God."
>
> Muhammad replied: "If he has come to work for his young children, then he is on the path of God; or if he has come to work for his aged and infirm parents, then he is on the path of God; or if he has come to work for himself in all moderation, then he is on the path of God. But if he has come to work only for luxury or self-glory, then he is on the path of Satan."

Acting in full awareness of the reality of God constitutes goodness in the Islamic creed. To quote once again from Tilman Nagel (2000: 18), "as a creature, man is created in the direction of God; if his nature can develop without being influenced from the outside, he is good." Here Nagel is referring to *fitrah* – the innate human capacity for goodness and openness to the entire creation (for any part of creation reflects the same source). The same belief explains a famous saying of the great 13th-century jurist Ibn Taymiyyah: "if you do not taste the sweetness of an action in your heart, suspect it; for the Lord, exalted is He, is the appreciative" (2006: xxv).

A host of disciplines has emerged over the course of Islamic history, all of them committed to discovering what constitutes "good action" and to giving concrete expression to what may count as an "action performed in awareness of God." Islamic jurisprudence is perhaps the most important of these disciplines; but Islamic philosophy too, and even Islamic art, are expressions of the same effort. We will shortly address the historical contexts within which these disciplines emerged and their central sources. But, generally speaking, the Prophets and prophetic dispensations – like holy texts – are the most important guides to good conduct.

Muslims believe that prophets, in their capacity as teachers, guide the human being toward correct behavior. There are numerous explanations for prophecy in Islam. Abu Nasr al-Farabi (d. 940), an esteemed Muslim philosopher, argued that prophets are endowed with a great mind, so that their intellect penetrates through the various layers of creation and comprehends the source of all things. The late contemporary American Muslim thinker Fazlur Rahman (2002: 32) argued in a similar vein that "a prophet is a person whose average overall character, the sum total of his actual conduct, is far superior to those of humanity in general."

Prophecy, one way or another, is regarded as a completely natural capacity, which is facilitated by the unity of all things. The Qur'an insists that Muslims be mindful of this and states:

> Say: "We believe in God, and in what was sent down to us, and in what was sent down to Abraham, Isma'il, Isaac, Jacob, and the Patriarchs; and in what was given to Moses and Jesus, and all the prophets from their Lord. We make no distinction among any of them. To Him alone we are submitters." (Qur'an 2: 136)

The Islamic acknowledgment that prophecy is a natural and universal phenomenon militates against dogmatism and exceptionalism; works define respect for prophecy, not particular beliefs:

> Say: Do you argue with us about God, when He is our Lord and your Lord? We are responsible for our deeds, and you are responsible for your deeds. To Him alone we are devoted. (Qur'an 2: 136–139)

Of course the Qur'an is an Islamic text; prophecy, however, does not belong exclusively to any nation. This state of affairs has given rise to another telling concept: that of the "people of the book" (*ahl al-Kitab*). Islam does recognize Judaism, Christianity, and monotheistic traditions more generally; it considers them akin to itself in their profession of *tawhīd*. The Qur'an says:

> Surely those who believe, and those who are Jews, and the Christians, and the Sabians – whoever believes in God and the Last Day and does good – they shall have their reward from their Lord. And there will be no fear for them, nor shall they grieve. (Qur'an 2: 62)

The Qur'an thus lays down the framework for a pluralistic, multi-confessional society; and indeed, throughout Muslim history, religious minorities have generally been free to worship as they pleased. Nevertheless, Muslims do not regard other faiths as equal to theirs. They believe that Islam is the most complete and perfect of the Abrahamic faiths, insofar as it is an unadulterated devotion to monotheism and rejection of dogmatism. They point to the development, in other traditions, of particular dogmas that they consider "deviations" from the universality of God. Particularizing God in any way would be a form of *shirk*. Thus the Qur'an says:

Oh, People of the Book! Commit no excesses in your religion, nor say of God anything but the truth. Jesus Christ, the son of Mary, was [no more than] a messenger of God and His Word, which He bestowed on Mary, and a spirit proceeding from Him. So believe in God and His messengers. Say not, "Trinity." Desist! It will be better for you, for God is one God, glory be to Him! [Far exalted is He] above having a son. To Him belong all things in the heavens and on earth. And enough is God as a disposer of affairs. (Qurʾan 4: 171)

And also:

They take their priests and their anchorites to be their lords in derogation of God, and [they take as their Lord] Christ the son of Mary. Yet they were commanded to worship but one God: there is no God but He. Praise and glory to Him! [Far is He] from having the partners they associate [with Him]. (9: 30–31)

Or, finally

Say: He is the one God, the eternal God, begetting not, nor begotten, and nothing bears comparison to the one. (Qurʾan 112: 1–4)

The above *surat* (chapter) is among the shortest in the Qurʾan; it is known as Surat al-Ikhlas (Pure Faith), but it is often referred to as Surat al-Tawhīd (Divine Unity). Prophet Muhammad thought that its value amounted to a third of the entire Qurʾan. Islamic tradition preserves the following account:

Aisha, the Prophet's wife, reported that the Prophet appointed an army commander who also led the men in prayers; this commander would always finish prayers with Sura al-Ikhlas. Prophet Muhammad asked why he does so. The man responded: "I do so because it mentions the qualities of the Most Beneficent and I love to recite it." Muhammad responded by saying: "God loves him." (Az-Zubaidi 1996: 1032, translation modified)

The Qurʾan: The Recitation

Thus far we have made references to the Qurʾan, the holy book of Muslims; let us now explain its content and essence properly. Although it may come naturally to compare the Qurʾan with the Hebrew and Christian Testaments – that is, with the Bible – this is not a useful comparison. The first reason is that Muslims believe the Qurʾan to be the word of God in a literal sense – and not the word of divinely inspired men. In the Bible it is believed that God inspires Paul as well as John, Matthew, and Luke to speak: they all speak under his inspiration. Muslims, on the other hand, believe the Qurʾan has one single author and this author is, literally, God. They are adamant that the Qurʾan is not the word of Muhammad being inspired by God but comprehensively the word of God. This may look like a subtle difference, but it has significant implications nonetheless.

Others find it useful, for the purposes of comparative religion, to compare the way Muslims approach the Qur'an to the way Christians view Jesus. In the Christian worldview, Christ is God's word incarnated in man; in the Islamic worldview, the Qur'an is God's word incarnated in word. This parallel is useful because, one way or another, Christians see in Christ the presence of God on earth; but the same could be said about the Qur'an. Indeed the Qur'an is God's word present in the world. So what does the word accomplish, and in what direction does it point humanity? In attempting to answer these questions we will discuss three aspects of Islam's sacred text: the Qur'an as revelation; the Qur'an as a source of ethics and law; and the Qur'an in relation to the five pillars of Islam.

Revelation

We will revisit the nature of the Qur'an as revelation all throughout this chapter; but here it is useful to introduce the Islamic view of revelation – a view shared, by in large, with other Abrahamic traditions. Revelation is fundamental to all of them, and in this sense it consolidates the very meaning of the phrase "Abrahamic tradition." God's word is the cornerstone of the Abrahamic worldview. In this section we will explain the significance of the word.

What is revelation? According to the Qur'an, creation itself is a revelation, as is language. Then there are the prophetic revelations of the Torah, the Psalms of the Prophet David, the Gospel, and (of course) the Qur'an. Let us begin with creation, since in the Qur'anic worldview the appearance of humanity is predicated upon the nature of creation itself.

The Qur'anic explanation of creation is not an historical account, and the Qur'an itself alludes to this; rather the Qur'anic description testifies to the essence of creation as revelation at all stages and consistently through all those stages. The Qur'an says:

> Verily in the heavens and on earth there are signs for those who believe. And in the creation of yourselves, and in the fact that animals are scattered [through the earth], there are signs for those of assured faith. And in the alternation of night and day, and in the fact that God sends down sustenance from the sky and revives therewith the earth after its death, and in the change of the winds, [in all these] there are signs for those who are wise. (Qur'an 45: 3–5)

Yet the Qur'an does not simply draw our attention to an omnipresent God – a God who is present in all acts; it also demands that the listener opens his/her mind to comprehend creation as revelation and therefore to take part in ascertaining the truth. Of the universe, the Qur'an says that "the heavens and the earth were joined together as one unit, before we clove them asunder" (21: 30). Then "it was He who created night and day, the sun and the moon; all [the celestial bodies] move along, each in its rounded course" (21: 33). In describing the earth, the Qur'an tells us that God "turned to the sky, and it had been [like] smoke. He said to it and to the earth: 'Come together, willingly or unwillingly.' They said: 'We come [together] in willing obedience'" (41: 11). And, finally, "the heavens, we have built it with power. And verily we are expanding it" (51: 47). Modern and contemporary Muslim thinkers, from Muhammad Iqbal (d. 1938) to Tariq Ramadan, have found in the concept of "universe as revelation" a dynamic feature of the Islamic worldview.

The Qur'an presents life on earth as revelation as well, implicating nature as part of a revelatory order: "And your Lord inspired the bee: build homes in mountains and trees, and in [the hives] they build for you." Verses like these were seized upon by Muslim scientists, who looked at the world empirically; they took them as an indication of the presence of laws and thus of a revelatory order. Islam has never had the problems with science that other religious traditions had; in fact during the Middle Ages it was Muslim contributions that laid down the groundwork for some of the quintessential elements of modernity, including the scientific process.

At this point we can consider the Qur'anic description of humanity at two levels: there is, first, a biological description; and, second, an ontological description. Biologically, life itself is always created from the same source. The Qur'an tells us that God "made from water every living thing" (21: 30), while another verse describes how "God has created every animal from water. Some of them creep on their bellies, some walk on two legs, and some walk on four. God creates what He wills, for truly God has power over all things" (24: 45). Concerning humanity in particular, the Qur'an refers to the embryonic process:

> we placed him as a drop of mixed fluid in a place of rest, firmly fixed. Then we made the sperm into a clinging clot [*alaqa*]. Then out of that clot we made a fetus lump of flesh. Then out of that lump of flesh we made bones, and we clothed the bones in flesh. Then we developed another creature out of it. So blessed be God, the best one to create! (23: 12–14)

An example of how the Qur'an stimulates thought and insists on the revelatory nature of created things is its use of the word *alaqa*. *Alaqa* denotes something leech-like. When the Qur'an referred to God making humans out of *alaqa* at a given stage (Qur'an 75: 37–38), the pre-Islamic Arabs were confused as to its meaning. How or why would God create a human out of a leech? It is not until the advent of modern science that exegetes could fully appreciate the value of the Qur'anic image: during the first trimester of life, the zygote clings to the uterine wall, much as a leech clings to human skin. This is not to make a case for the miraculous origins of the Qur'an, but rather to point out that this text provoked questions as much as it offered answers and encouraged a rational approach to the universe. There are numerous verses that refer to facts of geology, zoology, biology, and astronomy. The sheer number of these verses in a religious text helps explain why Muslims had a much easier time with science in the Middle Ages than their European counterparts.

The second level at which we could talk about the human being is ontological: the human being as revelation. In this context humanity is a revelation in the biological sense described above, where nature itself is miraculous and is deemed to be a sign; but human consciousness, as expressed through language, is the other dimension of accessible revelation. In spite of the heavy biological emphasis in the Qur'an, its treatment of the creation of Adam and Eve remains relatively consistent with that of the other Abrahamic traditions. Where and how it diverges from them is also significant, and some of those divergences will be addressed in the next section. But our concern here is the nature of language.

On the creation of humanity, the Qur'an poses an initial dilemma: "Behold, thy Lord said to the angels: 'I will create a viceregent on earth.' The angels replied: 'Wilt Thou place therein one who will make mischief and shed blood whilst we do celebrate Thy praises and glorify Thy holy (name)?' He said: 'I know what ye know not.'" Here we have one overarching theme: the human being is God's regent on earth and is thus bestowed with sovereignty within certain natural limits – these limits being humanity's intended purpose and potential ("I know what ye know not"). The following verse is revealing: it indicates the unique capacity of the human and the sacred role of language as revelation.

> And He taught Adam the names of all things; then He placed them before the angels, and said: "Tell me the names of these if ye are right." (Qur'an 2: 30–31)

> He said: "O Adam! Tell them their natures." When he had told them, Allah said: "Did I not tell you that I know the secrets of heaven and earth, and I know what ye reveal and what ye conceal?" (Qur'an 2: 33)

So that we do not undervalue the significance of the above passage for purposes of theology, consider the role of language for a moment: not only dialogical language, the words we speak to one another, but also the inner voice of consciousness, which is constituted by language as well. As the German theologian Heinrich Fries (1996: 219) points out, "language discloses the reality of the human being" in three ways. First, "it is the sign, the expression, and the medium of their creatureliness." Second, language sets humans free: "through speech human beings achieve distance from the speechless compulsion of instincts and habit, from the immediately present and existing, from the apparently inevitable, and are led to the possibility of decision." In addition, language brings up other possibilities or potentials, found in the past or in the future, through the language of history or that of planning. Third, language introduces humans "to an historical origin and tradition, to all kinds of relationships of belonging and communication, and they remain connected to these." So, on Fries description, language is revelatory in so far as it points to something beyond the words themselves – to the essence of things.

There is something I would like to add to Fries' description, something existentially more primal: this element or aspect is language/consciousness and its relation to the concept of the "Word" as revelation. The concept of the "Word" is closely bound up with notions of reason, logic, and language – all mutually interdependent. The concept of the "Word" embodies human beings' unique capacity to know, to be known by others, and to participate in knowledge. Consciousness is the individual's sole witness to reality, and it is through these mutually interdependent capacities, through consciousness, that reality is apprehended, reflected upon, and thus communicated – or *witnessed*. From a Qur'anic perspective, language/consciousness is the highest miracle; for it is literally impossible to be aware of God, let alone communicate God (which is the very purpose of revelation) in its absence. Language/consciousness is the very medium of the sacred, and thus it is itself sacred; remember that, in Islam, God taught Adam "the name of all things," in other words how to speak and think. Three things happened here. First, Adam was distinguished from the angels in this respect. Second, Adam was given authority through his ability to name all things, and thus to define them. Lastly, God endowed Adam (and by implication all of humanity) with the ability to speak, think, and reflect.

Language/consciousness is at the very heart and center of existence; for if you did not exist with consciousness, would reality exist? Yet you are a conscious being, and your consciousness has made you aware not only of yourself, but of the consciousness of others; thus your very consciousness has pointed to something beyond itself, namely reality. Hence, from a theological point of view, consciousness is revelation; for it implies the existence, beyond itself, of something greater.

With this in mind, we can now address the topic of the prophetic tradition in Islam. The Qur'an recognizes two types of prophetic tradition: one general, another specific. Both kinds are represented through theological commentaries, the former on humanity and existence, the later on various Abrahamic themes. The Qur'an says: "Before thee [Muhammad] We sent Apostles to many nations…" (6: 42). In fact the Islamic tradition suggests that prophets who professed *tawhīd* were sent to all the nations, and that revelation is a recurrent theme in history. More specifically, there are revelations that are tied distinctly to the Abrahamic tradition; these are too numerous to be all listed here, but here are a few examples:

> And remember we gave Moses the scripture and the criterion [between right and wrong]: There was a chance for you to be guided aright. (Qur'an 2: 53)

> We have sent Thee [Muhammad] inspiration, as we sent it to Noah and the Messengers after him: we sent inspiration to Abraham, Isma'il, Isaac, Jacob and the Tribes, to Jesus, Job, Jonah, Aaron, and Solomon, and to David We gave the Psalms. (Qur'an 4: 163)

> And in their footsteps we sent Jesus the son of Mary, confirming the law that had come before him: we sent him the Gospel: therein was guidance and light, and confirmation of the law that had come before him: a guidance and an admonition to those who fear God. (Qur'an 5: 46)

> When the Qur'an is read, listen to it with attention, and hold your peace: that ye may receive mercy. (Qur'an 7: 204)

Let us now look at the Qur'an as a source of ethics and law.

Ethics and Law

In order to understand the possibility of an ethical life among human beings, we must understand the Qur'anic view of human nature. We have repeatedly mentioned the lack of "original sin" in Islam; thus evil is not an inherent feature of mankind, but rather the byproduct of ignorant choices. More precisely, bad acts are caused by ignorance and arrogance, by forgetting one's true path. To appreciate this doctrine fully, let us look at the creation of human beings in the Qur'an. Qur'anic theology differs from Judaism and Christianity in its description of the cosmic crises around the confrontation between good and evil that occurred upon the creation of Adam and Eve. Adam and Eve are forgiven for their transgression against God's command "not to eat" from the forbidden tree; thus no fall occurs. Human beings are not inherently "sinful" but naturally reasonable, and thus free to choose the correct path. There is no dichotomy between the "saved" and the "damned." All humans have the same potential for salvation, so long as they remember God and behave accordingly. What does this tell us about the possibility of an ethical life?

In the last section we discussed revelation in relation to Adam (or humankind) in terms of communicating/consciousness. Veracious communication (i.e. logic) and experience come together to form reason. The ability to communicate or to produce understandable thoughts is an important aspect of reason. In order for words to communicate, they must be put together in such a way as to make sense. The words (signifiers) must signify something that makes sense to the listener, so they must *consistently* correspond to things in the world, and those things must be understood in a relatively consistent manner. Suppose I say to you: "I am jumping down to the sky." What do I mean? Not even I understand what I mean; the statement is meaningless and hence unreasonable. But sometimes you may understand a statement like "I am jumping up to the moon," but still consider it unreasonable because your everyday experience tells you that jumping up to the moon is impossible. Thus logic and experience constitute reason/rationality. In the Islamic worldview, the story of Adam proclaims humanity's rational nature and reason's association with the divine.

According to the Islamic worldview, human beings are by nature rational, since God endowed Adam with the ability to speak about things in the world. This is exactly what *distinguishes* Adam (or humanity) from the rest of creation – even from angels; and his possession of this ability takes us to the deeper ontological claim that the human being is inherently innocent and free to be moral. Here are three passages in the Qur'an that talk about the nature of humanity and immorality:

And behold, we said to the angels, "Bow down to Adam," and they bowed down. Not so Iblis: he refused and was haughty: and he was of those who reject faith. (Qur'an 2: 34)

O Iblis! What prevents thee from prostrating thyself to one whom I have created with my hands? Art thou haughty? Or art thou one of the high (and mighty) ones? (Qur'an 38: 75)

(Iblis) said: "I am better than he: thou created me from fire, and him thou created from clay." (Qur'an 38: 76)

In the Qur'an, the first act against humanity was Iblis' refusal to respect it. God commands respect for Adam – his rational creation, who was given life through his own breadth. But Iblis is arrogant and swears to be an enemy to humankind. The Qur'an provides the template for a dynamic between right and wrong – or perhaps between "good" and "evil." But what is important for us to remember here is that "evil" is not something inherent to the world; it is in fact an "enemy" to the natural state of things.

The Qur'an and the Five Pillars

By now you are familiar with the general ethos of Islam. There is only one source of true power – God. Entertaining fear or awe toward anything less than God is a result of intellectual dishonesty. From an Islamic point of view, the concept of *tawhīd* helps human individuals preserve their intellectual honesty by recalling the unique singularity of God.

Now, there are also practices that are designed to preserve the spiritual integrity of human beings; and these practices constitute the Muslim life. They are commonly referred to as "the five pillars." Although we have constantly referred to the emphasis that the Islamic tradition places on reason, the five pillars are a matter of faith. Revealed to Prophet Muhammad, these practices form the ascetic and social core of a Muslim's day.

Shahada

The first pillar is *shahada* – the Islamic confession. The process of becoming a Muslim is quite simple, which is consistent with the relative simplicity of Islamic belief. An individual becomes a Muslim by declaring: "I bear witness there is no God except the God and I bear witness that Muhammad is the Messenger of God." This simple statement is the foundation of Islamic belief. Theoretically, when an individual is of reasonable age, he/she declares the creed of his/her own will. In practice, Muslims tend to raise their children as Muslims, and thus the Islamic creed forms a part of their lives from a very early stage – as happens in all religions. Traditionally, many Muslims recite the *shahada* or the *athan* – that is, the Muslim call to prayer containing the *shahada* – in the ears of a newborn, so that this may be the first thing the child hears; this corresponds to the widespread Muslim theological belief that the oneness of God is the first thing a child intuitively knows. But these are folk traditions; they are not prescribed in the Qur'an.

If there is something we must immediately note about the Islamic confession, it is the role of rationality. The *shahada* is not a claim to have "faith" that there is no God except the God; it is a claim to "witness" it. Once again, this emphasizes the relative strength of reason and the senses in the Islamic worldview. The Muslim does not conclude that there is a single God *in spite of* the incoherence of the world around him/her; rather a Muslim concludes that the coherence of the world around him/her evinces God.

Salat

The second pillar is *salat* – prayer. A Muslim has to pray five times a day according to a prescribed ritual involving prostration and recitation of the Qur'an. According to an Islamic tradition, when the Prophet was asked why Muslims should pray five times a day, he answered: "If one bathed five times a day, would a speck of dirt remain on the body? Prayer is the same for the soul." As said before, the concept of *tawhīd* contains more than a simple statement to the effect that there is one God, as opposed to several gods. *Tawhīd* means that God is the sole source of reality; *salat* serves as an intellectual and spiritual peg of this idea throughout the Muslim's day. Five times a day, Muslims must take a few minutes to re-orient themselves toward the absolute, suspending their attention to the ephemeral and temporary world.

In addition to ritual prayer, a Muslim is required to purify him/herself ritually in preparation for it. *Wudu* (ablutions) involve washing the hands, the arms, the face, the neck, and the feet before *salat*. *Ghusl* (bathing) is required if a Muslim has had sexual intercourse between prayers. In our age this call to cleanliness may be lost on the reader; we are all accustomed to the daily shower. In the Middle Ages, however, such emphasis on hygiene was unheard of. Ritual bathing in the Islamic context underlined the importance of cleanliness and hygiene as a daily part of one's life.

Zakat

Zakat refers to almsgiving: every year a Muslim is required to give a fixed portion of his/her income to the poor. The function of charity is relatively straightforward; but, apart from contributing to social well-being, *zakat* does for one's livelihood just what *salat* does for one's spirituality: it ensures that money is not an end in and of itself and that the earner is consistently reminded of the larger social network s/he belongs to, depends on, and is in turn depended upon to sustain.

Sawm

The next pillar is *sawm* – fasting. Every year, during the month of Ramadan, a Muslim is required to fast from sunrise until sunset. The reason for the choice of this month is its auspicious place in the Islamic tradition: Ramadan is the month during which the Qur'an was first revealed to the Prophet. The Islamic calendar differs from the Gregorian in that it is lunar rather than solar; thus the Islamic calendar rotates throughout the Gregorian year, being shorter by roughly nine days. In some years a Muslim may fast with relative ease during the winter and with relative hardship in the summer, since the days are longer. During this month a Muslim abstains from any food and drink (including water), and also from smoking, having sex, and any other physical indulgence – every day, from sunrise to sunset. S/he is also expected to be at a higher level of spiritual awareness during this month, and s/he should refrain from outbursts of temper, gossip, and vain or superfluous talk. Although these things are always expected of Muslims, like anyone else, they may fail to deliver according to the highest standards of their humanity. The obligations of the month of Ramadan remind them of their spiritual discipline and of their ability to achieve it.

The fast during Ramadan has two main purposes. First, a Muslim must exercise authority over his/her body rather than allowing it to command the person. There are several prophetic traditions that may help explain what this means. The Prophet said: "A meal for two is enough for three, and a meal for three is enough for four." In other words, do not overindulge in eating and be mindful of sharing with others, we are all fully capable of doing so. Another tradition reports that "the man with an excessive gut is not a believer." If someone constantly pursues the need to satisfy bodily desires (such as a desire to eat in excess), that person has invested power in the body and has lost sense of the ultimate power of God. Overeating marks the absence not only of physical discipline, but of intellectual and spiritual discipline as well. The idea that obesity, alcoholism, sex addiction, drug addiction, or even addiction to ordinary smoking may be "diseases" is anathema to Islam. From the Islamic point of view, men and women command their body, not the other way around.

The second purpose of Ramadan is to offer Muslims the experience of going without basic things like food and water. In our environment of material abundance it is easy to forget the desperate need of others. Whereas the Muslim chooses to forgo food and drink during the month as an act of faith, the poor go without food or drink due to poverty, negligence, and, more often than not, human injustice. The hunger that the Muslim feels throughout the day should remind him/her of the hunger an innocent poor person feels throughout a lifetime. In addition to *zakat* and the innumerable insistences on charity given in the Qur'an, Muslims are reminded that they cannot turn their back on the poor; they are responsible for improving their conditions.

Hajj

Finally, the fifth pillar is *hajj* – the annual pilgrimage to Mecca, the birthplace of Islam. If s/he is physically and financially able to do it, a Muslim is required to attend *hajj* at least once in his/her lifetime. Every year, nearly 2.5 million Muslims from all over the world converge on their way to Mecca to perform the *hajj*. The purpose of *hajj* is to remind Muslims of the larger and extremely diverse community to which they belong. Apart from diversity, this pilgrimage also stresses the element of unity. All Muslims are required to wear the same type of clothing – a basic white tunic – in order to demonstrate their humility and their equality before God. Princes, paupers, generals, and farmers pray side by side, in unison, without regard for social status.

Like *salat*, the *hajj* involves rituals dictated by the Prophet. Some of these rituals are pre-Islamic; they were appropriated by the Prophet in the name of monotheism. Others affirm aspects of the larger Abrahamic tradition, particularly the Arabs' relationship to Ishmael, the son of Abraham. Mecca serves as a focal point, a place of gathering, and a common orientation.

Now that we have explained the basics of the Islamic creed we can turn to Islam's history, the development of its institutions, and its role in world history.

Notes

1   In fact these three consonants constitute the root of the noun "peace" in
Semitic languages as a whole; thus
"peace" is *salaam* in Arabic and *shalom*
in Hebrew. The first consonant is
known as *sīn* in Arabic and as *shīn* in
Hebrew; the remaining two are known
as *lām* and *mīm*.

2   In Arabic the word for "God" is "al-
Illah" or "Allah"; so "Allah" is not a
proper name, but simply the Arabic for
"God." Some argue that "Allah" cannot
be replaced by "God," since "al-Illah"
means "the God." I find this claim to
be misleading rather than to provide
greater accuracy; thus we will employ
the term "God." Now, what does it
mean, in Islam, not to believe? The
term for "unbelief" or "lack of belief"
is *kufr*, from the root *kfr-*, which has
two general meanings: to "cover and
hide"; and "hubris" or "arrogant ingrat-
itude." Thus infidelity is understood by
Muslims as an arrogant and ungrateful
or inconsiderate rejection of the reality
of God.

Discussion Questions

1   What is the nature of *tawhīd*? What are its theological implications?
2   What characterizes Muhammad's career, in both social and spiritual terms?
3   According to Islam and the Qur'an, the universe is a sign or a revelation ("Verily!
Our word unto a thing, when we intend it, is only that we say unto it: 'BE!' and
it is": Qur'an 16: 40). What implications could this have for science, or even for
philosophy?

Suggested Further Reading

Az-Zubaidi, Zain (compiler) (1996).
Summarized Sahih al-Bukhari, trans. Kuhsin
Khan. Riyadh: Dar-us-Salam Publications.

Esposito, John (2005). *Islam the Straight
Path*. Oxford: Oxford University Press.

Fries, Heinrich (1996). *Fundamental Theology*.
Washington, DC: Catholic University of
America Press.

Ibn Taymiyyah, Taqi ad-Din (2006). *The
Relief from Distress: An Explanation to the
Du'a of Yunis*, trans. Abu Rumaysah.
Birmingham: Daar as-Sunnah Publishers.

Khalidi, Tarif (1994). *Arabic Historical
Thought in the Classical Period*.
Cambridge: Cambridge University
Press.

Qutb (Koteb), Sayed (1945). *Al-Adalah al-
Ijtima'ya fi al-Islam*, trans. John Hardie.
Cairo: Maktabat Misr.

Nagel, Tilman (2000). *The History of Islamic
Theology from Muhammad to the Present*.
Princeton, NJ: Markus Weiner.

Rahman, Fazlur (2002). *Islam*. Chicago, IL:
University of Chicago Press.

4

Islamic Beliefs
The Development of Islamic Ideas

LAITH SAUD

Outline

Introduction

The Islamic scholar Vincent Cornell (1999: 67–69) observed that "the Qur'an is less concerned with defining creedal boundaries than with affirming the universal obligation to believe in One God." In the previous chapter we referred to this

An Introduction to Islam in the 21st Century, First Edition. Edited by Aminah Beverly McCloud,
Scott W. Hibbard, and Laith Saud.
© 2013 Blackwell Publishing Ltd. Published 2013 by Blackwell Publishing Ltd.

emphasis upon the oneness of God as *tawhīd*. In the previous chapter we referred to this emphasis upon the oneness of God as *tawhīd*. In this chapter we will discuss how *tawhīd* informs the central tenets of Islam, both as they developed during the lifetime of the Prophet and later throughout history. As a result, the fundamental premise of all Islamic thought is remarkably consistent: To be a Muslim is to act in accordance with one's awareness of God; and to be aware of God is to look beyond what is temporary in any given thing, to find the eternal source behind it. This worldview means that all things are valuable, since all things come from God and thus reflect his will and his creativity.

In the following pages we will explore the basic components of Islamic thought in light of the theme of *tawhīd*. By the end of the chapter the student will be more aware of the inner relationship between all the parts of Islamic thought and of how this relationship developed. The student will also be thoroughly familiarized with Islamic law, theology, and philosophy.

The *sunna* of the Prophet

As we said before, Islam is predicated on the belief that knowledge is fundamentally transformative. To know beauty is to experience beauty; to know love is to experience love. From the Islamic point of view, to know God is to experience peace of heart and mind. Moreover, such an experience is transformative. It is also the highest goal that one can achieve, and it reflects the ultimate purpose of human existence, which is to live in accordance with God's will. There are, then, two issues that inform the Muslim state of mind. First, there is the idea that knowledge of God returns an individual to his or her natural state or *fitrah*; this gives the individual a sense of being created with a purpose. Second, the Qur'anic insistence that one must act in an ethical (or moral) manner is based on a fundamental obligation to the creator of all life. One will be held accountable for his or her actions in the world. The Qur'an says: "And so, he who shall have done an atom's weight of good, shall behold it; and he who shall have done an atom's weight of bad, shall behold it" (99: 7–8).

A Muslim's actions, then, should reflect awareness of the creator (*taqwā*) and should be consistent with these basic moral obligations. To understand better how to live such a moral life, Muslims look at the example set by the Prophet. This is due to the general Muslim belief that no person exemplified the state of awareness of God better than Prophet Muhammad. Hence the *sunna* – the actions and sayings of the Prophet – constitute an important institution and tradition in Muslim society.

The concept of *sunna* dates back to pre-Islamic times. The *sunna* was composed of pre-Islamic traditions that the Arabs used to guide their own behavior and to determine right from wrong. But these traditions reflected the largely pagan and tribal mindset of the Arabs. When the Prophet proclaimed the absoluteness of *tawhīd*, the validity of these pre-Islamic traditions was discredited. Muslims refer sometimes to pre-Islamic Arabia as *jāhalīyaa*, the "age of ignorance," since they believe that in those days Arabs were guided by superstitions, not by knowledge of the one true God. The revelation of the Qur'an and the career of the Prophet were watershed moments in the history of the Arabs. Everything changed afterwards.

Fazlur Rahman (2002: 43) observes that, "so long as the Prophet was alive, he provided the sole religious and political guide for Muslims both through the Qur'anic revelation and by his extra Qur'anic words and behavior (i.e. *sunna*)." In the century following the death of the Prophet the unprecedented expansion of the Islamic polity raised practical questions. Unlike the Qur'an, which was written down in Muhammad's lifetime and codified very shortly after his death, tradition holds that the Prophet explicitly forbade the writing down of his own *sunna* or hadith (the sayings and actions of the Prophet), so that they may not be confused with the Qur'an. Oral traditions persisted in western Arabia and Iraq for a century, but they were often contradictory. Hence the need to codify the *sunna* of the Prophet soon made itself felt. Given the vastness of the Islamic Empire and the diverse makeup of its societies, it is not surprising that religious and legal questions of a specific and complex character arose. In order to deal with these questions in a satisfactory manner, one had to be able to distinguish the authentic sayings of the Prophet from spurious ones.

Malik ibn Anas

One of the first and most important codifiers of the *sunna* was Imam Malik ibn Anas (d. 795), from the Hijaz (a western province of Arabia). Imam Malik was a contemporary of the *Tabi'in* – the first generation of Muslims born after the death of the Prophet. These Muslims were the immediate descendants of Muhammad's companions. The Prophet's companions are known as *Sahaba*. Most importantly, this first generation actually heard what the Prophet had said and saw what he had done. Consequently its members were an invaluable source in documenting the Prophet's sayings and deeds.

Imam Malik employed a methodology that was useful for a society that relied upon oral traditions. His method involved the development of a verbal chain of transmission (referred to as *isnad*). Any report of the Prophet's actions or sayings was accompanied by a reference disclosing who heard or saw this report. Here is an example of a hadith that addresses the topic of speaking behind people's back (Rahimuddin 1985: 421; translation modified):

> Khalid ibn ʿAbd Allah ibn Sayyad reported that Muttalib ibn ʿAbd Allah ibn Hantab al-Makhzumi reported that a man asked the apostle of God: "What does backbiting [speaking behind one's back] mean?" Prophet Muhammad said: "Describing a man in such a manner that, if he should hear it, it should seem repugnant to him." The man said: "Even if it is true?" Muhammad responded: "If you speak falsely, it would be [an even greater] calumny."

Notice how the chain of transmission is documented? This is for verification purposes. Imam Malik's students edited their teacher's extensive collection of these reports into the *Al-Muwatta*. Imam Malik is thus known as a traditionalist in Islamic thought, since he valued the tradition and taught it. He should also be considered a traditionalist on account of the fact that he valued the authority of traditional practices over and above speculative reason *in determining good behavior* as well. This is not, however, the only position in Islamic thought. Many philosophers whom we will discuss later endorsed rationalism as a basis of determining right action. Nonetheless, since Imam Malik's work was so invaluable in the formulation of a normative code for later Islamic behavior, it is no surprise that he is considered the founder of one of the major schools of Islamic jurisprudence: the Maliki School.

Over the next few centuries other traditionalists would emerge who were more explicitly devoted to the authentication and exploration of the *sunna* and of various hadith. Naturally, with the passage of time, the length of *isnad* – the chain of transmission – increased, so an elaborate methodology had to be developed in order to test its veracity. The later traditionalists developed a set of methodologies, collectively known as *ilm al-hadith* (the science of hadith); they are known as *muhaddithun* (hadith scholars) and are credited with the maturation of these methodologies.

The Development of Islamic Jurisprudence, *Kalam*, and Philosophy

The emphasis on the life of the Prophet and the careful documentation of his words and deeds helped to develop a tradition of social–scientific historiography. Attention to the *isnad* has been commented upon by Ibn Taymiyya to Ibn al-'Arabi, the idea being that the ability to verify prophetic traditions roots Islam in some objectivity, and even empirical veracity. This emphasis upon verification and scholarship is also reflected in the Muslim approach to the Qur'an, particularly in regard to the "occasions of revelation" that inform the meaning and understanding of this text. Since the Prophet's revelations occurred within a particular historical context – and revolved around the life of the Prophet – studying his biography (*sira*) is a fundamental part of understanding Islam. Over the first two centuries of Islamic civilization these genres – hadith and sira – grew together and complemented each other, as did the methods by which they were validated. Since these matters had spiritual consequences, getting it right was very important.

An important part of the Islamic ethos – exemplified by the *isnad* – is its emphasis on knowledge and knowing. To take a position based on anything but knowledge was tantamount to guessing, which was considered an attribute of the age of ignorance. As Tarif Khalidi (1994: 18) observes, the Qur'an makes constant reference to "true wisdom," *ilm*, as opposed to "whimsical opinion," *zann*. These terms serve "to highlight the kind of wisdom acquired through the reflection upon the moral of Qur'anic narratives: real history as opposed to legend or illusion" (ibid.). The Qur'anic insistence that there is a single truth imposed an epistemological structure – or means of understanding what we know – on the community of Muslim believers. If there is a single truth, any part of that truth that has not been revealed *can* be discovered, either through an examination of traditions or through the use of speculative reason.

Imam Abu Hanifa

Abu Hanifa (d. 765) was born in Kufa, Iraq, which was an important center of Islamic learning, commerce, and military strategy. Abu Hanifa's life is of interest for several reasons. In the first place he was a major early jurist, and his juridical method influenced the development of Islamic law (*sharia*). Second, Abu Hanifa exemplifies one very distinct position on the intellectual spectrum that we discussed earlier. Lastly, he personifies the fierce independence of some Muslim intellectuals and their often tenuous relationship with government.

There are two major trends in Islamic jurisprudence: the Hijazi (Medinese) and the Iraqi (Kufic). Imam Malik, whom we discussed above, typifies the Hijazi trend. This trend is characterized by traditionalism, by which we mean a reliance on the traditions of the Prophet and his companions and on their institutionalization. It makes sense that Imam Malik is illustrative of the Hijazi trend: himself a Hijazi, he was in constant interaction with the *Tabi'in* and was based in Medina, the city of the Prophet and the heart of his career. Medina was home to the most important *Sahaba*, and thus to the most verifiable oral traditions. In short, traditions were strong in Medina, and Imam Malik valued them above all other sources for formulating normative behavior.

In Iraq the situation was very different. Since Iraq was further away from the seminal lands of Islam, the oral tradition there was neither as strong nor as valued as it was in Medina. Iraqi jurists developed methods based on reasoning – particularly analogical reasoning, which was known as *qiyas*. Abu Hanifa was an advocate of *qiyas*, which derived new legal opinions on the basis of prior analogous legal positions. Abu Hanifa also resorted to personal opinion (*ra'y*) and juristic preference (*istihsān*). These methodologies come together and explain the liberal nature of the Hanafi School of Islamic jurisprudence and its emphasis on the utility of human reason in solving legal problems. Contrast this with the approach of the Maliki School, according to which responding "I do not know" to a legal question was not only superior to speculative legal reasoning but essential to jurisprudence, since legal opinions should be based on sound traditions and little (if anything) more. This tension between "reason" and "tradition" is enormously important in the evolution of Islamic thought, and it will be taken up in the next section.

Abu Hanifa lived to witness the demise of the Umayyads, the rise of the Abbasids, and the political, cultural, and commercial ascendency of Iraq. Tradition has it that Abu Jafar al-Mansur, the second Abbasid caliph, appointed him Chief Judge (*Qadi*); this was one of the first appointments in a classical Islamic institution.

Abu Hanifa refused the post, however, preferring his independence; he was subsequently jailed and spent the remainder of his life in prison. Today one of the most important mosques in Baghdad stands in his honor.

The Hanifi School of Islamic jurisprudence was patronized by the Abbasid state and developed quickly. Roughly 800 years later, due to its liberal and flexible nature, this school was found useful by the Ottomans too – namely in the development of dynamic legal codes and new legal opinions in the face of radically changing circumstances. Ebu Su'ud, the greatest of Ottoman legal scholars, articulated legal opinions noted for their emphasis on progress and reason. He went so far as to endow the sultan with executive authority, thereby making sure that *sharia*, Islamic law, remained contemporary and to a large degree independent of tradition, according to his own vision.

The Islamic Epistemological Spectrum

We can now begin to define an epistemological spectrum of Islamic sciences: it ranges from traditionalism at one end to rationalism at the other. These two poles represent contrasting attitudes toward how the community of scholars understands certain knowledge and arrives at it. It is useful to become familiar with the whole spectrum, for it runs from the classical period to the modern age and persists throughout all genres of Islamic writing: jurisprudence, *kalam* (dialectics), philosophy, and literature.

Rationalism	Traditionalism
• truth is contemporary;	• truth is ancient, even eternal;
• authority is found in the present;	• authority is found outside of time;
• contemporary institutions or sages possess authority.	• only texts like the Qur'an or ageless traditions possess authority.

The spectrum above represents a broad typology, which incorporates many schools of thought; the central issue, though, that divides them is the disparate attitude toward human reason. Edmund Burke, the father of Western conservatism, famously argued that the reason of a single generation could never outweigh or outvalue the "collected wisdom of the ages." Imam Malik and the traditionalists parallel this point of view in classical Islamic society. This is why Imam Malik was so judicious in collecting the prophetic traditions; he believed that the past should be preserved – its endurance had to be safeguarded for future reference.

The rationalists, on the other hand, turned this logic on its head. They believed that the cumulative nature of knowledge inevitably endows the *present* with authority, since contemporaries possess knowledge of the past as well as of the changing conditions of the present. So, for example, the great *adib* (writer) al-Jahiz (d. 868) argued:

> books were transmitted from nation to nation, from era to era and from language to language until they finally reached us and we were the last to inherit and examine

them [...] our practice with our successors ought to resemble the practice of our
predecessors with us. But we have attained greater wisdom than they did, and those
who follow will attain greater wisdom than we have. (Khalidi 1994: 108)

Al-Jahiz is articulating an attitude of progress; he feels that progressive change,
or the accumulation of "greater wisdom" from age to age, necessarily *limits* the
ability of the past to govern the present. Rationalists therefore claimed the right
to reform and authorized such reform; rationalists also emphasized the need for
institutions endowed with the authority to lead such reforms.

At first glance the latter position may seem more reliable; a traditionalist,
however, would argue that rationalism/progressivism amounts to the blind
leading the blind. A traditionalist believes the past to be the only thing we can
claim to know with certainty; hence we should remain faithful to the tried principles of the past in order to maintain our course. Regarding the question of change,
traditionalists are not opposed to change altogether; they would simply caution
against what they perceive to be arbitrary and reckless change. Moreover, many
traditionalists would argue that radical change is simply the unwise abandonment
of the past. This creates new circumstances, which in turn create a perceived –
though not genuine – need to produce new answers. The inevitable result is society's setting course for unchartered waters and requiring, you might have guessed,
yet newer answers. So traditionalists can convincingly argue that rationalism in
fact leads society into darkness; for we have abandoned a "known" past for an
"unknown" future.

We must pause again, however, for the rationalist reply is equally strong. The
circumstances of Islamic society in 732 CE were radically different from the circumstances of Islamic society in 632 CE, when the Prophet died. A Muslim in Iraq, like
Abu Hanifa, did not have satisfactory access to authentic Prophetic traditions – let
alone a Muslim in Spain or in northern India. Yet Muslims needed solutions – and
solutions to questions for which there was no revealed truth, or no tradition to
provide guidance. Where else can one turn, then, apart from reason?

A brief look at the discussion above reveals the basic strength of both arguments. Had either pole been "more convincing" than the other, perhaps we could
dispense with the epistemological spectrum altogether; but this spectrum persists
in Islam (as it does in the Western tradition) precisely because of the relative
strength of both ends. In order for us to manage the inherent tension in the spectrum, for the purpose of understanding Islam, we need to understand that the
spectrum depicts two epistemological archetypes, and *not* definitive and clear-cut
attitudes. It will be common to see thinkers, movements, or trends that gravitate
toward one end of the spectrum but still exhibit characteristics found nearer the
opposite end. In addition, we will find that most Muslims – as groups or as
individual thinkers – occupy a place toward the middle of the spectrum.

Now that we have given some attention to the Islamic epistemological spectrum, let us discuss how this spectrum reveals itself through institutions. Islamic
law is such an institution; let us now look at its institutionalization.

Imam Muhammad ibn Idris al-Shafii

In early 9th-century Baghdad, the capital of the Abbasid Dynasty, not only had Islamic culture taken a definitive and recognizable form, but Islamic civilization was one of the most enlightened civilizations in the world. As Ahmad Dallal (1999) observes, the Islamic emphasis on verifiable knowledge made Muslims much more open to various sciences; in Islamic civilization "science was practiced on a scale unprecedented in earlier or contemporary human history" (155). This scientific attitude was displayed in all disciplines, including the law; and, like many poets, also philosophers and scholars were attracted to Iraq. Muhammad al-Shafii (d. 820) went to Iraq to participate in its high culture.

As we mentioned before, the Abbasids were beginning to institutionalize the law by creating posts like the "Chief *Qadi.*" A *Qadi* is a judge invested with the all-important task of arbitrating disputes on behalf of the state. His rulings become in turn precedents for future usage in determining the law. As Mohammad Kamali (1999: 114) notes, "the controversy between the Traditionalists and Rationalists had by al-Shafii's time accentuated the need for methodology." Al-Shafii studied with the Malikis in the Hijaz and with the Hanafis in Iraq, and in this manner he developed the general principles of jurisprudence (*usul al-fiqh*). *Fiqh* refers to the human effort to discover God's ideal law (*sharia*) through intellectual methods; thus there is always an understanding that Islamic law reflects an imperfect human interpretation of a perfect divine law. Here we can begin to see the usefulness of our spectrum: in order to ensure that society stays close to divine law, traditionalists stick to the sources they consider divine – the Qur'an and the *sunna* of the Prophet – while they severely limit the use of reason. Rationalists allow reason a greater role, as they emphasize the value of being contemporary. Al-Shafii brilliantly reconciled these two positions. As a result, he did not eliminate the spectrum, at least not in law, but actually secured its stability by anchoring both poles in common sources. Al-Shafii articulated the "four sources of the law" and articulated their respective relations with one another. Here they are:

1. Qur'an
2. The *sunna* of the Prophet (which occupies a position equal to that of the Qur'an)
3. *Ijma* – the consensus of the community
4. *Qiyas* – analogical reasoning

Imam al-Shafii argued that the Qur'an and the *sunna* enjoy equal status as legal sources insofar as the *authentically* reported actions of the Prophet could not have contradicted the Qur'an; in fact they personified the Qur'an. In other words, the Prophet is the best example of an actualized precedent, which can serve as a guide to understand what the Qur'an means in particular instances. Yet the Qur'an is not a legal text; the vast majority of Qur'anic verses are moral in nature, and there are questions that remain unanswered by the *sunna*. Al-Shafii allowed room for these questions to be addressed by way of human reason, yet he anchored reason. *Qiyas*, analogical reasoning – a method favored by Abu Hanifa – looks to known cases and addresses new ones using the similarities between the two categories. For example, the Qur'an explicitly prohibits the drinking of wine. The question then arose: Are other distilled drinks forbidden as well? Since the basis of the Qur'anic prohibition is that wine intoxicates the mind and inhibits human faculties, most legal schools prohibit other intoxicants as well, even though there is no explicit prohibition of them either in the Qur'an or in the *sunna*. Also, Imam al-Shafii allowed *ijma* – the consensus of the community, as represented by legal scholars – to be a source of the law (for Malik, *ijma* was restricted to the community in Medina). There is a proto-democratic flavor to this approach to the law, buttressed as it is by the well-known prophetic tradition according to which Muhammad says: "My community will never agree to an error" (Esposito 2005: 82). The followers of al-Shafii are known as Shafiis, but his methodology has pervaded all the legal schools.

Imam Ahmad ibn Hanbal and the Mihna

Kamali (1999: 114) notes:

> al-Shafii's degree of emphasis on tradition and his strong advocacy of the Sunna did not satisfy the uncompromising traditionalists, who preferred not to rely on human reason and chose instead to base their doctrines as much as possible on the precedents established in the Qur'an and hadith.

And indeed a major legal school emerges at this time – that of the Hanbalis, who trace their intellectual lineage back to the great Ahmad ibn Hanbal (d. 855). Hanbal was a staunch traditionalist; his conservatism cannot be understood merely within its intellectual context but must be couched in its historical and political environment. Two developments converge to contextualize the thought of Ahmad ibn Hanbal. First, the canonization of prophetic traditions had reached a much more mature stage during his lifetime, and thus traditions possessed much greater ideological authority. Second, and perhaps more importantly, the Abbasid state had itself become much more ideological; not only had it started to take rationalist schools of thought under its patronage, but it even attempted to impose certain dogmas on the community of believers, in an attempt to create an "orthodox Islam." Never before in Islamic history had the state had the authority to tell Muslims what to believe. The community was autonomous in its beliefs: this is why Muslims of different opinions have always been known to live more or less harmoniously together. The Abbasid state now moved to consolidate its authority by annexing Muslim beliefs and by conflating statecraft with matters of conscience; and it tried to force a certain belief on the community. In this effort, it would find no stauncher defender of the religious autonomy of the community than Ahmad ibn Hanbal.

In 833 CE the Abbasid Caliph al-Mamun initiated the Mihna. *Mihna* essentially means "inquisition" in Arabic. The Mihna sought to impose Islamic belief on the Muslims and was indifferent to other religious groups. But the scale of persecution of the Muslims who resisted the state is simply not comparable to that of the corresponding phenomenon in Europe. Caliph al-Mamun was deeply influenced by Greek philosophy and by Mutazilite *kalam*; for example, he founded the Bayt al-Hikma (House of Wisdom) in Baghdad – an institution commissioned to translate medical, scientific, mathematical, and philosophical works into Arabic, the *lingua franca* of the time.

An important Mutazilite doctrine was that of the "createdness of the Qur'an": we will address the Mutazilites in greater detail shortly. Their basic idea was that the Qur'an was *created in time*, as opposed to being co-eternal with God. This position reflects the highly rationalistic character of Mutazilite thought. The issue may seem trivial, but it is of tremendous theological import. If the Qur'an had been created in time, then, had it been revealed in a different time, it would have been a different Qur'an.

The central issue of the Mihna was the nature of the Qur'an. If the Qur'an was created in time, the Qur'an would only be relevant to its own time and place. The caliph would no longer have to show fealty to the Qur'an, the single most important source of Islamic law. The caliph could thereby assume much greater authority, not only on political matters, but even on matters of creed. This implication is consistent with the rationalist insistence on the authority of contemporary and novel knowledge. For the rationalists, the Qur'an is a source of Islam, but not the only one: human reason is also a source of Islam. There are a host of ideological and sociological reasons for this position, which will be addressed in the following chapter. In addition, one should remember that rationalism not only stresses the superiority of novel knowledge, but it also requires well-developed institutions to distribute various reforms. Thus, in time, we will come across cases of affinity developing between rationalists and the state, as happens in our own time. In Chapters 5 and 6 Scott Hibbard will outline how relations between scholars and state played out in modern times.

The main activity of the Mihna consisted in having scholars brought to the caliphal court to be questioned on certain issues, the nature of the Qur'an being the most significant among them. Those who adhered to the positions taken by the state, whether sincerely or not, were free to pursue their professional duties. Scholars who resisted the state's demands were imprisoned, tortured, and sometimes even killed. Imam Ahmad ibn Hanbal was a traditionalist and refused to make concessions to the official position of the state regarding the nature of the Qur'an; he was imprisoned and tortured.

Methodologically, Hanbal insisted not only on the exclusive authority of the Qur'an and *sunna*, but also on their literalness, thereby removing even the possibility that the Qur'an might require mediators who could rationally convey its "internal meaning." Hanbal was the most traditionalist of the traditionalists. For him, the Qur'an was both precise and timeless. But, most importantly, the Qur'an spoke for itself. A metaphorical Qur'an needs interlocutors to interpret it rationally and to convey its meaning to the believers; and such intermediaries would of course be appropriated by the state. Imam Ahmad ibn Hanbal insisted that the Qur'an should be read literally; this kind of reading would obstruct the generation of "official bodies" designed to mediate its meaning and thereby to claim authority in matters of religion. A literal Qur'an needs no spokesperson, for it says exactly what it says, and in so doing it maintains its autonomy.

The legacy of Imam Ahmad ibn Hanbal is rich and varied. Of the thinkers we have discussed so far, Hanbal gravitates furthest to the traditionalist side of our spectrum. He influenced the great 13th-century jurist Ibn Taymiyya significantly; and much of the latter's legacy, including our way of understanding him, bears the indelible imprint of Hanbal's influence. Ahmad ibn Hanbal strongly safeguarded the autonomy of the community and dealt a severe blow to the development of Islamic theocracy. But this high degree of autonomy and separation of the community is an ambivalent good for us today. On the one hand, it has become more difficult for the state to appropriate religion for political purposes; on the other hand, the lack of clearly defined religious authorities has opened a space for anyone to claim religious authority, regardless of how imprudent or uninstructed that person might be. Many of these issues are significant for the formation of an Islamic theocracy in 20th-century Iran and for the emergence of so-called "Islamist" movements.

Politics, Theology, and Mutazilite *kalam*

In all thought, there is an intimate relationship between history and ideas; this is no less the case in Islamic thought. Early historical events determined the development of theological ideas. Political events instigated questions that required doctrinal answers – theoretical answers. In 661 CE the success of Mu'awiya ibn Abi Sufyan against 'Ali ibn Abi Talib in assuming power raised a host of very serious questions for the community and induced self-introspection. Imam 'Ali ibn Abi Talib was no ordinary Muslim; he was the cousin and son-in-law of the Prophet and had been raised in the Prophet's house. In the cause of Muhammad, 'Ali was also a lion among men and one of Islam's greatest heroes. 'Ali occupies a central place for Shi'ite Muslims; hence we will elaborate on his life and influence later. For our present purposes we need only bear in mind that he was the fourth caliph and a legitimate leader at the time of his conflict with Mu'awiya.

Mu'awiya successfully defeated 'Ali in the first *fitna* (Civil War) and assumed the title of caliph. Mu'awiya was no ordinary Muslim either. He was a lifetime enemy of the Prophet and had converted to Islam only after the political successes of Muhammad ensured Islam's inevitable ascendency. Mu'awiya was also a brilliant tactician and a shrewd statesman, and he deployed the full range of his skills in his coup against Imam 'Ali. Upon his success, the following question arose: What does it say about my personal faith if I follow the rule of someone whose Islam may warrant little respect or who, at the very least, violated the law by challenging the legitimate ruler? The Kharijites answered this question for themselves, and in a quite definitive manner: they argued that anyone who violates God's law should be killed – and they went about trying to do just that. However, the vast majority of the community disagreed. The term *khawarij*, from which the anglicized name Kharijite is formed, means "exiled," thereby conveying the marginal place of its bearers in the wider Muslim imagination.

The vast majority of believers maintained a very moderate position, which was typified by the Murjites (those who "postpone" judging others). The Kharijites argued that, if someone was a "grave sinner," that person was no longer Muslim and therefore it would be right to stand against him/her, even by force. According to the Kharijites, the Umayyads were just such sinners, and hence they did not deserve legitimacy. The Murjites argued, on the other hand, that such judgments belong to God alone and will be issued by him on the Day of Judgment. The passivity of the Murjite position facilitated another doctrinal turn, which for many Muslims was, however, problematic; turn revolved around the idea that God had predetermined all things. The Qur'an is ambiguous on the issue of predeterminism; some passages clearly indicate that human beings are free, while others imply that one's fate is already determined. If God had willed all things, God had willed the rise of the Umayyads; and how was anyone to oppose the decree of God? The Umayyads had taken under their patronage scholars who collected traditions in support of this position.

Hasan al-Basri (d. 728) was a prominent Muslim thinker who advocated free will. Al-Basri is interesting by virtue of being a forefather of rationalist Islam, and in his interpretation of tradition we see how rationalism works. Hasan al-Basri wrote to the Umayyad Caliph Abd' al-Malik a letter in which he insisted on the fallacy of predeterminism; he argued that predeterminism was rationally incompatible with the belief in God's justice and mercy, which are major themes in the Qur'an. Al-Basri read metaphorically those passages that seemed to imply predeterminism, and he allowed his rational mind to parcel out their meanings; he did not read the text literally. Al-Basri went on to demonstrate that this, too, was the *sunna* or example of Muhammad, thereby authorizing his position vis-à-vis the authority of the Prophetic tradition. It is, however, al-Basri's hermeneutics (approach to interpreting the text) that we should be interested in; we will find in it a collaboration between metaphorical and rational interpretations of the text. Reading a text this way means that rationality is the fundamental prerequisite to approaching it; your rationality *leads* your reading of the text. Esoteric readings, supplemented by rationalistic philosophy, become a major feature of Islamic thought. In al-Basri's case we see rationality imposing itself as an authority over the text. As Tilman Nagel (2000: 39) writes, al-Basri "permitted himself a pointed polemical remark directed at the predestinarians: Most of those who claimed their faith or unbelief was predestined by God were careful not to let their worldly businesses run themselves without personally interfering!"

The Mutazilites are considered intellectual descendants of al-Basri. We have already been introduced to the Mutazilites in relation to the Mihna. The Mutazilites argued that their doctrines defended God's "justice" and "divine unity" against some of the other beliefs floating around at the time. "Influenced by the influx of Greek philosophical and scientific thought during the Abbasid period, with its emphasis on reason, logical argumentation, and study of the laws of nature, they relied on reason and rational deduction as tools in Quranic interpretation and theological reflection," observes John Esposito (2005: 71). These rationalists took issue with two major doctrines. The first doctrine involved the understanding of God's attributes; the second posited an uncreated, eternal Qur'an.

The Qur'an repeatedly refers, for example, to God "hearing" and "seeing." But if God "hears" or "sees," how are these distinct attributes to be reconciled with the Islamic notion of God's absolute unity? In addition, hearing and seeing are human faculties related to having a corporeal body. If God hears and sees, then does God have human characteristics? The Mutazilites insisted: "No!" To ascribe a "body" to God would be a form of anthropomorphism – a projection of human qualities onto God. In Islam this could of course fall into the category of *shirk*, since by separating the attributes of God we possibly construct multiple divinities – which, as we well know, is the single greatest transgression in Islam, and basically the only one that is universally recognized. Theologically, the idea that the Qur'an was co-eternal with God posed similar problems for the Mutazilites; and we have already seen its political implications. If the Qur'an is eternal, then it is co-eternal with God. If this is the case, then where does God end and the Qur'an begin? Al-Mamun, the great patron of the Mutazilites, summed up his position in a letter to one of his governors. "Everything apart from Him is a creature from His creation – a new thing which He brought into existence," insisted al-Mamun. In fact the doctrine of an eternal Qur'an replicated the same problem that Islam has with the various Christian doctrines of the Trinity; "they are, thus, like the Christians when they claim that Isa b. Maryam [Jesus son of Mary] was not created because he was the word of God" (Von Grunebaum 1953: 104). In fact the Qur'an refers to Jesus as being the word of God; nonetheless, for a Mutazilite, this passage should be read allegorically. Quite simply, ascribing eternity to anything but God compromises his unity; the eternal and the infinite cannot rationally be divided into parts, for the parts would delimit one another and contradict their eternal and infinite status. This is the Mutazilite position.

The Islamic Philosophical Tradition

Around the time when Mutazilite *kalam* and its Greek philosophical leanings were fully manifest, serious Islamic philosophy began to emerge. Towering figures like Hasan al-Basri set a high standard for Islamic thought. Figures like al-Basri not only reflected on Islamic doctrine but consistently tied it to the actions of an Islamic life. We have repeatedly referred to the all-encompassing nature of *tawhīd*; this framework unifies all acts. Prophet Muhammad once said that even a smile is an act of charity. Of course, charity is incumbent upon a Muslim; but what does this hadith mean? It means that a pleasant act persists at two levels. At one level there is the act, in and of itself, which contributes to a more pleasant world. At the second level, there is, simultaneously, the act as it pleases God. The belief in the multidimensionality of acts is a principal characteristic of Islam, as embodied in notions like *taqwā* (awareness of the creator) or *ihsān* (full realization of God). A good Muslim constantly strives to be conscious of this multidimensionality, and great Muslims achieve this state of consciousness. Hasan al-Basri was considered to belong in this latter class, and his life served as a model for many later Muslims who called themselves Sufis. Not all Muslim philosophers were – or are – Sufis, but the first Muslim philosopher we will discuss was.

Rabi'a al-Adawiyya was born in Basra, Iraq, in 717. Legend surrounds her circumstances, but it is believed that she was born into a very poor family. Her name, Rabi'a, essentially means "the fourth," perhaps as in "the fourth child." It is also thought that she was sold into servitude but released after being recognized for her piety. All we know of Rabi'a's ideas comes down to us in the form of anecdotes, many of which refer to Hasan al-Basri. The historical accuracy of these stories is of less importance than their intellectual and spiritual import. Rabi'a, the former slave girl, is constantly depicted as defeating the great Hasan al-Basri in intellectual debate. These debates encapsulate the very ascetic and profoundly witty ideas attributed to al-Adawiyya.

Michael Sells (1995b: 436) observes that "for Rabi'a affirmation of the one God was not a matter of mere verbal correctness. Divine unity could be authentically affirmed only by turning one's entire life and consciousness toward the one deity. To consider anything else was, in effect, a form of idolatry." We would be inclined to think of someone like Rabi'a as a straight ascetic, who completely forgoes the material world for a life of ascetic piety; but her personality is too brilliant for that. Rabi'a

> constantly criticized Hasan and other spiritual leaders for becoming attached to their ascetic piety and treating it as an end in and of itself. She offered a devastating critique of those claiming to despise the world for the sake of God; if they had truly achieved an affirmation of the one God, they would not be paying enough attention to anything else to bother despising it. (Sells 1995b: 436)

Rabi'a represents the perfect synthesis of the two dimensions referred to above. Sincere belief, in fact, entails the full absorption of the lower dimension into the higher one. Rabia contributes to the development of the doctrine of *sidq* – "sincerity." If I give in charity, the net secular effect of enhancing the world is dismissed. Even giving in charity out of fear of Hell is rejected by Rabi'a. Charity in the former case is given for the sake of others, while in the latter case it is essentially given for the sake of the self. In either case, one is not giving for the sole purpose of all things – God. A famous anecdote has Rabi'a carrying a bucket of water in her right hand and, in her left, a pot with a burning flame inside. Observers quickly crowded round, to ask her what she was doing. Rabi'a responded that she wanted to set Heaven on fire and put the fires of Hell out with water. Excited and shocked, the crowd asked why. Rabi'a responded that Heaven and Hell, hope for reward and fear of punishment, interfered with unconditional love for God.

This disregard for any end other than pleasing God is one of Rabi'a's great contributions to the development of Sufism. She rejected even acting in her own interest. This may seem harsh, but for the Sufis it is the perfect display of Islam. Remember, Islam means "peace achieved through submission to God." In Rabi'a's view, the human drama unfolding around us, with its pains and joys, hopes and disappointments, ambitions and schemes, belongs not to us but to God; she thus constantly strove to recognize it as God's. Rabi'a served God alone; the dramatic world around her did not *affect her* – rather the "her" is lost and absorbed into the acts of the one creative God. All things – good and bad – belong to God and to no one else. This annihilation of the self is an important concept in Sufism, where it is known as *fan'a*. The idea of losing oneself in God is analogous to that of a drop of water returning to the vast sea. Should the drop be beached, it will maintain its distinct identity as a drop, but it will soon dry and be no more. Should it be received by the waves – its place of origin – the drop will lose its distinct identity, but it will persist forever. Sufis devote themselves to returning the soul to its origin – God.

Beginning a discussion about Islamic philosophy with Rabi'a al-Adawiyya is not common, but it is useful for two reasons. First, she is an extremely important character in the original narratives of Sufism. Second, she also personifies one side of the epistemological spectrum that is more specific to philosophy. So far we have considered the spectrum as having two poles, rationalism and traditionalism. Since philosophy, by definition, involves speculation, philosophy generally gravitates to the rationalist pole of the spectrum. Staunch traditionalists are not much interested in speculation; they prefer to implement the known traditions inherited from the past.

Alfred North Whitehead famously remarked that the entire history of philosophy is nothing but a series of footnotes on Plato. He meant that the entire Western and Islamic philosophical traditions (which are organically related), are responses to the initial doctrines laid out before us by Plato (423–347 BCE). Of course, the person who most directly engaged with these doctrines was none other than Plato's student, Aristotle (384–322 BCE). The contrasting approaches to knowledge of these two classical philosophers create another important spectrum *within* the development of Islamic philosophy itself. Plato's thought deals in eternal truths and has sometimes been employed toward mystical interpretation. Aristotle's thought, on the other hand, emphasizes empirical analysis. Plato believed that Forms or Ideas were immaterial realities, and many of the Abrahamic scholars – Jews, Christians, and Muslims – freely practicing philosophy in the Islamic world were invoking doctrines of Platonist inspiration to explain the "immateriality of the soul," for example.

One of the first genuine philosophers in the Islamic world was Abu Yusuf al-Kindi. Al-Kindi served at the Abbasid court as a tutor. Al-Kindi represents very well the eclectic tendencies of the early philosophical movement; he composed treatises on medicine, arithmetic, geometry, astronomy, music, logic, and philosophy. He was also a skilled translator and editor of Greek texts and participated in the translation movement we mentioned above. The wide range of al-Kindi's interests reflects, once again, the nature of *tawhīd*: rather than remaining unrelated, these diverse interests run together and merge to form various manifestations of a single truth. The philosophers' common interest in medicine, for example, also involves an interest in the miraculous nature of the body, together with their responsibility to attend to its health.

In the hands of philosophers like al-Kindi, Islamic precepts militating against excessive materialism or consumption corresponded well to their own representation of Platonist ideas about the immaterial soul. In one of his philosophical treatises al-Kindi encourages us to imagine that we are on a ship heading for home. As the ship docks for a brief time, we the passengers file off to wander around for a time. Those who do not become too consumed with their surroundings return to the ship quickly and find large open seats awaiting them. Those who become attached to their surroundings take longer to return to the ship; nonetheless, they do not lose sight of the goal of returning home. When these passengers re-board the ship, they find seats with relative ease. Still others not only hesitate to return to the ship, but insist on collecting numerous things before they do so. These passengers find only a few seats left, and their comfort is even further hindered by their possessions. The last group of passengers grow so fond of their surroundings and the possibility of possessions that they do not hear the captain's call to board ship; they lose sight of the goal altogether. These passengers are left behind to perish. As Charles Butterworth (1995a: 440) points out, "as one who calls to the passengers, however, the captain may be compared to a prophet. Like a prophet, he calls only once."

Al-Kindi's allegory displays the Neoplatonist concern with materiality. It is not altogether clear whether al-Kindi was describing our transition from this world into the next (the topic of the afterlife is an important aspect of Muslim belief) or was offering advice for this life. At least in the Islamic framework, the allegory works in either case, and it may have been intended to cover both. Al-Kindi is an interesting early philosopher and he, like many other Muslim thinkers, found himself in and out of favor with the state. Three years after his death in Baghdad, one of the greatest philosophers of Islam was born: Abu Nasr al-Farabi (d. 870), who is widely regarded also as one of the greatest thinkers of the Middle Ages. Al-Farabi, along with Avicenna (d. 980) and following in the footsteps of earlier Greek commentators of late antiquity, made a concerted effort to reconcile Plato and Aristotle.

The basic difference between Aristotle and Plato in epistemology is this: for Plato, what counts as knowledge is knowledge of eternal entities – the Forms. For Aristotle, what counts as knowledge (as a valid claim to know something) is etiological knowledge – knowledge of that thing's cause. Obviously, Aristotelians feel more comfortable rooting claims to knowledge in the empirical world, where they can perceive causes and their effects. Platonists, on the other hand, feel free to contemplate a realm beyond sense perception. Muslims, as well as many others interested in philosophy, attempted to find a way to do both, and this brings us back to al-Farabi and Avicenna.

Here is an argument from al-Farabi's discussion of a famous Neoplatonist cosmological theory that goes back to Plotinus – the theory of emanation. There are necessary beings and possible beings. Necessary beings must exist, while possible beings may or may not exist. The latter require an external cause to bring about their existence. Had they not required an external cause, they would have been already in possession of sufficient conditions for their own existence. Had they possessed sufficient conditions, they would have *had to exist*; hence they would be necessary existents and not possible existents. See how philosophy works! Al-Farabi then goes on to say that, if we imagine a thing, for example a horse, and strip it of all of its coincidental attributes – attributes like color, height, weight, or existence (remember that "horse" is not a necessary existent, so its existence is a coincidental property) – the only thing that remains of the horse is its essence – or what it is to be a horse. The idea of a transhistorical essence is Platonist. The categories that al-Farabi employs and the deductive logic he prefers are Aristotelian. Al-Farabi saw the cosmos as a constellation of transhistorical essences to which existence is added – by an external cause, of course. But what (or who) was the external cause of the existence of the cosmos? Al-Farabi answered that this cause was God – a *necessary* being, he argued, whose existence and essence are one and the same. Al-Farabi also made famous contributions to logic and political philosophy; the latter seems to have corresponded with his metaphysical schema.

Something we should begin to see by now is the philosophers' attempt to prove the existence of God outside of religious texts like the Qur'an. Philosophers desired an independent verification of all kinds of beliefs, whether religious in nature or not. With regard to religious ones they thought that by and large they had achieved this desideratum, but only if the beliefs in question were not taken literally. With the Aristotelians in particular, the empirical nature of their methodologies prevented them from believing, say, in a literal, physical resurrection of the body, or in the creation of the world. Hence they interpreted these doctrines as symbols required to convey subtle and sophisticated truths to the masses. Islamic Aristotelians saw the prophets essentially as "public philosophers" – individuals who possessed great intellects and were able to penetrate the multilayered cosmos and see things as they are in themselves, then conveyed them in appropriate imagery, for the benefit of others. Here is a passage from al-Farabi:

> Once the images representing the theoretical things demonstrated in the theoretical sciences are produced in the souls of the multitude and the latter is made to assent to these images, and once the practical things together with the conditions of the possibility of their existence take hold of people's souls and dominate them, so that they are unable to resolve to do anything else, then the theoretical and practical things are realized. Now these things are philosophy when they are in the soul of the legislator [prophet]. They are religion when they are in the souls of the multitude. For when the legislator knows these things, they are evident to him by sure insight, whereas what is established in the souls of the multitude is [established] through an image and a persuasive argument. Although it is the legislator who also represents

these things through images, neither the images nor the persuasive arguments are intended for him. As far as he is concerned, they are certain. He is the one who invents the images and the persuasive arguments, but not for the sake of establishing these things in his own soul, as a religion for himself. No, the images and the persuasive arguments are intended for others, whereas, so far as he is concerned, these things are certain. They are a religion for others, whereas, so far as he is concerned, they are philosophy. (Al-Farabi 1969: 47)

Philosophers like al-Farabi were not comfortable with the idea that Prophet Muhammad (or any of the prophets, for that matter) was simply a mouthpiece. They argued for a more human-centric explanation of revelation. Prophets were exceptional people, endowed with exceptional mental capacities, who engaged with the cosmos; upon such an engagement they apprehended the truth and guided their peoples accordingly.

Avicenna gives us a similar theory on prophecy – a theory that emphasizes the strong faculties of mind possessed by a prophet. He also offers one of the most original epistemological theories of the Middle Ages, which pre-dates Descartes' similar theory by roughly six centuries. In the first chapter of *Kitab al-Shifa* (*The Book of Healing*) Avicenna postulates a hypothetical case, which is the basis of his epistemology. Imagine someone born without the five senses of touch, sight, hearing, smell, or taste; such a person would have no way of conceiving the outside world. "The only knowledge this person has is that of his or her own self, and the immediacy of this knowledge is such that the person is absolutely certain that if nothing else exists, he or she does," Mehdi Aminrazavi (1995: 451) explains. In other words, I think, therefore *I am* and I *know* that I am. It is the goal of epistemology to establish some kind of certainty in order to proceed with other philosophical goals; and this is what Avicenna did – like Descartes six centuries later. Along with Avicenna's renowned *Kitab al-Shifa* went his masterly work on medicine and physiology, the *Canon of Medicine*.

Avicenna was also the most reputable physician of his time, and his work set the standard for medical sciences in the Islamic world as well as in Europe. His *Canon of Medicine* was still in significant use in Europe until the 18th century. Once again, Avicenna's investigations into disease and health, including surgery and accurate diagnostics, testify to the great compatibility between Islam and science. People like Avicenna were outstanding and enlightened thinkers, who approached belief and practice with a significant degree of liberality. In terms of belief, they upset the traditionalists at times through their comfort with allegorical interpretation. Their liberality was also transparent at times in their personal lives. Avicenna is reported by his student, al-Juzjani, to have died of too much sex and drink, yet he never regarded himself as anything less than a believer.

As Islam spread through the Near East, it disseminated the Greek philosophical tradition. Bright thinkers like some of the ones mentioned above used the methodologies of philosophy to satisfy their need to understand the truth, and they felt that Islam obliged them to seek out the truth wherever it may be found. Prophet Muhammad had told his community: "He who leaveth home in search of knowledge walketh in the path of God" (al-Suhrawardy 1990: 94). This principle was put into practice by thinkers like al-Kindi, who subscribed to the ancient definition of philosophy as "assimilation to God." Armed with the intellectual rigor and judicious analysis of their discipline, to which they added the highly rationalistic tendencies of the Mutazilites, Islamic philosophers were becoming significant enough to challenge tradition. Did tradition have enough depth to challenge the new warriors of reason? Could reliance upon the past slow down (or even stop in its tracks) the seemingly inevitable advance of philosophically minded intellectuals, whose respect for the Qur'an took the form of allegorical interpretations? Only a truly astute mind and a large enough heart could rescue traditionalism from the abyss of mere sentimentality or, even worse, from the clutches of reactionary dogmatism. It could be argued that no thinker in Islamic history has enjoyed as much influence as the man who would successfully carry out the task not only of challenging philosophy but of putting it back in the bottle, nearly seven centuries before Hume and Kant had similar concerns. This was Abu Hamid Muhammad al-Ghazali.

Al-Ghazali (d. 1111) was born in Tus, Iran, into a family of scholars and mystics. Like many young Muslims who demonstrated an early talent, he studied with some of the most respected Sufis and scholars of his time, al-Juwaini being perhaps the most famous among them. Two opposing but complementary intellectual trends had long been established by Sufis, Mutazilites, and philosophers who shared a disposition toward rationalism. The first was advanced by many Sufis. Like Rabi'a al-Adawiyya, they perceived God everywhere and in everything and felt they had come so close to him that they had transcended basic Islamic requirements altogether. One such Sufi was the famous Mansur al-Hallaj (d. 922), who was often found performing the pilgrimage. Perhaps this in itself was not strange, but he would perform it... in his living room in Baghdad. When asked what he was doing, al-Hallaj would reply that he was on pilgrimage: what need had he to go to Mecca, when God was everywhere? But al-Hallaj was also – and strongly – in the tradition of Rabi'a, where total renunciation of the self and devotion to absolute *tawhīd* blur the line between worshipper and the worshipped.

This type of Sufism is characterized by "intoxication": the lover becomes so enamored with God, so taken by his/her own loving devotion that this state literally crushes all distinctions between subject and object, facilitating a rapture of the self into the absolute. Al-Hallaj was the most fearless, and also perhaps the politically most dangerous of these intoxicated Sufis. His most famous declaration was *anna al-haqq*, "I am the truth/real." As a proper name, "al-Haqq" is one of the 99 names of God in Islam. Was al-Hallaj claiming to be God? Of course not; he was testifying to *fan'a* – the successful obliteration of the ego or self that we referred to above. As in the prophetic tradition according to which Muhammad says *"ihsān is when you behave as if you see God"* (see Murata and Chittick 1994, *passim*), the idea here is that the believer fully relinquishes his/her own desire to act in his/her own interest and acts instead from a belief in the total acknowledgeability of the unity of all things. In spite of the very liberal atmosphere in Abbasid Baghdad, claiming *ana al-Haqq* was too much for the caliph, and after a lengthy investigation and trial Mansur al-Hallaj was executed. His execution did not, however, eliminate the presence of those Sufis who felt to be above certain obligations prescribed by Islam. Al-Ghazali would push back on this form of Sufism.

The other trend under consideration had been established by philosophers and Mutazilites. Being led by a rationalist hermeneutics, they often relegated Qur'anic passages to the allegorical realm; and they flouted prescribed Islamic rituals as well. In addition, these philosophers, al-Farabi and Avicenna in particular, undermined the literalness of basic Muslim beliefs, such as the belief in the resurrection of the body and in the creation of the world in time. Doubt about a resurrection of the body stemmed from the rationalist thought that something that had completely degenerated could not be regenerated; hence resurrection had to be spiritual and symbolic. The issue of creation in time is slightly more complicated. Imagine for a moment that I hold two fingers up in front of you; and now imagine that, with my other hand, I hold up another two fingers. Can I delay the persistence of four? Clearly I am holding up four fingers. Well, the philosophers made a similar argument about the world. They argued that, if God is eternal and unchanging, then God has always been creative and omniscient; but if this is the case, how could creation have been delayed? Just as the addition of two to two is a sufficient condition for four, omnipotence and omniscience combine to form the sufficient condition for creation. So how did the unchanging God change his mind and *decide* at a given time to create? The philosophers argued that the "creation" of the world in time was symbolic, and they preferred to argue from within an emanationist framework, where the universe is essentially eternal. Needless to say, these philosophers, like some of the more ecstatic Sufis, flouted traditional Islamic practices. Al-Ghazali would push back on this type of rationalism too.

The Asharite Response

Al-Ghazali's teacher, Abu al-Hassan al-Ashari (d. 936), was a student of the Mutazilite School, but he began to question some of its main teachings concerning the nature of the Qur'an and the literalness of God's attributes. As you may recall, the Mutazilites were committed to God's divine unity and justice, and this position entailed an allegorical understanding of descriptions of God in the Qur'an. Al-Ashari was not comfortable with blind traditionalism either; for him, this kind of traditionalism amounted to simple imitation. With regard to literalists and strict traditionalists he argued that rational thinking about matters of faith was a heavy burden for them; hence they grew inclined to blind faith and blind following. Asharite theology militated for a middle position between rationalism and traditionalism, and al-Ghazali was the Asharite who most perfectly articulated this position.

Al-Ghazali successfully challenged the possible extremism of all trends by attending to their legitimating principles; Sufis, philosophers, and strict traditionalists all claimed to possess *certainty* about their positions. The traditionalists claimed that the *sunna* of the Prophet gave them certainty; the philosophers claimed to have achieved certainty through reason; while the Sufis claimed to have experienced certainty through divine ecstasy. An intellectual master of moderation, al-Ghazali rigorously critiqued reason and outlined its limits in the discovery of the truth, thereby circumscribing the philosophers' enterprise. Second, al-Ghazali reconciled Sufism with traditionalist Islam; he argued that only a middle way provided the subject with certainty.

Al-Ghazali began his more mature spiritual life as a Sufi, studying Sufism's various practices and concepts under the auspices of ʿAli al-Farmadhi al-Tusi, such as the concept of *dhawq* or "taste." *Dhawq* has been an underlying principal of Sufism since Abdʾ al-Karim al-Qushayri (d. 1074), an eminent formulator of early Sufi concepts. *Dhawq* refers to actually experiencing God. In spite of his initiation into Sufi practices, al-Ghazali had not attained this ecstatic state. Frustrated, he then turned to philosophy and devoured its texts. Yet again his efforts were stifled by the limitations of philosophy. In spite of claims to the contrary, al-Ghazali argued that philosophers could be disproved on at least 20 points – by their very own methods no less. At this point, as al-Ghazali tells us in his spiritual autobiography, *Deliverance from Error* (al-Ghazali 2001: 62):

> An interior force drove me to research the reality of original human nature, and that of the beliefs which derive from conformism to the authority of parents and teachers. I tried to discern among the elements which are taught by rote and accepted without question which discrimination gives rise to so much controversy regarding what is true and what false. Then I said to myself: "My aim is to perceive the deep reality of things; I wish to seize the essence of knowledge. Certain knowledge is that in which the thing known reveals itself without leaving any room for doubt or any possibility of error or illusion, nor can the heart allow such a possibility. One must be protected from error, and should be so bound to certainty that any attempt, for example, to transform a stone into gold or a stick into a serpent, would not raise doubts or engender contrary probabilities. I know very well that ten is more than three. If anyone tries to dissuade me by saying, No, three is more than ten, and wants to prove it by changing in front of me this stick into a serpent, even if I saw him changing it, still this fact would engender no doubt about my knowledge [that ten is more than three]. Certainly, I would be astonished at such a power, but I would not doubt my knowledge. Thus I came to know that whatever is known without this kind of certainty is doubtful knowledge, not reliable and safe, that all knowledge subject to error is not sure and certain."

Al-Ghazali famously explored the limits of reason in his *The Incoherence of the Philosophers*. In this monumental work he addresses a host of philosophical issues, but we will concern ourselves here with only one: that of cause and effect. The relation between cause and effect is central to rationalism and for a long time coincided with the philosophical enterprise itself. Remember that Aristotle defined knowledge of something as knowledge of its cause. Furthermore, by understanding causes we hopefully disclose origins – the origins of ourselves and of the world around us. Philosophers typically argued from cause and effect: We know that there is a God because we cannot trace causes back *ad infinitum*; so there must be an ultimate cause, which would be God. Ironically, al-Ghazali, the believer, challenged the analytical veracity of the link between cause and effect in order to prove God's existence.

Of the 20 fallacies that al-Ghazali attributes to the philosophers, he considers only three to be heretical; and we will concern ourselves only with these. The first two have already been mentioned: the eternity of the world and the denial of the resurrection of the body. The third fallacy consists in God's knowledge of particulars. Al-Ghazali employed rigorous logic – the only philosophical discipline he deferred to – in his venture of deconstructing philosophy. At the heart of his argument is an attack on "causality and necessity" – that is, the idea that every effect is preceded by a cause. The relation between cause and effect is the foundation of rationalism, and we often see it employed by Muslim philosophers, for example in their arguments for emanation. Al-Ghazali observed that the so-called foundation of philosophy, causation (or the link between cause and effect), was analytically tenuous. The only reason why we assume the existence of cause and effect, al-Ghazali surmised, is that our experience tells us that event A and event Z have happened in the past simultaneously. For example, the only reason why you assume that fire causes burning is that, in the past, whenever you have witnessed fire you have simultaneously witnessed burning. Al-Ghazali argues that there is no reason to assume that the next time you see fire you will also witness burning: there is no logical necessity to this relation. In fact it is only the omnipotent God who associates fire and burning consistently, but the omnipotent God *could* suppress this association on any given occasion. This argument is very similar to the one that David Hume was to put forward in the 18th century (albeit without resorting to God), thereby changing forever the course of Western philosophy. Likewise, al-Ghazali's argument was a *tour de force* and changed the direction of Islamic thought for ever after.

Al-Ghazali's critique of the causal relation contributed to a long-standing discussion both in philosophy and in theology. And, although the great theologian dealt a decisive blow to philosophical methodology, this was by no means the end of the controversy. Averroes (d. 1198), Ibn Hazm, and contemporaries like Muhammad Abdel-Jabri have engaged in the debate on causation, and it was to become an important one. Contemporary critics have argued – just as Averroes did in the 12th century – that without cause and effect science is not possible. But what they fail to note is that al-Ghazali's argument, which is completely in line with rationalist thinking, was assessing the *logical* veracity of the link between cause and effect; and, according to the criteria of logic, the link is tenuous. In truth, analytically speaking, al-Ghazali was absolutely correct: there is no logical, deductive necessity between cause and effect, but only the consistent, inductive association of cause and effect in our past experiences. At this point there is a gap between inductive and deductive reasoning. When Hume encountered it, he tried to bridge the limits of philosophy through empiricism; he concluded that, epistemologically, we understand things as simple accumulations of empirical events. But how did al-Ghazali attempt to reconcile the limits of philosophy with the need for knowledge? He did it by appealing to gnosis.

Averroes, the Return of Aristotle, and the Gnostics

What made al-Ghazali's critique so brilliant was that he demonstrated the limits of reason quite decisively, without resorting to polemic or employing a low standard of logic. Al-Ghazali critiqued reason by using reason. It was not the theologian's place to discard logic; in fact al-Ghazali esteemed logic as the only branch of philosophy worthy of study. Yet he did not want to claim that we did not know anything. Remember that al-Ghazali wanted to quench his intellectual and spiritual thirst and, for him as a Muslim, faith alone did not suffice. The first part of the Islamic creed requires one to *bear witness* to the unity and singularity of God; it does not require one simply to have faith. So al-Ghazali needed to reconcile the limitations of reason with the need for knowledge in order to be able to practice as a Muslim.

Reason is useful to al-Ghazali so long as it remains confined within its own limits; once these limits are reached in spiritual matters, one must open one's heart and absorb the entirety of creation without mediation. Then, if God so wills it, the great spiritual truths will be revealed and *directly experienced*. According to al-Ghazali, the Qur'an gives us the practice by which we can acquire this direct spiritual knowledge. Of course, this type of epistemology is problematic. What if God does not will it? What are we to think about the world if God can, at any moment, cause fire to make us wet and water to burn our skin? In line with the powerful strand of rationalism in Islam, Averroes emerges to challenge al-Ghazali forcefully and restore the integrity of reason.

Abu al-Walid Muhammad ibn Rushd – or Averroes (d. 1198), as he is known in the West – is oftentimes considered the last great Aristotelian in the classical Islamic tradition; actually Ibn Khaldun (d. 1406) was (and he was perhaps also the most original thinker of the Middle Ages, and we will return to him shortly). Averroes was born in Cordoba at the highest point of its Islamic history – a period of great advances in civilization as well as of political upheavals. He descended from a long line of noted jurists and judges, and he was looked upon with favor by the court. Andalusian culture thrived under Muslim rule. Open, enlightened, and competitive, the Umayyad rulers of Muslim Spain aimed at patronizing an erudite court and initiated the cosmopolitan culture of Muslim Spain. Patronage of philosophy was part of "a deliberate attempt to rival the Abbasid caliphate of Baghdad," observes Majid Fakhry (1999: 284).

Two thinkers associated with this culture are Ibn Bajjah (d. 1139) and Ibn Tufayl (d. 1184). Ibn Bajjah was a rationalist who insisted that, "to the extent [that] man is close to reason, he is close to God. This is possible only through rational knowledge, which brings man close to God, just as ignorance cuts him off from Him." (ibid., p. 285). Here the philosopher points out that reason serves as a "bridge" between man and God. Our ability to reason is analogous with God's will and thus facilitates our ability to know God. We have seen precedents of this type of thinking in the Mutazilites.

Ibn Tufayl was perhaps the most original and celebrated philosopher of Andalusian rationalism before Averroes. Ibn Tufayl wrote a famous philosophical novel entitled *The Treatise of Hayy ibn Yaqzan*. In this literary piece our protagonist is born and grows up on an uninhabited island in the Indian Ocean. The novel is an elaboration on the theme of reason. Hayy grows up without a mother, a father, or society; hence he is not socialized into knowledge. Rather Hayy must discover knowledge with the help of nothing more than his own faculties: sight, sound, taste, smell, and touch. So, as our protagonist gets older on this island, he observes, remembers, and builds knowledge upon the accumulation of empirical experiences. Hayy's observations begin when he notices that he is different from the animals around him. When the doe that cared for him dies, Hayy performs an autopsy, in an effort to cure the animal. Upon finding out that her death was related to heart failure, Hayy is set on the path of scientific discovery and reflection.

Hayy ibn Yaqzan is a literary novel as well as a reflection on epistemological matters. Ibn Tufayl articulates there a theory of *tabula rasa* – the assumption that our mind is a "blank slate" at birth, and that we accumulate knowledge through sense experience. It is tempting to suggest that such thinking is a precursor to scientific inquiry, but in fact it is the culmination of the scientific mindset. Remember, Islamic culture was deeply immersed in the sciences. The empiricism of Ibn Tufayl characterizes the care and high regard in which Andalusian thinkers held the tangible. In spiritual matters, however, Hayy does rationalize to the point of discovering God – but,

> When he acquired knowledge of that superior being, whose existence was fixed and uncaused, and who was the cause of the existence of all things, he wanted to know how he had acquired this knowledge and by what faculty he had apprehended this being. He examined all the senses, namely: hearing, sight, smell, taste and touch, and found they could not perceive anything that was not a body nor [sic] in a body... (Khalidi 2005: 132)

That by which he was able to apprehend God was rather something "that was not a body, nor a bodily faculty, nor attached in any way to bodies" (ibid., p. 132). Here Ibn Tufayl is pointing to "soul" or "mind." This is a typical duality among Islamic philosophers: there is a tangible empirical world of which the body is a part, and there is a non-material world, through which we are connected to higher spiritual truths. What we need to keep in mind is the keen separation of the two. Al-Ghazali suspends the autonomy of the physical world and makes this world wholly subservient to the non-material will of God; in fact the physical world possesses no reality in and of itself, but is merely an extension of that all-powerful will.

Averroes was introduced at the Andalusian court by Ibn Tufayl, and he is known as Ibn Rushd in Arabic. As Fakhry (1999: 286) points out, "Ibn Rushd's contributions in philosophy, theology, medicine, and jurisprudence were voluminous and match in scope and thoroughness those of al-Farabi and Ibn Sina, his only equals in the east [Islamic lands]." What is most significant, however, is Ibn Rushd's command of the Aristotelian corpus and his use of it in matters of faith. Ibn Rushd did perhaps more than any another Muslim thinker to try to demonstrate the complete and inherent compatibility between reason and religion.

According to Ibn Rushd, knowledge takes on three forms: rhetorical, dialectical, and demonstrative. Rhetorical knowledge conveys sophisticated truths to the masses. Dialectics is employed by the theologians, who stand on higher ground than the masses; and, finally, demonstration, the highest form of truth, is understood by philosophers only. This categorization allows Averroes to argue for the reconciliation of revealed truths, which at times seem to contradict experience, with reason. Whatever disagreements the theologians had with the philosophers, they were due to the limits of language or of method, they were not inherent in philosophy itself. In fact Averroes (2001) argues in his *Decisive Treatise* that the Qur'an commands philosophy, since it encourages "people of understanding to reflect" (pp. 2–3). The truth cannot contradict the truth and, according to Averroes, reason is the foundation of our ability to think regularly about knowledge. Therefore reason, when employed correctly, can only confirm the truth of God or revealed knowledge.

The Qur'an itself points to two types of verse: clear and ambiguous. Whereas the former are clear to all, the latter are known only to God and those "well-grounded" in knowledge (3: 5–6). For Averroes, those "well-grounded" in knowledge were none other than the philosophers. Here we see the rationalist tendency toward progress: for our thinker, the accumulation of reason allows us to aspire to revealed truths not readily understood. The philosopher can deliberate and ascend to greater knowledge and thereby accumulate greater knowledge. In this manner we see a progress in spiritual matters that is similar to the progress in secular ones noted by al-Jahiz previously. But such a disposition can only be enabled by the use of reason and its cumulative nature.

Ibn al-'Arabi and Ibn Khaldun

The vigorous and systematic intellectual discourse that persisted throughout the Muslim world, from the 8th century until the turn of the 15th, fills out the epistemological spectrum that we have repeatedly referred to. In the latter part of this chapter we have privileged the rationalist end of this spectrum. In the next chapter we will engage with Ibn Taymiyya and others who were staunch traditionalists, and we will also examine more modern rationalists. And now we shall conclude this chapter by introducing two of the most original and highly celebrated thinkers of the Middle Ages: Ibn al-'Arabi (d. 1240) and Ibn Khaldun (d. 1406).

Ibn al-'Arabi was born in Murcia, Andalusia (Spain), in 1165. He was a young contemporary of Averroes and had a famed encounter with the master philosopher as a teenager. Averroes was reportedly stunned at Ibn al-'Arabi's insight and the depth of his spiritual wisdom; and, just as the meaning of that famed meeting eluded Averroes, Ibn al-'Arabi's legacy has far transcended any limitations of philosophy. Ibn al-'Arabi synthesized philosophy, theology, exegesis, jurisprudence, and history, to formulate one of the greatest and most sophisticated discourses of the Middle Ages. In addition, his thought has produced a school that has imposed itself on Islamic thought till this day. Whether in Iran or in the West, many philosophically inclined Muslims have been enlivened by his thought, and staunch traditionalists, for whom Ibn al-ʾArabi is a heretic, cannot ignore the Shaykh al-Akbar – the Greatest Shaykh – as he is commonly known.

Fully versed in the philosophical and theological disputes that preceded him, Ibn al-ʾArabi, it could be argued, successfully reconciled and transcended these disputes. As Michael Sells (1996: 17–18) points out, Ibn al-ʾArabi's thought represents the fourth major phase of Sufism. The early phase, typified by al-Hallaj and Rabiʾa, addressed the tension inherent in Islam's horizon of secular ethics and ascetic ritual.

> The tension between world-affirmation and world-transcendence (not rejection) is dramatized vividly in the life and sayings of Rabiʾa al-Adawiyya (d.185/801) a freed slave from Basra. Rabiʾa becomes the touchstone for a developing set of values that were to be the ethical ground of Sufism. The values included the affirmation of the divine unity interpreted as a relational absolute in which only the divine beloved is a matter of interest, or even consciousness [...]. (Sells 1996: 20)

At the next stage, developed by thinkers like Qushayri and al-Ghazali, Sufism is fully integrated into ritual and theological Islam. Ibn al-ʾArabi formulates a worldview quite unlike anything before it: comprehensive and exhaustive, immanent and transcendent, wholly pious yet beyond any sort of "orthodoxy" one can imagine. I cannot here describe to you in a few words the legacy of the Great Shaykh; we must simply look at it. But Michael Sells (1995a: 475–479) does outline the most important ideas of our thinker, which we will use as our reference table:

1. God (Reality/Absoluteness) transcends all names and logical categories, yet God is immanent in self-revelation in the world.
2. God cannot be known dualistically, as an object by a subject.
3. Human consciousness is the prism and mirror in which the undifferentiated God reveals and refracts itself into the God of attributes.
4. God can only be apprehended when the duality of subject/object are transcended by the human self.
5. God in transcendence is beyond polarities of Lord and Servant.
6. The manifestations of God are in constant flux.
7. True understanding occurs only to those who are themselves in constant self-transformation.

To these seven ideas or propositions I would like to add an eighth and ninth:

8. God in immanence signifies God in transcendence.
9. History (human and beyond) is a process of God's self-awareness.

For Ibn al-'Arabi, all of creation is a reflection of the absolute, and human consciousness is the most perfect mirror in this respect. And we are to understand the "role of humanity as the locus of a continuing kaleidoscope of divine manifestation" (Sells 1995a: 477). Without creation there is no creator, properly speaking. It is for reasons like these that staunch traditionalists are uncomfortable with Ibn al-'Arabi, for whom God's status as creator is independent and transcendent and anything beyond that is merely heresy. For Ibn al-'Arabi, however, when the human being's heart is pure and clear of attachments to wealth, status, fame, power, or even ideologies, political parties, ethnicisim, religious supremacism, or dogmatism, the human is free to participate fully in co-creation, in the manner outlined above. Once again, let us turn to Sells: "The Sufi re-creation is the mutual construction of the divine attributes and human categories within the polished mirror of the human heart" (1995a: 477–478). And this construction is revived in each moment.

The Qur'an attributes 99 names to God, but these names point to the elusiveness of God's nature rather than defining God. For example, in the Qur'an God is both "the merciful" and "the wrathful." Yet consider for a moment the contradiction inherent in these two names. One way to appreciate their meaning is to evaluate what remains when we eliminate the contradictory part: nothing remains. But, more accurately, no thing remains. God is not a "thing," as we are accustomed to thinking, observes Ibn al-'Arabi. To describe some thing, we must be able to delimit it, we must note where it begins and where it ends; otherwise it cannot be distinguished at all. For the Great Shaykh, God is beyond limitation, and "the unlimited must simultaneously be beyond all things, within all things, other than all things and identical with all things" (Sells 1995a: 477).

Ibn al-'Arabi's thought represents the culmination of the gnostic tradition. His work reveals one direction of Islamic philosophy and theology, but no more than one; and in Abdur-Rahman ibn Khaldun we find the expression of yet another direction. Ibn Khaldun was born in Tunis, in 1332, into a family of distinguished jurists and scholars. His aristocratic family served the court of the Hafsid rulers in North Africa, and Ibn Khaldun was brought up in the traditional sciences of exegesis and *ilm al-hadith*. In addition, Ibn Khaldun studied mysticism and philosophy and was particularly influenced by Aristotle. Aristotle's empiricism can be found in Ibn Khaldun's work. In fact the latter's use of empirical data gave rise to the single most original analysis in the Middle Ages. Ibn Khaldun initiated the science of sociology. As N. J. Dawood notes in his edition (Khaldun 1999: vii), Ibn Khaldun "was gifted with rare insight, enabling him to penetrate the essential of accumulated knowledge; so that, when he was ripe for his destined task, he was able to review historical experience on a universal scale and thus make his lasting contribution to the study of history."

Ibn Khaldun's interest in social patterns evolved out of two things. First, his study of philosophy and theology exposed him to the limitations of both, as we have seen from dynamic debates throughout Islamic history. This exposure allowed him to see in what ways systematic thinking could in fact be useful and in what areas it would be most successfully applied. Second, Ibn Khaldun was interested in establishing more objective historical narratives. The confident scholar in him observes:

> The critical eye, as a rule, is not sharp. Errors and unfounded assumptions are closely allied, familiarly in historical information. Blind trust in tradition is an inherited trait in human beings. Occupation with the scholarly disciplines on the part of those who have no genuine claim to them is widespread. But the pasture of stupidity is unwholesome for mankind [...] It takes critical insight to sort out the hidden truth; it takes knowledge to lay truth bare and polish it so that critical insight may be applied to it. (Ibn Khaldun 1999: 5)

For Ibn Khaldun, this "critical insight" was empirical analysis. Ibn Khaldun was interested in how physical conditions affect the nature of a society and, by its extension, its culture, including religion. It is not our point here to reiterate his approach to the growth and formation of political dynasties or to the relationship between sedentary peoples and nomads. Although his work in this regard is, according to Toynbee, "the most comprehensive and illuminating analysis of how human affairs work that has ever been made" (quoted by Dawood in Khaldun 1999: xiv), our aim is to examine only his method and how it involves Islam as religion and as law.

As has been the theme of our approach, Muslims understand Islam according to their epistemology or philosophy of knowledge. Ibn Khaldun's philosophy was rooted in empiricism and reveals empirical patterns. He believed that ideas, for example religious ideas, provided social solidarity or group feeling (*asabiya*). In turn, this social process drives the production of further ideas, religious ones included. Ibn Khaldun saw nothing incompatible between the empirical origins of faith and the divinity of revelation. As already mentioned, he was interested in the very fabric of civilizations, which for our thinker consisted of the group's unity. In this respect our thinker observes (Khaldun 1999: 120):

> The Bedouins are the least willing of nations to subordinate themselves to each other, as they are rude, proud, ambitious, and eager to be leaders. Their individual aspirations rarely coincide. But when there is religion among them through prophethood or sainthood, then this has some restraining influence in itself [...] When there is a prophet or saint among them, who calls upon them to fulfill the commands of God, rids them of blameworthy qualities, and causes them to adopt praiseworthy ones, and who prompts them to concentrate all their strength in order to make the truth prevail, they become fully united [...]

Conclusion

Classical Islamic thought does not end with Ibn Khaldun, but this is a convenient place for us to close the exposition on the classical period. In the next chapter we will examine some modern developments alongside classical ones, in an effort to understand "sects" in Islam. But in this chapter you have made a comprehensive journey through Islamic intellectual history. We have explored the rise of Islamic thought and how it emerged within its geographical and social contexts.

We can see now that Islamic thought began when critical scholars started thinking about Islam. What is Islam? How is the "Muslim life" supposed to be lived? Many different thinkers from different backgrounds offered different answers to such questions. Some argued from the point of view of reason, others from that of tradition. What is important to remember is that the intellectual spectrum persists to this day; furthermore, by examining such thought in a chronological order, we can see how time and place have often contributed to the way we think about certain things.

Discussion Questions

1   What is the significance of the epistemological spectrum?
2   What is the relationship between philosophy, theology, and Islamic law?
3   What are the hadith, what is *ilm al-hadith*, and why are these notions so important?
4   How does *ilm al-hadith* contribute to historiography?
5   What gives one permission to interpret the Qur'an literally or allegorically?

Suggested Further Reading

Al-Farabi, Abu Nasr (1969). *Philosophy of Plato and Aristotle*, trans. Muhsin Mahdi. New York, NY: Cornell University Press.

Al-Ghazali, Abu Hamid Muhammad (2001). *Deliverance from Error and Mystical Union with the Almighty*, trans. Muhammad Abu-Laylah. Washington, DC: Council for Research in Values and Philosophy.

Al-Suhrawardy, al-Mamun (1990). *The Sayings of Muhammad*. New York, NY: Citadel Press.

Aminrazavi, Mehdi (1995). Avicenna. In Ian McGreal (ed.), *Great Thinkers of the Eastern World*. New York, NY: HarperCollins, pp. 449–452.

Averroes (Ibn Rushid) (2001). *Faith and Reason in Islam: Averroes' Exposition of Religious Arguments*, trans. Ibrahim Najjar. Oxford: OneWorld.

Butterworth, Charles (1995a). Al-Kindi. In Ian McGreal (ed.), *Great Thinkers of the Eastern World*. New York, NY: HarperCollins, pp. 439–442.

Butterworth, Charles (1995b). Averroes. In Ian McGreal (ed.), *Great Thinkers of the Eastern World*. New York, NY: HarperCollins, pp. 465–468.

Cornell, Vincent J. (1999). Fruit of the tree of knowledge: The relationship between faith and practice in Islam. In J. Esposito (ed.), *The Oxford History of Islam*. Oxford: Oxford University Press, pp. 63–105.

Dallal, Ahmad (1999). Science, medicine, technology: The making of a scientific culture. In J. Esposito (ed.), *The Oxford History of Islam*. Oxford: Oxford University Press, pp. 155–214.

Esposito, John (ed.) (1999). *The Oxford History of Islam*. Oxford: Oxford University Press.

Esposito, John (2005). *Islam the Straight Path*. Oxford: Oxford University Press.

Fakhry, M. (1999). Philosophy and theology: From the eighth century to the present. In J. Esposito (ed.), *The Oxford History of Islam*. Oxford: Oxford University Press, pp. 269–303.

Ibn Khaldun, Abdur-Rahman (1999). *The Muqaddimah: An Introduction to History*, ed. N. J. Dawood, trans. F. Rosenthal. Princeton, NJ: Princeton University Press.

Kamali, M. H. (1999). Law and society: The interplay of reason and revelation in the *Shariah*. In J. Esposito (ed.), *The Oxford History of Islam*. Oxford: Oxford University Press, pp. 107–155.

Khalidi, Muhammad (2005). *Medieval Islamic Writings*. Cambridge: Cambridge University Press.

Khalidi, Tarif (1994). *Arabic Historical Thought in the Classical Period*. Cambridge: Cambridge University Press.

McGreal, Ian (ed.) (1995). *Great Thinkers of the Eastern World*. New York, NY: HarperCollins.

Murata, Sachiko and William Chittick (1994). *The Vision of Islam*. St. Paul: Paragon House.

Nagel, Tilman (2000). *The History of Islamic Theology from Muhammad to the Present*. Princeton, NJ: Markus Weiner.

Rahman, Fazlur M. (2002). *Islam*. Chicago, IL: University of Chicago Press.

Imam Malik (1985). *Muwatta of Imam Malik*, trans. Muhammad Rahimuddin. Lahore: Ashraf Printing Press.

Sells, Michael (1995a). Ibn al-ʾArabi. In Ian McGreal (ed.), *Great Thinkers of the Eastern World*. New York, NY: HarperCollins, pp. 475–479.

Sells, Michael (1995b). Rabiʾa al-Adawiyaa. In Ian McGreal (ed.), *Great Thinkers of the Eastern World*. New York, NY: HarperCollins, pp. 435–438.

Sells, Michael (1996). *Early Islamic Mysticism: Sufi, Qurʾan, Miʾraj, Poetic and Theological Writings*. New York, NY: Paulist Press.

Von Grunebaum, Gustave (1953). *Medieval Islam: A Vital Study of Islam at its Zenith*. Chicago, IL: University of Chicago Press.

5

Islamic Political Theology

LAITH SAUD

An Introduction to Islam in the 21st Century, First Edition. Edited by Aminah Beverly McCloud,
Scott W. Hibbard, and Laith Saud.
© 2013 Blackwell Publishing Ltd. Published 2013 by Blackwell Publishing Ltd.

Introduction

There is a coherency to Islamic thought that is reflected in the epistemological spectrum discussed in the previous chapter. In spite of the diversity of views among Muslim thinkers, there is a broad acceptance of the cosmology of *tawhīd* – the singular unified explanation of all existence. Where Muslim thinkers and theologians differ from one another is in their attempts to understand *tawhīd* and its implications for believers. Some of them emphasize the use of reason in this process, others the use of tradition. We have also mentioned esotericism (or mysticism) and gnosis. Regardless of these differences, the effort to understand *tawhīd* – and, hence, God's will – is a direct effect of the revelation of the Qur'an.

In Muslim belief, the Qur'an is the literal word of God, and hence the seminal expression of *tawhīd*. Not only did the Qur'an negate the pagan past of the Arabs but it also disqualified all non-monotheistic explanations of the cosmos as superstitions, and it characterized all knowledge that did not testify to this reality as ignorance. In other words, the Qur'an finally gave the pagan Arabs the ability to classify some forms of knowledge as more valuable than others, which led to the remarkable scientific and philosophical achievements in the later centuries of Islamic civilization. Of course such a legacy has not only epistemological implications, but political ones as well. In this chapter we will discuss the development of Islamic political theology, or what is commonly known as the rise of Islamic "sects."

Islamic Political Theology and the Qur'an

As noted earlier, Islam is a spectrum of beliefs – ranging from progressive to traditionalist – that revolve around the universally recognized concept of *tawhīd*. The tension, moreover, between the trends of progressivism and traditionalism is reflected in a tension between reason and tradition. As you will recall, some Muslims gravitate toward reason and argue that human reason should be used in reading and understanding a revealed text. The Qur'an may be the literal word of God, but there are metaphors that ought to be interpreted as such, and human reason is necessary for this kind of interpretation. Those who emphasize reason tend to allow for greater liberality in the reading and understanding of a text through metaphor and esotericism. On the other hand, many traditionalists are suspicious of human reason, of which they argue that it is limited in its ability to solve problems. In fact many such thinkers describe "reason" as little more than personal opinion. There is also a strong correlation between traditionalism and literalism; since traditionalists are suspicious of reason, they empower the literal word to stand on its own.

These debates inform the fundamental goal of Muslim intellectual endeavors: understanding revelation. The Qur'an is considered by Muslims to be the literal word of God. But how is it understood? Clearly, its author – God, according to the

Muslim worldview – is the authority when it comes to understanding the text; but who has the authority to interpret God's will? Who, in short, speaks on behalf of God? While all Muslims venerate the Qur'an, its *meaning* remains elusive at times and is a subject of contention. And the essence of the Qur'an's meaning is the central issue in Islamic political theology – what gives rise to Sunni, Shi'i, and Kharji positions. It is because of this elusiveness that we have difficulty in ascribing an orthodoxy to Islam.

Let us return to the beginning: during the month of Ramadan, in the year 610, Prophet Muhammad received the first in a series of revelations that, together, constitute the Qur'an. The Qur'an's central theme is the imperative to enjoin justice and do good, while also castigating injustice and wrongdoing. The Qur'an emphasizes the fate of humanity in both its secular and its sacred capacities. By secular I mean here the affairs of humans, including the rise and fall of civilizations; by sacred I mean the Qur'anic references to acts of worship like fasting and prayer. Lastly, the Qur'an is also a source of law.

Muslims agree that the Prophet delivered the word of God to his community and was the authority in understanding the Qur'an. But what was the nature of that authority and the meaning of the text? There are essentially three positions vis-à-vis this question and these positions bear the imprint of our epistemological spectrum. First, rationalists maintain that the divine cannot be understood at all, unless it is rendered through the human. This position does more than emphasize the role of reason in understanding the divine; it makes reason into a prerequisite to approaching the divine. The famous Mutazilite Abdul-Jabbar (d. 1025), for instance, argued that one can understand Islamic ethics only through reason. Traditionalists, on the other hand, claim that the imperfection of humanity renders it largely unreliable for the task of conveying the divine; this is the second position. For example, Abu al-Ashari argued that "the Qur'an is to be understood in its apparent meaning. It is not permissible to understand it any other way, except by proof" (quoted in Hourani 1985: 119). So a theologian like al-Ashari was willing to interpret the Qur'an by using reason, but only very cautiously. But puritan traditionalists would go so far as to argue that any human attribution ascribed to the Qur'an, including reason-based interpretation, negates the divine nature of the Qur'an, since divinity is, by definition, non-human; here God is not understood as speaking *through* humans but *to* them. This third line of thinking is represented, for example, by those who consider themselves followers of Ahmad ibn Hanbal.

We can begin to see how such approaches could affect the way one sees the role of the Prophet in understanding the Qur'an, as well as the nature of the word itself. Since the Qur'an is the literal word of God, the Qur'an is divine; since God is the only divinity, the Qur'an is completely synonymous with God's expression on earth. In short, the Qur'an is God on earth. Now, by this we do not mean that the Qur'an is the physical manifestation of God on earth, or the manifestation of what Muslims consider to be God's attributes – such as knowledge, power, or will. Rather, we mean that the Qur'an is synonymous with God's word on earth. We are now beginning to enter the realm of theology; and in the Islamic context theology is political just as much as it is metaphysical. The three major "sects" of Islam thus correspond in large part to different attitudes to the relationship between human reason and revelation.

Was Prophet Muhammad's reason a primary source in interpreting the Qur'an? Did the Prophet issue the law by applying his reason to revelation, or was he more or less a vessel of revelation, filled and emptied of its contents, but having no bearing on its understanding? Fazlur Rahman (2002: 33) argues, for example, that "the Qur'an is pure divine word, but, of course, it is equally intimately related to the inmost personality of the Prophet Muhammad whose relationship to it cannot be mechanically conceived like that of a record." Fazlur Rahman's position here is a rationalist one, as it highlights the centrality of the human being in mediating the divine message. We found in the previous chapter a similar articulation being made by the noted philosopher al-Farabi.

These spiritual types display a more open attitude toward revelation, which they regard as a natural concomitant to reason. This is an important point: for the rationalist, the ability to understand God (and, hence, truth) is ever present in human reason. What makes a prophet a prophet, according to this view, is his being more rational than ordinary people, so that his exceptional rationality allows him access to higher truths. Since rationality is a human characteristic, its persistence in the world leaves the door open for spiritual apprehension throughout all ages and cultures, not just in one or another; and revelation bares the imprint of socio-historical conditions.

With strict traditionalists, on the other hand, understanding revelation would be a process attributable exclusively to God, as would understanding the law. For the traditionalist, understanding God results directly from following God's own directives, and these are spelled out in scripture. Human reason plays little role, if any, in this process. The Prophet is an authority in understanding the Qur'an insofar as God *chose him* to be the recipient of this position. Not only had the Prophet's humanity nothing to do with understanding the Qur'an; the Prophet's humanity was decisively and miraculously *overridden* by divine revelation, and thus the Qur'an's total "otherness" – which translates into its total divinity – could be preserved. For strict traditionalist Muslims, then, Islam is a reality completely "other" than, or different from, humanity, while for rationalist Muslims there is no Islam outside of humanity.

Some of the major "sectarian" issues in Islam correspond to these theological issues, but the broad majority of Muslims, even when they represent different sects, take a position somewhere in the middle. Still, for the purposes of introducing the different spiritual types in Islam, we can say that Shi'ism and Sufism are more rationalist and gnostic in their approaches, while Kharijism is the most traditionalist. We will also explain in this chapter why this is the case. Finally, Sunnism falls, by and large, in the middle of the spectrum, and different Sunnis will take various different positions along it, just like all Muslims in general.

The Origins of Islamic Political Theology

In 632 Prophet Muhammad passed away. At the end of his life he had witnessed the completion of his career. He had advocated for the rights of women, the poor, and the unprotected and achieved social change; and, most importantly, he revolutionized the way his people saw the world. According to some historians, Muhammad was the single most influential man in history, so it is no surprise that after his death a crisis of succession occurred. The Prophet's succession began to be seen in the terms we have described above. The community, in an effort to secure stability and its hold on the prophetic legacy, elected Abu Bakr al-Siddiq as Muhammad's successor. Abu Bakr was the Prophet's best friend, one of the earliest people to embrace Islam, and one of Islam's most celebrated heroes. Abu Bakr was appointed "caliph" (*khalīfah*, successor/representative) – a term that comes from the Qur'an.

Two things are important about Abu Bakr's political vision. The first is that he acknowledged the authority of the community, both in the election of the caliph and in the guidance of his decisions, on which it acted as a correcting force. The second is the authoritative role played by the Qur'an and the Sunna under his administration. Community-based authority anchored in tradition is more or less the position of the Sunnis, to whom we will return later. Important here is to note that not everyone agreed with the election of Abu Bakr; many important companions would have preferred the accession of Imam 'Ali. Like Abu Bakr, 'Ali was one of the earliest to embrace Islam and one of its greatest heroes, but, unlike Abu-Bakr, he came from the Prophet's own household. 'Ali was Muhammad's cousin, was raised by him from a young age, and was the father of his grandsons.

Many felt that religious authority was an attribute inherent not only in the Prophet but in his entire clan, the Banu Hashim. This was the basis of the Shi'ite support for 'Ali. Although the Shi'ites are very conservative about extending religious authority to members of the Prophet's family, they do nonetheless open the doors to such claims. Had the Prophet's divinely mandated authority been exclusive to himself, as the Kharijites insist, then any occurrence of divine knowledge, in other words revelation or inspiration, which the Qur'an certainly is, could only be considered a total suspension of the natural order. If, on the other hand, people other than the Prophet are capable of such knowledge, then this phenomenon can be regarded as a natural manifestation of the general human capability to know. Shi'is see divine knowledge as continuing in the world after the Prophet's death.

Most members of the community recognized the succession of Abu Bakr. After him, Umar ibn Al-Khattab, and then Uthman ibn Affan, an Umayyad, succeeded to the office of caliphate. The succession of Uthman is significant, for the members of his clan, the Umayyads, were staunch opponents of Islam and its social reforms. Although Uthman was a highly respected companion of the Prophet, many Muslims felt that his clan was taking advantage of his position and relatively conciliatory personality. The socio-economic issues involved here cannot be overlooked either. The Prophet, as well as Imam ʿAli, came from the Banu Hashim, a respected but less powerful clan. The Banu Umayya, on the other hand, was seen by many as the old guard. With the re-emergence of this old order, concerns arose about the direction of the Islamic community and the watering down of the Islamic revolution. Three attitudes asserted themselves in regard to this crisis, and this is how the seeds of the emergence of the three major Islamic spiritual dispositions or "sects" were planted.

In 656 CE a group of dissenting Muslims fell upon the home of the third caliph, Uthman. It is reported that they took him by storm and stabbed him to death as he was reading the Qur'an. These dissenters argued that Uthman was not qualified to lead because he was *willing to compromise* with the powers that be. They were puritans and absolutists; they believed they were armed with the absolute authority of the Qur'an, and such authority empowered them to act from outside and above secular institutions, even institutions like the chief executive office of the caliphate. On the heels of Uthman's assassination, the community finally elected ʿAli as the fourth caliph. Thus the first four caliphs were one way or another elected to the office; this is the standard account of the early caliphate, and for this reason any "study of the political ideas of the Muslims is bound to concern itself with this standard account, since the elements mentioned in it – taking counsel, designation and acclamation – are widely held to be desirable" to Muslims, as W. M. Watt (1998: 37) observes.

ʿAli inherited a difficult situation. Members of Uthman's clan, particularly the powerful governor of Syria, Muʾawiya ibn Abi Sufyan, refused to recognize him until Uthman's killers were brought to justice. As noted earlier, Muʾawiya was a brilliant politician, and he put ʿAli into a corner. Although the puritans were rebels – and violent ones at that – they also represented the marginal classes of the still nascent community of believers. If ʿAli were to go against them, he would then be seen as defending the old Arab aristocracy. At the same time, the absolutism of the puritans was causing problems for the largely moderate community of Muslims, who were apprehensive about absolutes. Some puritans sided with ʿAli, seeing him as the most suitable and pious person for the job, but other rebellions of a puritanic character were sparking up in eastern Arabia and southern Iraq. This period of sedition and civil discord is known as the first *fitna* (Civil War) in Islamic history.

ʿAli first set his sights on the goal of stabilizing his immediate surroundings. Prominent companions who were not Umayyads were also troubled by the assassination of Uthman, and these frustrations culminated in the Battle of the Camel (or the Battle of Jamal) at Basra, Iraq, in 656. Although ʿAli was in no way involved in the assassination of Uthman, those who killed the caliph supported him. Several prominent companions, including the Prophet's widow Aisha, challenged ʿAli in the name of justice for Uthman. Before the battle ʿAli sent emissaries to the opposing camp – a camp composed of his friends and relatives; negotiations ensued, but peace was not secured and war broke out. Aisha, a prominent figure in Islamic history in her own right, sat atop a camel during the battle – hence the name. ʿAli's forces won, but he did not rejoice; he spent the next three days in mourning and attending to the burial of the dead on both sides. A subsequent conflict between ʿAli and the powerful governor of Damascus, Muʿawiya (a member of the Umayyad clan) divided the community once more and brought these competing armies into another direct confrontation. After three days of fighting, Muʿawiya's men hung a parchment of the Qurʾan on their lances and called for arbitration. They cried "let the book of God decide." After agreeing to arbitration, some of the puritans who supported ʿAli defected, claiming *la hukma illa lillah* – "no rule except the rule of God." The puritans argued that it was a sin to submit to human arbitration in matters decided by God. It is this logic that concerns us here.

The Shiʿat ʿAli and the Kharijites

The Qurʾan says: "if two parties of the faithful fight each other, then conciliate them. Yet if one is rebellious to the other, then fight the insolent one until it returns to God's command" (49: 9). For the puritans, God's command was clear and unambiguous. Human reason, with all its imperfection and personal interests, adulterated it. For these people the world was black and white, while for ʿAli, the leader of a community, the world was necessarily grey and needed to be negotiated through reason. It is this unwillingness to submit the word of God to human interpretation that characterizes Kharijite political theology. The Qurʾan was not to be understood through the mediation of institutions; even the caliphate, which was occupied by one of the most eminent scholars of Islam at the time, ʿAli ibn Abi Talib, had no institutional authority over how the Qurʾan was to be understood. From the Kharijite perspective, the Qurʾan speaks for itself, and it does so loudly and authoritatively.

This absolute traditionalism claims that true religious authority is located exclusively in the timeless ideals of God and can never be found in humanity. Hence human reason has no jurisdiction over the law of God, and interpreting the law means violating it. From the Kharijite point of view, ʿAli had done just that by submitting to arbitration. Consequently they left his camp; they came to be known as "Kharijites" after this episode and as a result of it (the word means "those who exit"). They held that, since God spoke unambiguously, anyone who subjected His command to human interpretation was a heretic. Moreover, the Kharijites took up arms against ʿAli: in July 658 he was forced to put down a Kharijite rebellion at Nahrawan, Iraq. Two years later, Imam ʿAli was assassinated – stabbed by a Kharijite.

As we noted previously, the early Kharijites read the Qurʾan and the *sunna* literally and reject alternative approaches to the tradition. So, for example, since racism and tribalism are explicitly forbidden in Islam, all Muslims are equal before God. The Kharijites embraced this ideal and repudiated the Arab custom of elevating certain tribes (or even the Arabs as a whole) above others. They insisted that any Muslim could be caliph, so long as he was pious and submitted completely to the letter of the law. They also took the Muslims' obligations to the *ahl al-Kitab* ("people of the book") very seriously. Christians and Jews were treated generously by the Kharijites – only fellow Muslims were exposed to their puritanical streak. The Kharijites raided towns and territories and subjected Muslims to inquisitions and persecutions. If Muslims were found not agreeing with them, they were summarily executed.

The cardinal principle of Kharijite belief, then, is the absolute authority of a literal Qur'an, and any Muslim who steps outside that authority is no longer protected by Islamic law. The three major branches of the Kharijites were the Azariqah, the Sufriyah, and the Ibadiya. Only the Ibadiya have survived into modern times; and the Ibadiya represent a moderate version of Kharijitism. These Muslims are found in Oman, where roughly 75 percent of the population is of the Ibadi disposition. There are spots in North Africa (for instance in the Mzab and Wargla), oases in Algeria, as well as the island of Jerba off Tunisia where Ibadis form communities. Small parts of Libya and Zanzibar are populated by them too. The Ibadis reject the appellation "Kharijite" and see themselves as more or less similar to Sunni Muslims. On the other hand, many modern traditionalist Sunni movements have gravitated toward classical Kharijite positions.

Modern Traditionalist Sunnism

An example of a movement that has adopted classical Kharijite doctrines is the unitarian movement of the Arabian Peninsula. Usually referred to in the West as the Wahhabi movement, this reform movement was founded by the scholar and reformer Muhammad Ibn 'Abd al-Wahhab (d. 1792). The 18th-century Muslim world that Shaykh Ibn 'Abd al-Wahhab was born into was grim. Arab lands were the backwater of an Ottoman Empire trying to turn the tide of decline, and Arabia in particular suffered. On the whole, Arabia was still populated by nomadic and semi-nomadic tribes; these tribes relied on scarce pasture for their sustenance. The scarcity of pasture forced some tribes to settle, so as to be able to cultivate the land, while other tribes roamed and invaded their neighbors. Dotted throughout the peninsula were settled tribes, many of which had fallen into idiosyncratic forms of Islam. For example, many tribes visited the tombs of pious Muslims, hoping for intercession – a practice of veneration that is still common in North Africa. Endless warfare characterized the region. Nomadic tribes rivaled one another for dominance and regularly invaded the towns, destroying wells and crops. Settled tribes, on the other hand, fought for commercial advantage and employed religious symbols to buttress their sense of aristocracy.

Despite this extreme division, stirrings for unification began in the Nejd region of the peninsula in the 1770s; they were instigated by the alliance between Muhammad Ibn 'Abd al-Wahhab and Abdul-Aziz ibn Saud. Shaykh Ibn 'Abd al-Wahhab was born in 1703. The son of an Islamic scholar and following in his father's footsteps, he traveled to the Hijaz ("the Barrier" in western Saudi Arabia) as well as to Basra (in southern Iraq) to study the Islamic sciences. Upon his return, Ibn 'Abd al-Wahhab began advocating a more austere Islamic temperament. He criticized tomb visitations and Sufism, arguing that they were corruptions of the primordial Islamic faith. The ideas of Ibn ʿAbd al-Wahhab became the ideological cornerstone of the Saudi movement: political reform was to be found in political unity, and political unity was to be found in religious reform and uniformity. And, of course, for Shaykh ʿAbd al-Wahhab religious unity was to be found in the unity of God – *tawhīd*.

Kitab al-Tawhīd (*The Book of Tawhīd*), a major work of ʿAbd al-Wahhab, is exemplary of modern traditionalist Sunnism. The work is composed of 66 very short chapters that relate traditions; the author then explains the benefit of those traditions. He remains as close as possible to the text and to its literal meaning. His understanding of the tradition is defined by a high degree of austerity. His emphasis upon *taghut* (overstepping, rebellion), for example, relates this concept to the spiritual corruption and oppression inherent in devotion to anything other than God. He argues that such devotion is based on self-delusion, which in Islam is always understood to be close to "evil" and to constitute ignorance.

Ibn ʿAbd al-Wahhab's teachings represented a significant challenge to common religious practices of the era. As mentioned, certain tombs became important shrines, not only in Arabia but also throughout the Islamic world. They were seen by some as being holy places, since they contained the remains of holy men and women. Many people believe that God is more accessible in such places. Ibn ʿAbd al-Wahhab, however, regarded such practices as being *haram* (forbidden), and he insisted that prayer to God "will reach from any location, however distant. There is no need therefore for physical closeness" (Ibn ʿAbd al-Wahhab 1992: 71). This metaphysical postulate is typical of a transcendental view. God is everywhere, but he can only be everywhere in transcendence. If it were otherwise, if God were everywhere in immanence (*tashbih* in Arabic), in other words if he were immanent everywhere or in all things, then God would be in bad acts as well as in good ones.

Immanence and transcendence are two major issues that inform theology. Those who hold the view that God is immanent – or hold dear the nearness of God – think of bad acts as a "lesser intensity of God" and of good acts as a "greater intensity of God." This is why the tombs of noble men or women become sanctuaries, or why certain places are holy; we will say more about his later. For the traditionalists, however, the veneration of saints and tombs was nothing but superstition. But remember these positions are just the extremes; the Islamic tradition reflects a rich blend between them. Traditionalist absolutists like Ibn ʿAbd al-Wahhab deny the possibility of "physical closeness" and remain committed to a more transcendent view of God. Theology and politics are closely related here. Ibn ʿAbd al-Wahhab's simple message was accessible and spread rapidly. Its austerity conveyed a purity and a simplicity in the understanding of God that freed the believer from unnecessary, time-consuming, and superstitious devotional practices.

The alliance between Ibn ʿAbd al-Wahhab and Ibn Saud proved fruitful. Within a few decades the two families had united the Nejd in central Arabia and began invading other nearby lands. In 1801 a confederation of their tribes, under the political leadership of the House of Saud and the religious guidance of Ibn ʿAbd al-Wahhab, invaded Iraq and sacked Karbala. Karbala was an important city for the Shiʿa, the supporters of ʿAli, for it was in Karabala that ʿAli's son al-Husayn, fought the forces of Yazid, the son of Muʾawiya.

Shiʿism

In 681 the Umayyad state was ruled by Yazid ibn Muʾawiya. The transfer of power from father to son marked the political break between the Al Khulafa Ar-Rashidun – the "Rightly Guided Caliphs" – and what would become the Umayyad Dynasty. According to the Sunni view, limited power characterized the rule of the Rightly Guided Caliphs: they came to power through election (or designation) and consulted others in their administration. Most importantly, they were bound by the laws of the Qurʾan and the *sunna* and accountable to the community. As Abu Bakr once said: "Obey me so long as *I obey* God and His Messenger. If I disobey them, you are not bound to obey me" (al-Tabari 1990: 201). The caliph had no authority in and of himself; he only had authority insofar as he implemented the Qurʾan and the *sunna*.

The ascent of the Umayyads complicates the issue of authority in Islamic history. Muʾawiya, although shrewd and able, ruled more like an Arab sheikh than like a Muslim caliph. Although there was a great deal of compatibility between Arab custom and Islamic law, others, particularly the Shiʿa and the Kharijites, insisted on fully implementing the Islamic revolution. According to them, all customs not validated by Islam were to be completely discarded. So how would these idealists – and by no means do I employ that term pejoratively – fulfill what they considered to be the complete Islamic vision? They would do so sometimes by fighting and, particularly in the case of the Shiʿa, by doing a great deal of brilliant writing.

With the death of Imam ʿAli, the Muslim community largely remained politically quiescent under the rule of Muʾawiya. Muʾawiya commanded a powerful army, but important Muslims were uncomfortable with the new political order – it reminded them of the days before Islam. The Kharijites resisted any type of central authority, while the Shiʿa rallied around Hasan ibn ʿAli (d. 669) and encouraged him to challenge Muʾawiya. After much consideration, Hasan chose not to oppose the Umayyad and abdicated rather than spilling more Muslim blood (especially when the outcome was so uncertain). After roughly two decades of rule, Yazid assumed the caliphate after his father's passing. Shortly thereafter, certain Muslims began to encourage al-Husayn, Hasan's younger brother, to challenge Yazid.

In 681 al-Husayn and a small camp of supporters marched toward Kufa, Iraq, to mobilize Shiʿa support where it was strong. On the way, al-Husayn received word that Yazid was sending a military contingent to confront him. Al-Husayn, more committed to moral principle than to political calculation, marched on. In al-Husayn's mind, his right to the caliphate was not only a birthright but part and parcel of the Islamic understanding of the office. For him the caliph was a successor to the Prophet not merely in administration, but in his entire capacity – that is, with

Shi'ism: God's absolute authority is immanent in the Imam, who is divinely chosen.	Sunnism: God's authority is immanent in the community but it is not absolute. God's absolute authority is transcendent and the community attempts to approximate it as best as possible.	Classical Kharijism: God's absolute authority is transcendent and is approximated by following the letter of the Qur'an and *sunna*.

Figure 5.1   The theological spectrum.

respect to both political and religious authority. Although Imam al-Husayn claimed no new religious message, he did maintain that the House of the Prophet was the repository of religious authority. In addition, since Islam is as much a social movement as it is a system of religious rites, the authority of the Imam was, ideally at least, both political and spiritual. This was also the view of al-Husayn's supporters.

From a Shi'ite perspective, the caliphate is *not* a secular office, limited to managing the affairs of the community and bound by Islam. Rather the caliphate is understood as the very extension of God's authority on earth. Imam al-Husayn, in his correspondence, described the caliphate as the "possession of God" and looked upon it to "guide" the community of believers; he argued that only the divinely ordained Imam can "unite us on the path of truth" (Jafri 1976: 178–181). Contrast this with the Sunni perspective we have continually presented: for the Sunnis, truth, or God's authority, cannot be found in *any* person, but only in the Qur'an and the *sunna*. And, since no one man or woman possesses the absolute authority of God, it is the community's mandate to approximate the truth as best it can. Political authority is different from religious authority; for the Sunnis the former is located in the caliphate, while the latter is found in the community.

For the Shi'is, on the other hand, God's authority on earth is embodied in the person of the Imam, the Prophet's true successor both in religion and in politics. The implications are significant. The first issue to deal with is the understanding of religious authority. God's authority is not sought in the past but is literally embodied in the person of the Imam – in the here and now. Similarly, according to the Shi'a, Islam is not to be understood *in spite of* the temporal character of humanity; in fact Islam can only be understood *through* humanity as embodied in the person of the Imam, who is divinely chosen. For the Shi'ites, you follow the Imam – just as the Prophet himself was followed. Lastly, although the Shi'ite conception of authority does not doctrinally extend authority to any person outside the House of Prophet, certain developments in philosophy, Sufism, and law open this door as well. For now, let us look at our spectrum (see Figure 5.1).

Although the Imam ideally succeeds the Prophet in all the latter's capacities, this was not the case on the ground; Imam al-Husayn did not possess political authority, so he asserted his religious authority:

I will soon come. But you must be clear about the fact that the Imam is only one who follows the Book of God, makes justice and honesty his conduct and behavior, judges with truth, and devotes himself to the service of God. Peace. (Jafri 1976: 179)

As Jafri (ibid.) observes, the last line of this letter from Imam al-Husayn may help us "understand Hussein's approach and attitude toward the whole problem". One should read the following excerpt from another letter that al-Husayn sent to the Kufans:

God has chosen Muhammad from among his people, graced him with his Prophethood and selected him for his message [...] We, being his family, his close associates endowed with the quality of guardianship, his trustees and vice regent, and his heir and legatee, are the most deserving among all the people to take his place. But the people preferred themselves over us for this privilege. We became contented, disliking dissension and anxious to preserve the peace and well-being of the community [...] If you listen to me and obey my orders I will guide you on the right path. May the Peace and Mercy of God be upon you. (Ibid.)

Jafri states:

the content of this letter is a complete statement of the Shiʿi doctrine of the Imamate even at this early stage [...] in these letters Hussein adequately explains the concept of *walaya*, which means that God has bestowed upon the family of the Prophet special honor and qualities, thereby making them the ideal rulers, and that through their presence on earth His (i.e. God's) grace is disseminated. (Jafri 1976: 180)

So why were the Imams not recognized as such? Obviously, not all Muslims agreed to this vision of Islam. For example, Umar ibn al-Khattab, the second caliph, famously said to al-Husayn's cousin: "the people did not want both the prophethood and the caliphate in the Banu Hashim" (Jafri 1976: 65–66). There are several implications to this statement, but the most important one is this: the separation between religious and political authority is the de facto reality of the early caliphate.

The doctrine of the Imamate – the belief that Muhammad's authority was passed on to ʿAli and then to subsequent Imams – was not altogether clear to early Muslims. The House of the Prophet was highly esteemed, of course. Many Sunnis benefitted from their knowledge and paid their respects, but they considered the career of the Prophet to be wholly unique and believed that God's authority is present only in the Qurʾan and the *sunna*, not in the Prophet's house. Nonetheless, disagreements regarding the caliphate were largely mitigated through the extraordinary character of all of the people involved. Their devotion to the cause of Islam and of the well-being of the community preserved their relations, although there is some evidence to suggest those relations were strained. Yazid, however, was a man totally devoid of character. He not only violated Qurʾanic norms, he ridiculed them. Consequently al-Husayn rose to fight him in the knowledge that, should he die in the fight, the principle would nonetheless live: goodness, justice, and truth are eternal values to which one gives oneself over fully. Politics, palace power, and wealth are temporal pleasures that should never be confused with eternal values; if one does that, s/he risks her/his salvation. Al-Husayn was making this distinction clear.

Al-Husayn faced an Umayyad army of 4,000 men with a camp of 72 supporters. Defeat and death were near, for al-Husayn swore that he would never recognize the rule of Yazid as legitimate. The battle began on the tenth morning of the month of Muharram, and even today Shi'i Muslims commemorate this day with lamentations. The passion of al-Husayn is related by the sources in touching terms. His supporters fell one by one throughout the day, and finally al-Husayn himself was killed and decapitated. The day of his death is known as "the Day of Ashura" (*ashura* meaning "tenth" in Arabic).

The Imamate

Moojan Momen (1987: 147) observes that

> the Sunnis and Shi'is are basically in agreement with each other over the nature and function of prophethood. The two main functions of the Prophet are to reveal God's law to men and to guide men toward God. Of these two functions, the Sunnis believe that both ended with the death of Muhammad, while the Shi'is believe that whereas legislation ended, the function of guiding men and preserving and explaining the Divine law continued through the line of the imams.

The Sunni concept of the Caliphate is essentially secular; the caliph is not designated by the Prophet but is a first among equals, recognized by consensus and having no religious authority. "To others, the theologians and experts in jurisprudence, is given the task of expounding upon religious questions" (ibid.). The Shi'i concept of the Imamate/Caliphate, however, is religious in its very nature. The Imam is God's divine representative on earth, and the earth is never without an Imam.

> The authority of the Imam derives from his designation by his predecessor to a spiritual station and is independent of his temporal standing, i.e. it makes no difference to the Imam's station whether he is acknowledged by the generality of Muslims or not, whereas this quite clearly does not apply to a Sunni caliph whose station is totally dependent on such acknowledgement. (Ibid.)

Muhammad al-Baqir and Jafar as-Sadiq

Two related issues are at stake here: first, designation (*nass*); second, epistemology. The Caliphate during the Rashidun period remained ambiguous in its function. Clearly, from the moment Abu Bakr assumed the position of caliph, a clear injunction was made that empowered the community and thereby secularized the office. "Now then: O people I have been put in charge of you although I am not the best of you. Help me if I do well, rectify me if I do wrong," the great caliph said (al-Tabari 1990: 201). Nonetheless, the early caliphs were still looked to for guidance by Sunnis when it came to understanding the faith, since they had been such dear and close companions to the Prophet, even though there was no feeling that they

Sidebar 5.1   Major distinctions between Sunni and Shi'i Islam

Both Shi'i and Sunni Muslims agree on the foundational concepts of the unity of God (*tawhīd*), prophethood (*nubuwwa*), and resurrection on the Last Day (*ma'ad*).

In addition to these, Shi'is have two more foundational concepts: the Imamate (*Im'mah*) and the justice of God ('*Adl*):

- *The Imamate* For Shi'i Muslims, the authority found in the succession of the Prophet resides in the Imam. The Imam's successor is designated by the Imam during his lifetime.
- *The justice of God* Individuals are responsible for their actions and will face just judgment from God. Also, God can only interact with the world in a just manner, as defined by himself.

Shi'i Muslims recognize three time periods of prayer in the day. Contrary to some assertions, Shi'i Muslims rehearse each day the same five prayers as Sunni Muslims do, but the way they distribute these prayers in the course of the day varies.

One final distinction between Sunnis and Shi'is regards the Shi'i practice of paying *khums* (one fifth): one fifth of a Shi'i excess income is paid as a tax to the religious establishment – for distribution, charity, and the like.

---

were divinely appointed authorities. With the rise of the Umayyads, however, this ambivalence was entirely dispensed with.

From the time of Hasan al-Basri, suspicion is evident on the part of Sunnis toward political officials and their role in the development of religious doctrines. The Shi'i concept of designation emerged precisely in order to preserve religious authority and protect it from the corruption of politics. Not only Prophet Muhammad, but Jesus, David, Moses, Abraham, Noah, Adam, and all the other prophets had brought perfected divine knowledge; thus they all had been the Imams of their times. They had been extraordinary individuals, who accessed divine truths, preserving and protecting them from corruption through their remarkable, world-changing work. Why would such perfect knowledge be liable to abuse and exploitation by political men? By the procedure of each Imam designating his successor, religious authority – perfect knowledge of the divine – is perpetually protected from less than perfect people.

Notice how on the one hand *nass* preserves divine knowledge from an often corrupt humanity, and on the other it preserves the ability to understand the divine through humanity. There is a sense of human centrality to this doctrine; in fact the Imams discussed the possibility of continued divine inspiration. Muhammad al-Baqir (d. 733), the fifth Imam, al-Husayn's grandson, commented: "Ali used to act in accordance with the book of God and the *sunna* of his messenger and, if something came to him and it was new and without precedent in the *Book or the Sunna*, God would inspire him" (Momen 1987: 149). Muhammad al-Baqir explained this type of inspiration as "not the inspiration of prophethood, but rather like that which came to mother Mary (Qur'an 3: 45) and to the mother of Moses (Qur'an 28: 7) and to the bee (Qur'an 16: 68)" (ibid.).

Perhaps the most important Imam after 'Ali and al-Husayn is Jafar as-Sadiq (d. 765). Imam Jafar was the sixth Imam and a great-grandson of Imam al-Husayn. He is responsible for developing the doctrine of *nass* and the doctrine of the infallibility of the Imam (*masum*). The Imam's infallibility is predicated upon his prophetic designation and his very high gnostic state of knowledge. No one occupies a closer state to God than the Imam. In the same way, no one was closer to God than Jesus in his own time, or than Muhammad in his own. The Imams continue this legacy, being the spiritual guides of their times. We mentioned earlier that this raises certain epistemological issues. For Sunnis, the collective reason of the community is superior to the rational faculty of any single person. The prophetic tradition that claims "my community will never agree on an error" buttresses this position for Sunnis. For Shi'is, however, the reason of the Imam supersedes that of the community at large. But notice that both traditions give reason jurisdiction: for Shi'is, the limits of reason are overcome by the gnostic authority of the Imam, which is exclusive, while for Sunnis the limitations of reason limit religious authority altogether.

Branches within Shi'ism

There are three major branches of Shi'ism: the Zaydis, the Isma'ilis, and the Twelvers. These branches stem from differences arising on the issue of succession. The vast majority of Shi'is are Twelvers, and for this reason we will briefly expound only Zaydi and Isma'ili doctrines here. Then we will discuss the consolidation of Sunnism and Shi'ism, the influence of Nasir al-Din al-Tusi, and the synthesis of Ibn Taymiyya. At the end we will move on to later developments.

Zaydis

Both politically and epistemologically, the Zaydis occupy a place between Shi'ism and Sunnism, standing proof that Muslims cannot be neatly divided into Sunni and Shi'i. Zayd al-Shahid was the brother of Muhammad al-Baqir and was recognized by Zaydis as the fifth Imam. Unlike the majority of Shi'ites, who consider designation a divinely ordained affair, for the Zaydis any descendant of Muhammad's daughter Fatima who resists the state in the name of pure Islam and is learned in Islam is a possible Imam. Unlike Muhammad al-Baqir, Imam Zayd initiated a revolt in Kufa against the Umayyad Caliph Hisham ibn Marwan in the year 737. Imam Zayd was killed, but in the eyes of the Zaydis his willingness to fight for his claim qualified him as Imam above his brother Muhammad al-Baqir, who devoted himself to religious study and remained aloof from politics. The Zaydis also consider Abu Bakr and Umar ibn al-Khattab to be legitimate leaders of the community, since they were brought to the caliphate through election by the community, and they were recognized by Zayd as Imams. This sheds light on another major difference between the Zaydis on the one hand and Twelvers and Isma'ilis on the other. For the former, the Imam is not *masum*; the limitations of reason are not overcome through gnosis, and they also limit religious authority to some extent. In general epistemological principals the Zaydis are very close to the Mutazilites, while in matters of the law they apply the jurisprudence of Abu Hanifa.

Isma'ilis

The Isma'ilis followed a different line of Imams. While the majority of Shi'ites accepted Musa al-Kazim, the son of Jafar as-Sadiq, as their Imam, some chose to accept Isma'il ibn Jafar instead. Imam Isma'il was Imam Jafar's oldest son. He predeceased his father, but not before having himself a son – Muhammad. Whereas in epistemology and politics the Zaydis found a place somewhere between general Sunni and Shi'ite positions, the Isma'ilis took gnosis to its extreme conclusion; thus they were the most gnostically inclined and progressive members of the Muslim community. Isma'ili hermeneutics revolves around the relationship between exoteric and esoteric aspects of revelation and of existence in general. Each external reality (*zahir*) has an inner meaning (*batin*), and all revelation (*tanzil*) is rendered meaningful through an esoteric exegesis (*ta'wil*).

For most Shi'ites, the Imam is the proof of God on earth. As we said before, the Imam occupies a higher spiritual station than others; hence his state of mind reflects divine reality perfectly and thus proves it. It is through the Imam's communication of a higher state of consciousness that followers achieve such a state, and thus approximate God. For the Isma'ilis, the proof of God – that is, the Imam – is also accompanied by a silent successor. The former speaks on behalf of God; the latter will succeed the speaker and, in turn, will have a silent successor. Numerology plays some role in Isma'ili cosmology, which makes sense, considering the significance Isma'ilis attribute to outer and inner meanings.

According to Isma'ili doctrine, a prophet, who is the perfect manifestation of knowledge of God (in other words, the perfect gnostic), can unfold the divine mysteries and initiate humans in them; this process is known as *walayat*. The Prophet has seven testamentary executors, and the seventh one is also a Prophet. According to the Isma'ilis, Noah was the seventh executor of Adam's message; Abraham was Noah's seventh, Moses was Abraham's seventh, Jesus was Moses' seventh, and Muhammad was Jesus' seventh executor of the divine message.

Once again, as we have repeatedly said, this cyclical orientation locates revelation *in the world* and not outside of it. For this reason the present moment is more significant to Isma'ilis than the past. The Isma'ili Imamate is as follows: 'Ali; Husayn ibn 'Ali (the Isma'ilis do not consider Hasan an Imam); 'Ali ibn Husayn al-Sajjad; Muhammad al-Baqir; Jafar as-Sadiq; Isma'il ibn Jafar; and Muhammad ibn Isma'il. Thereafter the Isma'ilis recognize seven descendants of Muhammad ibn Isma'il whose names remain secret, and then the first seven rulers of the Fatimid caliphate, a formal Isma'ili dynasty based in Egypt. The Fatimids were fascinating rulers: here for the first time in Islamic history, although perhaps not the last, a person is recognized as Imam in the fullest sense, actually holding power. As Paul Walker, a prominent Fatimid scholar observes,

> as imams of the Isma'ilis, the Fatimids controlled a network of missions (*da'was*, missionaries) that reached deep into areas inside the domains of their opponents. For his religious followers, the Fatimid ruler, in his capacity as Isma'ili imam, was the

absolute authority in all matters including most especially any issue of religion and religious doctrine and interpretation. (Walker 2002: 2)

In addition to missionary work, the emphasis on the present time in the Isma'ili tradition cultivated an appreciation for philosophy and for learning generally. It was the Fatimids who built the Al-Azhar University, which is today one of the most authoritative Sunni universities in the world.

Abu Yaqub al-Sijistani

In line with our constant reference to rationalism, the Isma'ili worldview maintains that all things, revealed scripture in particular, have an outward and an inward meaning. This approach enabled a broad, creative interpretation of the sacred text. Other Muslims, "when faced with a conflict between reason and revelation, cannot readily move from the obvious to the figurative or vice-a-versa. By contrast the Isma'ilis always sensed this possibility, which was, according to them, built into the very structure of revealed scripture" (Walker 1998: 10). This dynamism, enabled by reason, is exemplified in the works of al-Kirmani and in those of the thinker we will address here, al-Sijistani (d. 971).

The idea that there is an outward (*zahir*) and an inward (*batin*) meaning to a text is known as esotericism. Whereas the outward meaning may be apparent, it is the inward meaning that is essential according to this mode of thinking. Since the outward meaning is a symbol of the inward meaning, symbolism plays an important role in Shi'i hermeneutics and culture generally. Usually esotericism is considered irrational, or a-rational; however, that is a misunderstanding. The distinction between exoteric and esoteric meanings entails the liberation of the meaning of the text from a literal interpretation, which facilitates the possibility of *applying reason* to conclude a new interpretation, which is suitable for the times. This is similar to philosophers arguing that certain passages of the Qur'an were allegorical when such passages seemed to contradict reason.

Al-Sijistani devoted his intellectual abilities to the defense of Isma'ili doctrine. He was a fascinating thinker insofar as he employed reason to demonstrate the limits of Islamic philosophy and theology. In so doing, he argued that God can only be known through the law and the Imam. For example, al-Sijistani challenged the basic assumptions of metaphysics; he argued that metaphysics merely exposed the limits of reason rather than transcending them. In other words metaphysics requires understandable concepts to function. Cause and effect, being, things: these are examples of concepts important to metaphysics. Al-Sijistani challenged the capacity of such concepts to explain God.

Let us consider his argument against the philosophers who claimed that God was the "first cause." Al-Sijistani argues that God cannot be considered a first cause since that would imply that the world is eternal. If God is a cause, he is an eternal cause, and as such he would produce an eternal effect. This is blasphemous for al-Sijistani. Yet if God is not a cause, he cannot be known by his effects, an idea many Muslims would reject. In fact al-Sijistani's metaphysics results in agnosticism. For example, is God identical with his will? If so, then God and his will are the same, and *what God wills* is identical with God. This is pantheism. Perhaps God wills through a will other than his. Then there would be two gods, an eternal will and an eternal god. Of course the idea of two divinities is universally rejected by any and all Muslims. Perhaps the relationship between God and his will is not fully available to the human intellect. In this case we have a sort of agnosticism in which nothing about God can really be known, but this is not the position that al-Sijistani wishes to take.

"For the Sufis and neo-Platonists, the realization that God is not accessible to human thought does not result in agnosticism but rather in alternative forms of comprehension" (Walker 1998: 89). We saw this in al-Ghazali, who reconciled the limits of reason with gnosis. "Where the intellect fails," Walker observes, "a mystical attraction takes over and eventually allows" the direct apprehension of God (ibid.). For al-Sijistani, the intellect is incapable of comprehending God, but God is knowable – through the law. But how is the law to be understood? Through the Imam. God, for al-Sijistani, "is not and never was an object of reason" (p. 103). But the law can only be understood through the human Imam; thus, knowledge of the law is immanent in the world, contemporary with its events, and open to the reason of a human being.

Response to Esoterics: Toward a Consolidation of Sunnism and Shiʿism

Three thinkers from the classical period come together to form the backbone of contemporary Sunnism: Ahmad ibn Hanbal, Abu Hamid al-Ghazali, and Ibn Taymiyya. We discussed Ahmad ibn Hanbal at some length in the last chapter. As you may recall, Hanbal was a staunch traditionalist who resisted the state and insisted on the autonomy of the religious community. Ibn Taymiyya (d. 1328) is the single most influential Hanbalite of the classical period, and his influence continues to resonate today, as is evinced by the unitarian movement of Arabia, as well as by the thought of Sayyid Qutb (d. 1966). Al-Ghazali was another prominent influence in the development of Sunnism. He continued, however, to espouse the use of reason, although in moderation. Ibn Taymiyya's thought cannot be completely understood unless put in its context, and part of that context is responding to al-Ghazali.

As we have seen, al-Ghazali demonstrated that there were problems with philosophical approaches to Islamic questions. He was able to show that metaphysics was unable to prove beyond doubt the existence of God, or at least of the personal God of the Abrahamic traditions. This did not, however, prevent the great theologian from employing reason. Al-Ghazali regarded logic "as an 'instrument of thought' and as such religiously neutral or innocuous," observes Majid Fakhry (1999: 290). In other words the consistency of language and its ability to constantly describe the world still played an important role in al-Ghazali's approach to the text. Ibn Taymiyya, on the other hand, wanted tradition to occupy not only a superior place in terms of authority, but also an exclusive place.

In order to achieve this result, Ibn Taymiyya went further than al-Ghazali in his espousal of literalism and empiricism, the latter of which was embraced by figures like Ibn Hazm. Although al-Ghazali sought refuge in faithful adherence to the text of the Qur'an, his legacy vis-à-vis esotericism is more ambiguous – remember that he attempted to reconcile the limitations of reason with gnosis. Al-Ghazali took a middle position toward esotericism. He attacked the Isma'ilis' belief in the need for an Imam to interpret the Qur'an, and he did so by defending personal reason to a certain extent. He argued:

> For a person not sure of the direction of the Kibla [sic] [i.e. someone who has a problem locating the direction of prayer] all he can do is trust his own judgement. If he took the time to consult the Imam, he would miss the hour of prayer. Thus it is permitted to pray in the direction one estimates to be true […]. (Abu-Laylah 2001: 85)

So, although al-Ghazali shared with the Shi'is an esteem for the esoteric, he was radically at odds with them over the Imamate and the nature of authority. Roughly 90 years after al-Ghazali's death, another major Islamic thinker was born who must be discussed before we turn to Ibn Taymiyya. Nasir al-Din al-Tusi (d. 1274) is yet another heavyweight thinker of the period, who would exercise considerable influence – both philosophically and politically – in the consolidation of Shi'ism.

The Sustainer of the Faith: Nasir al-Din and His Influence

Al-Tusi was born in Tus, Iran, in 1201. At a young age he moved to Nishapur, the intellectual capital of the eastern Islamic lands, where he studied under Farid ad-Din Damad Nishapuri. As part of Nishapur's intellectual progeny, al-Tusi was literally five generations removed from the great Ibn Sina, as his teacher's intellectual heritage could be traced directly to him. And he would be the great philosopher's greatest disciple.

Al-Tusi also has a more ominous legacy, however. His life coincided exactly with the devastating Mongol invasions of the Muslim world. In 1255 Hulagu, the grandson of Chingiz Khan, invaded Khurasan, the large eastern part of Iran. One year later he captured the famous Isma'ili fortress of Alamut, where al-Tusi was staying. Al-Tusi showed his political tact by convincing the local prince to surrender to the Mongols, and in so doing he demonstrated his value. Hulagu retained him for more services, namely the sacking of the capital of the Muslim world, Baghdad, in the year 1258.

With the surrender of al-Must'asim, the Abbasid caliphate had come to a dramatic end. The Mongol invasions devastated the Muslim world. Baghdad was sacked; the symbolic seat of caliphal authority, an institution extending back to the Prophet, had been destroyed. Al-Tusi would remain in the service of Hulagu, then of his son Abaqa, until his death in 1274. He was buried in Kazimayn, just north of Baghdad.

Al-Tusi's service to the Mongols guaranteed the Shi'is a position in which they could flourish, as he was a Twelver himself. Their schools and thinkers went unharmed, or at least less harmed than those of their Sunni counterparts (including Ibn Taymiyya), who more diligently resisted the Mongols. Al-Tusi's influence is threefold. He had of course a great deal of political influence. Then there are al-Tusi's incredible philosophical and scientific achievements. And, lastly, he exerted an influence on al-Allama al-Hilli (d. 1325), who in turn initiated some of the legal developments that culminate in the modern period.

Al-Tusi wrote many works in the service of Isma'ili princes and, in many ways, he was able to reconcile philosophy with their cosmology. Since, as you will recall, the Isma'ilis believe that world history divides into prophetic stages, al-Tusi was able to legitimate Greek philosophy as part of an earlier period of wisdom. Thus he demonstrated that humanity is constantly moving forward and, as Antony Black (2001: 147) observes, he "did not consider the present Sharia as absolute as the Sunnis did."

In ethics, al-Tusi was more adamant than others on the themes of free will and the value of human reason. He argued that man's improvement is "entrusted to its own independent judgment" (quoted in Black, ibid.). This view is directly related to two things. First, it had an influence on later Imami jurists such as al-Hilli, who argued that independent reasoning must be employed by jurists in the absence of the Imams. This legacy would come into full force in the 1979 Islamic Revolution. Second, the view quoted above is related to al-Tusi's social theory. He argued that cooperation or the division of labor is the main impetus in forming society. Since we cannot do all of the things necessary for survival on our own, we must create societies to cooperate with others. As Black notes, "the ultimate factor in this explanation of human association is, surprisingly, love, which plays a more central part here than in any other Islamic social theory. Love engenders civilized life and social synthesis and is the 'connector of societies'" (p. 149). For al-Tusi, the cooperation of human beings in a society facilitates the process of human perfection and is a natural concomitant to spirituality.

In terms of a more direct political prescriptivism, al-Tusi continues the tradition of al-Farabi, equating Greek political concepts with Islamic ones. But, unlike in al-Farabi, in al-Tusi the community plays a larger role in giving consent to a ruler's authority. Al-Tusi argued that, by recognizing the authority of the Imams, the community was being empowered. This was, of course, a consequence of the Shi'i view that the Imams are a sign of God's favor bestowed upon the community. This type of logic only makes sense if we are willing to distinguish between Shi'i and Sunni views of the caliphate. For Shi'is, the Imam, who should assume total executive and religious power, embodies divine law perfectly; hence he is himself perfect and an extension of God's will toward the community. For Sunnis, on the other hand, no one after the Prophet embodies the law perfectly; the caliph is simply an administrator who should possess knowledge of the law and act justly, and his lack of religiosity does not condemn the religious community, for the religious community is autonomous from the state. But al-Tusi's thought not only advocated the role of the Imam; it incorporated old and persistent ideas from Persian theories of justice.

Al-Tusi stratified society into four groups: men of the pen (or men of knowledge and ideas); men of the sword (warriors); merchants; and agriculturalists. In Persian theories of justice, only a just ruler who is able to facilitate social justice across these groups rules effectively and therefore ensures the well-being of his community. Black insists that al-Tusi "transmitted elements of classical Islamic political philosophy into the modern world" (Black 2001: 152): his thought directly influenced the Safavids and the Ottomans insofar as these two dynasties facilitated the formation of premodern nation-states. One of these elements – al-Tusi's argument about "the agreement of the opinions of the community, who with respect to cooperation and mutual assistance are like the members belonging to one individual" (quoted in Black, ibid.) – reminds one of Rousseau. This idea of homogeneity can be seen to invite both a democratic ethos and totalitarianism.

And now let us look at a pillar of modern Sunnism: Ibn Taymiyya.

Enjoining the Good and Forbidding the Wrong: The Sultan–*Sharia* Synthesis of Ibn Taymiyya

By the age of 6, Ibn Taymiyya (d. 1328) was forced to flee his hometown of Haraan due to the Mongol invasion. He lived his life in the Mamluke domains of Syria and Egypt, where he reconciled the military authority of the sultan with the religious authority of the community. Ibn Taymiyya spent many years in prison, advocating his political ideas, and he died in prison in 1328. What characterizes Ibn Taymiyya's thought is the idea of the infallibility of the early community and a puritanism unmatched by his predecessors. Lastly, he insisted that power and faith go hand and hand. This would become the intellectual foundation of modern traditionalist states like Saudi Arabia.

With the collapse of the caliphate, a direct link to the Prophet no longer existed. And in many ways Ibn Taymiyya felt that Islamic practices were no longer directly linked to the Prophet either. He took al-Ghazali to task for arguing that there are four schools of Islamic thought – the Mutazilites, the Asharites, the philosophers, and the Sufis. For him, the *Sahaba* (companions of the Prophet) constituted another group, which was superior to the others in its proximity to the Prophet and lively support of his endeavors. This insistence on a pristine past is at the heart and center of traditionalist epistemology, where time is seen as an adulterating force. Although Ibn Taymiyya's thought is actually quite nuanced and he advocates the use of moderate reason and *ijithad* (effort), his legacy is nonetheless strictly conservative. Ibn Taymiyya encouraged reforms to the *sharia* so as to keep up with the times, but his methodologies were restricted to trying to emulate the opinions of the early companions. Thus, according to him, all things believed not to have existed in the days of the Prophet were innovations (*bid'a*) or heresies. On this list he would include the Imamate together with many Sufi practices, as well as philosophy.

From Ahmad ibn Hanbal on, the community maintained a tradition of fierce autonomy among Sunni Muslims. We are not suggesting that Sunnis were not ruled, but only that the caliph was not necessarily perceived as a natural extension of divine law – a status that remained the prerogative of religious scholars. This political disposition facilitated a kind of political quiescence, whereby Sunni Muslims were on the whole uninterested in who ruled, so long as stability was maintained and they could carry out their religious duties. But Ibn Taymiyya argued for a stronger link between political state and religious society. He argued that, unlike the other two revealed faiths – Judaism and Christianity – Islam provided the intellectual means to join the spiritual with the material (a legacy we find again in Sayyid Qutb).

As for the joining of spiritual and military authority, Ibn Taymiyya argued that power belonged to no one but was a trusteeship endowed by God. In consequence, although the sultan's authority derives from God, the interests that he must serve are those of the people, and God's law is the grace of the people. But, once again, unlike in Christianity, of which Ibn Taymiyya was a vocal critic, in Islam the law is manifested in society through prescribed punitive measures. Should those measures not be met, the law is not being enacted, and thus the grace of the community is suspended. In the spirit of this logic, Ibn Taymiyya argued for a staunch application of the law.

Premodern and Modern Developments
Built on Classical Legacies

Two things should be pointed out before we go on. First, none of the thinkers we have discussed thus far can be said to "typify" or completely "personify" Sunnism or Shiʻism; what these thinkers do illustrate are historical links between the Sunnism or Shiʻism of their times and what is generally understood today by Sunnism or Shiʻism. This brings us to our second point. To approach Sunnism or Shiʻism at any given time in Islamic history and to assume that the various historical manifestations we find represent these two doctrines in some atemporal form would be fundamentally flawed. Sunnism and Shiʻism (as well as puritanism) often overlap, or even switch positions altogether. This said, there are, however, some essential qualities that do distinguish them. Shiʻis have an Imam, and this Imam keeps authority immanent, in the world. Sunnis cut off the tradition of the Prophet's absolute authority, and, in trying to figure out Islam, they created a theology that contains a wide spectrum of approaches. At any given time, we can find among both Sunnis and Shiʻis people who have argued on either side of the controversy about the supremacy of tradition or reason over the other. For the purposes of an introduction to Islam for the 21st century, we will now examine two thinkers who have left an indelible imprint on Sunnism and Shiʻism as these are understood today: Sayyid Qutb (d. 1966) and Ayatollah R. Khomeini (d. 1989).

Sayyid Qutb and Jāhalīyaa at-Thani

Qutb was highly influenced by Ibn Taymiyya, particularly by his emphasis on the *Salaf* – the members of the first three generations of Muslims (which included the *Sahaba*). But it is difficult to discuss Qutb's thought merely in terms of ideas. He was a political dissident during the colonial period, as well as after the successful *coup d'état* of Gamal Abdel-Nasser's Free Officers' Movement in Egypt in 1952. He was educated partly in the United States, where, as an Afro-Arab, he witnessed up close the phenomena of racism and "Westernization." Back in Egypt he was imprisoned for his political activities, tortured, and eventually executed in 1966. And there can be no doubt that all of these experiences influenced his thought, just as experience influences anyone's thought. Here we will confine ourselves to the ideas produced by this influential man.

The various features of Qutb's thought coalesce into a radically anarchist political theory. It is his emphasis on Muslim society, as opposed to Islamic institutions, that qualifies Qutb as a contemporary "Sunni" thinker; and it should be mentioned from the outset that Qutb influenced everyone, including prominent Shi'ites such as A. R. Khomeini. Qutb argued that loyalty to the modern nation-state was a form of idolatry. In his view the nation-state was a modern political concept predicated upon notions of national identity and self-determination. Generally speaking, the idea that the French should rule the French, the Greeks should rule the Greeks, and the Americans should rule the Americans is associated with the nation-state; citizens should somehow legislate for themselves. Qutb takes issue with this mode of thinking and argues that it is analogous to that of the *jāhilīyyah* – the pre-Islamic "age of ignorance" mentioned in the previous chapter – as Muslims sometimes conceptualized this notion. Here are his words:

> It [*jahiliyyah*] is not now in that simple and primitive form of the ancient *jahiliyyah*, but takes the form of claiming that the right to create values, to legislate rules of collective behavior, and to choose any way of life rests with men, without regard to what God has prescribed. The result of this rebellion against the authority of God is the oppression of His creatures. Thus the humiliation of the common man under the communist systems and the exploitation of individuals and nations due to greed and wealth and imperialism under the capitalist systems are but a corollary of the rebellion against God's authority and of the denial of the dignity of man given to him by God. (Qutb 1978: 4)

Several features characterize the position expressed here, but the convergence of politics and theology is clear, and this is why we are discussing Qutb. For, whether one agrees with him or not, he remains loyal to the idea of delineating the relationship between politics and theology common to Islam. Qutb argued that devoting oneself to one's nation was a form of worship analogous to idolatry (*shirk*), and that it subjected the intellect to human conventions such as states, ethnicities, borders, and citizenships. For Qutb, when such things govern our behavior, they are false gods. If one goes to war to fight for the cause of ethnicity, or for one's flag, one commits the sin of *shirk*, because notions like ethnicity or citizenship are arbitrary. In Qutb's words:

> Only Islam has the distinction of basing the fundamental, binding relationship in society on belief; and on the basis of this belief black and white, red and yellow, Arab and Greek, Persian and African, and all nations which inhabit the earth become one community. (Qutb 1978: 65)

Qutb is opposed to certain political developments in the 20th century, and several elements of his thought can be construed as reactionary. What is his solution? He asks the reader to look back at the first generation of Islam; and here we see the influence of Ibn Taymiyya. But, unlike Ibn Taymiyya, who looks at the *Salaf* for legal guidance, Qutb invokes existential guidance. He respects what he considers to be the early community's mystical prowess, and he depicts two main characteristics of their concept of *tawhīd*. First, its proclamation challenged the "worldly authority that had usurped the greatest attribute of God, namely, sovereignty" (p. 13). Second, the first generation of Muslims allowed *tawhīd* to "penetrate into the deep recesses of the heart" and thus to "free" them (in Qutb's view) from adherence to social conventions (p. 19). In his commentary on the Qur'an, which he composed in prison, he says: "God's oneness is such that there is no reality and no true and permanent existence." He goes on to argue:

> This is the belief that should be entrenched in us. It gives us a full explanation of human existence. Once this belief is clear and the explanation has established itself in our minds, our hearts are purified of all falsities and impurities. They are thus released from all bonds except their bond with the Unique Being to whom alone the reality of existence belongs and who is the only effective power in this world. Thus, the human heart is released from bondage to anything in this world, even if it cannot shirk the notion that other beings exist. Indeed, why should our hearts aspire to anything that has neither a permanent reality, nor any independent power to function in this world? The only real existence is that of the Divine Being and the truly effective power is Divine Will. (Qutb 1990: 350)

Thus Qutb advances the idea that awareness of God (*taqwā*) should inform not only your personal and moral outlook, but also your social and political existence; you are bonded to others by *tawhīd*, not by citizenship or law. In fact Qutb argues that, when *tawhīd* is truly realized, the state will not even be needed, for the "Sharia harmonizes the external behavior of man with his internal nature in an easy way. When a man makes peace with his own nature, peace and cooperation among individuals follow automatically" (p. 60). Qutb's political theology remains a potent voice in today's Islam. He weaved together modern political concepts with classical Islamic concepts, which allowed Muslims who identified themselves as Muslims on a political level to engage with modern political discourse. A.R. Khomeini is an example of such a Muslim.

Ayatollah R. Khomeini: Revolutionary and Imam

Ayatollah ("Sign of God") Ruhollah Khomeini is perhaps the single most influential political figure of the last 50 years, for the Iranian Revolution of 1979 is comparable in scope and influence to the French Revolution of 1789. It has changed the world forever. The revolution of 1979 brought to power, for the first time in Islamic history, the clerical class; this phenomenon could be described as a theocracy. Iran is the only theocracy in the Muslim world, and the philosophical influences that contributed to its formation, unique and dynamic as they are, were brought together by Imam Khomeini himself.

Imam Khomeini was born in 1902, in a small village in Iran. His father died when Khomeini was still a baby, and his mother died when he was only 16. Nonetheless, Khomeini was educated in a traditional manner and introduced to Islamic science from a young age. Throughout his life he argued with the political authorities, thus replicating the unease between Muslim thinkers and politicians. He was exiled to Iraq and eventually to Paris, from where he led a campaign to overthrow the shah (king) of Iran, Mohammaed Reza Pahlavi. His political career was prepared for by his religious career; moreover, Ayatollah Khomeini had an eclectic background in Islamic sciences and taught philosophy, *fiqh*, and mysticism in seminaries in Qum, an important religious center in Iran. Let us now review some of the thinkers who influenced his ideas.

Mulla Sadra and Illuminationist Philosophy

Some consider Mulla Sadra (d. 1640) to be the last great classical Muslim philosopher and a bridge between classical and contemporary Islamic thought. Indeed you have already been introduced to his thought. Sadra advanced brilliant doctrines in epistemology, and, in the hands of a luminary like Khomeini, his philosophy in general had a profound political impact. Mulla Sadra himself was deeply influenced by Avicenna, Ibn al'Arabi, and the Persian mystic Suhrawardi. He was also marked by Shiʻism, which, as you will remember, is more permissive than traditionalist Sunnism: it admits of divine inspiration (*wahy*) extending into the human world.

Sadra regarded Being as the primary reality and, by using Ibn al'Arabi as well as philosophical analysis and mysticism, he identified Being with God. This doctrine is known as *wahdat al-wujud* – "the unity of existence." Ibn al'Arabi is credited with this doctrine, although he never employed the label. For our purposes it is not necessary to explore its highly sophisticated and nuanced contours, only to address its implications in simple terms. The unity of existence, particularly in its Sadrian form, implies that all things are unified in God's knowledge. But God's knowledge is itself a comprehensive reality. As Mehdi Aminrazavi (1999: 487) observes, "since God's essence and Being are the same and all things emanate from Him [His knowledge], He is at once the knower, the known, and the knowledge." So, if everything is unity, why do we perceive multiplicity? For Mulla Sadra multiplicity is a figment of the imagination, and it is reinforced through language. As Ibn al-'Arabi argued, reality is the mirror of God. God's complexity is reflected in this splendid universe, and God himself is most perfectly reflected in the perfect man (*insan al-Kamil*).

Once again, to put it in simple terms, there is no reality without God "perceiving himself," if you will; thus reality is an extension of God. It is possible, then, for someone to penetrate the layers of reality and have direct knowledge of God, which is a kind of inspiration. This is the power of Ibn al'Arabi and Mulla Sadra, and Ayatollah Khomeini not only understood it but was committed to it. In this philosophy, a person's insight could be "illuminated" through direct apprehension of God. Khomeini taught such doctrines. But other developments in Shi'i jurisprudence also contributed to his vision.

In the late 18th century a fierce debate was taking place between Shi'ite religious scholars concerning the nature of their authority. As you will recall, the Shi'ites invest the Imam with authority. Ever since the 10th century Twelver Shi'ites have believed that their Imam is in occultation: he has disappeared, but will resurface one day, and they await his return. Thus Shi'ites are more messianic, or at least this worldview has been more formalized in their culture. So, in the absence of the Imam, should clerics have the authority to interpret the law (the *usuli* position), or should they simply follow the traditions of the Imams (the *akhbari* position)? Here you can see the same tension persisting between the freer use of reason and the guidelines of tradition. The *usuli* position won, however, and the clerics gained greater authority in interpreting and articulating the law, particularly by comparison with their Sunni counterparts.

Ayatollah Khomeini's deep entrenchment in the Islamic sciences exposed him to all these ideas. By informally synthesizing them, he empowered himself to effect change in the world. His most original contribution is the theory of *velayet-e faqih* – the authority, governance, or jurisdiction of the jurist. He argued, for the first time in Islamic history, that the jurist should rule, or at the very least possess an ultimate veto power in a Muslim state. Thus jurists should not only articulate Islamic law; they should be able to execute it. The jurist has inherited the mandate of the Imam, and the idea that jurists are custodians of political authority until the Imam returns is fundamental to the Iranian revolutionary outlook. Once again, as you may recall, it is the features of the Imamate as Shi'ites conceive of it that allow such a political and religious mandate to exist. When the political and the religious are not only combined, but synonymous, the result is a theocracy. As we already noted, Iran is the only theocracy in the Muslim world; and let it be said that, at this moment at least, what permits the existence of a theocracy is the particular structure of the Shi'ite worldview. Of course, not all Shi'ites adhere to Khomeini's vision; besides, some Shi'ites consider it blasphemous – an usurpation of the divine mandate of the Imam. But what the Islamic Revolution undeniably accomplished was to raise a challenge to the secular state and to the political passivity characteristic of religious scholars today.

Political Theology Summarized

We have attempted here an unorthodox approach to the phenomenon of Islamic "sects." Textbooks usually pin them down, pointing out a few fundamental beliefs with bullet points. We have explored instead the meaning of "sects" as different spiritual types that are in some way shaped by beliefs. We have also noticed that some Sunnis look like Shi'is and some Shi'is look like Sunnis; and this is due to the absence of an orthodoxy in Islam. We must also point out that we have chosen to highlight the more dynamic figures of a political theology – in other words most of those engaged in politics. There are many among the apolitical ones who manifest spirituality in the terms described above.

An important reminder: we have examined the phenomenon of "sects" in historical contexts. This is because no movement (in Islam or anywhere else) is ahistorical: all movements and doctrinal claims are intimately related to their environment and to the needs of their own times. In the following chapters we will examine how these doctrines have affected world politics.

Discussion Questions

1   What is the relationship between traditionalism and literalism, rationalism and esotericism, transcendence and immanence?
2   According to the various views presented above, what is the relationship between human reason and the understanding of revelation?
3   Is Islam theocratic? If so, how? If not, why not?

Suggested Further Reading

'Abd al-Wahhab, M. (1992). *Kitab al-Tawhid*, trans. Ismail Farooqi. Kuwait City: Al-Faisal.

Al-Ghazali, Abu Hamid Muhammad (2001). *Deliverance from Error and Mystical Union with the Almighty*, trans. Muhammad Abu-Laylah. Washington, DC: Council for Research in Values and Philosophy.

Al-Tabari (1990). *History of Prophets and Kings*. Vol. 9: *The Last Years of the Prophet*, trans. I. Poonawala. Albany, NY: SUNY Press.

Aminrazavi, Mehdi (1999). Mulla Sadra. In Ian McGreal (ed.), *Great Thinkers of the Eastern World*. New York, NY: HarperCollins, pp. 484–488.

Black, Antony (2001). *The History of Islamic Political Thought: From the Prophet to the Present*. New York, NY: Routledge.

Daftry, F. (2007). *The Isma'ilis: Their History and Doctrines*. Cambridge: Cambridge University Press.

Esposito, J. (ed.) (1999). *The Oxford History of Islam*. Oxford: Oxford University Press.

Fakhry, M. (1983). *A History of Islamic Philosophy*. New York, NY: Columbia University Press.

Fakhry, M. (1999). Philosophy and theology from the eighth century to the present. In Esposito (ed.), pp. 269–303.

Hourani, George (1985). *Reason and Tradition in Islamic Ethics*. Cambridge: Cambridge University Press.

Jafri, S. H. (1976). *The Origins of Early Development of Shi²a Islam*. Qum: Ansariyan Publications.

MacGreal, Ian (ed.) (1995). *Great Thinkers of the Eastern World*. New York, NY: HarperCollins.

Momen, M. (1987). *An Introduction to Shi²a Islam*. New Haven, CT: Yale University Press.

Qutb, Sayyid (1978). *Milestones*. Salimiah, Kuwait: IIFSO.

Qutb, Sayyid (1990). *In the Shade of the Qur²an*. Leicester: The Islamic Foundation.

Van Ess, J. (2006). *The Flowering of Muslim Theology*. Cambridge, MA: Harvard University Press.

Walker, P. (1998). *Abu Ya'qub Al-Sijistani: Intellectual Missionary*. New York, NY: I. B. Tauris.

Walker, P. (2002). *Exploring and Islamic Empire: Fatimid History and Its Sources*. New York, NY: I. B. Tauris.

Watt, W. M. (1998). *Islamic Political Thought*. Edinburgh: Edinburgh University Press.

Part II

Islam and the Modern World

6

Islam and the State

Part I

SCOTT W. HIBBARD

Outline

An Introduction to Islam in the 21st Century, First Edition. Edited by Aminah Beverly McCloud, Scott W. Hibbard, and Laith Saud.
© 2013 Blackwell Publishing Ltd. Published 2013 by Blackwell Publishing Ltd.

Introduction

Muslims have long debated the proper relationship between Islam and the state. Although it is argued that Islam is a totalizing religion – one that rightfully governs all facets of human life, including the political – in practice this has not always been the case. On the contrary, there have been long-standing tensions between religious authorities on the one hand and their political counterparts on the other. Although the early caliphates merged religious and political leadership in a single person, subsequent Islamic history saw a division of labor – and often a competition – between religious scholars and Muslim rulers. Political actors, for example, regularly sought to limit, co-opt or otherwise regulate religion in public life. At times they even tried to eradicate it. Similarly, Islamic scholars struggled to maintain their independence from political manipulation and debated the relative merits of a close association of religion and political authority. While many argued that a truly Muslim society needs government to enforce Islamic law, others have been concerned about the corrupting influence of politics on religion.

Although these debates are not new, the context in which they have taken place has changed dramatically over the past century. Gone are the early caliphates, as well as the empires and sultanates of the Middle Ages. In their place, the nation-state has emerged as the dominant form of political organization. While it is commonly assumed that modern states are, by definition, secular, in practice this is clearly not the case. On the contrary, modern nation-states have taken a variety of forms: democratic and authoritarian, religious and secular. The assumption that such states would be secular reflects the dominant trends of the early to mid-20th century. At that time there was a conscious effort to create secular political structures to govern – and modernize – societies in the Middle East, in South Asia, and elsewhere. This was particularly evident in the 1950s and 1960s, when many government leaders believed that economic and political development required the elimination of religion from public life. This trend has been, however, reversed in recent years, as calls for a more overtly religious state have found new support.

The following two chapters examine these issues and look at the debates during the past century surrounding the role of religion in public life. More specifically, these chapters will focus on the differing ways in which governments (and government leaders) have understood the proper relationship between Islam and the modern state. In the present chapter we examine the secular tradition within the Islamic world and we look at a variety of states where conscious efforts were made by government authorities to constrain or otherwise control the influence of Islam in public life. A central feature of this entire section is an examination of the historical debates about whether or not Islamic societies require a close association between religious and political authority. The next chapter will review other cases where religious and political authority are closely intertwined and where Islam is more explicitly embedded in the institutions of the modern nation-state.

It is important to note from the outset that these two examples – a "religious" (or "traditionalist") state and a "secular" one – represent poles on a spectrum rather than distinct models of governance. Since most states seek some form of religious or cultural legitimacy, Islam has always been a central part of political discourse. Moreover, the relationship between Islam and the state is different from the relationship between Islam and politics. If the first deals with the formal structures of government – and with the relationship between religious authority and political authority – the second concerns the interaction between people, political parties, and other organized social actors. In this latter and broader sense, politics is more than just government; it includes the efforts of diverse actors to define collectively (though often in competition) a vision and a direction for society. These two issues are of course related, but they are also distinct. The purpose of this and the next chapter is to focus only on the first – the relationship of religion and state; other chapters in this volume will examine the broader issue of Islam and politics.

The Historical Context

The End of Empire and the Rise of Nation-States

The original sources of the Islamic tradition provide little guidance on what form of government is required for a truly Islamic state. The Qur'an, the example of the Prophet (the *sunna*), and his sayings (hadith) are all relatively silent on the issue and do not call for a particular form of government, be that a monarchy, a democracy, or an oligarchy. Nonetheless, early Muslim society was both a religious and a political community, and issues of governance and succession (who should rule and under what conditions) were extremely important for both religious and political reasons. The question of Muslim governance was subsequently clarified through the contributions of Islamic jurisprudence (*fiqh*) in the early centuries of Islam. As discussed in Chapter 3, this body of Islamic law (*sharia*) was derived from the sources of the tradition – the Qur'an and the *sunna* – but it was also informed by analogous reasoning (*qiyās*), textual analysis, and human improvisation. The development of large-scale political organizations during the Umayyad and Abbasid caliphates was also influenced by other factors, including Arab tradition and Persian and Byzantine practices. As the early Muslim community conquered new lands, it adopted many of the mechanisms and practices of imperial rule that defined earlier empires.

It was during the Umayyad period that separate centers of religious and political power began to develop. This trend continued under the Abbasid Dynasty, where the interpreters of religious tradition were growing increasingly distinct from the political elite that managed the temporal affairs of the community. The division between these two sources of authority was particularly evident after the fall of Baghdad in 1258. In the aftermath of the Mongol invasion, the Abbasid caliph (the spiritual leader of the Muslim community) was installed in Cairo, but he had only ceremonial functions. Real political power remained in the hands of the Mamluk sultanate.

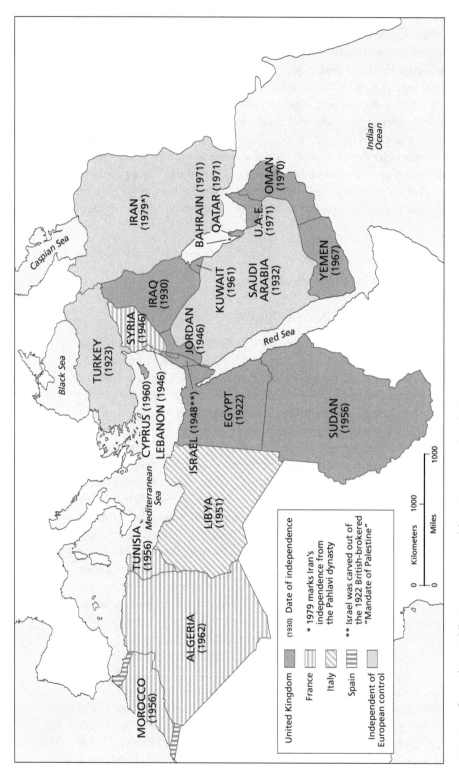

Map 6.1   The modern Middle East as it emerged from European colonial rule.

The argument, then, that there has never been a separation between religion and politics in Islam (and, consequently, between Islam and the state) is somewhat misleading. Rather, this period in Islamic history witnessed the evolution of separate centers of religious and political power and a system of dual authority that was replicated throughout the Islamic world. Of course, there was a high degree of cooperation: political rulers required moral legitimacy, while religious leaders needed the state to uphold Islamic law. Nonetheless, the relationship was difficult. Political elites sought to dominate religious figures – as well as the doctrines of Islam – in order to pursue their own ends more ably, and they were often willing to use force to attain compliance. On the other hand, the community of religious scholars (the *ulamā*), jurists, and philosophers struggled to maintain its independence and integrity, recognizing the corrupting influence of political power, both upon themselves and upon Islamic doctrine. Imam al-Ghazali, the 12th-century Sunni scholar, summed up the suspicion many jurists had of political rulers:

> Three kinds of relations are possible with princes, governors, and oppressors. The first and worst is that you visit them. Somewhat better is the second, whereby they visit you; but best of all is the third, in which you keep your distance so that neither you see them nor they see you."[1]

If the premodern era was characterized by a system of dual authority – each trying to gain the upper hand – the early modern era was defined by the dominance of the political. With the growing influence of European political power in the 19th century and the corresponding decline of the Ottoman Empire, Islamic societies throughout the world were exposed to the modernizing influences of European political, economic, and ideological thought. The internal transformations that this trend inspired pit traditional religious elites against an emerging, Western-oriented political elite. These early modernizing elites used the state to create a more secular society and to gain greater control over social life. By reforming the economic and political basis of social life, the emerging elites sought to separate the *ulamā* from its traditional source of economic livelihood – tax farms and religiously endowed properties (*awqāf*); the intention was to make the *ulamā* dependent upon the state. Other reforms sought to minimize the control of the *ulamā* over education and the law. The corresponding social revolution helped to establish the dominance of a political elite in areas traditionally controlled by religious scholars and left to the latter a very limited – and re-conceived – realm of religion.

Religion and State-Led Secularization

During the early modern era religion remained a dominant feature of Islamic society, but debates about the proper relationship between religion and government continued. These debates were central to the Islamic reform movement of the late 19th and early 20th century. What drove the reform movement – and the debates – was the challenge of European colonial rule (see Map 6.1). At issue was the question of how to explain the relative decline of the Islamic world vis-à-vis Christian Europe. There were various interpretations, both of the nature of the problem and of the proper response to it. One perspective, articulated by Islamic reformers Jamal al-Din al-Afghani and Muhammad 'Abduh, was that Islam had become mired in medieval scholasticism and this did not allow for the innovation and dynamism demanded by the modern age. Muslim societies, in short, could not compete with the West because intellectually they remained trapped in the past. Consequently, these early reformers saw the reformation of Islamic thought and practice as a necessary means for revitalizing their communities and challenging the West.

A central part of the argument for reform was that Islam is entirely compatible with the modern world. What was needed, however, was to break away from literal interpretations of the religious tradition and to abandon the "unquestioning imitation" (*taqlīd*) perpetuated by earlier scholars. The "modernist" reformers also brought a distinctly critical and liberal approach to the Islamic tradition. They advocated *ijtihād* (interpretation) as a means of changing Islamic thought and institutions. With their emphasis upon individual conscience and reason, they also saw enlightenment norms as being entirely compatible with the Islamic tradition.

A related concern of these early reformers was the persistence of political autocracy and the support it received from religious sources. By political autocracy we mean a system of government where the ruler remains unaccountable to the population over which he (or she) rules. From the reformers' perspective there were two dimensions to this problem. The first was the unjust (and hence un-Islamic) nature of the sultanate – or autocratic state. The second and related dimension was in the fact that religion had been too commonly used to legitimize tyranny. This was perceived as an abuse of religion, and it undermined the integrity of both religion and society. A truly Islamic system, from the reformers' perspective, would entail constraints on the ruler and a greater degree of justice in the exercise of power. Hence the constitutional reforms carried out during the late 19th century in the Ottoman Empire and elsewhere were seen as consistent with Islamic teaching. The success of such reforms, however, required a greater degree of individual freedom. It would also require divesting political authority of any claim over religious belief and liberating "the creed from the act of political exploitation" (Belkeziz 2009: 34). From a reformist perspective, it was the rulers who should serve Islam, not the other way around.

A second response to the question of Muslim decline was offered by conservative activists such as Rashid Rida (a disciple of 'Abduh) and Hasan al-Banna (the founder of the Muslim Brotherhood in Egypt). These individuals were very much influenced by the reform movement's emphasis on religious revitalization and political change. However, they viewed the underlying problem in a very different light. For them, the problem was not a matter of religious interpretation; rather it was the loss of belief, and failure to adhere to the basic tenets of Islam, that produced Muslim weakness. Nowhere was this abandonment of Islam more evident than in the Muslims' effort to emulate the West, be they the "modernists" who sought to incorporate European ideas into the Islamic tradition or leaders who embraced secular forms of governance. By mimicking their colonial rulers, al-Banna and others argued, Muslims were internalizing the values of imperial subjugation and betraying their cultural heritage.[2] The answer, then, was to "return to Islam" and create a true "Islamic order" (*al-nizām al-Islāmī*). Although vague, this argument provides the basis for the modern Islamic state, which will be discussed at length in the next chapter.

A third interpretation of the Islamic decline was offered by the early secularists. For this group, the problem was not a matter of interpreting Islam or a decline in religious belief, as al-Banna would argue; quite the opposite, in fact. For the early secularists, the weakness of the Islamic world vis-à-vis Europeans was rooted in what they saw as the continuing influence of a backward tradition in Muslim society. Religion and traditional patterns of social organization, in short, hindered economic and political development and kept Muslim societies from the technological advancement necessary for military competitiveness. Consequently, secularists believed that there was much to learn from the West, even if the European powers were the primary threat to the Muslim world. Moreover, they believed that the full potential of society could only be achieved by diminishing the hold of religion both on the community and on individuals. These assumptions constitute the basis for the early secular project and for the conscious effort to diminish the grip of Islamic tradition upon society. Secularizing political elites consequently sought to break the power of traditional elites – such as the *ulamā* in the Arab world, the mullahs (leaders or teachers versed both in religion and in canon law) in Iran, or the religious leaders of Turkey. Hence the nationalization (and secularization) of education, law, and the economy was intended to extend the control of the modern state into realms of society historically dominated by religious leaders and other traditional elites.

The most dramatic example of this trend was the secular revolution in Turkey (see below). In the aftermath of World War I, Mustafa Kemal Ataturk consciously sought to remove Islam from Turkish public life and to construct a secular state on the remnants of the Ottoman Empire. Central to this effort was a state-directed cultural revolution that sought to re-orient Turkish society toward Europe and to modernize both state and society. The assumption, common at the time, was that secularization was associated with modernity and progress, whereas religion was tied to a backward tradition. Moreover, Westernization and modernization were commonly seen as one and the same thing (see Sidebar 6.1).

Sidebar 6.1   Westernization or modernization?

What does it mean to be modern? For many, particularly in the early 20th century, to be modern was to be Western and secular. Hence "modernization" entailed the adoption of Western-style political institutions, legal codes, and economic models. It also commonly entailed the adoption of attitudes toward religion that were informed by Enlightenment rationalism. In short, modernization entailed "Westernization." This was the assumption behind Ataturk's revolutionary reforms and behind the development strategy of Reza Shah (as well as of his son) in Iran, and it informed many of the development strategies in the 1950s and 1960s in many parts of the Islamic world. In more recent years, however, it has become apparent that there are many forms that "modernity" can take. The real issue, then, is the challenge of all societies to reinterpret their traditions in a contemporary context.

Hence Ataturk's efforts were designed in large measure to replicate, within Turkey, the kind of modern economic, military, and political structures that allowed the Europeans to dominate the planet. This was part and parcel of a broader state-building project and of Ataturk's effort to create a modern nation-state out of the remnants of the Ottoman Empire. A similar strategy was evident in early 20th-century Iran, though it was not carried through in such an extreme manner.

The secular trend was also evident in Gamal Adbel Nasser's Egypt and in the Pan-Arab movement that informed the 1950s and 1960s (see below). Although not as dramatic as Ataturk and his reforms, the Arab nationalists were similarly keen to break with the traditional elites that had cooperated with British colonial rule. Nasser's secular Arab nationalism also posed a threat to the traditional monarchies of the region, particularly those in the Gulf countries. In Nasser's view, conservative religion was an obstacle to the kind of economic and political reform that he and his fellow Arab nationalists wished to implement. The Islam of the Muslim Brotherhood and of the establishment *ulamā* was tainted, in Nasser's view, by its association with reactionary elites. For Nasser and other modernizing state actors, secularism was a prerequisite for both freedom and development.

It was in this context that the relative merits of a "secular" and a "religious" state were widely debated. In what would come to be known as the "secular–integralist" debate, the Islamists (most notably Egypt's Muslim Brotherhood, but others as well) argued for a central role for Islam in the modern state. By "Islamists" we mean those groups and activists commonly referred to as "fundamentalist" or Salafist, who advocate a return to the fundamentals of the tradition. The basic argument is that Islam provides a "comprehensive program" meant to regulate all facets of human existence. To preclude a central role for Islam in government would, according to this view, be a violation of God's revelation. While there was some questioning as to what this meant in practice, the *need* for an Islamic state, it was argued, was clear. (The next chapter will examine this argument in greater detail.) The secular Arab nationalists, on the other hand, disagreed and argued that the type of state structure adopted by the country was, from a religious perspective, immaterial. They believed that there was nothing inconsistent between Islam and a secular state as long as certain minimal prohibitions were upheld. The secularists were also concerned about linking religious and political power too closely. As Khalid Muhammad Khalid argued in 1950, a religious state would hinder Egypt's socio-economic development, since the unification of religious and political authority would have corrupting effects on both. What was truly needed, he argued, was a social revolution. Such an alternative, though, would be hindered by a "priesthood" that "colluded with tyrants," and, in its pursuit of power, used religion to "keep the people poor and ignorant" (Hourani 1991: 353).

These debates have periodically recurred, in Egypt and elsewhere, and were a central feature of the Islamist challenge of the 1990s. The same question as the one posed in 1950 has remained central – namely whether a secular or an Islamic (that is, "traditionalist") state is preferable. The competing arguments remain largely the same today. As in earlier years, the secular perspective generally takes one of two approaches. The first argues that nowhere in the Qur'an is a particular form of government specified; hence a secular form is consistent with the Islamic tradition. The second claims that social life needs to be free from the dominance of any institutionalized religion – if for no other reason, the diversity of the national community requires it. The Egyptian Wafd Party's slogan in the early part of the 20th century, "religion belongs to God, the nation belongs to all" (*al-dīn llāh, wa al-watan li al-jami*), reflects this idea that social harmony is best ensured by relegating religion to the private sphere.[3] It was not that the early Wafdists were hostile to religion. Rather they were concerned about the politicization of religious authorities and about the manipulation of religion by political actors.

One of the complicating factors in this debate is a lack of clarity regarding the essence of the secular idea. On the one hand, secularism is commonly interpreted as state neutrality in matters of religion and religious doctrine. According to this understanding of secularism, the state is *not* meant to be the enforcer of religious law or the regulator of religious orthodoxy. On the contrary, it is up to individual conscience (or at least that of religious authorities) to determine which interpretation of religious doctrine reflects God's will. Moreover, it is believed that efforts on the part of governments to coerce individual conscience will likely promote hypocrisy (*nifāq*), not true belief. There is also the argument that the politicization of religion leads to its corruption. Hence, separating religious authority from political authority is intended to preserve the integrity of religion. According to a second interpretation, secularism does not, however, involve a state of neutrality, but rather one of active hostility toward religion. If, in the first interpretation, this concept was compatible with religious expression in public life, in the second it is not: the second interpretation sees religion as a detrimental force in society and seeks its marginalization. This is what informs the French conceptions of *laïcité* (discussed in Chapter 8), as well as Ataturk's ardent secularism. Not surprisingly, this interpretation leads Islamists to believe that secularism is either a form of unbelief (*kufr*) or an active hostility to religion, religious authority, and public expressions of religion. From an Islamist point of view, the alternative to an Islamic state is not a "civil state," but rather a non-religious one.

Cases

Turkey

Although Islam was a central feature in Ottoman rule, the collapse of the Ottoman Empire ushered in a new era of secular nationalism. Ataturk, the father of modern Turkey, saw Islam as part of a backward East and embraced secular norms as a means of re-orienting Turkish society toward a European and Western vision of modernity. In an effort to create a modern nation-state from the remnants of the Ottoman Empire, Ataturk and his allies developed a secular political structure, which separated religion from government and consciously sought to diminish the influence of Islam upon society as a whole. The secular project was driven by the belief that a complete transformation of society was necessary in order for Muslim countries to compete with Europe economically, politically, and militarily. The social revolution that ensued was defined by an active opposition to religion – both at the societal and at the individual level – and by a conscious effort to create a new Turkish citizenry out of the former Ottoman subjects. This new nationalist vision created the ideological basis for the modern Turkish state.

While some of Ataturk's reforms were superficial – the ban on traditional dress such as the fez and the headscarf, for example – others were more far-reaching. For example, Ataturk established a constitutional republic in place of the Ottoman sultanate (the sultan was the political leader of the empire) and replaced Islamic law and law courts with Western legal codes modeled on the ones in Switzerland and Italy. Ataturk also created a secular educational system and imposed the Latin script instead of the Arabic. Perhaps the most significant reform was the elimination of the Islamic caliphate – the religious institution by which the Ottomans claimed leadership in the Islamic world: Ataturk abolished it in 1924.

These various reforms were premised on the idea that modernity and secularism were synonymous and that Islam was one of the key factors that had held the Ottoman Empire back. Ataturk's goal, then, was to break the hold of religion on what he perceived to be a stagnant, traditional society. Thus the social revolution of post-World War I Turkey – which entailed a complete separation of religion from politics and government – was part of his larger program of economic and political transformation. But Ataturk was also motivated by his need to exert control over the new state. In short, the successful construction of a new political order required him and his allies to disempower the traditional elites that had dominated throughout the Ottoman period until then. Many of the secular reforms – not least among which was the abolition of the caliphate – were intended to overturn the power structures of the Ottoman era and to pave the way for a new, secular order.

Ataturk's legacy survives to this day. Secular Turkish nationalism – commonly referred to as "Kemalism" – remains extremely influential, as is the strong, centralized state that it helped to create (see Sidebar 6.2). The interpretation of secularism that defines Ataturk's legacy, however, is one of active hostility to

---

Sidebar 6.2   Kemalism

The ideology known as Kemalism (named after Kemal Ataturk) was developed and institutionalized in the early Turkish state. It comprised of six principles: populism, nationalism, statism, secularism, revolutionism (i.e. reform), and republicanism. This revolutionary ideology was a response to the Ottoman legacy and consciously sought to break both with the monarchical and with the religious moorings of the Ottoman Empire. Kemalism's interpretation of secularism brings it very close to the concept of *laïcité* in France, insofar as it sought to remove religion (and religious influence) from the public sphere. It meant secularizing education, abolishing the Islamic caliphate, and removing religion entirely from the public sphere. From the perspective of Ataturk and his followers, this was essential for the modernization of Turkey and Turkish society. Others, however, have taken a different view. Particularly in more recent decades, Kemalism is seen as an authoritarian and divisive ideology that represses ethnic difference and infringes upon fundamental rights of religious expression.

Figure 6.1   The Sultanahmet Mosque (better known as the Blue Mosque) in Istanbul, Turkey.

religion, not one of neutrality. This is evident in the continuing effort to remove all forms of religious expression from public life, for instance the headscarf and overt references to Islam. The Turkish state and Turkish politics have not, however, been entirely free of religion. In the 1950s, for example, Adnan Menderes, Turkey's prime minister, appealed to traditional identities in his political campaigns. Similarly, President Turgut Ozal used religion as a means of cultivating popular support during his tenure in the 1980s. In both instances, the willingness of political leaders to invoke religion demonstrated the continuing salience of Islam to large segments of the Turkish population. Moreover, despite efforts to eradicate religion from society, Islam has remained a significant element in Turkish culture and the country is still divided over the question of religion. This is evident in the current tensions between Islam and secularism in contemporary Turkish politics. The Justice and Development Party (AKP), which came to power in 2007, is more overtly Islamic. Consequently it has been trying to reinterpret secularism as an attitude of impartiality toward religion rather than as one of hostility. This subtle difference allows for overt expressions of religion within society and government, without necessarily abandoning Turkey's secular tradition. The Turkish military, however, the last bastion of Kemalism, still views any form of religious expression with suspicion and trepidation.

Secular Arab Nationalism in Egypt

Numerous other states also embraced a secular vision of political development in the early 20th century. This was evident in Iran, where the first Reza Shah (the father of Muhammad Reza Shah) sought to replicate Ataturk's state-building enterprise in the 1920s and 1930s. Although the Iranian experience was less extreme than the Turkish, Reza Shah reformed the education system, secularized the legal system, and took other steps toward transforming his society and culture. The Iranian experiment was informed by the same kind of secular nationalism as its Turkish counterpart and was driven by many of the same motivations. Its success was, however, limited on account of the fact that Iran's religious establishment and other traditional elements of society continued to be just as strong. Reza Shah's son similarly supported a secular vision of national development and worked to curb the influence of the Iranian mullahs in public life. The residual strength of Islam in society and the popularity of the clerics set the stage for the 1979 Iranian Revolution, which deposed Muhammad Reza Shah and brought to power the current government. All this will be discussed in Chapter 7.

After World War II and the collapse of European colonial rule, similar efforts to redefine the relationship between religion and political authority were commonly made in other countries throughout the Islamic world. Countries as diverse as Indonesia, Algeria, Tunisia, Syria, and Iraq all sought to eradicate the colonial economic and political structures that had long governed their societies. For many, a secular vision of national development played a central role in leading this revolutionary spirit. At the time, secular nationalism brought with it a progressive vision of reform, which contrasted sharply with the religious traditionalism perpetuated under colonial rule: the traditionalism of a feudal order. In the 1950s and early 1960s, the wave of secular nationalism seemed to bring the tide of the future.

The Nasserist Revolution in Egypt is perhaps the best example of this kind of postcolonial secular nationalism. Gamal Abdel Nasser, along with his fellow "free officers" in the military, deposed the Egyptian monarch, King Farouk, in 1952 and set up a new socialist government. A defining feature of the social revolution initiated by Nasser was the secular vision of Arab nationalism that it embodied. A second key feature – and aspect – was the revolutionary effort to displace the traditional elite, including the landowning class and the Egyptian monarchy, and to redistribute the country's wealth among the impoverished masses. Though this movement was not as dramatic or radical as Ataturk's revolution, Nasser sought on the one hand to reconfigure the economic basis of Egyptian society, and on the other to break the hold of traditional elites (both religious and political) on society. This latter effort was accomplished through a reform of the educational system that brought key religious institutions such as Al-Azhar University under direct government control. In a nutshell, the modern state was the tool by which the new political leadership would reshape Egyptian society and religion.

Figure 6.2   A street scene in Cairo, Egypt, near the Bab al-Futuh.

It is important to keep in mind the fact that religion was not absent from Egyptian politics during this time. The Nasserist state sought to co-opt and marginalize Islam rather than to eradicate it. Subsequently it supported a modernist interpretation of the religious tradition, one consistent with the regime's secular and socialist policies. An important goal of this effort was to build an inclusive Arab national identity, one that was *not* based on religion, but on a common culture, language, and history. Arab Christians were very much involved in articulating and promoting this vision of Arab nationalism.

The Nasser regime faced two political and ideological challengers. The first was the Muslim Brotherhood, which had both political ambitions and ideological disagreements that put it at odds with the Arab nationalist agenda (the debates over such issues have already been discussed). This conflict was resolved largely through the persecution and imprisonment of members of the Muslim Brotherhood. The government's effort to eradicate the Brotherhood and its ill-treatment of the latter's members in prison helped to breed the radicalism that would become manifest in the writings of Sayyid Qutb. Qutb articulated the religious basis for the militant violence of later decades (which will be discussed in Chapter 12).

The second challenge to Nasser's government came from the Arab monarchies in the Gulf, particularly Saudi Arabia. The conflict between Egypt and these monarchies formed the basis of what came to be known as the Arab Cold War, which embodied issues of strategic and ideological competition (see Sidebar 6.3).

Sidebar 6.3   Arab Cold War: The ideological division between Gulf monarchies and Arab socialist states

The Arab Cold War, a phrase coined by Malcolm Kerr (1971), refers to the Cold War rivalry between the Gulf monarchies and the Arab socialist states. The rivalry was both ideological and strategic. Nasser's government in Egypt, for example, perceived the conservative monarchies of the Gulf region as forces of reaction, and their continued adherence to traditional conceptions of Islam as a major obstacle to the modernization of the region. The monarchies, in turn, feared Nasser's socialist and republican ideas and saw the military coups in Iraq, Egypt, and Syria as representing a clear threat to traditional patterns of authority. This rivalry became more significant in the late 1950s and early 1960s, as the US and the Soviets became increasingly involved in the region. The US backed the Arab monarchies (including Jordan, Kuwait, and Saudi Arabia) as well as Turkey, Israel, and Iran. The Soviet Union, on the other hand, supported Algeria, Egypt, Iraq, Syria, and other socialist states.

While much of the regional competition was over power and resources, religion and ideology played a central role in the conflict. Each side appealed to competing interpretations of Islam in order to have their respective claims to regional leadership sanctioned, and each had very different ideas about Islam and the state. For example, the House of Saud's role as guardian of Medina and Mecca – along with its close association with Wahhabist Islam – was invoked as a sanction for the Saudi monarchy and was used to legitimize Saudi control of the vast wealth that flowed from the oil fields. The austere understanding of Islam and of the link between Wahhabist or Salafist ideals was very much at odds with the secular and modernist ideas of the Arab nationalists. Similarly, Nasser invoked a theologically liberal Islam to have his program of socialist reform sanctioned. These different readings of the

(Continued)

Nasser's secular nationalism was enormously influential throughout the region until the war with Israel in June 1967, when Nasser's armies were defeated in a matter of days.

Secular Nationalism in Iraq, Syria, and North Africa

Similar tensions between Arab nationalist forces and traditional elites were a regular occurrence throughout the Middle East and North Africa in the early postcolonial period and were evident in the political turmoil that characterized the 1950s and 1960s. In Iraq such tensions came to fruition in 1958, in the overthrow of the Hashemite monarchy. In a manner reminiscent of Egypt's 1952 revolution, a group of military officers took control of the state and attempted to transform the existing power structure and to redefine the basis of Iraqi national life. The overthrow of the monarchy and the death of King Faisal II, together with much of his family and entourage, sent shock waves through the region. There were of course differences between these events in Iraq and what had happened in Nasser's Egypt. One difference was the violence used here to eliminate – or rather exterminate – the royal family; another consisted in the ruthlessness and divisiveness that characterized the Ba'ath Party's rule for some time. (*Ba'ath* means "renaissance" in Arabic.) The ethnic and religious factionalism in Iraq, so different from the relative homogeneity of Egypt, was another complicating factor. Iraq's sectarian divisions pitted the Arab Sunni minority against both the Shi'i population and the Kurdish community in the north. Nonetheless, support for a secular vision of Iraqi society was widespread among the dominant political actors.

While cooperation with other Arab countries proved elusive, the Iraqi Ba'ath Party emerged as the dominant force in Iraqi politics. Its commitment to Arab unity was rhetorical rather than real, but the party did adhere to a strict secularism. The formal separation of religious authority from government was a hallmark of the Iraqi regime up until the Gulf War of 1990. As in Egypt, the traditional religious elites here had strong ties to the traditional landowners and formed a significant block of opposition. Hence the Iraqi government sought to subjugate these elements of society, in order to avoid a religious challenge to state authority. It was only in the context of the Iraqi invasion of Kuwait – and of a pending US counter-invasion of Iraq – that the Iraqi leadership, then under the rule of Saddam Hussein, turned to religion. Although still ostensibly secular, the Hussein regime recognized the utility of Islam as a means of appealing to popular sentiment and of articulating moral purpose.

Islamic tradition embodied very different visions of society and governance (religious versus secular, progressive versus traditional), and gave a religious foundation to the ideological rivalry.

The war of words between Nasser and the Gulf monarchies turned violent during the Civil War in Yemen, which broke out in 1962. Egypt and Saudi Arabia backed opposing sides in this war and supplied both troops and funding to their respective allies. The intra-communal conflicts within Egypt – and within Islam – were subsequently replicated in the region as a whole. This "Arab Cold War" only came to an end with the defeat of the armies of the Arab nationalist states by Israel in 1967, which set the stage both for a rapprochement of the rival Arab powers and for the subsequent dominance of the Saudi vision of religion in public life.

In the immediate postcolonial period Syria was defined by many of these same issues, including commitment to a secular vision of national development. As in Egypt, here too young military officers took control of the government and (theoretically) sought to use it in order to transform Syria into a more just and prosperous society. Syria is particularly notable for its contribution to the development of the secular ideology of Arab nationalism. It was there, for example, that the Baʿath Party was founded – by Michel Aflaq and Salah al-Din al-Bitar. The Baʿathist ideology sought to merge Arab nationalist ideals with an emphasis upon social justice and egalitarianism. Like Nasser's Egypt, the Syrian Baʿathists placed a strong emphasis upon state-led economic development and social revolution, both of which were part of a broader effort to dismantle the hierarchical social structure of the *ancien régime*. The Syrian Baʿathists also saw the Arabs as a single nation, though one divided (and weakened) by European intervention. Hence they were committed to Arab unity as a means of reforming and empowering their region.

Secularism was at the heart of the Baʿathist ideal. On the one hand, as in Turkey, Egypt, and elsewhere, traditional religious leaders were commonly tied to the traditional elites that had previously ruled the societies now being overturned. Religion, in short, was seen as part of the old order, which was passing away. On the other hand, there was a recognition that Arab weakness was the result of internal division. Hence, what was needed was a sense of national identity that was not based on religion or sect, but on more inclusive cultural (and linguistic) features. Particularly in a region defined by a high degree of religious variation, a national identity that transcended religious divisions was seen as a necessary prerequisite for political stability and empowerment. Secular Arab nationalism seemed to be uniquely able to play that role. It is not surprising that the ideology of the Baʿath Party – and secular nationalism more generally – resonated with Arab Christians, even if Baʿathism included references to Islam.

However, instability in Syria during the 1950s and 1960s greatly undermined the viability of the Baʿath Party and its lofty vision. Despite the rhetoric, different factions in Syrian society and in the military fought one another for power. While there was a short-lived political union with Egypt (1958–1961), Syria's divisions greatly undermined the dream of Arab unity (for more on this, see Ajami 1992). When this period came to end, however, what emerged was a secular dictatorship under the rule of Hafez al-Assad. Assad was from the ʾAlawī community, a minority sect of the Shiʾi community. This helps to explain his continued commitment to a secular vision of society. The ʾAlawī ruled uneasily over a predominantly Sunni population, and this contributed to the view that separating religion from state was a practical necessity. It is not surprising, then, that the most staunch opposition to the secular vision – and to Assad's rule – came from the Sunni Islamists affiliated with the Syrian Muslim Brotherhood. As in Nasser's Egypt, the competition between the government and the Islamists and between their rival visions of society turned violent. In 1982, for example, the Assad regime sent the military into a city called Hama, which the Muslim Brotherhood had taken under their control. Over the course of two weeks, the Assad regime destroyed entire sections of the city, killing more than 10,000 civilians and leaving a legacy of sectarian division that has been resurrected in the uprisings of 2011.

Finally, the contemporary history of North Africa was influenced by many of these same trends. In Algeria, for example, the socialist National Liberation Front (FLN) came to power in the aftermath of independence from French colonial rule. The struggle for independence was a brutal one, and it left the country scarred and divided. The FLN ruled for most the following three decades and was explicitly allied with Nasser's Egypt in the larger struggle against the West and the Gulf monarchies. The FLN, however, in its war against the French (1954–1962), appealed to Islam as a means of mobilizing popular Algerian sentiments. Islam was subsequently assimilated into postcolonial nationalism and became the official state religion, although on the basis of a modernist understanding of Islam, similar to that of Nasser's Egypt. In other words, the Algerian state promoted many of the same policies as other Arab nationalists regimes – for instance in areas like education and the emancipation of women – even though the government continued to invoke Islam as a means of sanctifying its authority. In the 1990s tensions among different factions, and among different visions of Islam and public life, ultimately led to civil war between Islamists and the FLN regime.

Secularism in South Asia

Debates about the proper role of religion in public life were a central feature of politics in colonial India (see Map 6.2 and Map 6.3). Secularists, both Hindu and Muslim, argued against a close affiliation of religion and government; Muslims, did so because of their minority status – and in full knowledge of the fact that it would not be *their* religion that the government would promote – and Hindus because they recognized the potential abuse of religion in such a system. On the other hand, "communalist" organizations took the opposite view. By "communalism" we mean the belief that members of a particular religious or cultural community share the same economic or political (in other words secular) interests and that differing communities have opposing interests. Communalists – whether Hindu, Muslim, or Sikh – felt that their religion ought to be integrated into the governing structures that ruled over their communities, much to the consternation of other religious groups. In the lead up to Independence, these debates were central to questions of whether or not to divide India and create an independent Muslim state. For many, including Muhammad ʿAli Jinnah and Muhammad Iqbal, there was a fear that Muslims could not expect fair treatment in a Hindu-dominated state, even if that state was ostensibly secular. Consequently they argued for a separate state, where Muslims would form the majority. This constituted the basis for the partition of India and the subsequent creation of Pakistan in 1947.

Within India, Hindu communalists called for the creation of a Hindu state even after Independence. It was argued at the time that Muslims had their state; why should Hindus not have a religious state of their own? Such appeals, however, were rejected by the leadership of India's ruling Congress Party. What emerged instead was an explicitly secular form of government, which included constitutional protections for ethnic and religious minorities. By secularism, in this instance, we mean neutrality in matters of religion and belief, not hostility to religion (as in the Turkish example). As Jawaharlal Nehru, the first prime minister, noted at the time:

> We call our State a secular one. The word "secular" perhaps is not a very happy one and yet for want of a better, we have used it. What exactly does it mean? It does not obviously mean a society where religion itself is discouraged. It means freedom of religion and conscience, including freedom for those who may have no religion. It means free play for all religions, subject only to their not interfering with each other or with the basic conceptions of our state. (Jawaharlal Nehru, cited in Chandra, Mukherjee, and Mukherjee 2008: 48)

Nehru's support for secularism was premised upon a belief that a secular government – on an inclusive understanding of this nation – was necessary for integrating India's diverse ethnic and religious groups into a common political framework. Particularly in the aftermath of the partition experience, which was marred by violence, any politicization of religion was avoided, for fear that it would fan the flames of sectarian division. Moreover, Nehru believed, like Nasser, that the modernization of society required a lessening of religion's influence. It was believed by many that some of India's worst social ills – casteism, denigration of women, and poverty – were associated with traditional religion. Hence developing the country economically and politically required a far-reaching social revolution as well.

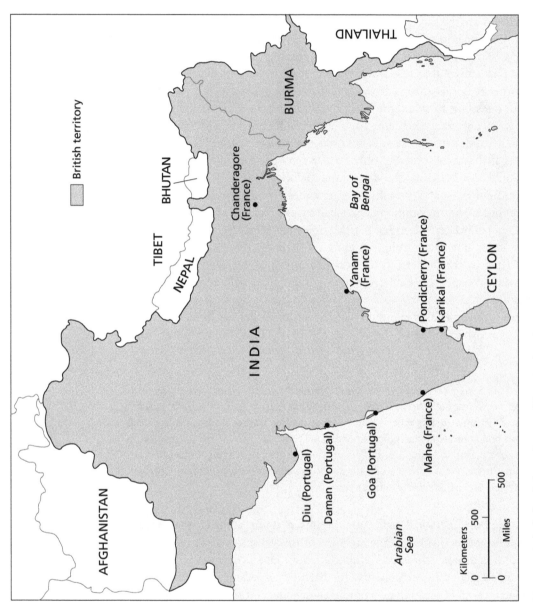

TIBET

NEPAL

BHUTAN

AFGHANISTAN

INDIA

BURMA

THAILAND

Chanderagore
(France)

Bay of
Bengal

Yanam
(France)

Pondicherry (France)

Karikal (France)

CEYLON

Diu (Portugal)

Daman (Portugal)

Goa (Portugal)

Mahe (France)

Arabian
Sea

British territory

Kilometers
0   500

Miles
0   500

Map 6.2   India before Independence and Partition (1947).

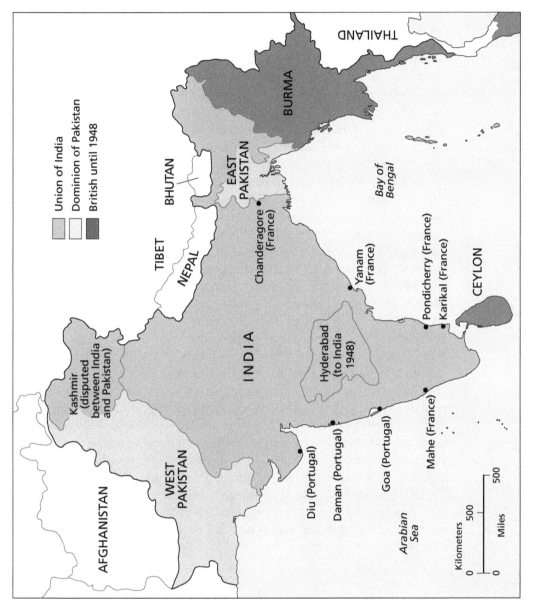

Map 6.3 India after Independence and Partition (1947).

Living up to Nehru's secular ideal has been a challenge. While the Nehru era (the 1950s and 1960s) saw the institutionalization of secular norms in India, this commitment faded in subsequent decades. A defining feature of the 1980s and 1990s was the resurgence of Hindu communalism and of the same kind of sectarian violence that characterized earlier decades. The destruction of the Ayodhya Mosque in 1992 and the 2002 Gujarat massacre (which targeted Muslim Indians) are only the most extreme examples of a much broader trend. Nonetheless, the secular idea remains a part of Indian politics. This is due in no small part to the religious diversity of the country. Aside from the many Buddhists, Christians, and Jains, India remains home to a Muslim population of over 150 million people. Moreover, the Muslim community is well represented in government, business, sport, and entertainment. Some of the most influential directors, actors, and actresses in India's famed "Bollywood" are Muslim. This has contributed greatly to a cosmopolitan outlook, particularly among younger generations. More to the point, the Muslim community remains an integral feature of Indian society and a reminder of the necessity of religious tolerance for social cohesion.

On the other side of the border, Pakistan has faced similar challenges. Originally Pakistan was created to provide a separate state for Muslims in South Asia, and it was not clear at the outset what kind of government it ought to have. The debate over this (discussed in the next chapter) hinged on whether or not the government ought to define – and enforce – religious orthodoxy for the population, or whether the new state would simply be a homeland for the Muslims of South Asia. Muhammad Jinnah, the father of Pakistan, was very "secular" in his outlook – he was a largely non-observant Muslim – and opted for the latter interpretation. Although he readily invoked Islam in the campaign for a separate Muslim state, once this state was created, he believed that it was not the role of government to resolve intra-religious disputes. This was an important matter for the newly created Pakistan, given its diverse ethnic groups and its own religious division between Sunni and Shi'i Muslims (among other sects). These divisions created the initial impetus for a government that did not meddle in religious affairs and sought an inclusive national identity, one that did not privilege one ethnic group over others. The failure to find this balance, however, led to the Civil War that separated East and West Pakistan into what is today Pakistan and Bangladesh. The subsequent emergence of an explicitly Islamic state in Pakistan during the 1980s and 1990s is discussed in the next chapter.

Conclusion

As the case studies illustrate, the politics of many Muslim societies during the mid-20th century was dominated by secular nationalists intent on building independent modern nation-states. In realizing their intention, they consciously sought to minimize the influence of religion in public life and to build government institutions that were based on secular models. The leaders of this era were cognizant of the continuing religiosity of the population and for the most part did not attempt to banish Islam, as Ataturk had done, but they were also skeptical of those who called for an explicit "Islamic order." During this period modernization was commonly equated with secularization (or Westernization), and those who advocated return to a more overtly "Islamic" state were seen as remnants of an era gone by. The economic, political, and social development of society, it was believed, necessarily entailed the marginalization of religion in the public sphere.

The end of the secular idea came in the second half of the 20th century. Some argue that it was the defeat of the Arab armies in June 1967 that destroyed Arab nationalism and, with it, the secular vision. Whether or not the Six-Day War is a sufficient explanation, it is clear that the defeat of Nasser's Egypt and of the other Arab regimes diminished the popularity of the nationalist vision. More to the point, the 1967 war prompted renewed debate on the causes of the defeat. Like the ideological debates of earlier years, this, too, revolved around religion and politics. Many on the political left argued that the defeat in 1967 was the result of Nasser's failure to carry out a true social revolution and to break the hold of a backward tradition on Arab society. The Islamists, on the other hand, argued that it was precisely the effort to break with tradition, and the straying from Islam, that were behind the 1967 fiasco. The military officers' embrace of foreign ideologies and their attempt to reshape Egyptian society on foreign models, it was argued, was their downfall. As one Syrian writer noted at the time: "The Arabs had turned away from God, and God had turned away from them" (cited in Ajami 1992: 74).

This debate reflected the deeper tensions within Arab and Muslim society about whether Islam ought to rule over all facets of life, or whether it should be relegated to the realm of individual conscience and private morality. Does a truly Muslim society require an "Islamic" or "traditionalist" state, or should the state be neutral in matters of religious belief? Although this debate has never been resolved, events in the 1970s and 1980s dramatically changed the political dynamic. Anwar Sadat succeeded Nasser as president of Egypt after the latter's death in 1970, and he abandoned Nasser's secular project. Similarly, the influence of Saudi Arabia became increasingly pronounced throughout the Arab world in the aftermath of the 1973 war with Israel. On the one hand, the Arab oil embargo, which was such a central feature of that war, appeared to validate the Islamic turn in the Arab world. By the same token, the rise of Saudi Arabia as an economic and political force in the region appeared to validate the call for an Islamic state. The dramatic increase in the price of oil also provided Saudi Arabia with money to fund groups and *madāris* (religious schools; singular *madrasah*) that embraced the Saudi vision of Islam throughout the Middle East, South Asia, and elsewhere. Finally, the Iranian Revolution shocked the world with its establishment of an explicitly theocratic state. It is to these issues that the next chapter will now turn.

Notes

1   Abu Hamid Al-Ghazali, *Ihya' 'Ulum al-Din* [*The Revival of Religious Sciences*]. Book 14: *Kitab al-Halal wal-Haram*. Cited in Cabrini Mullaney 1992: 120 (translation modified).
2   See Mitchell 1969, particularly chs. 8 and 9; see also Abu-Rabi 1995: ch. 3.
3   See Najjar 1996: 21; more on these debates can be found in Hibbard 2010.

Discussion Questions

1   What are the different interpretations of secularism, and how are they reflected in Turkey and Egypt? What were their primary motivations?
2   What are the arguments for separating religious authority and political authority? Is this act meant to protect politics from religion or religion from politics (or both)?
3   What is the difference between modernization and Westernization? What does an Islamic version of modernity look like, or an Islamist vision of modernity?
4   Should religion govern all aspects of community life, or should there be a distinction between public and private realms? What does Islam say about this? What does your tradition have to say on this topic?
5   How does secularism in India influence your view of the secular tradition? Why has the Nehurvian ideal of secularism been so difficult to live up to? Does this reflect the experience of secularism in other countries?

Suggested Further Reading

Abu-Rabi, Ibrahim (1995). *Intellectual Origins of Islamic Resurgence in the Modern Arab World*. New York, NY: State University of New York Press.

Ajami, Fouad (1992). *The Arab Predicament: Arab Political Thought and Practice since 1967*. New York, NY: Cambridge University Press.

An-Na'im, Abdallahi (2010). *Islam and the Secular State: Negotiating the Future of Shari'a*. Cambridge, MA: Harvard University Press.

Belkeziz, Abdelilah (2009). *The State in Contemporary Islamic Thought: A Historical Survey of the Major Muslim Political Thinkers of the Modern Era*. New York, NY: I.B. Tauris.

Cabrini Mullaney, Francis (1992). *The Role of Islam in the Hegemonic Strategy of Egypt's Military Rulers (1952–1990)*. Unpublished dissertation, Harvard University, Massachusetts.

Chandra, Bipan, Aditya Mukherjee, and Mridula Mukherjee (2002). *India after Independence: 1947–2000*. New Delhi, India: Penguin.

Flores, Alexander (1997). Secularism, integralism and political Islam: The Egyptian debate. In Joel Beinin and Joe Stork (eds.), *Political Islam: Essays from Middle East Report*. Berkeley, CA: University of California Press, pp. 83–96.

Hashemi, Nader (2009). *Islam, Secularism and Liberal Democracy: Towards a*

Democratic Theory for Muslim Societies. New York, NY: Oxford University Press.

Hibbard, Scott W. (2010). *Religious Politics and Secular States: Egypt, India and the United States.* Baltimore, MD: Johns Hopkins University Press.

Hourani, Albert (1991). *Arabic Thought in the Liberal Age: 1798–1938.* New York, NY: Cambridge University Press.

Ismail, Salwa (2006). *Rethinking Islamist Politics: Culture, the State and Islamism.* New York, NY: I. B. Tauris.

Karakas, Cemal (2007). *Turkey: Islam and Laicism – Between the Interests of the State, Politics and Society.* Frankfurt, Germany: Peace and Research Institute Frankfurt.

Keddie, Nicki (2003). Secularism and its discontents. *Daedalus,* 123(3): 14–30.

Kerr, Malcolm (1971). *The Arab Cold War: Gamal Abd al'Nasir and His Rivals, 1958–1970.* New York, NY: Oxford University Press.

Kuru, Ahmet (2009). *Secularism and State Policies toward Religion: The United States, France and Turkey.* New York, NY: Cambridge University Press.

Mitchell, Richard (1969). *The Society of the Muslim Brothers.* New York, NY: Oxford University Press.

Najjar, Fauzi M. (1996). The debate on Islam and secularism in Egypt. *Arab Studies Quarterly,* 18(2): 21–37.

Navaro-Yashin, Yael (2002). *Faces of the State: Secularism and Public Life in Turkey.* Princeton, NJ: Princeton University Press.

Roy, Olivier (2009). *Secularism Confronts Islam.* New York, NY: Columbia University Press.

7

Islam and the State
Part II

Scott W. Hibbard

An Introduction to Islam in the 21st Century, First Edition. Edited by Aminah Beverly McCloud,
Scott W. Hibbard, and Laith Saud.
© 2013 Blackwell Publishing Ltd. Published 2013 by Blackwell Publishing Ltd.

Introduction

In this chapter we will look at examples of modern governments that are defined by a close association between Islam and the state. The chapter will begin by examining the basic argument that Islam, properly understood, is both a religion and a state (*din wa dawla*). Those who make this claim argue for the creation of a form of government where religious authority and political authority are closely intertwined and where the state actively promotes a particular vision of religious orthodoxy in public life. Examples of such states include the current government of Iran – which is defined by clerical rule – or that of Saudi Arabia, which has a long-standing connection to the Wahhabist vision of Islam. As noted in the previous chapter, the distinction between "Islamic states" (or what we will refer to as "traditionalist states") and "secular states" is not always sharp or clearly defined, particularly for secular governments that invoke religion as a basis of support. Nonetheless, the distinction remains a useful means of differentiating between categories of states and their varying relationship with Islam and religious authority. The chapter will also examine the claims of religious opposition groups that have argued for a more central role for Islam in government. In either instance – whether religion is tied to a particular regime or to the political opposition – the arguments for a traditionalist state are similar: God is the ultimate source of sovereignty, and Islam ought to provide the basis for legislation, law, and governance.

As will be discussed below, the idea of an Islamic or traditionalist state is commonly argued to be a more authentic rendering of the Islamic political tradition. The model for this form of rule is the early Muslim community, where the Prophet and his immediate successors were considered to be both the political and religious leaders of the *ummah* (community of believers). Consequently, religious authority and political authority were closely intertwined in the early Muslim community. Islamist thinkers of recent years call for a return to a similar model of governance and demand that state leaders rule in accordance with Islamic teachings. They also refuse to recognize the legitimacy of states that do not fully implement their interpretation of Islamic law (*sharia*). The Islamists (or Salafists) throughout the 20th century believed that it was precisely the failure of political leaders to abide by such practices, together with the effort of Arab and Muslim political leaders to emulate Western styles of governance, that led to the weakness and subjugation of Muslims worldwide. Hence contemporary Islamists continue to argue that only by returning to a political order where Islam is central can the Muslim community once again find its strength in this world. The "return" to Islam, in short, is seen as essential to the political reassertion and revitalization of the Muslim community.

In addition to a discussion of these ideas in their historical context, this chapter will examine several governments that are defined by their efforts to construct an explicitly religious or traditionalist state. These governments are Saudi Arabia, Iran, Sudan, Pakistan, and Afghanistan. In each instance, government leaders have sought to address the challenge of applying traditional conceptions of Islamic law to a contemporary setting. In doing so they have offered a variety of visions of what an Islamic state ought to look like. These societies have continued, however, to be plagued by various ills, including autocratic governance, sectarian division, and poor human rights records. As these contemporary examples illustrate, the close association of religion with the state does not necessarily produce just, let alone wise, rule.

The Theoretical and Historical Context

Many look at the history of Islam and see not a tradition of activism, but one of "political quietism." This was evident in both the Sunni and the Shi'i traditions during the medieval period. Faced with rulers who were tyrannical and often changing, the *ulamā* of the Sunni tradition and the clerics of Shi'i Islam commonly argued for obedience to political authority. Their argument was based on the fear that the alternative to tyranny was worse. The great concern for many early Islamic scholars was civil war and *fitnah* (anarchy or strife), both of which weaken the community of believers and undermine the integrity of the Islamic tradition. There were also outside threats, such as the crusader armies of Europe and, later, the Mongol invasion discussed in Chapter 2. These foreign interventions endangered the lands of Islam and fostered the perception that Islam needed a ruler who should be able to defend the religion and the community. Such fears formed the basis for a religious obligation to obey political authority regardless of its nature. During times of political uncertainty, it was argued, the need for a *strong* governing authority superseded the need for a *just* authority (Brown 2001).

This tradition of political quietism came to an end with the rise of European predominance and Europe's intrusion into the Islamic world. As noted in the previous chapter, the advent of European colonial rule sparked a process of internal reform and reflection. Why, it was asked, were Muslim societies dominated by the Christian West, and how does one explain the relative decline of Islamic civilization? What, in short, had gone wrong? While the last chapter looked at two answers to this question – the liberal reformers and the secular alternative – the following section will examine the Islamist perspective. Unlike the liberal thinkers of the reform movement in the early 20th century and unlike secularists such as Ataturk, Islamists argued that the source of Muslim decline was its loss of religion. By seeking to emulate the West, Islamic governments and society as a whole had lost touch with their heritage, and this would explain their subsequent weakness. It followed, then, that by "returning to Islam" the political community would be redeemed. Moreover, unlike the liberal reformers, Islamists did not seek to reconcile religion with Western ideas. Rather the Islamist – or Salafist – perspective argued for a return to religious literalism and sought to create an Islamic order modeled on the example of the Prophet and on what they saw as the golden age of Islamic rule.

Some of the earliest examples of Islamic revivalism included the Mahdist revolt in Sudan, the 18th-century Wahhabist movement in Saudi Arabia, and the Sanusi movement in Libya. In each instance, indigenous groups responded to internal decline or foreign intervention by calling for a return to the basic tenets of the Islamic tradition. Many of these activists – the Wahhabists in particular – were concerned with what they perceived as un-Islamic practices that had crept into the tradition, such as Sufi mysticism, the veneration of saints, and simple differences over doctrine. Although the emphasis was on religious reform, the goal was ultimately political. In the case of Saudi Arabia, the 18th-century religious leader Muhammad ibn 'Abd al-Wahhab promoted a strict and literalist reading of the Islamic tradition and joined forces with the al-Sa'ud family to promote both religious and political change. Two defining features of this movement were the religious zeal with which it pursued its ends and the military capability of the al-Sa'ud family. Combined, they were able – temporarily – to throw off Ottoman rule and to establish the first Saudi state in the Arabian Peninsula.

Similarly, in Sudan, the Mahdist forces were able to unite the indigenous tribes in opposition to the Anglo-Egyptian rule. The leader of this movement, Muhammad Ahmad (1840–1885), came to be known as the *mahdi* (literally, the Messiah), and was able to mobilize the Sudanese tribes through a mixture of religious and political appeals. Though short-lived, Mahdist rule in Sudan sought to replicate the experience of the Prophet and to establish a society based on Islamic teachings. Similarly, the Sanusi movement in Libya was able to unite politically different tribal factions under a banner of Islam. As in the other movements of this era, ridding Islamic tradition of cultural accretions was part of a broader effort to revitalize both the political and the religious life of the community. In a manner similar to that of the Mahdist movement in Sudan, the Sanusi movement had for its goal the creation of a traditionalist state and the expansion of Islam beyond Libya's borders. Much of the impetus, moreover, was to check the growing encroachment of European colonialism (see Sidebar 7.1).

The Islamist (or "fundamentalist") movement of the early 20th century echoed the basic themes of these premodern revivalists. The Muslim Brotherhood in Egypt, the Jamaat-e-Islami in Pakistan, and other fundamentalist groups were responding both to a perceived sense of internal decay and to the external intervention of European powers. They also worked to promote political reform

---

Sidebar 7.1   The Mahdist revolt in the Sudan

The Mahdist revolt in Sudan took place in the late 19th century and temporarily ended foreign rule in that country. The revolt is named after its leader, Muhammad Ahmad, believed to be the Mahdi ("Redeemer"), who invoked Islam as a means of uniting the various northern Sudanese tribes and communities by way of creating an opposition to Egyptian and European rule. The early successes of the Mahdi appeared to validate his message and quickly garnered widespread support for his cause. The final victory came in 1885, when Khartoum fell to the Mahdist forces and its then governor, Charles Gordon, was captured and put to death. The Mahdist government remained in power until 1899, when British forces under the command of Lord Kitchener were sent up the Nile, ended the Mahdist state (the Mahadiyya), and established British colonial rule over Sudan. This rule would last until 1956.

through religious revivalism. The term "fundamentalism," though a source of contention, is relevant because it refers to the reaffirmation of certain fundamental or foundational beliefs and to the corresponding effort of religio-political groups to transform society in light of these foundational principles.[1] In this sense, the Muslim Brotherhood and Jamaat-e-Islami are good examples. The Brotherhood, which was founded by Hasan al-Banna in 1928 in Egypt, is noteworthy because its influence extended throughout the larger Middle East. In its early stages the organization had an extensive grassroots network, an active political party, and a military wing; however, it was the ideology and the combination of religious message and political activism that defined the group. For the Brotherhood it was important to capture, or influence, state power and to use the mechanisms of modern government to reform civil society along Islamist lines. The close association of Islam and the state was thus a central feature of the organization's goals.

As noted in the previous chapter, the heart of the Brotherhood's message was a belief that the social ills of Muslim society were attributable to the irreligious or secular nature of government leaders. The problem, from this point of view, was that the effort to emulate the West had led to internal fragmentation and to external weakness. Al-Banna was consequently very much concerned with the influence of European ideas and with what he referred to as the process of "mental colonization." By emulating Western patterns of thinking, governance, and lifestyle, Muslims were validating and perpetuating their own subjugation. This position put al-Banna and

Sidebar 7.2   Hasan al-Banna

Hasan al-Banna founded the Muslim Brotherhood in Egypt in 1928. By doing so he helped to create the organizational structure and the ideology that would shape the Islamist movement for the rest of the 20th century. His primary concerns were the intrusion of Western ideas and political power into his native Egypt and the corresponding willingness of his fellow countrymen to embrace Western culture. Al-Banna's work consequently focused on education, political action, and grassroots mobilization, all with the intended goal of making Islam the organizing principle of society. In reaction to the decline of society under colonial rule, al-Banna believed that only a "return to religion" could be a viable basis for political unity and cohesion in Muslim society. In short, the source of Muslim weakness was a perceived loss of religion; hence the return to religion would be a source of newfound strength:

> After the last war [World War I] and during the period I spent in Cairo, there was an increase in spiritual and ideological disintegration, in the name of intellectual freedom. There was also a deterioration of behavior, morals and deeds in the name of individual freedom [...] I saw that the social life of the beloved Egyptian nation was oscillating between her dear and precious Islamism which she had inherited, defended, lived with and become accustomed to [...] and this severe Western invasion which is armed and equipped with all the destructive and degenerative influence of money, wealth, prestige, ostentation, material enjoyment, power and means of propaganda. (Hasan al-Banna, cited in Abu-Rabi 1996: 65)

other Islamists distinctly at odds with the secular and liberal reformers, who sought to accommodate European ideas and to adopt Western models of law and governance. Al-Banna was particularly concerned about the corrupting influence of Western liberal education, "which cast doubt and heresy into the souls [of our sons]" (Abu-Rabi 1996: 80). It was this type of cultural intrusion – linked to the secular patterns of social order promulgated by indigenous, secular elites – that the early Islamists saw as a primary threat to Islam.

The political program of the early Islamists consequently sought to counter these trends by calling for a return to Islam as the organizing principle of society. In practical terms, this entailed the creation of an "Islamic order" (*al-nizām al-Islāmī*), defined above all by the application of Islamic law (*sharia*). The close association of religion and political authority was central to this vision. Since the absence of religion (or what was perceived as true religious values) was the source of Muslim decline, a recommitment to the fundamentals of Islam was required. These basic themes were similarly articulated by Mawlana Mawdudi, an influential activist and writer from South Asia and the founder of the Jamaat-i-Islami, a political party in Pakistan. Mawdudi's influence derived in part from his effort to systematize and clarify the Islamist message. In doing so, he defined the "Islamic state" as "an ideological state that should be run only by those who believe in the ideology on which it is based [the Qur'an and the sunna] and in the divine law which it is assigned to administer" (Mawdudi, cited in Ayubi 1993: 128). Central to this was the claim that sovereignty lay not with the people or with the state, but with God alone. Moreover, the Jamaat called all true believers to action, arguing that it was not enough to accept Islam; there was a similar obligation to "command good and forbid evil," and this required political action.

During the postcolonial period the primary opponents of the Islamists vision changed, but the basic message did not. As noted in the previous chapter, secular Arab nationalists came to power in a variety of countries – including Egypt, Syria, Iraq, and Algeria – in the immediate postcolonial period. These secular governments posed a serious threat to the Arab monarchies that were supportive of the Islamist vision. More to the point, from the Islamist perspective, the secular leadership of this era seemed to be moving precisely in the wrong direction. Its representatives were

---

Sidebar 7.3   Mawlana Mawdudi

Mawdudi helped to define the concept of an Islamic (or traditionalist) state in the mid-20th century. Writing first in colonial India and later in Pakistan, he helped to systematize Islamist thought. His ideas about the Islamic state were particularly influential. He argued that God alone – and not the population or the monarch – is the source of sovereignty and that the only source of law and legislation is God's word. More to the point, he argued that Islam is an all-encompassing tradition, therefore an Islamic form of government has jurisdiction over all aspects of human existence. An Islamic form of government, then, needs to serve as an instrument of reform, to shape society in a manner consistent with Islamic teaching. As Mawdudi wrote,

A state of this sort cannot evidently restrict the scope of its activities. Its approach is universal and all embracing. Its sphere of activity is co-extensive with the whole of human life. It seeks to mould every aspect of life and activity in consonance with its moral norms and programme of social reform. In such a state no one can regard any field of his affairs as personal and private. Considered from this aspect [*sic*] the Islamic state bears a kind of resemblance to the Fascist and Communists states. But you will find later on that, despite its all-inclusiveness, it is something vastly and basically different from the modern totalitarian and authoritarian states. Individual liberty is not suppressed under it nor is there any trace of dictatorship in it. It presents the middle course and embodies the best that human society has ever evolved. (Abu-L-Ala Mawdudi, cited in Donohue and Esposito 1982: 256)

charting a path for their societies that was inimical to the Islamist vision. In a nutshell, the Islamists' enemies were no longer the Europeans – the external threat – but rather the indigenous inheritors of the secular alternative. In the ideological cauldron of the Cold War, Islamists sought to offer an alternative to liberal democratic capitalism on the one hand and to Soviet-style socialism or communism on the other. In this context the Islamist vision was meant to be both culturally authentic and consistent with the Islamic tradition. Islam was consequently viewed as an "organic ideology of unity," which was, at least theoretically, outside of the ideological battles that pitted East against West during the Cold War.

The Traditionalist State

The idea of an Islamic or traditionalist state is ultimately rooted in the tradition of the caliphate. While there are differences (particularly between the caliphate of the Abbasid or Ottoman period and the modern Islamic state), the underlying commonality is the merging of religious authority and political authority. From this perspective, the Islamist call for a traditionalist state is rooted in the perceived historicity of a religious tradition that rightfully extends its influence into all realms of social (and individual) life. This conception of Islamic rule is based on the assumption that Islam will – and ought to – regulate all aspects of human existence. The state within an "Islamic order," then, serves as the enforcer of Islamic law and actively promotes and regulates religious belief among members of the community. This understanding of the proper relationship between Islam and the state is significant partly because it rejects the basic premise of the secular tradition, which not only removes religion from the purview of government authority, but also differentiates between various social realms: public and private, religious and secular. In the secular tradition governments cannot rightfully interfere in matters of personal conscience, religion, or belief. This is clearly not the case for those who advocate an Islamist understanding of a traditionalist state.

The question remains, however, as to what exactly a traditionalist state would look like. While interpretations differ (as we will see below), the basic elements of such a state include the application of Islamic law and the corresponding enforcement of religious orthodoxy by state actors. Significantly, the ruler is not above the law within this idealized vision of an Islamic state. On the contrary, those who control the state ought to be subject to Islam's commandments, not least to the tenet of doing good and forbidding evil. Failure to abide by this rule warrants rebellion among the population. It follows, then, that an Islamic state would be a constitutional one insofar as there are foundational principals that restrain the governor and hold rulers accountable to the population (*ummah*). The underlying assumption – which is also found in liberal conceptions of constitutional governance – is that, without some constraint on state leaders, there will be no justice, but only oppression. Where this Islamic ideal differs, however, from the Western tradition is in the source of its foundational principles; rather than emerging from a document, or from consensus among people, the foundational principles of an Islamic state are found solely in the Qur'an, the sunna, and the *sharia*.

While there remain disputes over the content of an Islamic state, its necessity is self-evident for its advocates. The root of their argument is that creating such a state is a religious obligation. There are two key aspects to this argument. First, a state is essential for the prevention of chaos and *fitnah* and for the preservation of the unity of the Islamic community. Second, Islam is not simply a religion, but also a social and political system; hence a state is necessary if one is to implement the Islamic mandates in society and to fulfill the Islamist vision. A defining feature of this argument is its social character. The assumption here is that, in order to truly live according to God's will, one must live within a community that is regulated by laws handed down from above. Consequently, it is incumbent upon the state to create the kind of society in which Islam will flourish and where individuals can live according to God's mandate. Moreover, this is not simply a matter of choice; from the Islamist perspective the establishment of an Islamic state is a foundational precept of Islam.

There are several important assumptions that underlie this line of thought. First, as noted earlier, the proponents of the Islamic or traditionalist state argue that, according to tradition, all aspects of human existence are meant to be regulated by God's will. This means that a close affiliation between Islam and state is essential for the actualization of Islam in the world. Proponents also assume that without Islam there will be no foundation for a moral life, and hence no basis for a just political order. This amounts to saying that Islam – both Islamic values and Islamic law – is the only viable means of constraining the arbitrary use of government power and of securing the basis for a more just rule. Secular states, runs the claim, simply do not have this capability.

The advocates of a traditionalist state also argue that secular norms and secular governance are simply inappropriate in a Muslim context. They base this idea on the claim that secularism is a Western phenomenon, which emerged from the European experience of a dominant church. Within the Islamic tradition the situation is different, because there is no formal church, no conflict between religion and science, and no distinction made between the spiritual and the material realm. Hence secularism is simply not applicable to Islamic society; it is culturally inauthentic (see Flores 1997). This argument is persuasive partly on account of the historical experience of secular governments in the Muslim world, first during the colonial period and then under secular dictators later on. In the first instance, secular forms of government and law were imposed upon society from above, and, it is argued, they did not accord with popular will. In the second instance, secularism was associated with the military dictatorships that emerged in the postcolonial period and that have long lost popular support. For many, then, the association between secularism and despotism – either European or Arab nationalist – has tainted the secular idea and linked it with injustice, misrule, and weakness.

These arguments in favor of a close relationship between Islam and the state have been reiterated in more recent times by religious thinkers such as Yusuf al-Qaradawi and Ṭariq al-Bishri (among others). Their efforts to develop a more moderate "Islamic constitutionalism" are intended to allay concerns that a "return to Islam" would impact adversely on minorities or women, while they stress the positive contribution that Islam can make to national unity, cultural autonomy, and political independence. Like those who came before them, these more recent thinkers emphasize the centrality of Islamic law – *sharia* – as a mechanism for guiding state and society and its source in the Qur'an and in the example of the Prophet. *Sharia* is the legal and moral basis of the spiritual community, and hence it is right for it to guide political governance. These contemporary scholars see the state as an important mechanism for transforming both the individual and society and consider such changes to be legitimate functions of an Islamic state. Government thus acquires an intrusive role in regulating religion, morality, and education. A key assumption in this argument is the belief that individual conscience can be wrong, and that it is up to the state to protect the community from those who do not understand God's will. By enforcing religious law – and religious orthodoxy – in this manner, the state is said to "represent the justice of God on Earth" (Yusaf al-Qaradwai, cited in Rutherford 2008: 122).

Realizing that there are areas within Islamic tradition that are silent – or unclear – on particular issues of governance, the Islamic constitutionalists recognize the role of interpretation, consultation, and analogous reasoning. They argue, nonetheless, that the specifics ought to be guided by the central principles of *sharia* and that positive law must be derived from divine law. In the Islamic tradition, this process of interpreting *sharia* in a contemporary context is known as *fiqh* – Islamic jurisprudence (see Chapters 3 and 4). Similarly, one of the key arguments made by the Islamic constitutionalists is that the state itself ought to be constrained by Islamic law and values. This includes limiting the power of the executive (the president or other rulers), removing the military from politics, strengthening the judiciary, and creating greater autonomy for religious scholars and institutions. While this sounds a great deal like liberal constitutionalism, al-Qaradawi and others would differ. They argue that earlier efforts to adopt European law helped to fragment the Muslim community and produced governments that were largely alienated from their populations. By returning to Islamic sources of governance and ensuring that the laws governing society are derived in a manner consistent with Islamic tradition, the community would once again find its cultural and religious moorings, and this would constitute the basis for a revitalized society and for greater political autonomy (as has been frequently argued before).

The Critique of the Islamist Vision

The arguments in favor of a traditionalist state beg numerous questions, and this invites a critique of the close association between Islam and state. What, specifically, would an Islamic state look like in practice, and how would it differ from existing governments? More to the point, which interpretation of *sharia* is one to implement? In the Islamic tradition there are 1,400 years of Islamic jurisprudence and a variety of schools of thought that disagree on any number of issues. Which school would be authoritative? Similarly, there remains a question as to *who* is to interpret Islamic law on contemporary issues, for which there is no classical precedent. Who, as Noah Feldman notes, "is in charge of specifying the meaning of the *sharia* and by what authority?" (Feldman 2008: 13). Critics of the religious state seize upon these various issues. First, critics argue that the positions described above rely on a narrow interpretation of Islam, which draws only selectively from the Islamic tradition, serving particular interests and not others. Second, there is significant concern that both the interpretation and the implementation of Islamic law would be done by fallible humans and human institutions. Far from ensuring God's rule on earth, religion would simply become a means of political oppression.

These criticisms get to the heart of the basic political problem of a traditionalist state: whose interpretation of religion is to be taken as authoritative, and which government official is to determine the will of God? While many take a literalist interpretation of the Qur'an and assume that the meaning of the divine text is self-evident, others disagree on this question of self-evidence. As noted earlier, particularly in matters of governance, there is an absence of clarity within the Qur'an and sunna on issues that arise in the context of the modern world. Who, then, will resolve disputes among Islamic scholars over the implementation of Islamic commandments? This is less of a problem within the Shi'i tradition, where there is an authoritative ruler – the *vali-e-faqih* or "guardian jurist," who serves as both religious interpreter and political leader – but it remains a significant challenge within the Sunni tradition.

Related to these concerns are the implications of institutionalizing one interpretation of religion at the expense of all others. This is particularly evident in questions regarding dissent, sectarian differences, and human rights. With regard to the first issue, there is concern that the invocation of divine authority precludes any form of political dissent, because the latter would be readily equated with religious dissent or unbelief. Several of the states discussed below have consequently sanctioned the maltreatment of those deemed to fall outside the community on account of their religious opinions or political views. Similarly, the question of the religious state raises significant concerns for minority populations, whose members see themselves as second-class citizens within a state where civil status is determined by religious identity. There is also the question of cultural practices and their relevance in the 21st century. For example, what should be done about the forms of corporal punishment known as hudud, which include stoning, severing the hands, and the use of the lash? Are these forms of corporal punishment still applicable in the modern world, no matter how "evident" their applicability is in the religious tradition? And what about issues such as the veil, or the low status of women? These tend to be matters of culture, not religion; yet states such as Iran, Saudi Arabia, and Afghanistan have made it clear that their governments see them as religious matters. In the process, these states have caused concern that modern state officials are reshaping the content of Islamic tradition by including cultural practices that have little or no grounding in the Qur'an. This, then, ties into the final critique: Are modern state elites faithfully implementing Islam, or are they simply using it to justify their own (often sordid) motives? This is one question that secular critics and Islamist activists alike raise in the context of contemporary politics.

Cases

Saudi Arabia

Saudi Arabia is an example of a modern state that actively enforces religious orthodoxy. While it is not a theocracy – which means that clerics do not rule – it has a government that is defined by its adherence to, and implementation of, a strict interpretation of Islam. Moreover, the religious character of the state is part of the country's self-proclaimed identity. The origins of the contemporary Saudi government lie in the 18th-century Wahhabist movement discussed above. As previously mentioned, Muhammad ibn 'Abd al-Wahhab's call for religious revival and reform was linked with the military capability of a local tribal leader, Muhammad ibn Sa'ud. Together, they were able to occupy the holy cities of Mecca and Medina and create a nascent state in the central Hijaz. Although the first Saudi state was crushed by an Ottoman army led by Muhammad 'Ali of Egypt, a subsequent state was resurrected by the heirs of ibn Sa'ud in the early 20th century. With material support from the British, 'Abd al-Aziz bin al-Sa'ud, son of Muhammad ibn Sa'ud, was able to once again establish control over much of the Saudi Arabian Peninsula and to unite the different regions and tribes under his rule. The discovery of oil in the 1930s and the subsequent exploitation of these resources in the post-World War II period greatly facilitated the development of state institutions and the consolidation of power on the part of the House of Sa'ud.

Even today, the defining feature of Saudi Arabia is its close association of religion and government. The particular interpretation of Islam that informs the Saudi state is commonly described as "Wahhabism" – a label that refers to the 18th-century religious leader. Wahhabist ideals are the moral and religious foundation of the Saudi state, and they are regularly invoked to sanction state policies. This particular interpretation of Islam is rooted in the Hanbali School of Islamic jurisprudence and is greatly influenced by the thought of the 13th-century legal scholar Ibn Taymiyah. The *sharia* courts that are at the heart of the Saudi legal system similarly draw from the Hanbali tradition (although there are also other courts, which hear cases in areas that fall outside the jurisdiction of *sharia*). Within the Saudi political system, the official *ulamā* plays an important role in governing society. Its members interpret Islam for the Saudi state, serve as judges and jurists in *sharia* courts, and sanction government policies. There is also a religious police, whose role is the enforcement of Islamic morality. This includes policing public behavior and dress and making sure that fasting is observed during Ramadan, that business close during prayer times, and that alcohol is not consumed.

The primary challenge to the Gulf monarchies in the post-World War II period – both in terms of religion and in terms of politics – consisted in the Arab nationalist forces discussed in the previous chapter. As we have already seen, Saudi Arabia was deeply troubled by the populist rhetoric and revolutionary policies of the Egyptian regime. Nasser's Arab nationalism challenged directly the legitimacy of Saudi Arabia's ruling family and its control of the region's oil wealth. On the other hand, Nasser perceived Saudi Arabia as a bastion of conservative reaction, actively working against his interests. The Gulf monarchies' alliance with the West was, in Nasser's view, a perpetuation of the colonial relationship and kept the Arabs divided and weak. Both the Saudis and the Egyptians subsequently worked against each other's influence in the region and set up competing Islamic institutions to promote their respective agendas. Each of these organizations appealed to a different interpretation of Sunni Islam; together they promoted the interests of competing states. In this way the debate over the proper relationship between Islam and the state – and over the proper interpretation of Islam – became part of the Cold War competition in the Arab World.

The Arab Cold War peaked in the mid-1960s and took a decisive turn with the defeat of Nasser and his allies in the 1967 war. Nasser's death three years later further deprived the Arab nationalists of their leading voice. While the socialist states of the region remained largely intact, the stage was set for the resurgence of a more theologically conservative and Saudi-influenced Islam and for the abandonment of secular ideals. This was evident in Egypt, where Nasser's successor, Anwar Sadat, actively sought a rapprochement with the Saudi royal family (a trend begun under Nasser) and distanced himself from the secular nationalism of his predecessor. Sadat's subsequent embrace of a more traditional conception of Islam helped to validate the ideological claims made by the Saudi royal family. The Arab success in the 1973 war with Israel further influenced this trend. A central feature of the 1973 war was the Saudi oil embargo, which targeted the West and was seen as demonstrating a newfound strength in the Arab world. The embargo also increased the price of oil dramatically. The subsequent influx of oil revenues increased Saudi Arabia's influence throughout the region and, with it, the success of the Wahhabist vision of Islam. In short, the oil boom of the 1970s and early 1980s helped facilitate an ideological shift in the region, as the Saudi interpretation of Islam became more influential and the secular nationalism of the previous decades was increasingly eclipsed.

Saudi Arabia has promoted its version of Islam throughout the Middle East and South Asia over the past few decades. For example, the Saudi state (which controls the country's oil revenue) has funded Islamic schools (*madāris*) throughout these regions, has funded or subsidized the publication of religious material, and has funded scholars and organizations sympathetic to its aims. The Saudi government also provided funding for the Muslim Brotherhood in Egypt and for the Jamaat-e-Islāmi in Pakistan and helped to finance the holy warriors (*mujahidin*) fighting the Soviet

Union in Afghanistan throughout the 1980s. It was also a significant supporter of the Taliban government in Afghanistan after the Afghan War. Saudi support for these forces was intended to counter the influence of opposing ideas – including the revolutionary Shiʿism of Khomeini's Iran (which is discussed below) and the lingering influence of leftist secularism. It was also meant to promote what the Saudi's perceived as the true Islam, and particularly the conception of an Islamic order defined by a close relationship between religious and political authority. The revival of Islamist ideas in recent years is a testament to the success of this strategy, but also to its costs. Osama Bin Laden, once a recipient of Saudi support, turned on his former ally and actively called for the overthrow the House of Saʿud. As the case of Pakistan illustrates (see below), support for Islamist militancy can be a two-edged sword.

Iran

Nowhere is the resurgence of Islamic fundamentalism more evident than in Iran. In 1979 the Iranian Revolution shook the world. By deposing the shah of Iran – a close ally of the United States – and by replacing monarchy with clerical rule, Ayatollah Khomeini and his followers demonstrated the continued power of religion in modern politics. The Islamic Revolution was particularly surprising given Iran's secular past. As discussed in the previous chapter, Iran under the first Reza Shah sought to build a secular, modern state in the 1920s and 1930s and was greatly influenced by Ataturk's ambitious reforms. Like Ataturk, Reza Shah sought to restrain religion, centralize political control, and extend his own control over the entire country. While unable to replicate Ataturk's experiment and to remove religion from public life, Reza Shah could contain the influence of the Shiʿi clerics. His pro-German leanings, however, prompted a British invasion in 1941, and his son Muhammad Reza Shah was put on the throne. Western intervention in Iranian politics continued throughout the post-World War II period. In 1953, for example, the Central Intelligence Agency (CIA) orchestrated a coup to depose the nationalist forces that had recently taken control of the Anglo-Iranian oil company. The coup undermined the parliament within Iran's constitutional monarchy and ushered in 25 years of secular – and repressive – rule under Muhammad Reza Shah.

The 1979 revolution was prompted by popular disdain for the shah and his policies. While grievances were largely political – a response to political repression, economic mismanagement, inflation, and uneven development – the critique was articulated primarily in religious terms. This was due in part to the reverence in which Iranians held their religious clerics, particularly Ayatollah Khomeini, and to the continuing salience of Shiʿi Islam to Iranian national identity. Another important factor was the centrality of the mosque in organizing society against the regime. Islam was important to the revolution because it provided a moral language of opposition. Khomeini's interpretation of Shiʿi Islam was infused with Marxist ideas (the legacy of an activist named ʿAli Shariʿati), and decidedly anti-Western. Drawing on the themes of other Islamists, he decried the influence of Western culture and power on Iranian society (which was commonly referred to as "Westoxification," or *gharbzadegi*), and the exploitation of Iranian resources by Western companies. Given the history of great powers intervening in Iran, it was not difficult to attack the shah's strong ties to the West as culturally inauthentic.

Despite the religious nature of the rhetoric and of the leadership, the coalition against the shah was diverse, and many participants called for a return to the liberal constitution of 1906. Here the struggle among different elements of the opposition for determining the meaning and direction of the revolution took a dramatic and

ugly turn. Between 1981 and 1982, the leftist elements of the opposition were purged from the ruling councils: 50 to 100 people were executed daily while others were jailed, tortured, and forced into Soviet-style confessions aired on national television. The "reign of terror" that characterized this period ended with the consolidation of power in the hands of the ruling clerics.

What ultimately emerged in post-revolutionary Iran was a form of government that had the constitutional framework of a republic – including a parliament (*majlis*), elections, and several branches of government – but nonetheless gave to the head of state or supreme leader the power to make final decisions on matters of religion and governance. This newly created institution was the Velayat e-faqih – "guardianship of the jurists / clerics" or "rule by jurisprudence" – a political and theological innovation that constituted the basis for direct clerical rule. Iran's Islamic Republic was clearly a theocracy, and it differed from states such as Saudi Arabia through this element of direct clerical rule. The concept of the Velayat e-faqih was articulated by Ayatollah Khomeini years earlier, in a series of speeches – and later on in a book – that gave a religious foundation to this innovative form of government. In the Shi'i tradition, the rightful leader is drawn from the line of imams who descend from the Prophet's nephew, 'Ali. With the disappearance (or occultation) of the twelfth imam, the task of governing devolves to the clerics. Their responsibility is to implement the *sharia* in a just and knowledgeable way. There is no precedent for this vision of rule; hence Khomeini's concept embodies a high

Sidebar 7.4   Khomeini and the Velayat e-faqih

The Velayat e-faqih – the jurist's (*faqīh*) governance – is a revolutionary concept in Islamic thought; it gives the right to, and the responsibility of, political rule to a single pre-eminent religious cleric: the "guardian-jurist" (*vali-ye faqīh*). This marks a departure from traditional concepts of governance, whereby political authorities have a responsibility to rule in a manner that is consistent with Islamic teachings, but it is not the clerical class that is actually ruling. Ayotollah Khomeini, who pioneered this vision, argues that there is a clear need for an executive to administer or implement Islamic law: only in this way can God's will be manifest on earth. Consequently, many of Khomeini's writings focus on the need for an Islamic government. Their purpose is also to differentiate it from other kinds of rule, where laws are made by men. Implicit in Khomeini's arguments is an assumption that God's will is rightly understood by the ruling clerics and that the implementation of the divine mandate is not subject to human whim. In his own words:

> The Islamic Government is not despotic but constitutional. However it is not constitutional in the well-known sense of the word. It is constitutional in the sense that those in charge of affairs oversee a number of conditions and rules underlined in the Quran and the Sunna and represented in the necessity of observing the system and of applying the dictates and laws of Islam. This is why the Islamic government is the government of the divine law […]. (Ayatollah Ruhalla Khomeini, cited in Donohue and Esposito 1982: 317)

degree of interpretation, but it is nonetheless drawn from the sources of the tradition.

The ultimate source of authority within this system remains the will of God – not that of a monarch, or that of the people, or even that of the *sharia*. However, to determine God's will in any given situation is the responsibility of the Velayat e-faqih. This has led to a central critique of the institution: it is not God's will that is being served, but the will of those in power. Since all humans are fallible, and since it is in any case unlikely that anyone can truly know God's will, the concentration of religious authority and political power in the hands of one man is likely to have corrupting effects. It has also led, in the Iranian case, to rampant human rights violations and the mistreatment of minority populations (see Sidebar 7.5). As Nazih Ayubi noted, after Khomeini became the first beneficiary the new institution of Velayat e-faqih – the first "guardian-jurist" (*vali-ye faqīh*), a function commonly referred to in the West as "supreme leader" – he portrayed "his guardianship (now analogous to that of the Prophet) [as] absolute, even if it contradicts the stipulation of the *shari'a*. It is now the government that is supreme, not the *shari'a*; the State, not the ideology" (Ayubi 1993: 151).

Pakistan/Afghanistan

Pakistan was created in 1947, when British colonial rule ended and India was partitioned into two separate states. The defining feature of this new country was its Muslim identity. Pakistan was created specifically to be a homeland for Muslims who feared second-class status in a Hindu-dominated India. The question remained, however, whether the new Pakistani state would simply have a Muslim identity – and thus be largely secular in orientation – or whether the state would be committed to creating the kind of Islamic order discussed above. In other words, would the state be religious or

---

Sidebar 7.5   Human rights and minorities in Iran

The following excerpt is taken from the US Department of State 2010 Report on International Religious Freedom:

The constitution [of Iran] states that Islam is the official state religion, and the doctrine followed is that of Ja'afari (Twelver) Shi'ism. The constitution provides that "other Islamic denominations are to be accorded full respect," while the country's pre-Islamic religious groups – Zoroastrians, Christians, and Jews – are recognized as "protected" religious minorities. However, the fourth article of the constitution states that all laws and regulations must be based on Islamic criteria. In practice the government severely restricted freedom of religion.

During the reporting period, government respect for religious freedom in the country continued to deteriorate. Government rhetoric and actions created a threatening atmosphere for nearly all non-Shi'a religious groups, most notably for Baha'is, as well as Sufi Muslims, evangelical Christians, members of the Jewish community, and Shi'a groups that do not share the government's official religious views. Reports of government imprisonment, harassment, intimidation, and discrimination based on religious beliefs continued during the reporting period. Baha'i religious groups reported arbitrary arrest and prolonged detention, expulsions from universities, and confiscation of property. During the reporting period government-controlled broadcast and print media intensified negative campaigns against religious minorities, particularly the Baha'is. All non-Shi'a religious minorities suffered varying degrees of officially sanctioned discrimination, particularly in the areas of employment, education, and housing.

(Continued)

Although the constitution gives Christians, Jews, and Zoroastrians the status of "protected" religious minorities (as long as they do not proselytize), in practice non-Shi'a Muslims faced substantial societal discrimination, and government actions continued to support elements of society that created a threatening atmosphere for some religious minorities.

secular? The founder, Muhammad 'Ali Jinnah, was a lawyer educated in the West who had little interest in using the state to promote Islam. Moreover, the diversity of the Pakistani population – which was made up of secular Muslims, a large Shi'i minority, numerous ethnic and linguistic groups, and sects like the Ahmadiyya, which many in Pakistan did not consider truly Muslim – made the question of imposing a particular vision of Islam a sensitive matter. Early constitutional debates reflected these divisions and demonstrated a lack of consensus over such basic issues as what is Islam and who is a Muslim (Esposito 1998: 115). Consequently, the early Pakistani state did not seek to implement a particular interpretation of Islam or Islamic law even though it embraced Islam as part of its nationalist discourse. Groups such as the Jamaat-e-Islami advocated a more active role for the state in religious matters and consistently called for the creation of an Islamic order, but they remained on the margins of Pakistani political life.

Debates between modernists and fundamentalists over religious interpretation and over the proper relationship between religion and state fluctuated quite dramatically throughout the 1970s. In 1971 the Civil War led to a division of the country and to the subsequent creation of Bangladesh. It also ushered in a period of democratic rule. With his calls for a secular and socialist state, Zulfiqar 'Ali Bhutto – leader of a leftist party, the Pakistan People's Party (PPP) – attracted support from both the lower classes and the large Shi'i population. Bhutto's government, however, increasingly sought to co-opt the discourse of Islam throughout the 1970s as part of an effort to cultivate ties with, and to secure financial aid from, the oil-rich Gulf states. Bhutto conceded a number of issues to the traditionalists in Pakistan – declaring the Ahmadiyya sect as non-Muslim, for example, or prohibiting alcohol and gambling – though he retained the country's commitment to socio-economic reform. In the 1977 national elections the PPP was opposed by a coalition of religious parties that included the Jamaat-e-Islami, and each side was invoking Islam to justify its competing political agenda. This situation reflected the degree to which Islam had re-emerged as a central feature of Pakistani identity and its function as a language of political discourse.

Despite Bhutto's impressive victory in the 1977 elections, his tenure in office was short-lived. Three months after elections, in July 1977, the military removed him from power and installed General Zia al-Haqq as president. The new government subsequently put Bhutto on trial in 1979, convicted him, and put him to death. This marked the beginning of a new period of military rule.

The defining feature of General Zia's tenure in power was his conscious effort to create an Islamic system of government that closely tied Islam to the state. In attempting to create such a system, Zia embraced the vision of the Jamaat-e-Islami Party and its call for an Islamic order. This meant that the state actively pursued an active program of Islamization, which included, among other things, the implementation of Islamic law and the reform of education (more on this below). From the government's perspective, the program of Islamization was an important means of unifying a society deeply divided along ethnic, linguistic and sectarian lines (see Map 7.1). Only by cultivating an overarching Islamic identity, it was

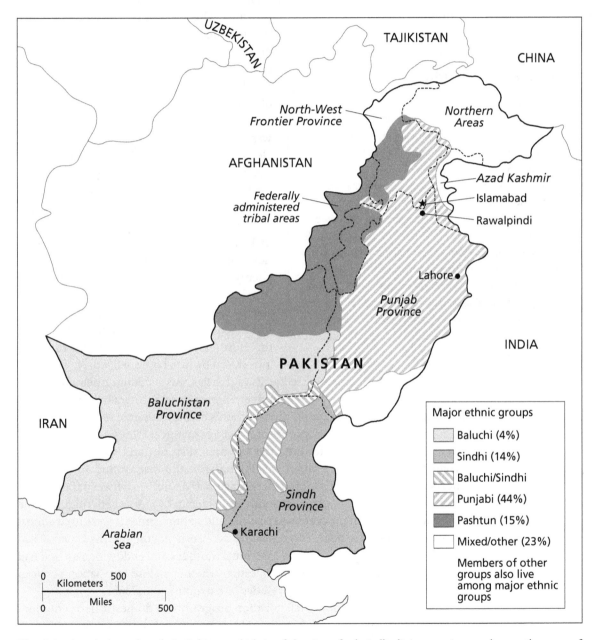

Map 7.1   An ethnic patchwork. In Pakistan, which is a federation of ethnically distinct provinces and areas, the sense of national identity has been fragile for a long time.

believed, could Pakistan transcend these divisions and come together as a nation. While the Jamaat supported the program of Islamization – and members of the Party took important positions within the Zia government – the leadership of the party was troubled by the undemocratic nature of the regime and the way in which it came to power.

Zia's program of Islamization included a range of polices affecting the law, education, the economy, and religious practice. This program included for instance the introduction of laws that imposed the observance of fasting during Ramadan, the integration of hudud punishments into the penal code,[2] and the establishment of a new set of *sharia* courts, which were specifically created to determine whether or not existing law was consistent with Islamic mandate. Other elements of this program pertained to the Islamization of the public sphere through the media and education. An Islamic taxation system was also created, and other changes were introduced to the economic system, to make it more consistent with Islamic prohibitions on interest. The state also passed a blasphemy law, which made the denigration of the Prophet and of the teachings of Islam punishable by death or imprisonment. Although Zia was killed in a mysterious plane crash in 1989, the close association of Islam and the state introduced by him has remained.

Sidebar 7.6   Hudud punishments

Hudud means "restriction" or "limit" in Arabic, but this noun has come to designate physical punishments associated with the implementation of Islamic law in particular countries. These punishments include measures such as stoning (for adultery), amputation (for theft), and flogging (for a variety of offenses such as alcohol consumption). Hudud punishments are incorporated into the legal codes of Pakistan, Afghanistan, Saudi Arabia, and Sudan, although their application has been limited, owing to the strict requirement for evidence in the Islamic tradition. Nonetheless, critics of Islam have been quick to seize upon these punishments in order to characterize the tradition as antithetical to modernity.

One of the criticisms directed at Zia's policies was its Sunni orientation. The state supported Sunni institutions and seminaries, but not their Shiʻi counterparts. Sunni doctrines were taught in public schools as the authentic understanding of Islam, and other minority sects were portrayed as heretical. This greatly aggravated Sunni–Shiʻi tensions and fostered the sectarian division (and violence) that has plagued the country ever since. This is similar to the case of Sudan, where the efforts to impose Islamic law on society exacerbated tensions between the Muslim North and the Christian/Animist South (see Sidebar 7.7). Another critique of the Pakistan Islamization program was that the hudud punishments were used almost exclusively against the poor. There was also a concern that the state had encroached upon Islamic institutions – such as individual mosques and endowments – and had politicized them. All this raised the question whether a close association between religion and state was sanctifying politics or corrupting religion.

While much of Pakistan's Islamization program was domestic in orientation, the role of Islam – and of Islamic militancy – in Pakistan's foreign policy is of particular significance. In this context, traditionalist conceptions of Islam were closely tied to policies associated with the Cold War and with efforts to marginalize both leftist and Iranian (that is, Shiʿi) influence in the region. This was evident during the 1980s, when Pakistan's intelligence services, the Inter-Service Intelligence (ISI), served as the main conduit for funding the *mujahidin* in Afghanistan during the latter's war with the Soviet Union. The tendency toward this kind of foreign policy continued well into the 1990s (and even after), as the ISI provided – and still provide – military, financial, and political support for Islamist militant groups and used them as "proxies" to further Pakistan's own goals. The ISI helped to create and fund militant groups such as Lashkar-e-taiba, Jaish-e-Mohammad, and others, which are active in the Kashmir region of India. The ISI also helped to create the Afghan Taliban, which came to power in Afghanistan in the mid-1990s and consisted of Pashtun, the largest ethnic group in the country. Control over Afghanistan has long been perceived as a strategic goal of Pakistan – which is why it supported the Taliban until the American invasion of Afghanistan in 2001.

As is widely known, the Taliban government was defined by its strict interpretation of Islam and by a close affiliation between religion and state. The Taliban movement itself emerged during the Civil War that followed the Soviet withdrawal from Afghanistan, when it was able to bring order and some degree of stability to a nation ravaged by war. The Taliban government was associated with a Wahhabist interpretation of Islam, and it received funding and support from Saudi Arabia as well as from Pakistan. It also earned a reputation for brutality. Its laws instituted severe corporal

Sidebar 7.7   The Civil War in Sudan

Originally a British colony, Sudan gained independence in 1956. Almost immediately, however, civil war broke out between the Muslim north and the predominantly animist and Christian south. While the war was driven by economic and political considerations, religion and the role of Islam in society were vital contributing factors. Northern political parties argued for a central role for Islam in governing the country, arguing that political unity required a high degree of religious and cultural uniformity. Southerners, on the other hand, were concerned about Muslim domination in a religious state and ultimately about becoming second-class citizens in their own country. This was a central issue in the Civil War. The war raged between 1956 and 1972 and broke out again in 1983. The conflict itself only ended in 2005. It led to a final separation of the country between north and south in 2011.

Since 1989 the Sudanese government has been led by General Omar Bashir and has been defined by its commitment to an Islamist ideology. The government has extended Islamic law to the entire country and has used the state as an instrument for promoting an exclusive vision of religion and society. It has severely restricted all forms of political opposition, committed extensive human rights violations, made itself guilty of genocide in the Darfur region of western Sudan, and supported tribal militias that have in turn perpetrated numerous atrocities against the local population (torture, rape, and murder). These allegations and the evidence supporting them have led the International Criminal Court to issue an arrest warrant for General Bashir in 2009. The general is charged with war crimes and crimes against humanity.

punishment, such as stoning for adultery or amputation for theft. The government also prohibited women from working outside the home and banned music, television, and kite-flying (among other things). All of these prohibitions were enforced by a religious police force that answered to a government department dedicated to the propagation of virtue and suppression of vice.

It is important to keep in mind that the Taliban and the Islamist militants of South Asia represent only a very narrow slice of the Islamic experience. Moreover, one can argue that this is what happens when political actors manipulate religion without regard for the consequences. The international jihadist movement, which spawned the Taliban and the other militant groups, was the unintended consequence – the "blowback" – of the Afghan War against the Soviets. Again, at the time, support for Islamist militancy (jihadism) was seen as a necessary means of fighting the Cold War. The promotion of conservative religion by pro-Western governments was driven in part by the belief that Sunni fundamentalism could serve as a bulwark both against the influence of the Soviet Union and against the resurgent Shiʿism of the Iranian revolution. The result, however, is that US and the Saudis' support for *mujahidin* fighters inadvertently fostered the proliferation of loosely connected Islamist militant groups worldwide. This set the stage for the spread of Islamic militancy throughout the Middle East and North Africa during the 1990s; for the creation of al-Qaeda; and, ultimately, for the events of 9/11.

Conclusion

The argument in favor of a close relationship between Islam and the state has a long and varied history. Originally seen as a response to fragmentation and decline, in more recent years it has taken the form of sophisticated modern ideologies. At its core is the belief that the state ought to implement – and be guided by – Islamic values and laws. And this belief, in turn, can be found at the basis of increasingly common governments and policies around the globe. In practice, however, the close affiliation of religious authority and political power has proven to be divisive – unable to bring political unity to religiously diverse societies. The states examined in this section – Saudi Arabia, Pakistan, Iran, and Afghanistan – illustrate this trend. Ironically, their effort to cultivate political unity through religious uniformity has had the opposite effect: it has fueled sectarian division and pitted different members of the Muslim community against one another. The human rights abuses affiliated with these regimes, however, ought not to be used to indict either Islamic religion or the desire to have a politics informed by religious values. The secular governments discussed in the previous chapter have not offered more humane forms of rule, particularly if one takes into account Saddam Hussein's Iraq or Assad's Syria.

It is also important to remember that the debates reviewed here are not unique to Islam but are a common feature of human history. The proper relationship between religion and state and the problem of which religion ought to be given precedence in public life informed the religious wars of Europe that pitted Protestants against Catholics and ripped the continent apart in earlier centuries. Moreover, these questions inform the culture wars of contemporary American politics, where secular Americans find themselves to be at odds with religious conservatives. In that context, debates about whether the United States is a Christian or a secular nation are strikingly similar to the debates transpiring throughout the Islamic world.

Perhaps what this section illustrates above all is the difficulty of living up to professed ideals and the fallibility of political leaders. Believing that God is on one's side may be empowering, but, if it justifies actions that are morally objectionable and that contravene basic elements of the faith, such a belief is likely to be wrong. In instances of this sort it is not religion that is the problem, but rather human arrogance, greed, and lust for power. Religion may have an enormous impact upon politics in such a context, but it is also clear that political manipulation has impacted religion adversely.

Notes

1 For purposes of clarity, this chapter will tend to use the term "Islamist" to refer to fundamentalist groups, ideas, or individual activists.
2 The hudud punishments derive from the Qur'an, which prescribes severe corporal punishment for offenses such as adultery, the drinking of alcohol, theft, and bearing false witness – namely punishment through flogging (whipping), the severing of hands, or stoning. Interestingly, John Esposito (1998: 173) notes that amputations did not occur during this period because physicians in Pakistan refused to carry out court orders to this effect.

Discussion Questions

1 What are the arguments in favor of a close relationship between religious and political authority within the Islamic tradition? Are these arguments persuasive? Is a "traditionalist" state a more authentic rendering of the Islamic political tradition? What are the pros and cons?
2 How has the legacy of European colonial rule affected Muslim views on the secular state and on the traditionalist state? Why do Islamists believe that the need for an Islamic (or traditionalist) state is self-evident regardless of the institutional "content" of the state?
3 What are the differences between Iran's form of government and that of Saudi Arabia? In what are they similar, and in what do they differ? Does either live up to the ideal of an Islamic state envisioned by Hasan al-Banna or Mawlana Mawdudi?
4 What are the concerns regarding the application of Islamic law (*sharia*)? How have these concerns been manifest in countries like Iran? Does the human rights record of Iran (or countries such as Sudan) justify the broader critique of the Islamist vision, or is it simply a failing of the ruling elite?
5 What is the Velayat e-faqih, and why is it such a novel concept?
6 How have debates over the relationship between religion and political authority played out in contexts with religious traditions different from Islam? Would your views on this debate be different if one were to discuss your faith tradition?

Suggested Further Reading

Abu-Rabi, Ibrahim M. (1996). *Intellectual Origins of Islamic Resurgence in the Modern Arab World*. New York, NY: State University of New York Press.

Ayoob, Mohammad (2007). *The Many Faces of Political Islam: Religion and Politics in the Muslim World*. Ann Arbor, MI: University of Michigan Press.

Ayubi, Nazih (1993). *Political Islam: Religion and Politics in the Arab World*. New York, NY: Routledge.

Belkeiziz, Abdelilah (2009). *The State in Contemporary Islamic Thought: A Historical Survey of the Majro Muslim Political Thinkers of the Modern Era*. New York, NY: I. B. Tauris.

Brown, L. Carl (2001). *Religion and State: The Muslim Approach to Politics*. New York, NY: Columbia University Press.

Donohue, John, and John Esposito (2006 [1982]). *Islam in Transition: Muslim Perspectives*. New York, NY: Oxford University Press.

Esposito, John (1998). *Islam and Politics*, 4th ed. Syracuse, NY: Syracuse University Press.

Eubens, Roxanne (1999). *Enemy in the Mirror: Islamic Fundamentalism and the Limits of Modern Rationalism*. Princeton, NJ: Princeton University Press.

Fadl, Khaled Abu (2007). *The Great Theft, Wrestling Islam from the Extremists*. Harper Collins Publishers.

Feldman, Noah (2008). *The Fall and Rise of the Islamic State*. Princeton, NJ: Princeton University Press.

Flores, Alexander (1997). Secularism, integralism, and political Islam. In Joel Beinin and Joe Stork (eds.), *Political Islam: Essays from Middle East Report*. Berkeley: University of California Press.

Hourani, Albert (1983). *Arabic Thought in the Liberal Age*. Cambridge, UK: Cambridge University Press.

Mitchell, Richard (1993). *The Society of the Muslim Brothers*. New York, NY: Oxford University Press.

Qutb, Sayyid (2000). *Milestones*. Cedar Rapids, IA: Mother Mosque Foundation.

Rutherford, Bruce (2008). *Egypt after Mubarak: Liberalism, Islam and Democracy in the Arab World*. Princeton, NJ: Princeton University Press.

8

Muslims as Minorities in the West

Aminah Beverly McCloud

Introduction

Muslims living as minorities in the West face several dilemmas, all of which stem from the competing pressures of integration on the one hand and exclusion on the other. The first issue involves the ongoing question of assimilation and of the degree to which one can, or should, relinquish former customs and cultures in

An Introduction to Islam in the 21st Century, First Edition. Edited by Aminah Beverly McCloud, Scott W. Hibbard, and Laith Saud.
© 2013 Blackwell Publishing Ltd. Published 2013 by Blackwell Publishing Ltd.

order to integrate into Western society. Conversely, within dominant populations there is always resistance – often coupled with a high degree of intolerance – toward minority cultures, and this precludes a full embrace of diverse populations and peoples. Even if individuals and communities wish to integrate, there is the question of whether or not they will be accepted by the majority community. Instances of discrimination and abuse – which are evident in the rise in Islamophobia discussed in Chapter 15 – are symptomatic of this latter issue. Such phenomena highlight a key challenge for Western societies and the values they espouse. The treatment of Muslims as second-class citizens in the West represents a "challenge [to] the popular notion most Western countries have of themselves as plural, tolerant, secular and modern [...]" (Ahmed 1993).

The United States is home to the largest indigenous population of Muslims in the West and this has created unique challenges, which are different from those of groups that migrated from other countries. The large African American Muslim population in the US has had to deal with issues of racial discrimination and with the legacy of slavery, as well as with religious intolerance. In Europe, the three countries with the largest Muslim populations are the UK, France, and Germany. In the UK and in France most of these communities come from former colonies, whereas Germany's large Turkish population migrated after World War II. Muslims in these countries are refugees, entrepreneurs, freedom seekers, opportunists, and political exiles – to name just a few of the categories into which they fall. Most did not leave their homelands in search of religious freedom; however, issues of religious freedom and the right to build houses of worship permeate their existence in the West.

The relationships between Western societies and the minority communities they host are complicated by the fact that Muslims who have migrated to the West frequently come from places that had previous relations with the West, and these relations were often hostile. Such relations have been captured in negative stereotypes, in prejudices, and in a lingering perception that Islam (and Islamic civilization) is a rival to Christianity. Nonetheless, most Muslims are drawn to the West by their search for solace, freedom, economic opportunity, and political stability. Like other immigrant communities, Muslims seek to maintain their cultural habits and attitudes and to pass these values on to their children. However, this often puts them in tension with the dominant communities, as they resist cultural assimilation. Much of the perceived conflict of values, then, is indeed a conflict between traditional cultures (and the desire to retain them) and that of the secular West. Of course dissolute behavior, greed, and corruption, as well as the abuse of sex, alcohol, and drugs, are not found only in the West; nonetheless, Muslims from more traditional societies commonly equate these trends with the secularism that informs Western understandings of modernity.

Western countries in general have promoted themselves as lands of freedom, openness to all persons, liberty, and access to opportunity, education, and employment. These are some of the factors that draw migrants to Western society. However, Muslim minorities have found that their religion is frequently imposed upon them as a matter of identity, rather than their nationality – in other words they are identified as Muslim rather than as Indian or Algerian. This religious identity is frequently imbued with particular stereotypes. Fluctuating economic conditions also affect popular receptivity toward minority communities. When the economy is good, the adherence to the professed values of tolerance is high. Foreign workers, both professional and skilled, have even been recruited from countries all over the Muslim world. During times of economic decline, however, Western societies again become nativistic and have made those same skilled immigrant workers targets of fear and despair. Now, in the 21st century, many Muslim immigrants in the West are citizens under a microscope.

Our examination looks broadly at the most prominent issues raised in current research –

> ### Sidebar 8.1   East and West
>
> References to the "East" or the "West" reflect a Euro-centric categorization that differentiates between Europe and America (the West) and the Arab and Asiatic lands (the East). Although these terms designate geographical spaces, historically they have also accumulated assumptions about levels of economic, intellectual, and political development. One old essentialist argument against Islam is that it is intolerant, oppressive of women, and inimical to "the West" and its "Enlightenment" values; moreover, the religion determines all aspects of its believers' lives, in a way in which Christian faith and Judaism do not. This was central to the "clash of civilizations" thesis offered by Samuel Huntington in the early post-Cold War period.

education, the building of masajid (mosques), freedom of religious expression, and political opportunity in the United States, the UK, France, and Germany. Each of these states has its own particular history regarding post-Enlightenment ideals about the nature of citizenship, pluralism, and societal relations, and these ideals are firmly in place in the 21st century. Conversely, particular Muslim cultures have migrated to particular European states that have used many of those Enlightenment ideals to form viable and productive societies.

The United Kingdom and the United States

In the first decade of the 21st century both the United Kingdom and the United States experienced heightened tensions with Muslim residents and compatriots. The tragic events of September 11, 2001 and July 7, 2005 negatively reshaped understandings of multi-religious social and political engagements in both countries. On one hand, the necessity of inter-religious and inter-ethnic dialogues was apparent. On the other hand, both countries began to experience a resurgence of nativism, not in the citizenry as a whole, but by several very influential people, groups in government, and the media. The economic downturn following the financial collapse of 2008 has exacerbated such tensions.

Prior to September 11, both the UK and the US had largely been hospitable to immigrants, though their policies differed. Indeed Margaret Thatcher and Ronald Reagan had made both countries leaders in a "new world order," whose neoliberal policies provided an incentive for large numbers of Muslims to migrate. Public policies encouraged immigration, and the government made available a myriad of

Sidebar 8.2   The European Union

The European Union (EU) was created through the Maastricht Treaty and became effective from November 1, 1993. It is an international organization "comprising 27 European countries and governing common economic, social, and security policies" (Maastricht Treaty 1992). The purposes of the Union are to enhance European political, social, and economic integration, to project a unified foreign and security policy, and to advance cooperation in other areas such as immigration and judicial affairs. The first step toward the current EU was taken in 1951, when Belgium, France, Italy, Luxembourg, the Netherlands, and West Germany signed the Treaty of Paris; this treaty created the European Coal and Steel Community.

work visas that rendered engineers and computer software specialists from foreign countries eligible for citizenship. Though immigrants in both of these countries chafed under some of the assaults of racism and discrimination, these experiences were miniscule when compared to post-9/11 Islamophobia. Both the US and the UK embraced a degree of cosmopolitanism that welcomed diversity (though they dealt with it in competing ways). After 9/11 immigration policies were revisited, revised, and restricted. Improved surveillance techniques went into effect, along with improved "homeland security" policies. As a result, the lives of all citizens in both countries have changed forever.

Cultural pluralism in its various forms – multiculturalism, melting pots (forced assimilation), and so on – often did little to address the very real social issues generated by economic changes, and particularly the simmering anger over racism, discrimination, and prejudice that former immigrants (now citizens) continued to suffer. Such discriminatory treatment undermined the immigrants' pursuit or enjoyment of any success. For Muslims in both countries, the treatment had taken a curious turn. Most of them do not describe themselves as religious, yet all those born and/or practicing Islam were lumped together in the monolithic category of "Muslim." In the UK, however, because of the class origins of a majority of the country's former colonial subjects from South Asia, there are much higher numbers of those whose cultural habits suggest greater religious affiliation. There is also a tendency on the part of these communities to stay together. British Muslim enclaves are seen as Indian/Pakistani ghettos where the dress is ethnic, the language is Urdu, and the masajid is full of men on Friday prayer. How significant these observations are regarding the religious adherence of British Muslims as a whole is unknown. In the United States the angst is against Arabs and, subconsciously, the category "Muslim" is conflated with that of "Arab" almost universally, although there is no prior colonial relationship.

On the other hand, in the United States the number of self-identified "practicing" Muslims has been estimated liberally at 40 percent of roughly 6 million in official surveys, while researchers put the number at 10 percent. Many Muslims immigrated to the US as students and as professionals seeking highly paid employment. As a result, surveys (for instance Pew Forum on Religion and Public Life 2011) show that the average income in the immigrant Muslim community is higher than the average American income. Both the US and the UK are experiencing the presence of an unprecedented, extremely diverse population of Muslims from all over the world, but their attitudes toward this population are influenced by many old stereotypes and by a number of devastating new ones, which follow the patterns usually discernible in hard economic times. Extremely disconcerting is the fact that both countries designated all these people as "Muslims" rather than as members of an ethnic group. This is peculiar in view of the religious nature of the designation. For example, in the United States, Mexicans are Mexican, not Catholic or Protestant Christians; Puerto Ricans are who they ethnically are, not Christians; and so are Poles, Germans, or Brits. One other exception is the Jewish community, which is defined by Judaism, but Judaism is regarded both as an ethnicity and as a religion. In the 21st century, Muslims alone are defined by their religion alone, which is further qualified though stereotypes originating in the 18th century, and the media supports and fuel the transmission of these stereotypes in the 21st century.

This simultaneous bombing of three US targets in 2001, the US attacks on Afghanistan (2001) and Iraq (2003), and the subsequent subway and bus bombings in London in 2005 affected US and British societies in unprecedented ways. In the US, that these attacks were carried out by Muslim "extremists" – and were portrayed as an assault upon Western values – greatly damaged communal relations in both societies. It also opened the door for more resentment, physical assaults, and a targeting of Muslim communities as objects of law enforcement. And it contributed to a sharp

Sidebar 8.3   The great powers

Throughout the 20th century the list of the world's great powers has been predictably short: the United States, the Soviet Union, Japan, and Western Europe. The 21st century will be different. The list of great powers will also include formerly colonized nations such as China, India, and Brazil.

rise in Islamophobia – literally, the fear of Islam – and to the corresponding fraying of the cosmopolitan fabric of society. These trends were exacerbated by US media pundits and by some politicians who blamed all Muslims for the attacks and criticized their religion as a whole for fostering such antagonism. The British response was markedly different: the authorities only blamed those responsible as individual criminals and did not seek to extend the burden of culpability to the larger community. In both countries, a few vocal and influential politicians argued that Islam was an unwanted, potentially dangerous presence in the West, and they used their access to the media to foster anti-Islamic sentiments (as discussed in Chapter 14).

Both President George W. Bush and British Prime Minister Tony Blair contributed to this trend by defining the state of affairs at the beginning of the 21st century in ideological terms. For them, the so-called "war on terror" was a "struggle for civilization," and this created in their public's mind a vision of the West being under attack from Islamic militancy. While the two leaders made a distinction between the ideology of al-Qaeda and the tradition of Islam, others were not so judicious. The end result was a common perception that the Muslim world wanted to attack the freedoms enjoyed in the West. It is particularly ironic, then, that in pursuing this conflict, both governments readily abandoned many of the individual freedoms customary in their countries and engaged in an unprecedented surveillance of citizens and imposition of restrictions on their freedom of movement. Both societies put their immigration policies under review and severely restricted immigration from Muslim countries. As a result, the old tensions of the last decades of the 20th century have joined in and in some ways have been exacerbated by the violence that opened the 21st century.

Religious Expression

Freedom of religious expression has been of the utmost importance in both countries. After World War II religious pluralism was reflected in the variety of Protestant churches, and the question of religious freedom was focused primarily on willingness to tolerate both Catholicism and Judaism, without discrimination. Despite lingering anti-Semitism, Jews were largely integrated into societies where Christianity was dominant, both communities making accommodations to each other. The other challenge to religious expression in previous decades was the orientation of the secular state toward such expression and the various restrictions placed on the official ties between political authority and formal religion. The UK managed this delicate balance despite the establishment of the Anglican Church; and so did the US.

The United States gives constitutional guarantees for the freedom of religious expression and prohibitions against government interference. This is embodied in the first amendment of the US constitution, which prohibits the establishment of an official church (or religion), but also precludes any restrictions on the free exercise of religion. The UK offers no constitutional protections for one's religious freedom, but common law tradition is in firm support of religious pluralism, and thus of pluralistic religious expressions. Generally, Muslims have enjoyed the accommodations made in pervious eras; they have also sought to expand these basic freedoms so as to make them include Islam specifically. Unfortunately, violent events and actors in the Muslim world affect directly the Muslims living in the West. This is all the more problematic as some of these Muslims in the West are tied to "violent" people, organizations, and events – as was revealed in the case of the London bombings of July 2005. For instance, some Muslims living in the West had belonged to student organizations in the home country or had family members who had initiated or supported charitable foundations that were subsequently labeled "terrorists" by Western governments; thus the Muslims in question found themselves labeled as supporters of terrorism. Additionally, religious communities, especially in the United States, found themselves challenged by rapidly growing secular demands in the public sphere.

A particularly interesting example of the UK's approach to multiculturalism can be found in the existence of courts that rule on matters of personal law. Taking advantage of a clause in the UK Arbitration Act of 1996, the Muslim Arbitration Tribunal (MAT) runs *sharia* courts in London, Bradford, Birmingham, Manchester, and Nuneaton. This five-court network rules on cases ranging from divorce and financial disputes to ones involving domestic violence. The MAT is considered an alternative dispute resolution program, and being classified this way allows it to operate in a manner that is not perceived as supplanting British common law. Jewish Beth Din courts have operated in the same way for more than 100 years. Such trends, however, are not found in the US. On the contrary, there is a current of hostility toward multiculturalism in the US, where greater emphasis is placed on assimilation than on allowing distinct communities to exist outside of the dominant culture. This hostility toward genuine diversity in the use of religious law as a form of religious expression is manifest in anti-*sharia* movements that are going on in a dozen states. This is in stark contrast to uses of religious law by Christian and Jewish communities.

Education

Education is critical to social cohesion in multicultural and multi-faith societies. The state school system is the primary mainstream social institution through which young people can have sustained contact with one another. Education is also a key factor in determining opportunities for future employment and career. In the UK, the main educational issues that worry Muslim parents are the poor academic results of their children in state schools, the need to eradicate institutional racism (racist or Islamophobic bullying), the lack of recognition or support for their children's faith identity, and the inadequacy of the spiritual and moral education provided in state schools. These issues are not limited to one country. For instance, events involving the bullying of Muslim schoolchildren by their classmates, with the support of their teachers, have occurred both in the UK and in the US. Sometimes such incidents have had tragic results.

In general Muslims oppose a purely secular education, which is devoid of shared religious values. More specifically, they oppose state schools that, in one form or another, teach Christian religious values alone, omitting the values of other faiths. The general public in the UK and in the US has been made aware that this is not only a matter of texts and students, but one involving the teachers' and school administrators' attitudes toward Islam and Muslims.

The UK provides financial support for its religious schools. This phrase has traditionally encompassed Christian schools and a few Jewish schools. Muslims have had to petition strenuously for the same benefits and have been put under special scrutiny. In the US Muslim parochial schools have generally not relied on, or expected, any of the benefits enjoyed by other religious schools. This is in spite of the long US legal history of making specific accommodations for religious schools. The most recent debates have been over the content of social studies texts regarding Islam and Muslims. Both parochial and state schools use the same texts, and those that include Islam are being investigated for biases.

In the UK it is reported that the levels of academic achievement of Muslim students are low, but improving. Explanations for these low levels are usually framed around factors such as poverty, social deprivation, and language difficulties, but there are further obstacles to Muslim children's full achievement of their potential, obstacles that relate more specifically to their experiences as Muslims. These obstacles are the prevalence of religious prejudice and Islamophobia; the lack of Muslim role models in schools; the low expectations that some teachers have of Muslim students; and the lack of recognition for the students' Muslim identity.

In the US the picture is slightly different. While Islamophobia prevails in some school districts, in others many school administrators and teachers have gone out of their way to make their Muslim students feel comfortable. Perhaps due to the educational and professional levels of many Muslim parents, Muslim students tend to be among the highest achievers in schools. A legal prohibition on teachers and administrators wearing religious garb has had a detrimental effect on the presence of female Muslim teachers in public schools. The problem generated in the UK by the absence of Muslim role models in schools is somewhat ameliorated in the US through the presence of African American Muslim administrators and teachers.

The school curriculum has an important role to play in encouraging cross-cultural understanding. Two shifts in the curriculum might help to make this happen. The first would be a more global focus, whereby European, American, and Christian culture could be contextualized in terms of world civilization. The second would be the inclusion of references to Muslim contributions to European learning and culture, particularly in the fields of art, literature, mathematics, geometry, science, history, philosophy, astronomy, and medicine.

Masajid-Building and Political Participation

An estimated 1.6 million Muslims live in England, Wales, and Scotland, and there is roughly one masajid or one prayer room for every 1,000 Muslims. On the whole, masajid-building has not been particularly controversial in the United Kingdom, but it has been something of an issue from time to time. Most of the antagonism comes from resident and business complaints around traffic snares and parking spaces. Sometimes, in some cities, Muslims are even given first choice on a piece of land. This state of affairs is closely tied to the building of resources by local organizations.

The situation in the United States now, at the beginning of the 21st century, is different. After 9/11 residents were goaded by conservative politicians to be alarmed about any masajid building and to regard it as part of a program of "stealth Islamization" of the country. As a result, since 2008, 39 proposed masajid and community centers have faced significant resistance (as reported in the Pew Forum on Religion and Public Life 2011). It is estimated that there are at least 2,000 masajid in the US today, without counting various other prayer spaces or rooms, which serve approximately 6 million Muslims. Many of the fears invoked by residents echo the rhetoric of republican politicians. The building of a masajid is thus perceived as an impending threat of *sharia* takeover.

The political participation of Muslims is steadily increasing in both countries. In the UK, Muslim communities are concentrated geographically, which assists in maintaining a separate institutional and economic infrastructure for perpetuating religious and cultural norms. This geographic concentration also secures the resources for a political base at the local level, which allows these communities to negotiate with local politicians and other residents. The community groups have studied the political strategies of other well-organized groups in the UK, and this has greatly increased their effectiveness. Muslim community groups published their own first voter guide in 1997. This started, and then facilitated a process of educating the larger communities about candidates who were sympathetic to their problems. There are two Muslim Members of Parliament (MPs), 217 Muslim councillors out of 25,000, and the government recently appointed its first two Muslim Members of the House of Lords. All this has happened despite the fact that Muslims are not well organized at the national level. They are divided by language, race, theology, and national origin. Unity at local levels comes directly from communities of the same national origin. There are serious efforts to get beyond these obstacles, and the Labour government provided assistance in the years prior to losing its Parliamentary majority in 2010. As mentioned previously, British Muslims, unlike US ones, are in general disadvantaged by economic deprivation and low educational attainment. Nevertheless, with the help of state structures in the UK that can intervene and assist, the future looks bright.

In the US, at the national level, two African American Muslims serve the nation, while at the state level there are ten Muslim representatives. It is forecast that, despite the rhetoric of the Republican Party, these numbers will increase in the 2012 elections.

France and Germany

Just as in Britain, the Muslim communities that settled in France have largely come from former colonies of North Africa and the Levant. In Germany, on the other hand, most Muslims migrated from Turkey. This was a direct consequence of treaties signed in the 1950s and 1960s, which were consciously designed to encourage immigration with a view to rebuilding the country's workforce, devastated as it had been during World War II. Politically and legally, France and Germany require the state to remain neutral in religious affairs and to protect citizens' individual rights of religious expression. Both France and Germany, however, have made concessions to Catholic and Protestant Christianity and to Judaism in matters of support for schools and the building of houses of worship. The impetus for religious freedom in these countries is rooted in the bitter history of their religious wars and in the corresponding recognition that social peace in multi-religious societies requires, at a minimum, tolerance and equal rights of religious expression.

France and Germany, as well as most of Western Europe, are subject to the secularizing trend of recent decades. This is reflected in declining church attendance, lower church membership, and a diminished emphasis on personal faith. Religious belief has increasingly been consigned to the private sphere, even if these societies do have an established church and religion continues to affect public policy. In France, for example, the Catholic Church is the established church, while Germany has a de facto plural religious establishment through its acknowledgment of religious corporations.

Sidebar 8.4   *Laïcité*

Laïcité ("secularism") is a concept that renders the French interpretation of the secular tradition, and it is defined by a sharp separation between church and state. The concept emerged out of the French Republic's desire to minimize the continuing influence of the Catholic Church on state and society alike. Subsequently *laïcité* came to differentiate between the public and the private sphere and to restrict religion to the latter. This differentiation was seen to be essential for the protection of freedom of religion and freedom of thought. As Olivier Roy has noted, however, *laïcité* does not necessarily entail the rejection of religious values or of a broader notion of the sacred. Rather, the political doctrine entailed by this concept simply "aims to free political, but also public, space from religious control. [It] does not aim to replace religious discourse by a new ethics [...]" (Roy 2007: 22). *Laïcité* has become controversial in recent years because of the manner in which it has been interpreted, particularly in the context of debates over headscarves and other outward symbols of personal faith. Many perceive this manner as discriminatory and as an infringement on the individual religious freedom it is supposed to protect.

Of all of the countries that, after the Enlightenment, made efforts to achieve a separation between church and state, France is the only one to engage in this process through the law. *Laïcité* is promoted as a concept blind to religion and race in public social and policy matters. Nevertheless, the Catholic Church remains, and the tension between state and church subsists as well. *Laïcité* defines religion in sociological and cultural terms rather than as a part of personal identity: the citizens of France are first and above all else French.

As in England and the United States, in France too Muslims began to arrive in significant numbers after 1960. Many of the country's imperialist / colonialist efforts in the Muslim world had been expended in North and West Africa. Although its colonies stretched to Southeast Asia (most notably to Indochina, or today's Vietnam), French colonists settled in Algeria in relatively large numbers and governed the neighboring countries of Tunisia and Morocco. After the Algerian War of Independence (1954–1962), hundreds of thousands of Algerians who fought on the side of France were granted asylum and fled to France. About another million laborers (Senegalese, Algerian, Moroccans, Tunisians, Ivoirians) subsequently migrated to France, in search of work in a growing post-World War II economy. France granted citizenship to asylum seekers and others, who worked their way through the immigration process. This is different both from the situation in the United States – which imported highly professional Muslim workers along with opening the doors to immigrants and issued citizenships through regularized (though tedious) policies – and from the situation in England, where citizenship was extended to former colonial subjects. In all three countries, however, Muslim populations have expanded through legal birthrights, illegal entrants, and the exceptional cases in which family reunifications were allowed.

The values embodied in the concept of *laïcité* and the public policies it generated have caused some of the most significant tensions between French Muslims and the state. The French model of societal organization is based on the belief that any recognition of "difference" can lead to the division of society into a number of antagonistic factions. As a result, the French approach to immigration is one of stressing assimilation and the adoption of French mores and customs – in contrast to the British emphasis on multiculturalism. Challenges to this approach started to appear early on in the mid-20th century. One case that rose to national attention was that of Amadou Diop, who at the age of 23 signed up as a volunteer in the French army in Senegal in 1940. African recruits were treated like French soldiers until they docked at Marseille. Remarkably these veterans, victims of unequal treatment, received pensions until 1959; then their pensions were frozen, while French veteran pensions rose with inflation. Amadou Diop sued for his 22-year severance pay in 1996, and after five years of postponements he won (though he died before receiving notification). For some people of color and for those religious individuals whose adherence spills over into the public space, French ideals are hollow at best.

In Germany Islam was treated as a "guest religion" for many decades, and thus the state had no obligation to accommodate Muslims under the law. Until recently, the religious needs of a growing Muslim population were either neglected or referred to the immigrants' home country – Turkey. Joel Fetzer and Christopher Soper (2004) assert that the German church–state system strikes a middle ground between Britain's established church and France's *laïcité*.

Education

All discussion and debate on the education of Muslims in France centers on a small number of schoolgirls who wish to wear scarves over their heads. Although there are many other issues, this one topic has generated the greatest amount of attention and controversy. France's foundational legal documents guarantee freedom of religion to all French citizens. Unlike in Britain but like in the United States, in France the national curriculum does not include religion as a formal subject, nor does it provide for religious education after school. Islam itself only appears in one unit, namely in the French curriculum for the *cinquième* history and geography class. Due to the early start of children's education in secularist values, boys and girls sleep in the same room on overnight field trips, and in some schools they take their physical education classes together, including swimming. Many Muslim parents are extremely uncomfortable with this situation. In Germany, as in Britain, religion is included in the national curriculum. The subject does not, however, encompass all major world religions. The separation of church and state is taken there to mean not taking a stance on religious doctrine, but just helping the churches teach their own doctrines by employing in schools teaching staff selected by the churches themselves (Fetzer and Soper 2004).

Thus the churches select both the teachers and the textbooks for the teaching of religion in German schools. Parents can enroll their children for an Evangelical Protestant course or for a Roman Catholic one, or they may withdraw their children entirely from religion courses (Fetzer and Soper 2004). Unfortunately for the Muslim children, there are no religion courses on Islam; they receive instead courses in general religious studies, and even this feature varies from one local government to the next. As the obvious needs of a diverse population have been brought to the attention of authorities, some teachers have begun to plead for an inter-religious education.

Metropolitan France does not have any state-funded Islamic schools, although it does have Catholic and Jewish parochial schools that receive state funds. The French government has set a series of criteria that, it claims, Muslim schools have been unable to meet. These criteria are: acceptance of students from any religious background, coupled with the voluntary nature of attendance at in-school religious instruction and practice; a general curriculum similar to that used in public schools; and proof of a continuous five-year history, during which the school had a large number of students (Fetzer and Soper 2004). Though a few Muslim schools did meet all of these criteria, so far the authorities have failed to approve any of the applications for state funding. There are, however, privately funded Islamic schools.

Masajid-Building and Political Participation

In France, as in the US, local political opposition has weakened Muslims' efforts to build new masajid or to convert existing buildings into places of worship (Fetzer and Soper 2004). Nevertheless, places of worship continue to increase in number – but not rapidly enough to keep up with the growing numbers of French Muslims who need to use them. In 2001 about 2,000 masajid were reported to exist in France, while 150 were in the process of being built. Many former Catholic churches have turned into masajid (Fetzer 2004), and Muslims are asking to pray in Catholic churches that are now empty. This situation arose through lack of space: Muslims were forced to have their Friday prayers in the streets, where they caused traffic disruption. Ironically, members of the Catholic clergy were the ones who asked city officials in cities such as Lyons to assist Muslims in getting buildings: they argued that it is psychologically damaging for Catholics to convert their empty churches into masajid.

Elections of right-wing politicians, along with violence in the Muslim world, have been the two most damaging factors hindering the efforts of French Muslims to become an integral part of France's religious landscape. Anti-immigration officials and racists have taken to the streets, attempting to force the government to reaffirm its commitment to *laïcité* and to deport its Muslim citizens. The recent election of left-wing President François Hollande has already initiated a policy change through the appointment of three Muslims to his cabinet.

One frequently raised topic regarding the political participation of Muslim citizens in both France and Germany is that of their lack of participation in the historical compromises that led to the inherited religious establishment. The French model of a strict separation between church and state has limited the ability of Muslim groups to take their case for public recognition of their religious rights directly to the state. Regarding its political ideology, the concept of *laïcité* represents a very powerful reality, both for the elite and for the general population. France's secular, republican creed shuns notions of special lobbies or communities, although it clearly has tackled such notions with other religious communities. In addition to not receiving funding for Islamic schools, Muslims are unable to get aid for Muslim social service organizations either.

In Germany the church–state policy legacy has been relatively amenable to Muslim religious demands – at least potentially, though not in actuality. The question there, as in Britain and France, is whether the state is willing to expand its formal religious establishment so as to consider Islam as a public corporation despite the fact that Muslims were not party to the original compromises that enabled a more positive church–state relationship. In 2006 the German government decided to move the issue of Islam to the top of the political agenda. After a long period of outsourcing the responsibility for Islamic life in Germany to institutions in the countries of origin, attempts are now being made at de-transnationalization with regard to religious matters.

Conclusion

As noted in the introduction, the immigration of Muslims to the West is character-ized by certain fundamental tensions. These include the challenge of integrating or becoming assimilated into the culture of the dominant community or, alternatively, of resisting and remaining apart from mainstream society. There are also obstacles within Western societies to genuinely embracing minority communities, particularly if that requires tolerating diverse expressions of religious faith. None of these chal-lenges is easy to deal with, but they do reflect the core issues associated with the migration of peoples. Moreover, as we have seen, different countries have dealt with these challenges in different ways. In the United Kingdom the emphasis on multicul-turalism – tolerating and attempting to embrace distinctive communities and cul-tures – has often limited the ability of minority communities to genuinely integrate; they remained instead isolated in enclaves. France – a country that ostensibly empha-sizes complete assimilation – has nonetheless faced its own problems with integrating minority communities; for instance, it left many of them economically marginalized. Germany and the United States have both encouraged immigration at different points in time, but, like the others, they find genuine tolerance and inclusion a continuing challenge. Despite the widespread adoption of religious neutrality and of secularism understood as an attitude of non-discrimination in matters of religion, genuinely embracing the diversity in our midst continues to be a value more commonly sup-ported in theory than in practice.

Discussion Questions

1   What are the relative merits of the different approaches to Muslim immigrants discussed above?

2   Is multiculturalism a more effective approach to social harmony than assimilation, or is it the other way around? What are the pros and cons of each approach?

3   Why do some see the constructions of mosques (masajid) as being so threatening to their society? How can such an opposition be addressed constructively?

4   Is the French vision of *laïcité* so different from other countries' approach to secularism? How does it compare with the United States' separation of church and state?

Suggested Further Reading

Ahmed, Akbar [presenter] (1993, May). *Living Islam* [six-part series]. BBC Two.

Al-Azmeh, Aziz (2008). *Islam in Europe.* New York, NY: Cambridge University Press.

Fetzer, Joel and J. Christopher Soper (2004). *Muslims and the State in Britain, France, and Germany.* New York, NY: Cambridge University Press, 2004.

Gilliat-Ray, Sophie (2010). *Muslims in Britain: An Introduction.* Cambridge: Cambridge University Press.

Huntington, Samuel P. (1996). *The Clash of Civilizations.* New York, NY: Simon & Schuster.

Leiken, Robert (2001). *Europe's Angry Muslims: The Revolt of The Second Generation.* New York, NY: Oxford University Press.

Maastricht Treaty (1992). Treaty on European Union. At http://eur-lex.europa.eu/en/treaties/dat/11992M/htm/11992M.html (accessed Sptember 20, 2012).

The Pew Forum on Religion and Public Life (2011). At www.pewforum.org/topics/religious-Affiliation/Muslim/ (accessed September 20, 2012).

Roy, Olivier (2007). *Secularism Confronts Islam.* New York, NY: Columbia University Press.

Part III

Regional Studies

9

Islam in Africa

Babacar Mbengue

Outline

An Introduction to Islam in the 21st Century, First Edition. Edited by Aminah Beverly McCloud, Scott W. Hibbard, and Laith Saud.
© 2013 Blackwell Publishing Ltd. Published 2013 by Blackwell Publishing Ltd.

Introduction

About one in every five Muslims (in total, between 400 and 450 million of them) lives on the African continent. In 2010 the Pew Research Center revealed that more than 230 million among them live in countries south of the Sahara (Pew Research Center 2009: 19). Today, Muslims represent the overwhelming majority of the population in all countries located in North Africa and in most countries of the western part of the Sahel, a region stretching from the Atlantic Ocean in the west to the Horn of Africa in the east, from the southern fringes of the Sahara desert in the north to the wet Savannah in the south. Muslims are also predominant in Sudan, Chad, and Tanzania. They represent important minorities in numerous countries throughout the African continent (Ottayek and Soares 2009: 10–13; see Map 9.1).

The division of Islam, along geographic lines, into a core and a periphery has been an almost classic feature of most studies of Islam in the West. Albeit academically convenient, such an approach usually fails to capture the originality and dynamism of the history of Islam and of scholarship in Africa. Due mainly to its Arabic heritage, North Africa is often treated as a part of the core of Islam, which leaves the rest of the continent on the periphery. This conception of Islam in Africa, which neglects a host of diverse representations, often implies a reified and static religious phenomenon. Islam in Africa, or what is sometimes suggestively called "African Islam," is in reality understood as sub-Saharan Islam. In its relationship with "core Islam" (Islam in Arab lands) it has generally been perceived at best as an echo chamber, a backyard of sorts, where issues already dealt with in the "core" regions receive a second life.

According to that perception, it is in Sufism that the localized African Islam finds its best form of expression, especially Sufism understood as the most ecstatic dimension of Islam. In many cases indeed, the recognizable Sufi dimensions of Islam in Africa are viewed as a mere veneer, a legitimization of rituals going back to pre-Islamic traditions that are deeply entrenched in the African. As a matter of fact, Sufism has not been, historically, the predominant form of Islamic practice anywhere on the continent. In many parts of the Sahel, for example, the establishment of Islamic practices has been documented well before Sufism became part of mainstream Islam. Important Khariji, Sunni, and Shi'i communities existed in that part of the continent as early as the 10th century. Sufism, especially organized Sufism in the form of brotherhoods, did not start to take hold until the beginning of the 17th century. African Muslims across the continent, just like their counterparts in other Muslim cultures, have incorporated a blend of the spiritual practices of Sufism into Islamic legal norms. Sufism is understood to bring a spiritual augmentation to normative Islamic life, not to suppress it. Even as Sufism grew and became an important aspect of Islam in Africa, the scholarly contributions of African Muslims in building Sufism are often overlooked.

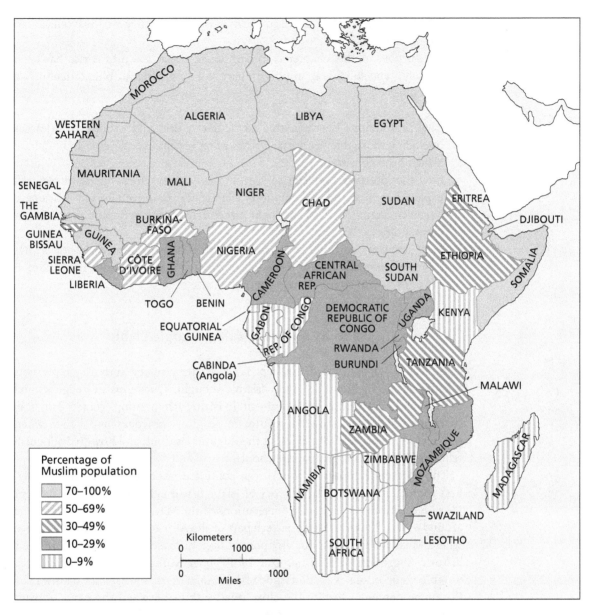

Map 9.1   The Muslim population in Africa.

It is important to emphasize African agency in shaping Islam, and this is what the present chapter proposes to do. Certainly the vastness of the African continent and the diversity of its people and experiences represent a formidable challenge for any attempt at capturing the multi-faceted Islamic experiences on that continent into one single framework of study. Thus our analysis of Islam in Africa will deliberately take strong regional biases. Here we will focus on those regions where historical and modern contributions to the body of Islamic knowledge have been the greatest and where issues and concerns in the 21st century are most relevant to our volume as a whole.

The purpose of this chapter is to demonstrate that Islam in Africa has been historically – and still is – an important part of a global Islamic phenomenon. We will examine:

- how interactions between this particular region and other Islamic areas (including those that are variably seen as representative of "core Islam") have always been consistent;
- how the interplay between reform and continuity works in Islam: we will explore how past and contemporary Islamic reform movements in Africa have been consistently crafted and legitimized across many generations of Muslim communities;
- how activism and quietism in the context of Muslim Africa did not always espouse uniformly one or the other of the two dominant aspects of Islam in the region – Sufism or Sunni legal thought.

Islam in Africa: A Kaleidoscopic Debut

The diversity of cultures that accept Islam as the primary authority represents a kaleidoscope of blends of early Islamic thought. Questions of religious and political authority were most prominent. In Islam such questions centered on how to choose leadership, how to legitimate religious practices and belief when teachers were coming from different theological positions, and how to distinguish relationships between competing schools.

The northeastern part of the African continent, more precisely Ethiopia, figures prominently in the early history of Islam. It was in Ethiopia that the nascent Muslim community fleeing the persecutions of the Meccans found its first refuge around 615 CE. This makes the eastern part of the African continent the first place where Muslims lived without any persecution, at least seven years before their historic migration to Medina. One of Prophet Muhammad's first and most notable companions was the famous first muezzin of Islam, Bilal, who was of Ethiopian descent. Despite the close relationships between the early Muslim community and some parts of the African continent, Islam did not, however, become a major religious movement in Africa until after the multi-phased conquest of Mediterranean Africa, starting with the conquest of Egypt in 641 CE. The relatively rapid introduction and consolidation of Islam in Mediterranean Africa and the latter's subsequent Arabization turned out to be exceptional phenomena in the African history of Islam in that, generally speaking, elsewhere on the continent Islam spread progressively and through relatively peaceful means, especially along commercial routes.

The direct contacts between the already Islamized North African merchants and the populations living on the southern edges of the Sahara Desert – contacts made through the age-old trans-Saharan commercial routes – were vital for the expansion of Islam into the Sahel. The advent of Islam in the northern part of the continent seemed to have expanded and consolidated the commercial links between the regions on both sides of the Sahara. Unlike in Mediterranean Africa, where Islamization generally followed an east–west direction, in central and western Sudan Islam moved progressively from the border regions of the Sahara southwards, from the savanna of the Soudano-Sahelian region to the edges of the Guinean rainforest. This

> ### Sidebar 9.1   The Sahel
>
> Derived from the word *sāhil*, which means "coast, litoral" in Arabic, the name Sahel designates the region of Africa immediately south of the Sahara Desert, which was considered for a long time to be a sea. This is the sub-Saharan region that first came into contact with Islam. It extends east–west from the Atlantic to the Indian Ocean and north–south from the fringes of the Sahara to the fringes of the Sudanian savannas.

expansion of Islam over the course of many centuries was mainly the result of the combined actions of itinerant merchants, rulers, militants, charismatic scholars, and religious families. The effect, as might be expected, was an uneven spread of knowledge about Islamic beliefs and practices.

Yet despite the almost unfettered spread of Islam across the continent, there was resistance to it too. This phenomenon took several forms. The dislocations caused by the transition to Islam are most recognizable in disruptions of cultural integrity and authority, along with disruptions in knowledge transmission and religious legitimacy. Many cities – especially those located on the edges of the Sahara (both west and east), where trade was heaviest – were structured as twin cities. One side was Islamized and contained mosques and important Muslim communities, while the other side preserved the traditional architecture and cultural practices. For a time, these cities demonstrated dual authority. In Mali, for example, the king (*mansa*), who was Muslim, kept up residence in the traditional city while governing the whole of Mali – which indicated perhaps that some synthesis was necessary for identity. Other places were completely immune to the influence of Islam, yet they continued their commercial exchanges with Islamic cities and they maintained their networks in the north. Some communities chose to move to isolated regions. After the advent of Islam in parts of present-day Mali, for example, the Dogon moved into mountainous areas, in order to resist the new religion. Disputes over authority began to spark off between traditional wisdom and the new wisdom of Islam; these often implied a certain mastery of the Arabic language as well as some knowledge of the Qur'an and other important Islamic texts. These issues continue today.

The economic and political fortunes of many cities and places on both sides of the Sahara that were predominantly Muslim depended on their location on trans-Saharan trade routes. Until the rise of the Almoravid movement, which was strongly grounded in Sunni Islam, and until the Arabization of North Africa after Banu Hilal's invasion – two events that started in mid-11th century and produced a combined effect – Islam in sub-Saharan Africa mirrored North African Islam, which was essentially Khariji in character. In major sub-Saharan cities – such

Sidebar 9.2   The Kharijites

The Kharijites put forward the view that any Muslim could be the leader of the Muslim community. They also insisted that when a leader violated guidelines known from the example of Prophet Muhammad, that leader could be removed.

Sidebar 9.3   Maliki

Maliki here refers to the Maliki School of jurisprudence. This school relies on what Prophet Muhammad did and said in the second part of his prophethood, by way of guidance, in the city of Medina.

as Gao, Awdaghost, or Kumbi Saleh in the west, or Zaghawa in the east – Islam remained strongly influenced by Kharijism at least until the mid-11th century (Lewicki 1964). Kharijism had enjoyed a strong presence there thanks to its commercial strength – and also thanks to traveling teachers and relatively consistent diplomatic activities. After its decline another movement emerged in its place, and that movement was to become even stronger than its predecessor.

To begin with, the Almoravid movement took its inspiration from ʿAbdallah ibn Yasin, a jurist and scholar from the stronghold of al-Qayrawan (Kairouan or Kirwan) in North Africa, and then it rapidly gained momentum in the sub-Saharan state of Takrur, on the lower Senegal River. It did not take long for the movement to spread southwards into sub-Saharan Africa and northwards into almost all of North Africa and southern Spain. It was a Sunni Maliki movement, puritanical in its orientation, and it swept across the entire region and beyond; the bastions of Shiʿism and Kharijism on both sides of western and central Sahara were turned into predominantly Sunni Maliki areas. From then on, the prevalence of this school of religious law in the western and central parts of North and sub-Saharan Africa continued by and large undisturbed. Certainly, other forms of Islam – such as Sufism – would emerge later on; however, they never altered the underlying Sunni Maliki element, which remained fundamental to Islam in this region.

Islam in Africa in the Era of the Great Sudano-Sahelian States

Far from representing a barrier to trade, the Sahara Desert has long been used as a bridge, a transit point for the long-standing commercial links between North and sub-Saharan Africa (Lydon 2009). The spread of Islam certainly brought greater homogeneity in important sectors like the economy, because uniform commercial laws based on Islam became the norm on both sides of the Sahara. It is important to recall here that the trans-Saharan commercial routes pre-date Islam. But the Islamic expansion in the region surely helped in terms of establishing uniform commercial and cultural codes (Insoll 1996).

Naturally, the commercial relationships were accompanied by an important movement of people and ideas. As a transit point to the pilgrimage to Mecca, Egypt, an important Islamic center, counted a large community of people from sub-Saharan Africa, including a large contingent of students, especially during the period between the Tulunid and the Mamluk era (10th–16th centuries). Important numbers of sub-Saharans also lived in other key Islamic centers throughout North Africa. Successive states that existed in the Muslim-dominated Sahel between the 9th and the 16th centuries maintained important relationships with their counterparts north of the Sahara. One can mention the medieval empires of Takrur, Ghana, Mali, and Songhay among the Sudano-Sahelian states of that era whose history has been greatly influenced by Islam.

By the end of the 16th century Islam was well established in the Sahel from the Atlantic to Lake Chad. Many localities of the region were inhabited by Muslims who had come to Islam through different routes. Generally speaking, the first African Muslims arrived at Islam through interactions with Muslim traders from the north. The trans-Saharan commercial relationships played a major role in the introduction of Islam into the Sahel and further south. That first wave of Islamization was followed by another, which involved for the most part the ruling elites of important Sudano-Sahelian states.

Takrur, Ghana, and the Rise of the Almoravids

As previously stated, the history of Islam in the western and central Sudan has been marked very early on by the emergence of an important reform movement, which would ultimately sweep across major parts of the Muslim world and beyond: the Almoravid movement. This movement was initiated by Yahya ibn Ibrahim, a native Berber from the tribe of the Judala in western Sahara who wished to consolidate an orthodox Sunni Islam in the wider Sanhaja confederation to which his tribe belonged. (The Sanhaja was a nomadic confederation of Berber tribes such as the Masufa, the Lamtuna, and the Judala itself.) The Almoravid movement was spearheaded in 1039 by 'Abdallah ibn Yasin, a Sunni scholar from the Maliki School of jurisprudence. But ibn Yasin's puritanical and egalitarian views encountered fierce opposition from the Judala Berber leaders, who finally expelled him. Ibn Yasin then retreated south and allied himself with the leader of Takrur, Lebu, son and successor to War Jabi. He also managed to win the support of the Lamtuna, who were then in dispute with their Judala brethren and set out to conquer Sijilmasa in the north – a Khariji stronghold until then. Through the conquest of Sijilmasa, the Almoravid state increasingly gained political legitimacy, as is attested by the establishment of a mint where the Almoravid *dinār* (golden coin) was struck – in large part thanks to gold bullion coming from the Sudan. The movement gained strength in the Takrur, unified North Africa and Spain, and altered forever the nature of Islam in the Sudan, giving it its long-standing Sunni Maliki character. It also contributed to rerouting westwards important north–south trans-Saharan commercial routes from Awdaghost to Takrur, which ultimately allowed Takrur to experience some economic expansion. Certainly the fame of Takrur among some Arabic-language historians and other scholars seemed to have coincided with this new politico-religious situation. Awdaghost, a major trading post and city in Ghana, was conquered in 1054; then

Ghana's capital, Kumbi Saleh, fell to the Almoravids in 1076. This precipitated the fall of traditional Ghana, and the Sunni Maliki School became the predominant form of Islam in the western and central Sudan.

Sidebar 9.4   The Almoravid Empire

The Almoravid Empire extended over present-day Morocco, Mauritania, southern Spain and Portugal, present-day western Algeria, and a part of what is now Mali. The Almoravids have built the city of Marrakesh.

Among the Almoravids' maneuvers to consolidate power, one can detect a move away from the initial contestations of authority, and also new competition for authority inside the Muslim community. The Almoravids' call for a return to a puritanical Islam was mainly directed at the grassroots – first at the Berbers and the Sudano-Sahelians and subsequently at all people within their reach. Following the Almoravids, other movements of reform would emerge, such as that of the Almohads, but the ideas of Islamic reform that would most impact the Sudan – or, more precisely, some ruling elites of the Sudan – came mostly from scholars of the 16th century.

Mali and the Mansa

Once Ghana was defeated, the sub-region briefly fell under the domination of the kingdom of Sosso. Unlike Ghana, however, Sosso was not known to be particularly attracted to Islam; it was known rather as a kingdom where traditional African beliefs were predominant. The Sosso kingdom was to be relatively short-lived: around 1230 it would fall to the Mande, a largely Islamized people. The Mande founded the state of Mali. Mali would eventually grow to comprise a territory at least three times the size of ancient Ghana; at its apogee, Mali's sovereignty stretched from the Atlantic in the west to the borders of today's northern Nigeria in the east and from the fringes of the Sahara Desert in the north to the borders of the Guinean forest in the south. Mali derived its strength mainly from control of the southern termini of the trans-Saharan trade routes. In the rest of the Muslim world, this new empire became famous essentially for the tradition of high-profile pilgrimages to Mecca that its rulers established. These pilgrimages served as opportunities to establish diplomatic ties with other Muslim states on the path to the holy sites of Islam and to gain a favorable opinion from the ordinary Muslims in and around those sites. They also created an opportunity for intellectual exchanges between the Sudan and the rest of the Muslim world. It was under the reign of Mansa Musa (1312–1337) that such exchanges with the Muslim world south of the Mediterranean intensified. Mansa Musa commissioned

---

Sidebar 9.5   Mansa Musa

Mansa Musa was the ruler of Mali in 1324 who had, among his escort, a suite of up to 100 camels with a total load of gold estimated at 15 tons, which he liberally distributed in Cairo and other stops along the way to and from the holy sites of Islam.

a number of public and private works in major cities, for instance mosques-universities in cities like Jenne and Timbuktu and a palace in Niani, the capital of the empire. He developed a policy resolutely directed at promoting Islamic knowledge through scholarly connections with important Islamic cities in North Africa, such as Fez in Morocco. After Mansa Musa, Mali continued its relationships with Fez, which was dominated by the Sunni Maliki at the time, therefore consolidating the Sunni and Maliki tendencies in the Sudan.[1]

Important centers of learning with a focus on Sunni Maliki orthodoxy started to take shape in urban centers such as Walata, Jenne, Gao, and Timbuktu. At the time of Mali's decline, Timbuktu, which had been no more than a stop along one of the trans-Saharan commercial routes, grew into one of the most important Islamic centers of learning in the Muslim world. The combination of the Almoravids' past activities in the region in the 11th century, the expansion of the Mali polity, and the rise of a major center of Islamic training in the 14th century contributed to a greater uniformity of Islam in the Sudan. In the central and western Sudan Islam was thus increasingly characterized by greater adherence to Maliki orthodoxy, a homogenized regime of training for Muslim scholars, the rise of a typical Sudano-Sahelian Arabic script, the consolidation of a typical Sudano-Sahelian architecture – especially through the large number of public and private works commissioned by Mansa Musa in cities such as Jenne and Timbuktu – and a pronounced tendency toward Sufi Islam. The major issues of authority were settled through adherence to one school of jurisprudence, Maliki, and through a variety of spiritual experiences (especially Sufism). The beginning of Mali's decline in the early 15th century did not prevent the development of important centers of learning in the Sudan. Timbuktu's prestige among them subsisted and Islamic learning and scholarship quickly spread to modern-day Nigeria in the south.

Songhay and the Issue of Syncretism

Mali, already weakened by internecine fights over succession in the second half of the 14th century, clearly started to lose its sovereignty over some of its vassals in the western and southern parts of the empire. Indeed, at the turn of the 15th century, Songhay, until then a principality with its capital at Gao, increasingly started to assert its autonomy from the central power of Mali. The further weakening of the Malian central regime emboldened this quest for independence, which was led by the Sonni Dynasty. Under the leadership of Sonni Silman Dandi, Songhay even expanded its authority around the bend of the Niger River. Within a few years of his accession to the crown of Songhay in 1464, Sonni ʿAli Ber took over Timbuktu, which was already under the control of the Tuaregs around 1433. This move was apparently dictated by a call for help from the people of Timbuktu, who were facing exactions from the increasingly aggressive Tuaregs. Sonni ʿAli then embarked on an ambitious campaign of expansion of this new Songhay state; he captured other important cities, such as Jenne around 1473, and conquered more territories along the Niger River. At his death in 1492, after a 28-year reign,

Sonni ʿAli had established an empire at least equivalent to that of Mali. But his rule also inaugurated an unprecedented hostility toward Muslim scholars, especially in cities like Timbuktu, where Sonni ʿAli earned the unflattering title of *khariji* ("rogue"). This ruler is usually seen as representing a segment of the Sudan that was less favorable to Islam and more attached to traditional African beliefs.

Sonni ʿAli would be succeeded by his son Sonni Baro, whose leadership was quickly contested by one of his father's generals, Muhammad Ture. Muhammad took up arms against the newly appointed emperor and was declared leader of Songhay. He ushered in the rule of a new dynasty: the Askiya. Askiya Muhammad, as he would become known, promoted a resolutely pro-Islamic policy. A few years after assuming the leadership of Songhay, he resumed the high-profile imperial pilgrimage to the holy sites of Islam – a tradition inaugurated by the leaders of Mali. At his return from pilgrimage, freshly imbued with the desire to give an authentic Islamic imprint to his rule, Askiya Muhammad sent a series of questions on Islamic governance to three noted Islamic scholars of his day: the Maliki jurist ʿAqib ibn ʿAbd Allah al-Ansamuni of Takkeda, Muhammad ʿAbd al-Karim al-Maghili, and the Shafiʿi Jalal al-Din al-Suyuti from Cairo. The answers of al-Maghili seem to have had the farthest echo and are, not surprisingly, the ones that interested the historians the most. In fact al-Maghili – a Maliki jurist originally from Tuwat – advocated a non-compromising attitude toward both non-Muslim rulers and Muslim ones who mixed other beliefs or practices with Islam. In this he was unlike al-Suyuti, who sounded a little more accommodating on matters such as the legality of talismans. Al-Maghili's intolerance for what he saw as syncretism (*takhlīt*) and his position on issues to do with non-Muslims in Muslim-dominated lands were applied on the ground in Tuwat in 1492, shortly before his trip to Gao. At Gao al-Maghili met with Askiya Muhammad in 1498; then he proceeded south to Kano, where he advised its king, Muhammad ibn Rumfa. Even though al-Maghili's positions were not immediately implemented by Askiya Muhammad, they nonetheless remained relevant for key figures of militant Islam in the Sudan until well into the second half of the 19th century.

Askiya Muhammad's pro-Islamic policy was noticeable in his appointment of Islamic judges and in the establishment of Islamic courts in key areas of the Songhay Empire such as Timbuktu, Jenne, and other important cities. With these new appointments, Askiya Muhammad introduced a fully independent judicial authority essentially along the lines of Maliki orthodoxy, thereby making the Maliki School the official school of the empire. One should note, however, that a shift of sorts occurred in Sudan's scholarly relationships with Egypt. Egypt was ruled by the Mamluks to the detriment of the Maghreb, whose scholarship was seen as stagnant. The shift, which was apparent in Askiya Muhammad's choice of scholars to be consulted in matters of Islamic governance, could also be explained by the fact that Cairo was on the path to a pilgrimage to Mecca and many scholars in cities like Timbuktu and Jenne studied with 15th- and 16th-century scholars based in Cairo. The Shafiʿi exegete al-Suyuti, the Maliki jurist al-Maghili, and the Sufi al-Bakri had a considerable and enduring influence on Islamic learning in the Sudan.

Overall, Askiya Muhammad showed a lot of deference and generosity toward the Islamic scholars of the empire, in ways that indicated a greater role for Islam in the administration.

In 1528 the aging Askiya Muhammad who had lost his sight, was deposed. He was succeeded first by his son, Askiya Musa, and shortly afterwards by his nephew, Askiya Muhammad Benkan. Within the same decade, in 1537, Muhammad Benkan was deposed and the crown passed on to Isma'il, a son of the old Askiya Muhammad. This was another short-lived reign: one year later Isma'il died of natural causes and was succeeded by his brother Ishaq. In 1549 Ishaq died too, leaving another son of Askiya Muhammad, Dawud, to be the new Askiya. Both Ishaq and Dawud were devoted Muslims who had received a thorough Islamic education. It was especially under Askiya Dawud that Timbuktu reached its peak as a center of learning. With its three mosque-universities – Sankore, Jingerey Ber, and Sidi Yahya – Timbuktu boasted some of the most brilliant Islamic scholars of the day. The pursuit of Islamic learning at these universities and in other private schools was well supported and channeled into by the existence of a broad base of primary schools, whose number came close to 600 at the beginning of the 16th century.

During his 33 years of reign Askiya Dawud scored numerous military victories; thus he was able to consolidate the Songhay Empire and to promote his pro-Islamic policy fully. In the north, however, the Askiya had to face an increasingly unstable situation, especially regarding the termini of the trans-Saharan trade routes. In fact the fall of the Marinids and the rise of the Sa'dis (also as known Sharifians), coupled with the territorial advances and combined ambitions of the Portuguese, Spaniards, and Ottomans in the Mediterranean, left the lucrative trans-Saharan trade routes and their coveted gold supply more and more exposed to the ambitions of these new powers rising in the Mediterranean. Meanwhile Songhay maintained relatively good relationships with Morocco, which was under great pressure from Portugal. For example, as a gesture of friendship and support, Askiya Dawud sent ten thousand *mithqāl* of gold (the equivalent of 4.25 grams, or a dinar of pure gold) to the Sa'di sovereign of Morocco, Sultan Mawlay Ahmad al-Mansur, after his great victory over the Portuguese in 1578.

Askiya Dawud died in 1582 and was succeeded to the throne of Songhay by his son Askiya Muhammad Bani. Interestingly enough, al-Mansur imposed a period of official mourning, to be held at his court upon Dawud's death. Al-Mansur had the ambition of recreating – if not in the whole of Muslim Africa, then at least in parts of it – a caliphate similar to the one that the Abbasids had possessed between the 8th and the 11th century. In 1591 this ambition eventually pushed him to send across the Sahara Desert, to the south, an army of up to 4,000 soldiers armed with cannons and muskets, whose goal was to conquer Songhay and to take control of its lucrative gold and salt mines. Al-Mansur's army was led by Judar and met the army from Songhay at Tundibi near Gao. The latter's traditional weaponry proved to be no match for the former's firepower: Gao and important centers like Timbuktu fell to al-Mansur. On October 20, 1593 – which the people of Timbuktu have called "the Day of Tribulation" ever since – the Moroccan army took into custody the leading scholars of Timbuktu. Some died, others were taken to Marrakesh. The brilliant Ahmad Baba, for example, spent two years in jail there and afterwards was put under house arrest, where he remained until al-Mansur's death in 1607. He returned to Timbuktu in 1608 and died there in 1627. But Ahmad Baba's scholarship was not wasted on the Moroccans: he ended up imparting knowledge during his custody in Marrakesh, where he composed 40 of his books (these numbered more than 70 titles altogether).

Substantial wealth was taken from Songhay in the form of spoils of war. This helped al-Mansur pay his army in gold – he was already nicknamed "the Golden," al-Dhahabi, due to the value of his coinage – and undertake major construction projects in his kingdom. His invasion changed the face of Songhay forever, and with it that of western Sudan. For one thing, it turned what used to be the largest Sudano-Sahelian state in history into a handful of small political entities beset by problems of all kinds.

One of the motives given by al-Mansur for the invasion was the increasing pressure exerted by the rising European powers on Muslim lands situated in the southern part of the Mediterranean basin. Indeed by the second half of the 16th century the Portuguese had established a few ports in places like Arguin and a few trading posts along the Atlantic coast of the Sudan. These fledgling maritime points were ultimately intended to divert the commercial flux across the Sahara and to capture the supply of gold and slaves from the Sudan. The rise of the European powers was to culminate in the colonial enterprise, which peaked in the 19th century.

Sufism in Africa

After the Moroccan invasion and the subsequent fall of Songhay no major state of comparable size was to emerge in the Sudan ever again. Former Songhay dependencies such as the Muslim states of Kano, Katsina, or Zamfara gained greater autonomy, but the vacuum left by the disappearance of the empire seemed to exacerbate problems that were recurrent in the Sudan, such as slavery. Apparently the existence of smaller competing states increased instability in the region and their in-fights led to endemic enslavement. In 1614 Ahmad Baba called slavery "a great calamity whose adverse consequences have engulfed these times and these lands" (Hunwick and Harrak 2000: 58). The growing presence of the rising European maritime powers – the Portuguese, the Dutch, the Spanish, the French, and the British – in the Sudan did not alleviate matters; rather it turned slavery into a major commercial activity, especially with the beginning of the triangular slave trade. Meanwhile the trading posts and forts built by Europeans along the Atlantic coast of the African continent, from the Mediterranean in the north to the Gulf of Guinea in the south, became objects of intense rivalry between the European powers, which competed for a greater share in the trade with the Sudan; and so they were to stay until well into the 18th century.

By the middle of the 17th century Sufism, which was already present in the Sudan but almost exclusively in the form of individual asceticism, was making large inroads into the region through organized brotherhoods known as *tarīqa* (plural *turuq*). The *Tarīkh al-Sudān* (*History of Sudan*), a chronicle composed around 1655 by ʿAbd al-Sadi that documented the history of Islam in the western Sudan and in Timbuktu, uses a lot of Sufi terms without mentioning any particular Sufi brotherhood. Likewise, when he describes certain Muslim populations of the Sudan in his fatwa *Miʾrāj al-Suʾūd* (*The Ladder of Ascent toward Grasping the Law about Transported Blacks*), the erudite Ahmad Baba uses terms such as "ascetics" (*fuqarā*) without mentioning any specific brotherhood. At least one celebrated Sufi master from 16th-century Cairo, Muhammad al-Bakri, seems to have enjoyed a lot of respect throughout the western Sudan during his lifetime. He is mentioned a few times in the *Tarīkh al-Sudān* by the Sufi title "the pole" (or "the pivot": *Quṭb*), as someone close to the scholars of Timbuktu.

Meanwhile in North Africa Sufi brotherhoods had been part of the Islamic landscape since as early as the sixteenth century, through the strong presence of the Jazuliyya in southern Morocco and of the Tlemcen, the Qadiriya, and the Shadhiliya (one of the latter's branches) in Algeria and Fez. Egypt, too, had a relatively long history of accommodating Sufi brotherhoods such as the Rifaʿiyya (another offshoot of the Qadiriya), founded in 1183, the Ahmadiyya, founded toward the end of the 13th century, and others. Historically, as a main point of transition in the pilgrimage to the holy sites of Islam, the city of Cairo has played a crucial role in the spread of Sufi affiliations throughout the African continent, both in the Maghreb and in the Sudan. The role of Cairo-based Al-Azhar University has been especially important. In the Maghreb, Sufi brotherhoods emerged as main stalwarts against the increasing European advances in the 16th and 17th centuries.

Some of the brotherhoods present in North Africa started to gain ground in the Sudan especially from the 17th century on. It was mainly through trade and family networks that the diffusion of Sufi brotherhoods in the western Sudan first started. In the mid-16th century for example, the Kunta family, noted for its affiliation with the Qadiriya, started to gain notoriety in the Sahara and beyond for its erudition and piety. By the time this family settled in Tuwat – an important intersection for the trans-Saharan routes, where it founded a Sufi lodge known as the Zawiya Kunta – its reputation was well established throughout the region. In the early 18th century two branches from this family, both descending from Ahmad al-Bakkaʿ, moved in two different directions: one, led by Muhammad al-Saghir, settled in the southern part of present-day Mauritania, while the other, led by ʿUmar al-Shaykh, settled in parts of central Sudan, along the trans-Saharan trade routes. The former clan gave birth to the Qadiriya-Fadiliya, which took its name from Muhammad Fadil Mamin (c. 1795–1868). Centered in the Hawd region, in the southwestern part of today's Mauritania, the Qadiriya-Fadiliya spread to Senegal in the south and to Morocco in the north at a later date, especially under Muhammad Fadil's nephew and sons Sad Buh (d. 1910) and Maʾ al-Aynayn (d. 1917). Around the mid-18th century al-Mukhtar ibn Ahmad ibn Abi Bakr (1729–1811), a member of the latter clan who was noted for his piety, scholarship, and charisma, founded a base in al-Hilla in the Azawad, along the Middle Niger River, and this became a main center of diffusion for the Qadiriya-Mukhtariyya, as this branch would become known. Al-Mukhtar (who is best known as Sidi al-Mukhtar Kunta) maintained a successful trade network. He was instrumental in the spread of the Qadiriya throughout the western Sudan. In the mid-19th century the Qadiriya in the western Sudan came to be identified with the Kunta family. One notable disciple of Sidi al-Mukhtar Kunta was the Mauritanian Shaykh Sidiyya (1775–1868), who after studying under him moved back to Mauritania and became a respected authority in matters of Islam.

The Qadiriya also spread to the east of the continent, but this happened at a much later date. In Somalia, for example, this brotherhood surfaced in the 1820s, under the leadership of Shaykh Uways ibn Muhammad al-Barawi (1847–1909), who also propagated it to Zanzibar, Mozambique, Madagascar, and other eastern parts. Finally, the Qadiriya reached Malawi, where it was brought by Malawi students returning from Zanzibar.

The other major Sufi brotherhood whose diffusion throughout the African continent was successful is the Tijaniya. The Tijaniya was founded by Shaykh Ahmad al-Tijani (d. 1815). Although this brotherhood was relatively young by comparison with the Qadiriya, its expansion and diversification in Africa were very rapid. By the end of the 19th century, a little less than a decade after the death of its founder, the Tijaniya unmistakably represented an integral part of Islam in Africa. Often perceived as the standard bearer of militant Islam, the Tijaniya order has often-times challenged the European colonial enterprise and has been integrated as an organic element of Islam in many communities throughout the African continent. Tijaniya first expanded southwards, into western Sahara, thanks to Muhammad al-Hafidh ibn al-Mukhtar (d. 1830) of the Idaw ʿAli clan (which was based in Shinguitti, in present-day Mauritania); he was a direct disciple of the founder of the Tijaniya order. Under Mawlud Fal, a student of Hafidh, the Tijaniya spread throughout Mauritania, then reached central Sudan in Cameroon and Chad and Nilotic Sudan further east. (For an example of how the long-standing relationships between North and sub-Saharan Africa are reflected in the architecture of today, see Figure 9.1.)

The principal propagator of the Tijaniya in Africa remains, however, al-Hajj ʿUmar Tal (d. 1864), a scholar from Futa Toro (today's northern Senegal). Al-Hajj ʿUmar received his formal affiliation to the Tijaniya during his pilgrimage to Mecca, namely from Muhammad al-Ghali, himself a direct disciple of Ahmad al-Tijani. Some sources indicate that Al-Hajj ʿUmar might have been introduced to the Tijaniya even earlier, while he was a student in Futa Jallon (today's northern Guinea). He spent about five years studying Islam in Futa Jallon (c. 1822–1827). Upon his return from the pilgrimage to Mecca he traveled to different places in the western Sudan – for instance Sokoto (today's northern Nigeria), where he stayed for just under a decade, or Masina (in today's Mali) and Jegunko in (the Northern part of today's Guinea). Al-Hajj ʿUmar had read the work of al-Maghili and subsequently

Figure 9.1   Interior courtyard of the Grand Mosque in Dakar (Senegal) in the Andalusian North African style. Photo taken in 2008 by the author.

engaged in a jihad, seeking to spread Islam in its Tijaniya form throughout western and central Sudan. The Tijaniya branch that originated with him proved to be very prolific, because almost all the later branches of that order in the western Sudan were in one way or another connected to the descendants of al-Hajj ʿUmar.

Another major Sufi brotherhood that took roots in Africa was the Shadhiliya. Founded by Abu Madyan Shuʾayb (d. 1197), the Shadhiliya derived its name from that of his disciple, Abu Hassan ʿAli al-Shadhili (d. 1258). This brotherhood was very successful in East Africa, where it became the next largest Sufi order after the Qadiriya. This was due especially to Muhammad Maʾruf (d. 1905), a member of the Hadrami family in the Comoros Island. Through his travels, Muhammad Maʾruf actively helped spread the order in Madagascar, Tanzania, and Malawi. The Shadhiliya reached Nilotic Sudan quite early, in the 17th century, mostly due to this area's proximity to Egypt. However, it did not become highly organized until one century later, through the influence of the Moroccan Ahmad ibn Idris (d. 1837), who spent most of his career in the Hijaz and Yemen.

Muhammad ibn ʿAli al-Sanusi (1787–1859), one of Ahmad ibn Idris' students, founded the Sanusiya, another Sufi order that was diffused in North Africa, in the Hijaz, and, following the trans-Saharan trade route to the south, in the Chad area, in Wadai, and along the Middle Niger. There was widespread affiliation to the Sanusiya among traders in Bornu and in the regions north of Hausaland.

Movements of Islamic Reform in Africa through the Jihad: The Fulani Thread

The development of Sufi orders throughout Muslim Africa has also been the result of large movements of population from areas where Islam was dominant to less Islamized parts, especially from the 17th century onwards. These movements were determined mostly by the search for better economic opportunities – particularly through trade – but also motivated by instability. They generally took a north–south direction. In the western Sudan, for example, the populations involved were largely Muslims: the Banu Hassan, the Fulani, the Soninke, the Mande, and the Hausa. The successive movements of the Banu Hassan, a clan of Arab nomads, from the eastern Maghreb to the southwestern Sahara during the 15th century changed considerably the dynamics of populations north of Senegal River. The influx of these Arabic-speaking nomads into the region north of the Senegal turned the entire society from one dominated by Sanhaja Berbers into a Moorish society comprised of Hassan, Zawaya, and Lahma. During the hegemony of the Hassan, the Zawaya were subjected to the payment of a tribute, *gharām*, which was ultimately rejected because the Hassan were not capable of providing protection in return. The tense situation that resulted led to the emergence of a movement of reform led by the Islamic scholar Awbek ibn Ashfaga, later known as Nasir al-Din. While recruiting mostly from the Banu Dayman, a subgroup of the Zawaya, Nasir al-Din later projected a movement that would transcend ethnic considerations and would put in place a society modeled on the early community of Islam. He appointed a prime minister (*vizir*) and at least four judges (*qādī*), and he set up the basis of a state by requiring allegiance from the Zawaya leaders. In 1673 his movement launched a jihad in the south, across the Senegal River, in Futa Toro. There he gained the support of the Torodbe, a class of Muslim clerics among the Fulani, and he deposed the non-Muslim ruler, who belonged to the less Islamized Denianke. Back on the north side of the Senegal River, he imposed the payment of the zakat on the Lahma, who resented it and called in the Hassan for help. Some of the Hassani scholars rejected Nasir al-Din's legitimacy as caliph and his imposition of the zakat. After two violent encounters with the Banu Hassan, he was finally killed in 1674. Some of Nasir al-Din's successors would try to revive the idea of an Islamic state levying zakat, but without much success. Nasir al-Din's failure backfired on the Futa Toro, where his former Torodbe allies lost power to Denianke once more. This triggered successive waves of migration of the Islamized Torodbe southwards, mainly along the Senegal River. They settled in Bundu, in the Upper Senegal, in Futa Jallon, and further south in Hausaland, around the Niger Delta.

Many movements of Islamic reforms were initiated by the Torodbe in lands where they settled. In the 1680s, for example, the Torodbe Malik Sy, an Islamic cleric originally from Futa Toro, created the first Fulani-led Islamic state in Bundu, on the Upper Senegal River, and he assumed the title of *elimāni* (imam). Originally this state was a coalition of independent villages; Torodbe Malik Sy expanded it by defeating the former suzerain, the neighboring state of Gadiaga.

Further south of Bundu, in Futa Jallon, a group of Torodbe clerics came together in 1725, created a state of their own, and elected as leader Ibrahim Sambighu, also known as Karamokho Alfa. Ibrahim was an Islamic cleric who doubled as political leader of the province of Timbo, the later political capital of the Islamic state, and he remained in power until his death in 1751. His more aggressive successor Ibrahim Sori undertook ambitious military campaigns beyond the borders of Futa Jallon. Ibrahim Sori's army was finally defeated by Wasulu, a neighboring state mainly populated by the less Islamized Bambara. The Bambara overtook Timbo in 1767 and threatened the entire Islamic state. It was not until 1776 that Futa Jallon could decisively push back the repeated assaults of the Wasulu army and secure the state. Futa Jallon was a reputed place of Islamic education in the sub-region, and it preserved this status for a long time. Islam served as the ideological foundation of the state, and the *sharia* was considered the rule of the land, at least in theory.

Futa Toro had been for a long time a stronghold of the Denianke, who resisted many attempts on the part of Islamic conquerors to impose the *sharia* as the law of the land. But even this state turned Islamic when Sulayman Bal, a Torodbe Islamic cleric trained in Futa Jallon, went back to Futa Toro and succeeded in establishing an imamate there in the 1760s. After this success, Sulayman Bal endorsed the nomination of 'Abd al-Qadir as *almamy* (imam) in 1775. Almamy 'Abd al-Qadir immediately set out to expand the influence of this new polity in neighboring states around the Lower Senegal River Valley. He intervened in the north, in Mauritania, where he settled the disputes between Banu Hassan in 1786; he imposed new tolls on the French, who were engaged in commercial activities in the region; and he also intervened in Bundu. By 1796 Almamy 'Abd al-Qadir could impose the supremacy of the new imamate all the way to the Middle Senegal in Bundu and south up to Kayor, in central Senegal. However, his attempt to invade Kayor ended in great humiliation: not only was his army defeated, but he himself was captured and subjected to hard labor for three years before his release. In 1806 the aging Almamy, who had lost most of his aura through his experience in Kayor, was defeated and killed by the allied army of Bundu and Kaarta.

Among all the Islamic reform movements initiated by Torodbe-Fulani in the Sudan, probably the most successful and enduring was the one initiated in Hausaland toward the end of the 18th century. In the early 19th century Usman dan Fodio, a scholar of Torodbe origins whose ancestors were settled in Hausaland started a jihad movement that would mark the history of Islam in the Sudan. Born in 1754 in Marata, Gobir, in northern Hausaland, Usman dan Fodio received an Islamic education from an early age, as usually expected of a Torodbe. In consequence he grew up as a member of an intellectual elite of Muslim clerics in Gobir – a kingdom in the Hausaland that had known Islam from as early as the 14th century. In Gobir as in most of Hausaland, Islam was generally limited at that time to the ruling classes. The general population, for the most part, practiced traditional African religions or an Islam mixed with traditional African elements. This syncretism was the subject of heated debates among lettered Muslims in Hausaland, who were conversant in the classical Arabic of the 18th century. Among them were Muhammad al-Barnawi who condemned any deviation from strict orthodoxy, and Shaykh Jibril ʿUmar, a teacher of Usman dan Fodio, who regarded any sin, including that of syncretism, as a form of apostasy. Positions such as these were in tune with with the views of al-Maghili, the Maghreb scholar who visited Hausaland three centuries earlier; in fact al-Maghili was very influential in shaping Usman dan Fodio's views. Somewhat on the margins of the debate were Muslim clerics who found a way of accommodating Islamic practices into traditional African religions; for the most part, these clerics developed close working relationships with leaders in Hausaland who incorporated elements of traditional African beliefs in their rules. As an affiliate of the Qadiri Sufi order, Shehu Usman joined the debate later on, in his book *Ihyā al-Sunnah* (*Revival of the Sunna*), with rather moderate positions. In his early twenties, he set out to preach against syncretism among the Muslims of Gobir, Zamfara, and Kebbi. It was not until 1784, ten years after his first preaching, that he took his message to the rulers of Gobir, demanding greater conformity to Islamic orthodoxy. Yet Usman and his supporters met with increasing hostility from Gobir's rulers, who allegedly attempted from time to time to liquidate them. Tensions escalated into an armed conflict that forced Shehu Usman and his supporters to leave and to settle in Gudu, an area outside the jurisdiction of Gobir's ruler. It was there, in Gudu, that Shehu Usman set up the organizational basis of his reform movement. His main target was the corrupt and tyrannical rule in Hausaland. The organization set up by Shehu Usman soon grew into a state, where he took the title of Amir al-Muʾminin or Emir of the Believers. At the same time Shehu Usman composed a series of books denouncing the corruption and lack of belief of the elite and the oppression and heavy taxation it imposed. In 1804, with the support of Hausa peasantry, he launched a series of campaigns that ultimately toppled the kingdom of Gobir when its capital Alkalawa was captured in the same year. He then captured the neighboring Hausa states of Katsina, Kano, and Zaria, sweeping south into Nupe and the lands of the Yoruba. The campaign culminated with the creation of the largest state in the Sudan at that time: the caliphate of Sokoto, between the Niger River and the Chad. Shehu Usman died in 1817. He was succeeded by his son Muhammad Bello, who ruled until 1837. Both father and son, and especially Usman's daughter Nana Asmau (d. 1864), left an extensive body of literature, both in classical Arabic and in Ajami. Indeed, very early on in the life of the Sokoto caliphate, its founder Shehu Usman devoted much of his time to composing written justifications for his actions and to producing literature destined for the education of Muslims – and possibly of non-Muslims, too. His example was then followed throughout the empire he created. It was followed especially by the class of educated Muslims, who used not only classical Arabic but also local languages in order to express themselves. The caliphate of Sokoto survived until 1804, when it was occupied by the British troops.

Islam in Africa: The Colonial Paradox

The Europeans' persistence, from the 15th century on, in attempting to gain some foothold along the western coast of the African continent paid off for the most part. By the end of the 18th century some European enclaves existed along the African coast in places like Cape Verde, Goree, Saint Louis, or Almina. However, until 1870 European influence in Africa was basically limited to the coast. The European presence was to be consolidated over the next century, by the end of which European colonial administrations were well implanted in the whole of Africa. The continent was essentially carved up among the European powers, especially after the Berlin Conference of 1885. France and Britain took the lion's share. The French took possession of most of North and West Africa, while the British took the bulk of East and South Africa. The possessions of the Portuguese, Italians, Germans, Belgians, and Spaniards were comparatively minimal. By 1895 most of western and central Sudan was part of French West Africa; a consolidated administration was headquartered first in Saint-Louis and then in Dakar, while the British controlled the Gambia, Sierra Leone, Ghana, and Nigeria.

Naturally the colonization process met fierce resistance from the Africans, most of it under the banner of Islam. Indeed the establishment of colonial states did not interrupt the course of Islamic reform, which was already underway in most of the Sudan since the early 16th century. The consolidation of the colonial administrations actually added a new dimension of Islamic reform to the resistance movement, especially from the second half of the 19th century. From a different perspective, the strong Islamic presence in parts of the Sudan shaped in many ways the types of policies implemented by colonial administrations. In theory, the doctrine specific to the colonial enterprise should also determine the reaction of the African Muslims directly concerned: generally the British model of colonial administration is identified as one based on the notion of indirect rule, while the French model was more geared toward assimilating the subjects to French ideals, and therefore it necessarily required a direct type of rule. Whether or not such theoretical nuances were perceived by those directly impacted by the colonial presence to a point where they shaped such people's agency is, however, something yet to be established. In any case, the African efforts to counter the European colonial enterprises took many forms, including military, cultural, and intellectual resistance. As outsiders, the European colonial administrations in Africa had in general to rely heavily on the collaboration of some African informants or employees to calibrate their actions and reactions to certain events.

Although it fell within the tradition of Islamic reform already established in western and central Sudan and it continued the series of reforms initiated by the Fulani-Torodbe, the movement of al-Hajj ʿUmar Tal undoubtedly illustrated an aspect of the military resistance to colonial domination.

Al-Hajj ʿUmar Tal spent two years in the Hijaz, between 1828 and 1830, and performed the pilgrimage three times. His stay in the Hijaz offered him the opportunity to be officially initiated in the Tijaniya order and appointed as a representative (caliph) of the Tijaniya in the Sudan. On his way back from the Islamic pilgrimage, he stopped in Cairo. He then traveled to some Sudano-Sahelian Muslim states of great importance – such as Bornu, Sokoto, Masina, and Futa Jallon. Up until that time the Qadiriya, and especially the branch led by the Kunta clan, remained by and large the dominant Sufi order in western and central Sudan. Ruling elites in most of the Muslim Sudan – including the leaders of Sokoto, Masina, and Bornu – were then members of the Qadiriya-Mukhtariyya. Meanwhile the scholarship, charisma, and prestige of al-Hajj 'Umar since his return from the pilgrimage to the holy sites of Islam contributed (among other factors) to a remarkable increase in membership to the Tijaniya in a relatively short time. Through his various trips all across western and central Sudan after the pilgrimage to Mecca, al-Hajj 'Umar was able to gain a substantial number of disciples to the Tijaniya. These new followers either formed circles of their own in their localities or followed al-Hajj 'Umar in his travels. He visited Futa Jallon, a place where he studied, spending there some of his younger years (from 1840 to 1845). This had been a decisive stage in his career, both as a writer and as the leader of a nascent community; during that time he composed his major works, for instance the famous *Al-Rimāh* (*The Lances*). In his numerous books he denounced the double enslavement of Muslim Africans – to their fellow Africans and to Europeans. He managed to create a community of followers in Jigunko, a town in Futa Jallon. After an absence of almost 20 years from his home country of Futa Toro, al-Hajj 'Umar returned from his travels and gathered an important following in Senegambia, both in Futa Toro itself and further south, including in the neighboring Jolof (today's Senegal). It is important to note that Futa Toro had been since the defeat and killing of 'Abd al-Qadir in 1806 subjected to frequent slaving raids by the ruler of Kaarta, with the latest expedition in 1846. After a few years in Futa Toro, al-Hajj 'Umar decided to move back to Futa Jallon. However the political situation in Futa Jallon by then had changed: the new ruler was less welcoming to al-Hajj 'Umar and his followers, making their stay in Jigunko difficult. To avoid confrontation, al-Hajj 'Umar and his followers retired to Dinghiray, a dependency of the neighboring non-Muslim kingdom of Tamba, in 1849/1850. This movement was seen as an equivalent of a Hijra, especially for later followers of al-Hajj 'Umar. Located beyond Futa Jallon and east of the Bafing River, a tributary of the Upper Senegal River, Dinghiray offered the main characteristics of a fortress, in many ways similar to those of a *ribāt* (frontier post). In fact Dinghiray turned out to play the double role of the traditional *ribāt*: it served not only as a walled military city, but also as a spiritual refuge. It was therefore renamed Tayba – one of the old names of Medina, Prophet Muhammad's city. A few years after the move to Dinghiray, the relationships between al-Hajj 'Umar and the king of Tamba, which had been cordial to begin with, degenerated – especially when the former refused to turn over for punishment one of the king's close collaborators, who had joined the ranks of the Muslims in Dinghiray. In 1852 a war broke out between the two sides. The relatively easy victory of al-Hajj 'Umar's army in this confrontation

marked the onset of a series of battles against different armies in the sub-region –
both non-Muslim such as Kaarta and Segu (1861) and Muslim such as Masina
(1862) – and brought al-Hajj 'Umar's army in direct collision with the French, who
were seeking at that time to consolidate their hegemony along the Senegal river
and throughout the entire region. By 1863, al-Hajj 'Umar controlled almost the
entire Middle Niger River. A Muslim coalition pushed him back from Masina into
the mountainous region of Bandiagara, where he died in 1864.

Al-Hajj 'Umar's influence in the Sudan, on the Tijaniya in particular and on Islam
in general, is significant. He inspired a number of Islamic reform movements and
armed resistance to colonial penetration in the Sudan – for instance the resistance
mounted by his former Tijani disciple and fellow Fulani Maba Jakhu Ba in central
Senegal against the French in the 1860s. After al-Hajj 'Umar, Sufi Islam in the form
of the brotherhoods spread quite rapidly throughout western Sudan, especially
during the second half of the 19th century. The rapid expansion of Islam and Sufism
in western and central Sudan paradoxically coincided with the establishment of
French, Portuguese, and British colonial administrations in these areas. Interestingly
enough, the policies of colonial administrations toward Islam in general and toward
Sufi brotherhoods in particular were ambivalent over the years.

At first the reaction of colonial administrations, especially the French and British
administrations in the Sudan, toward Sufi brotherhoods was mainly one of hostility. During the second half of the 19th century, when these administrations were
barely put in place, many Sufi brotherhoods were generally labeled as hostile to
the colonial domination; such was the case for example with the Sanusiya in the
Lake Chad area, the Tijaniya in western Sudan, and the Muridiya in parts of the
Senegambia. In the case of many of these, the colonial administration resorted to
violent means and downright repression to deal with any perceived resistance to
its authority. Some of the best known cases are the uncompromising stance of the
colonial authority against the Sanusiya order, which was always seen as inherently
dangerous to the colonial enterprise, or the repeated exile of some Sufi leaders
such as Ahmadu Bamba, the founder of the Muridiya in Senegal, whose charisma
was perceived as crystallizing African resistance to the European colonial
domination. When they realized that Islamic reformers in the Sudan were for the
most part people freshly returned from pilgrimage to the holy sites of Islam, colonial administrators, and especially French ones in western and central Sudan, took
it upon themselves to regulate and control the flow of pilgrims to Mecca. In order
to counter the prestige and charisma of the pilgrims to the holy sites of Islam and
minimize their contact with Muslims in the Middle East and North Africa, these
administrators started to condition the pilgrimage on their authorization.
Furthermore, they changed the traditional itinerary to the holy sites, which
normally went across the Sahara and made stops at major Islamic centers such as
Cairo; now pilgrims had to take the road across the sea and make stops at Marseille
in southern France. The colonial authority would later establish a commissioner in
charge of the pilgrimage, whose ultimate task was rather the surveillance of the
activities of Sudano-Sahelian pilgrims during their presence at the holy sites of

Figure 9.2   Mosque on Gorée Island, Senegal, built during the colonial era. Photo taken in 2008 by the author.

Islam and beyond. (See Figure 9.2 for an example of the mosques built by the French colonial administration to accommodate the Muslim population.)

As a foreign entity, a colonial state in the Sudan was in general highly central-ized and autocratic – especially from the end of the 19th century, when such states succeeded in imposing their authority after they defeated all armed resis-tance. In order to effectively govern large swaths of population and lands that had never been put under the same jurisdiction, a colonial state needed at least some measure of viable local support. In Muslim-dominated lands in Africa, that support was often sought from influential Islamic groups or personalities. Over time, the colonial state managed to develop a policy of collaboration with Islam and with the Sufi orders in the Sudan, and it was thanks to this policy that its authority gained relative legitimacy among Muslims in the Sudan. These groups or personalities often played the key role of brokers between the colonial state and grassroots Africans. The phenomenon was not only observable, but striking in colonies such as Senegal, which had what some authors call a Rustovian accommodation – that is, a long-standing antagonistic situation where neither of the opposing parties could dislodge the other (Stepan 2012: 9). The policy of co-optation in fact turned out to be one of the hallmarks of the colonial state in the Sudan – and in many ways this would be the policy pursued by the future postcolonial states.

The role of intermediary, played by the Sufi orders, further reinforced the dynamism of these Islamic organizations in many parts of the Muslim-dominated Sudan. Naturally, the dynamism of Sufi Islam preceded European colonial domination in Africa; the colonial states' recognition of the importance of Sufi brotherhoods came to be added to the latter's popularity at grassroots level. During the colonial era in the Sudan, Islam as represented by the Sufi orders emerged as the main and most dynamic anchor for resistance to cultural and

> ### Sidebar 9.6   The Muridiya
>
> The Muridiya is one of the most studied Sufi brotherhoods in sub-Saharan Africa. Founded in 1883 by Shaykh Ahmad Bamba, this brotherhood is known for its emphasis on work and discipline. It currently has networks in many parts of the world, including Europe and the United States, where some its followers live.

religious domination. During this era the Qadiriya remained the main Sufi order in the region. As for the Tijaniya, the Sudan turned out to be a fertile ground for its expansion, especially at the hands of charismatic religious leaders who, although still rooted in the main branch of the Tijaniya, left behind important social structures that were going to be later on offshoots of the original Tijaniya. This is the case for the late 19th- and early 20th-century Islamic scholars such as al-Hajj Malik Sy, al-Hajj ʿAbdullah Niass, and Shaykh Hamahullah who left behind important spinoffs of the Tijaniya. The evolution of Sufism in the Sudan in the late 19th and early 20th century is better captured in the history of one Sufi order that stood out particularly as local in origin, even if its founder was at some point affiliated to the Qadiriya: the Muridiya, founded in 1883 by the Senegalese Shaykh Ahmad Bamba. At its creation, the Muridiya was perceived by the French colonial administration as the last rallying point for all failed armed resistance to colonial domination. This prompted colonial authorities to exile its founder – first in the remote and dense tropical forests of Gabon in central Africa, where he had to stay for at least seven years; then to Mauritania – before they put him under house arrest in Diourbel, Senegal until his death in 1927. This policy of repression – which, ironically, had the effect of increasing the popularity of the Muridiya order among Africans – was also applied until well into the 1930s against other Sufi sub-orders, such as the group led by Hamahullah and its branch, the Yacoubi (Hanretta 2009; see Figure 9.3 for the mosque in the city of Touba, center of the Muridiya).

In the early 1960s, by the end of the colonial era, Sufism was strongly established as the main face of Islam in such important parts of Muslim Africa as western and central Sudan, and in fact on most of the African continent. Islam was, in turn, the main monotheistic faith on the continent, stretching south into regions that had little or no place for it in their historical past. Certainly the regional polities set in place by colonial powers throughout the continent stimulated interactions between the northern half of the continent, where Islam was predominant, and the southern half, which had little or no Islamic presence. Naturally, the history of Islam in postcolonial Africa will reflect these disparities in the distribution of the Islamic faith.

Figure 9.3   Grand Mosque in Touba, Senegal, a city established by the founder of the Muridiya Sufi brotherhood in the nineteenth century. Photo taken in 2008 by the author.

Islam in Postcolonial Africa: Between Reform and Continuity

A proper study of Islam in postcolonial Africa would necessarily have to distinguish cases where Islam has long been the main religious tradition from cases where the Islamic presence is only recent. Similarly, a distinction should be made between cases where Sufism has been a long-standing phenomenon and cases where it has little or no history. The idea of an Islamic reform is often assimilated to anti-Sufi attitudes, because Islamic reformism is commonly seen to be anti-conformist, while in recent history Sufism has represented conformism.

Of course, Islam in Africa has not been immune from the reform movements that shaped most of the Muslim world, from the 18th century to the 20th – from the movements led by Muhammad ibn ʿAbd al-Wahhab to the Iranian Revolution of the late 1970s. These movements took, however, peculiar forms within different African contexts. For example, from 1848 on some movements of Islamic reform started to emerge in some urban centers of colonial Senegal under the leadership of Muslim scholars such as Ahmad Ndiaye Ann, Muhammad Seck, and Ndiaye Sarr, who advocated greater consideration for Islam in the legislation process and a better organization of the pilgrimage to Mecca. These early movements were consolidated later on in such organizations as the Union Fraternelle des Pèlerins Musulmans de l'AOF, created in 1922, and Liwaʿ Taʿakhi al-Muslim al-Salih (The Good Muslim Brotherhood Brigade, or La brigade de la fraternité du bon musulman) founded in 1934. These early reform movements, mostly based in urban areas, were often embedded in Sufi orders, especially the Tijaniya (Loimeier 2003).

It was not until the 1950s that a reform movement – the Union Culturelle Musulmane (UCM), led by Cheikh Touré – started to challenge the hegemony of the Sufi orders. Strongly influenced by the Jam'iyya al-ʿUlama' al-Jaza'iriyya (The Association of Algerian Religious Scholars), an Algerian reform movement, the UCM was the first embodiment of modern Islamic reform.

Following the UCM in Senegal, the Islamic reformer Abubakar al-Gumi created in northern Nigeria the Jama'a Izala al-Bid'a wa-Iqama al-Sunnah (The Society for the Eradication of Blamable Innovations and the Establishment of the Sunna) in 1978. Al-Gumi's ideas of Islamic reform were also directed against the hegemony of Sufi orders, which were predominant in northern Nigeria.

In East Africa one of the most noted reformer was Shaykh ʿAbd Allah Salih al-Farsi, who was particularly active in Kenya and Zanzibar in the 1970.

Although the African postcolonial state inherited – and sometimes preserved – many traits of its predecessor, the colonial state – and such traits included legislation and political institutions – important movements of Islamic revival appeared, from the 1970s onwards, in many predominantly Muslim nation-states across the African continent. With the exception of Sudan in East Africa, where a regime of Islamic law was introduced in the early 1980s, the movements of Islamic revival in sub-Saharan Africa remained for the most part self-contained; they had few or no political ambitions, despite some connections to Islamic movements in areas of the Muslim world like North Africa, the Middle East, and South Asia. Significant Islamic states or non-state actors – such as Iran after the 1979 Islamic Revolution, the Egyptian Muslim Brotherhood, Southeast Asia's Tablighi Jama'at – as well as the Ahmadiyya movement and Saudi-supported organizations like the World Muslim League and the World Assembly of Muslim Youth developed relations with some locally run Islamic movements in the 1970s and 1980s. These sub-Saharan Islamic movements – movements of a new kind – competed mainly with each other and against the dominant homegrown Islamic educational system, which had been nurtured by long-established Sufi groups. The rise of the Islamic movement of revival in sub-Saharan Africa during the 1980s coincided with the implementation of different programs of economic austerity in many countries – programs that, under the dictates of Bretton Woods institutions such as the International Monetary Fund and the World Bank, forced those states to considerably decrease investments in social sectors like healthcare, education, and welfare and to privatize hitherto publicly run sectors of the economy. One consequence of these policies was the substantial increase of the informal sector, which emerged as the only sector purveying jobs, especially to the less educated and most vulnerable sections of the society. As a result, in some predominantly Muslim countries of sub-Saharan Africa, Islamic movements emerged as the main institutions organizing the networks that are often necessary to run an informal economy. Some of these networks extended beyond the limits of national borders.

This increase in the importance of the role played by some Islamic movements in sub-Saharan Africa continued unabated, especially in the aftermath of the Cold War, when the continent ceased to be a battleground for the two main protagonists in that war. In that context, many Islamic movements of revival developed still further their relationships with Islamic regimes or organizations in the larger Muslim world. In Nigeria, for example, the Islamic movement, which was a Shiʿi organization, consolidated its relations with Iran and the Lebanese organization Hizbullah.

Islam in Africa and the "War on Terror"

The end of the Cold War and the subsequent rise of non-state actors resorting to unconventional forms of armed struggle brought Islam – and Islam in Africa – to the forefront. The African continent became a notable battleground in the protracted and asymmetric warfare that mainly opposed the United States and a non-state actor such as al-Qaeda, especially following the attacks on the American embassies in Nairobi, Kenya, and Dar es-Salam, Tanzania in 1998. The events of September 11, 2001, a little over two years after the attacks on the US embassies in East Africa, and the ensuing global "war on terror" highlighted new forms of Islamic militancy on the continent. Certainly the Islamic landscape in sub-Saharan Africa remains predominantly Sufi; however, the start of a "war on terror" seems to have goaded the rise of new forms of religious militancy, which were thus far almost unknown in sub-Saharan Africa. The failing Somali state, for example, and the absence of any central government there since the fall of the regime of General Siad Barre in 1991 created a situation of lingering conflict that ultimately led to the rise of the organization known as al-Shabab ("the Youth"), which seeks to fill the political void. The organization is a splinter group of the Islamic Court Union (ICU), itself a loose coalition of factions from Al-Ittihad Al-Islami (AIAI, "the Islamic Union"). This coalition was founded after the fall of Barre's regime and its ultimate goal was the establishment of an Islamic state in greater Somalia. Al-Shabab recruited among young people of Somali background living mainly in the West – the United States, Canada, and Western Europe.[2] This organization, which joined the fray boldly, claims alignment with some global networks of Islamic militancy and expanded the battlefront to some neighboring states such as Kenya and Ethiopia, especially after direct involvement of troops from these countries in the Somali crisis.

More recently, in 2009, an Islamic organization in Nigeria known as Boko Haram came to the limelight in a series of violent clashes essentially with the police, starting with the riots in the northern Nigerian states of Bauchi, Borno, Kano, and Yobe in late July 2009. Boko Haram (which means "Western education is sacrilege" in Hausa, one of the main languages in northern Nigeria) emerged mainly as an organization opposed to any Western influence, and its members were identified as perpetrators of many recent attacks on Nigerian police and on other institutions perceived as signs of the Nigerian secular federal state and of Western influence. Like the Somali Al-Shabab, Boko Haram evolved in the 1990s as the offshoot of a pre-existing Islamic organization known as the Islamic Movement of Nigeria – a Shi'i movement led by Ibrahim al-Zakzaky, whose objective was the establishment of an Islamic state. Certainly long years of mismanagement, corruption, and economic stagnation at the hands of the Western-trained Nigerian ruling elites helped fuel the appeal of the organization among the disenfranchised youth. The often heavy-handed policy of the state toward Boko Haram, as illustrated by repressive campaigns of the police against the organization,[3] contributed to further radicalization. To this day, the multiple violent attacks attributed to Boko Haram pose a serious challenge to the Nigerian federal state; and the spread of such attacks to other states does not help assuage the long-standing ethno-religious tension often associated with that West African nation.

Elsewhere on the African continent the wave of popular revolutions that have been sweeping across the Arab world starting in December 2010 toppled a number of authoritarian regimes in North Africa – for instance those of Tunisia, Egypt, and Libya. One of the consequences of these revolutions has been the election of so-called moderate Islamists in positions of power in many of the countries where they occurred. Parties and candidates affiliated with long-standing Islamic movements, such as the Muslim Brotherhood in Egypt and al-Nahda in Tunisia, have been voted to power, sometimes in a landslide victory. A less talked about consequence of these revolutions is the shift in the balance of power – precarious until now – which it created in neighboring regions, especially in the Sahel. In Mali, for example – a country for a long time in the grip of a low-level Tuareg irredentism – on April 6, 2012 a heavily armed group of Tuaregs from the organization known as the National Movement for the Liberation of the Azawad (MNLA in French) chased the Malian regular army from the northern part of the country and declared the lands under their control to be an independent entity under the name Azawad. Prior to their incursion into northern Mali, these members of the MNLA were thought to have taken part in the violent events that led to the fall of the Khadafi regime in Libya; they fought on Khadafi's side. But the independence was to be short-lived: almost immediately after their declaration of independence, the leaders of the Azawad were chased and defeated by an Islamist group known as Ansar Dine (Helpers of the Religion), whose members helped the MNLA conquer the northern part of Mali. The Ansar Dine have since taken control of important cities in northern Mali and declared Islamic law as the law of the land under their control. Important cities such as Timbuktu and Gao, whose place in the history of Islam in Africa has been discussed in this chapter, are under the Ansar Dine's control. In Timbuktu members of the Ansar Dine carried out some public flagellations and destroyed some historic Sufi shrines that were deemed to be un-Islamic.

Although they may draw inspiration from some transnational militant organizations, the Islamic movements resorting to militant tactics that have recently appeared in sub-Saharan Africa – such as al-Shabab and Boko Haram – remain mostly self-contained. Certainly they add a new dimension to the Islamic landscape, which is still very much dominated by Sufi organizations.

Conclusion

The history of Islam in Africa has been marked by frequent movements of reform. From the Almoravid movement in the 11th century to contemporary currents of Islamic reform in postcolonial states, one dominant aspect of these movements of Islamic reform is that they are directed against what is perceived to be unorthodox religious practices, either at the leadership or at the grassroots levels. Throughout the continent, the success of the reform movements has consistently depended on many factors, including the long-standing Islamic presence, the existence of a Sufi tradition, and the attitude of modern public authority (colonial or postcolonial) toward Islam in particular. To some degree, western and central Sudan have sometimes in the past served as a ground for competing ideas of reform, specifically from the northern part of the Muslim world. In the late 15th century, for example, the Egyptians al-Maghili and al-Suyuti, two Islamic scholars who advocated reform, saw their ideas gain favor, and their advice was solicited by Askiya Muhammad, the ruler of Songhay. Al-Maghili would also be consulted by another ruler from the Sudan, the king of Kano. Following these royal consultations, al-Maghili composed two handbooks of sorts, destined for African rulers. In his handbooks this scholar advocated an uncompromising attitude toward those he called "false Muslims" and a strict adherence to the tenets of Islam. Although his advice was not immediately put into practice, it was implemented much later, in the 19th century, by Usman dan Fodio, the founder of the Sokoto state in today's northern Nigeria. As for al-Suyuti, his influence in the western and central Sudan almost never disappeared, since his commentary of the Qur'an – entitled *Al-Jalālayn* – has always been the one most widely known across the region.

For the most part, in western Sudan Islam in general and Sufism in particular are viewed in quite monolithic terms. However, throughout its history, Islam in Africa has been marked by movements of reform that took a quasi-cyclical form. Even Sufism, which appears as the default form of Islam in recent history, has been the vehicle for important reform movements. The period of European colonial domination, which lasted from the mid-19th to the mid-20th century, has been largely regarded as a period marked by the greatest number of attempts at Islamic reform. The end of the Cold War, the retreat of the postcolonial state from social welfare coupled with resolute policies of economic liberalization and privatization, and especially the global war on terror have all contributed to the emergence of new forms of Islamic organizations in sub-Saharan Africa in the 21st century.

Notes

1   "Sudan" is used to mean "black Africa." "Western," "Central" and "Nilotic" refer to Muslim regions in black Africa. "Nilotic Sudan" refers to the east-African region that includes modern-day Sudan, Ethiopia, Somalia, and Tanzania.

2   There are controversies as to when al-Shabab was exactly created. Some date its creation to 2006, following the Ethiopian invasion of Somalia; others put it a little earlier, in 1998, when al-Shabab was an elite group of the Islamic Court Union (ICU). See Vidino, Pantucci, and Kohlman 2010.

3   The raiding of the organization's headquarters in the northern Nigerian state of Bauchi in July 2009, and especially the capture and killing of its charismatic leader, Ustadh Mohammed Yusuf, together with the death of more than 700 members in the subsequent clashes could have contributed to the fact that the organization resorted to violence; see Adesjoli 2010, especially p. 98.

Discussion Questions

1   Would you consider a good understanding of Islam in Africa to be helpful for a better understanding of global Islam in the 21st century? Why – or why not?

2   Could you identify some specific aspects of Islam in Africa?

3   Would you include Islam as a component of African identity? Why – or why not?

Suggested Further Reading

Adesoji, Abimbola (2010). The Boko Haram uprising and Islamic revivalism in Nigeria. *Africa Spectrum*, 45(2): 95–108.

Hanretta, Sean (2009). *Islam and Social Change in French West Africa: History of an Emancipatory Community*. Cambridge: Cambridge University Press.

Hunwick, John and Fatima Harrak (ed. and trans.) (2000). *Miʿrāj al-Ṣuʿūd Aḥmad Bābā's Replies on Slavery*. Rabat: Institute of African Studies.

Insoll, T. (1996). *Urbanism, Archeology and Trade. Further Observations on the Gao Region (Mali), The 1996 Field Season Results*. British Archaeological Reports S829. Oxford: BAR.

Lewicki, T. (1964). Traits d'histoire du commerce trans-saharien: Marchands et missionnaires ibadites au Soudan occidental et central au cours des VIIIe–XIIe siècles. *Etnografia Polska*, 8: 291–311.

Loimeier, Roman (2003). Patterns and peculiarities of Islamic reform in Africa. *Journal of Religion in Africa*, 33(3): 237–262.

Lydon, Ghislaine (2009). *On Trans-Saharan Trails: Islamic Law, Trade Networks, and Cross-Cultural Exchange in Nineteenth-Century Western Africa*. Cambridge: Cambridge University Press.

Messier, Ronald A. (2010). *The Almoravids and the Meanings of Jihad*. Santa Barbara, CA: Praeger.

Oliver, Roland (ed.). *The Cambridge History of Africa*, vol. 3: *c.1050–c.1600*. Cambridge: Cambridge University Press, 1977.

Ottayek, R., and B. Soares (eds.) (2009). *Islam, état et société en Afrique*. Paris: Karthala.

The Pew Research Center (2009, October). *Mapping the Global Muslim Population: A Report on the Size and Distribution of the World's Muslim Population.* At http://www.pewforum.org/Mapping-the-Global-Muslim-Population.aspx (accessed September 22, 2012).

Stepan, Alfred (2012). Rituals of respect: Sufis and secularists in Senegal in comparative perspective. *Comparative Politics*, 44(4): 379–401. (23).

Vidino, L., R. Pantucci, and E. Kohlman (2010). Bringing global Jihad to the Horn of Africa: Al-Shabaab, Western fighters, and the sacralization of the Somali conflict. *African Security*, 3(4): 216–238.

10

Islam in South Asia

Saeed A. Khan

Introduction

South Asia is home to one of the largest Muslim populations in the world. Out of a world population of approximately 1.6 billion Muslims, nearly half a billion live in one of the four nations that comprise the region: Sri Lanka has 1.8 million; Pakistan 178 million; Bangladesh 149 million; and India 177 million (Pew Research Center 2010). A region where Islam has a long history, South Asia also has a

An Introduction to Islam in the 21st Century, First Edition. Edited by Aminah Beverly McCloud, Scott W. Hibbard, and Laith Saud.

tremendously diverse Muslim society, featuring a mosaic of ideological, political, cultural, and economic complexity.

History

Islam has maintained a presence in the Indian subcontinent since the earliest days, when the faith formed in the Arabian Peninsula (see Map 10.1). Commerce proved to be the primary vehicle for initial contact with the region, when Arab merchants and traders sailed to the Malabar Coast, along India's southwestern shoreline, and established outposts in the early 7th century. Such interaction led to conversion among indigenous peoples; in fact a mosque was built in the Indian state of Kerala in 629, only seven years after Muhammad's migration to Medina.

While maritime trade brought Islam to India, this was not the only migration of its kind. In the 8th century Muhammad Bin Qasim, a general in the Umayyad army, conquered the province of Sindh in present-day Pakistan. He was able to take advantage of an unpopular Hindu ruler presiding over a Buddhist majority and established a tolerant and economically vibrant region, where Islam's egalitarian ethos served as a compelling counter-narrative to the caste system that dominated the existing social structures. Bin Qasim's efforts made the Sindh Islam's easternmost province in the Umayyad caliphate (661–750); this region would eventually come to include parts of the Punjab.

Further campaigns led by Muslim armies were successful in solidifying an Islamic presence militarily, politically, economically, and culturally throughout the Indian subcontinent. In the early 10th century Mahmud of Ghazni completed the conquest of the Punjab begun two centuries earlier, while Muhammad of Ghor captured Lahore, Gujarat, Tarain, and Delhi by the end of the 12th century. Advancing Muslim armies often confronted and defeated Hindu forces. Apart from this, there were several occasions when conflicts involved intra-religious engagements.

Trade and military conflict were not the only vehicles for the spread of Islam in South Asia. Arguably, a more successful and sustained one was the spread of Sufism and its ecumenical appeal. The indigenous religions of India, particularly Hinduism, Buddhism, and Jainism, have a very strong ascetic component. Sufism's inclination toward favoring the metaphysical over the mundane gained considerable currency in South Asia, which transcended those religious boundaries that were deemed to be artificially created by society. In addition, Sufism's inherent mysticism and egalitarianism were highly attractive to lower caste Hindus and to members of the

Sidebar 10.1   The shrine of Khwaja Muinuddin Chishti

The shrine of Khwaja Muinuddin Chishti, a 12th-century Sufi master, is located in Ajmer, in the western Indian state of Rajasthan. Known as Gharib Nawaz, the "Benefactor of the Poor," Chishti is revered by Muslims and Hindus alike, and his tomb is the popular destination for millions of worshippers annually.

Map 10.1 Map of South Asia.

Untouchable community. Several Sufi leaders, including Khwaja Muinuddin Chishti, Nizam Uddin Awliyah, Shah Jalal, and Baba Farid, developed into cult figures beloved to Muslims, Hindus, and other religionists. Many Sufi masters have become objects of veneration, long after their death, as saints possessing the power of intercession. For their followers, their shrines have become centers of pilgrimage from all over the Indian subcontinent, irrespective of religious affiliation.

Sidebar 10.2   The Taj Mahal

Emperor Shah Jahan (r. 1628–1658) ordered the construction of the Taj Mahal, one of India's (and the world's) most recognizable monuments, as a mausoleum to his wife Mumtaz, in Agra near Delhi.

After several centuries of Muslim presence in South Asia and a variety of regimes in power, Islamic political sovereignty attained its apogee in the subcontinent during the Mughal period, which spanned over 300 years. Tracing his ancestry to the Timurid Empire, which had dominated Central Asia, the first emperor of the Mughal era, Babur, advanced south from Khorosan and defeated the Muslim Delhi sultanate in 1526. Babur and his descendants created a hereditary dynasty that dominated India as a Muslim minority governing a largely Hindu majority population for three and a half centuries. Babur was succeeded by his son Humayun, who was in turn followed by his son Akbar; then Jahangir, Shah Jahan, and Aurangzeb followed in the same way. This was the beginning of the golden period of the dynasty (1526–1707).

Politically, the Mughal Dynasty may well have dominated the Indian subcontinent – either by conquering rival Hindu adversaries or by entering with them into alliances that recognized the Muslim regime's power in the region. Yet, as a result of its encounter with other religions of South Asia and of a generally tolerant relationship with them, Islamic culture developed as an indigenous and in many ways unique civilizational phenomenon under the Mughals. Islam in South Asia became a syncretistic faith-culture, in which some social customs (such as marriage or cultural expression) absorbed Hindu characteristics. Under the reign of Akbar, for example, this syncretism was both a source of praise – from those who welcomed recognition of South Asia's non-Muslim communities – and a source of criticism – from those who were suspicious of undue compromise and deference to those populations.

As emperor, Akbar (r. 1556–1605) recognized the demographic complexities of his subjects. Well aware of being a Muslim who ruled over a majority non-Muslim region, Akbar embarked upon creating an institution that reflected such a phenomenon; and this was the Din-e-Ilahi. The central doctrine of this movement was a shift from orthodox Islam toward the Sufism favored by Akbar. The movement also privileged a spirit of ecumenism and tolerance across religious lines. Akbar built the Ibadat Khaana (House of Worship) in Fatehpur Sikri, near Agra, and declared it open to people of all religions. The faith of the Ibadat Khaana was universalistic in nature, blending Islam and Hinduism, Buddhism and Jainism, while also acknowledging Islam's relationship to other monotheistic faiths, such as Christianity and Judaism.[1]

But Akbar went further than simply establishing a perception of egalitarianism among the religions of South Asia; he also implemented policies that removed differences among them in society. He repealed the Jizya, the special tax paid by non-Muslims for protection in an Islamic polity – a move hailed by Hindus and others but sharply critiqued by Muslims, particularly the ones more traditionally oriented. Akbar also enacted measures that appealed to Hindu sensitivities, such as a ban on the slaughtering of cows. His belief that no faith had a monopoly on truth placed South Asia's numerous religions on a level ideological footing. Nevertheless, Akbar's vision and actions won him animosity from the Muslim orthodoxy, which was offended by his theological and political concessions relating to Islam's dominance on the subcontinent.

The end of Mughal rule in South Asia and the concomitant demise of Muslim dominance occurred not at the hands of competing religious factions, but rather as a result of the British colonization of India. The last Mughal emperor, Bahadurshah Zafar, ended his reign in 1857, which was also the year of the Sepoy Mutiny and of the establishment of imperial rule under Queen Victoria. Islam did, however, remain as a political presence, albeit on smaller scale – namely as the Nizamate of Hyderabad, a princely state in southern India.[2]

With the advent of British colonial rule, the Muslims of South Asia played a pivotal role in the independence movement. Muhammad ʿAli Jinnah, the eventual founder of Pakistan, Liaqat ʿAli Khan, its first prime minister, and Abul Kalam Azad, a leading figure in the Indian National Congress, were some of the key figures of the Quit India struggle, which culminated in the withdrawal of British sovereignty over India and subsequent partition of the subcontinent in 1947. With Jinnah, the creation of Pakistan was based on the conceit that the Muslims of India would require a separate homeland in a post-British South Asia to ensure their political rights and cultural identity, given rising tensions with the majority non-Muslim population.

Pakistan was founded in the midst of a civil war between Indian Muslims, Hindus, and Sikhs, while an independent state, separated by 1,000 miles from a hostile country in the middle, was being crafted. As the rationale for the new nation was to create sovereignty in regions holding Muslim majorities and these existed on either side of India, that country was none too pleased about this division of territory and the violence and population displacement that occurred in its aftermath. Though the acrimony was shaped across religious lines, the conflict was a matter of religious identity through a political lens rather than a theologically driven war. In fact both India and Pakistan were ostensibly established as secular nations. Tensions between the two countries have remained political in nature since 1947 over several issues, chief among them being the disputed territory of Kashmir, a Muslim majority province in northern India that is claimed by both nations. In addition, India's involvement in the 1971 war, which led to Pakistan's division and the creation of Bangladesh from East Pakistan, has been a diplomatically contentious matter, yet it has demonstrated that religious difference is not necessarily a strong line of demarcation in South Asia.

Islamic Movements in South Asia

The religious diversity of South Asia is self-evident; virtually all major faiths of the world are represented in varying measure within the region. Yet there also exists a tremendous amount of variation within South Asian Islam itself: there are several sects and sub-sects, and religio-political movements abound, a good number of them being unique to the subcontinent and a function of its historical, demographic, and political pecularities. While the overwhelming majority of South Asians are Sunni, there are several divisions within this group, just as there are considerable distinctions among the assorted Shi'a factions. In either case, theological and philosophical variations are informed and affected by political factors and motivations. Of course Sufism remains a strong presence and influence throughout the Indian subcontinent, both as a religious and as a cultural imperative.[3]

One of the most influential of the Sunni movements in South Asia is the Deobandi School, which is named after the eponymous city in the northern Indian town that houses the Darul Uloom institution for learning. Established as a seminary in 1867 by Muhammad Qasim Nanautawi and Rashid Ahmed Ganobi, Deoband sought to address the Muslim community's decline in British India following the 1857 mutiny and the end of Mughal rule. With its curricular focus on Qur'anic and hadith studies and on Islamic law and sciences – all conducted in an Urdu medium – Deoband purposely omitted English and Western disciplines from its program, arguing that they represented British oppression and, more perniciously, a threat to Islam in India. Originally catering to the subcontinent's Muslim elite, Deoband was grounded in classical Sufism and trained its pupils to achieve a focus on spiritual discipline. At the same time, however, the institution was vehemently against certain aspects of Sufism – such as saint veneration or its hierarchical structures.

Although founded as an anti-colonial Islamic institution, Deoband has maintained its position as one of South Asia's leading centers of learning, and its influence extends beyond India. Initially the school was against the founding of Pakistan, because of its opposition to a perceived paradoxical concept – namely a secular Muslim state. Deobandi scholars have exerted considerable religious authority over the nation, especially with regard to other sectarian factions, whether Sunni or Shi'a.

Deoband has played an undeniably critical role in shaping Islamic discourse in South Asia since the imposition of British colonial rule; it was, however, not the only response of its kind to foreign imperial authority. In 1875 Sir Sayyid Ahmed Khan (d. 1898) founded the Muhammadan Anglo-Oriental College (also known as the Aligarh Muslim University) at Aligarh, in the Indian province of Uttar Pradesh. Without question, Khan designed Aligarh to be the antithesis of Deoband. Modeled on the Oxbridge system of British higher education and decidedly secular in its orientation, Aligarh offered a curriculum and a campus architecture fashioned after the two most prestigious collegiate universities of England. The courses included engineering, law, and medicine, as well as Western liberal arts. Khan believed that, for Indian Muslims to survive (and perhaps even to thrive), they needed to move beyond denying, with so many others, the irreversible loss of power in the subcontinent and to face the realization that Britain and the West were now on the way up. Muslims needed to maintain their buoyancy in a society that no longer privileged them, in fact was forcing them to compete for space and success with a majority non-Muslim population that had already embraced Western ways and modalities of knowledge.

Aligarh's curriculum and its stated mission have been successful in cultivating generations of Muslim professionals in the Indian subcontinent – professionals who subsequently became prominent leaders both at home in India and in Pakistan or Bangladesh. Although Aligarh is almost diametrically opposed to Deoband in focus and vision, both institutions have helped shape the narrative of Islam in South Asia through their differing approaches to educating Muslims.

Both Deoband and Aligarh created educational centers and curricula to address the needs of South Asia's Muslims, and in the process they became ideologies and approaches in their own right. The Sunni Muslims of the subcontinent also have movements and imperatives that define Islamic identity and manners of engagement with society. One such movement is the Barelvi, which received its name from the hometown of its founder, Ahmed Riza Khan (d. 1921): Bareilly in Uttar Pradesh Province, India. Barelvism represents the popular strain of South Asian Sufism, which has three foundational aspects: the hagiography of Prophet Muhammad, which is sometimes accused of approaching a divine perception of its subject; the belief in the intercession of Sufi saints – that is, the Pir/Murid system; and the commemoration of popular festivals, particularly the ones that celebrate the Prophet's birth.

> ### Sidebar 10.3   Pir and Murid
>
> Pir is a term designating the Sufi master, while Murid is used of someone who gives his oath of allegiance to a particular Pir, recognizing him as his spiritual master and even intercessor. This relationship is not recognized by the Islamic orthodoxy, which sees the practice as an un-Islamic innovation and a heresy.

Barelvism enjoys widespread support throughout South Asia, especially among the Muslims of Pakistan. Its syncretistic nature and lack of rigidity – by comparison with the austere orthodoxy associated with the Deobandi School – has given Barelvism popular appeal, but also exposed it to severe criticism on account of its being outside the purview of acceptable Islam. Deobandi scholars such as Ashraf ʿAli Thanvi (d. 1943) have issued religious opinions – fatwas – condemning Barelvism and calling its adherents illegitimate Muslims. Still, such opposition has neither deterred the movement nor prevented it from maintaining a strong position in the Muslim culture of South Asia.

While some Sunni movements in South Asia have concentrated on education and others on ideological orientation, the Jamaat-e-Tabligh employs engagement as its principal point of departure. Founded in 1927 by Muhammad Ilyas in the northern Indian town of Tabligh, the Jamaat is primarily concerned with intra-faith rather than inter-faith. Originally a Deobandi, Ilyas recognized the merit of missionary work in spreading Islam; however, the object of his efforts was to reach fellow Muslims. Ilyas was concerned that Muslims in South Asia had been exposed to an Islam tainted by foreign innovations and encroachments; he sought to refine the Islamic practices of Muslims instead of teaching Islam to others from scratch. Since the movement has chosen to limit the scope of its focus as such, the Jamaat-e-Tabligh is seen as an apolitical, non-controversial effort, both within South Asia and in its relatively recent global project.

Not all Islamic movements in South Asia have been able to escape politicization, in spite of their efforts to stay out of the political arena. The Ahmadiyya (Qadiani) movement is considered one of the subcontinent's more controversial factions. The group traces its roots back to the town of Qadian in the province of Punjab and to its founder, Mirza Ghulam Ahmad (d. 1908). Around 1898 Ahmad made a claim to prophethood, in direct contravention to the orthodox Islamic belief that Prophet Muhammad was the last such divinely ordained messenger. With the exception of this albeit significant factor, Ahmadis generally adhere to a fairly conventional Sunni expression of Islam. They have nonetheless been subject to a pervasive campaign of discrimination, demonization, and persecution in Pakistan since the 1950s. As a small, though cohesive and organized minority group, the Ahmadis have faced public derision as well as official condemnation from the government of Pakistan, which declared them to be non-Muslims by amendment to the Constitution of Pakistan in 1974.

> ## Sidebar 10.4   Shiʿa
>
> The Shiʿa constitute roughly 15 percent of the population of Pakistan; less than 10 percent of the Indian population; and less than 2 percent of the population in Bangladesh.

The diversity among the various Sunni movements of South Asia has been informed by, and has in turn affected, the complexities of the majority Muslim denomination of the region. Shiʿa Islam, though represented by a small population, enjoys a similarly wide spectrum of ideological and social differences. The largest component in this minority community is the Twelver (Jafari) Shiʿa sect. The Twelvers, though few in number, occupy a major position in shaping Islamic history in South Asia. During the 16th century, Shiʿa kingdoms presided over the Deccan Plateau in the southern part of India, and in 1732 the Twelver sect had founded the state of Awadh in northern Indil, its capital was Lucknow, a city that served as one of South Asia's epicenters of Islamic culture and education. With the advent of colonial rule in the 19th century, the British authorities sharply enervated the Shiʿa aristocracy, thereby diminishing its political power. In addition, the colonial divide-and-rule strategy politicized latent sectarian differences, constructing new lines of demarcation for identity politics and discord, along Sunni–Shiʿa lines. With the upheaval of power structures and the loss of Muslim power in South Asia, Sunni theologians, worried about the impact on Islam's continued coherence, began to target Shiʿism and certain practices, issuing declarations that they were un-Islamic. Long-standing Shiʿa religio-cultural traditions, such as the commemoration of passion plays (Taaziyat), were deemed to be in violation of Islam.

In recent decades the Sunni–Shiʿa divide in South Asia has attained a more corrosive and violent dimension, especially in Pakistan. As a small and beleaguered community, the Shiʿa of Pakistan are often made scapegoats for political and social dysfunctionality and are easy targets of extremist acts. In addition, foreign interventionists supply aid and weapons to both Sunni and Shiʿa factions, thus forwarding their own agenda at the expense of domestic stability in Pakistan. The bloodshed tends to intensify during major Shiʿa days of commemoration, when the carnage and its visibility can be maximized.

The Twelver Shiʿa are a minority among Muslims, both in South Asia and throughout the Islamic world as a whole; however, they are still in the majority within the overall Shiʿa community. The Indian subcontinent is home to significant numbers of these "minorities within minorities" – for example non-Twelver Shiʿa such as the Ismaʿilis. Being small yet cohesive and prosperous groups, they have been very adept at navigating a sometimes treacherous political, ideological, and social landscape in South Asia, though by and large they avoided the larger sectarian and inter-religious conflicts in the region.

Of the two denominations of Ismaʿili Islam in South Asia, the Mustali, also known as the Bohra, have a longer history in the Indian subcontinent, having arrived there in the middle of the 11th century from Yemen. Being a vestige of the former Fatimid line of Ismaʿilis, which ruled over Egypt and other parts of the Middle East, the Bohras follow the instructions of the Daʿi al-Mutlaq, the unique representative of the Hidden Imam, a central figure in Shiʿa belief. Settling mostly on the western coast of India and on the southern coast of Pakistan, the Bohras are a tightly knit community that maintains strict codes of piety and social conduct. The Daʿi in fact assigns identity cards to his followers on the basis of the depth of adherence to his teachings that each one demonstrates. These cards, colored green, yellow, or red, indicate and determine the level of access and acceptance within the community that their holders will enjoy.

The Nizari, or Khoja, constitute the second of India's two Ismaʿili denominations. Led by their spiritual leader, the Aga Khan, the Khoja have been established in India and Pakistan; their headquarters are in Bombay, since the movement migrated from Persia in the 19th century. The Khoja are a very cohesive, self-sufficient, and prosperous community. They place a very high premium on education, the pursuit of business, and other professional careers. Two million Khoja reside in Pakistan, a number that represents 2 percent of their population worldwide. They maintained well-established communities in East Africa until the early 1970s, when political turmoil forced many of them to resettle in Europe and North America. The Khoja, both through the Aga Khan and as a community, have contributed economically and politically to South Asia, creating endowments and educational institutions and engaging in philanthropic work. Muhammad ʿAli Jinnah, one of the leaders of the Indian independence movement and the founder of Pakistan, was himself a Khoja.

Political Islam in South Asia

For Muslims in South Asia, political participation is a multi-faceted phenomenon, spanning the whole spectrum from disengagement to active, identifiably Islamic expression. While postcolonial India has maintained a democratic system since its independence, its more Muslim neighbors – Pakistan and Bangladesh, respectively – have each endured a history of vacillation between democracy and dictatorship. In all three countries Muslims have been extensively involved in the political process and have certainly exercised their freedom to opt for a secular form of participation or party affiliation. At the same time, however, several political parties on the Indian subcontinent have been demonstrably Islamic in their rhetoric and outspoken ideological orientation, creating a mosaic of political alliances, adversities, and alignments. These parties see themselves not only as political actors but also as agents for social change and cultural identity in their respective countries.

The Ahl-e-Hadith (not to be confused with the Ahl-e-Sunnah Wal Jamaah, a branch of the Barelvis) do not follow any of the recognized schools of Sunni Islam, claiming that such methodological distinctions are artificially created and have no theological foundation or requirement.[4] As adherents to an unaffil-iated model, members of the Ahl-e-Hadith believe in *ijtihad* (independent reasoning of the individual) instead of *taqlid* (blind imitation), which they claim is the result of the institutionalization of Sunni schools of thought. The Ahl-e-Hadith have organized as a political party in Bangladesh, where they have enjoyed limited success, and the Pakistani version maintains an even smaller presence in that country.

By far the most prominent Islamic political movement in South Asia has been the Jamaat-e-Islami, founded in 1941 by Abul Ala Mawdudi (d. 1979). The Jamaat's initial objective was to form an Islamic state in the context of impending independence from Britain and while its main political opponent, the Muslim League, was seeking a potentially secular alternative. For this reason the Jamaat opposed the formation of Pakistan in 1947; but eventually it accepted it and accord-ingly moved its base of operations to the new nation. Once there, Mawdudi led the Jamaat into the country's political process, asserting a clearly Islamic tone and platform in spite of the secular trajectory envisaged by Jinnah, the founder. Pakistan's political turmoil and instability as it moved back and forth between civilian and military governments caused public cynicism about the viability of a secular polity, allowing the Jamaat to gain considerable currency in the political debate. Mawdudi leveraged his own ideological vision through the Jamaat by calling for a return to original Islamic doctrine. Declaring all Western ideologies – theological, political, and other kinds – morally and Islamically bank-rupt, Mawdudi called for an Islamization of the state that was to be achieved through the implantation of a rigid construal of the Qur'an and Prophetic tradi-tion. In fact Mawdudi was even critical of traditional Islamic scholars (*ulamā*) for being quiescent or complicit in the decline of Islam in the daily lives of South Asia's Muslims.[5]

The Jamaat-e-Islami proved to be an influential political force in Pakistan, particularly against religious minorities. While embarking on its anti-Ahmadiyya campaign in 1953, the Jamaat was finally successful in its efforts to have the government declare the Ahmadiyya a non-Muslim group through constitutional amendment in 1974. Further success was achieved under the military regime of General Zia ul-Haq, an ardent supporter of Mawdudi's Islamic state model. With consultation and guidance from the Jamaat, Zia implemented *sharia* law in several areas of civil society, among the most contentious of his measures being the Blasphemy Ordinance, which punishes any statement or publication deemed offensive to Islam, the Prophet, or the Qur'an as a potentially capital crime.

Today the legacy of Mawdudi and of the Jamaat in Pakistan has led to the establishment of Islamic parties as well-mobilized and influential actors in the country's political discourse. Similarly, albeit to a lesser degree, the Jamaat's analogous organization in Bangladesh has helped bolster an Islamic presence in the nation's political process; for example, in 1988 Islam was declared state religion. By contrast, however, the Jamaat's Indian incarnation has assumed a less strident posture, advocating the protection of minority Muslim rights and the social reform and spiritual renewal of the individual.

Various extremist movements have taken shape in South Asia that claim an Islamic impetus for their actions. Some are descendants of the *mujahidin* fighters, who were supplied and financed by Western powers to fight the Soviet army during its invasion of Afghanistan in the 1979–1989 campaign. The formation of the Taliban in the Afghan refugee camps of Pakistan during the 1990s changed the country's cultural landscape even after the Taliban left to fight in the Afghan Civil War. For many participants in these movements, the Taliban's subsequent alliance with al-Qaeda in Afghanistan further entrenched an Islamic narrative in the rhetoric and motivation of armed struggle and resistance. As a result, an entire generation of religiously motivated fighters emerged, recasting Islam as a liberation theology in order to justify efforts to redress old and existing grievances across the region, chief among these being the ongoing Kashmir conflict. Groups like Laskhar-e-Taiba, Jaish-e-Muhammad, and Lashkar-e-Janghvi have conducted extremist activities in Indian-controlled Kashmir and more recently have claimed to have orchestrated attacks in Bombay and other Indian cities.

Gender and Islam in South Asia

The treatment of women has been a measure commonly applied to Islamic societies for gauging their purported development and progress. Islam in South Asia has not been exempted from such an analysis. However, like religion itself, the subject of Muslim women is a highly complex matter in the region, because faith and its various theological interpretations do not alone inform sufficiently the myriad factors that affect this topic or allow for convenient generalizations. Muslim women throughout the Indian subcontinent are affected by local cultural particularities, socio-economic conditions, political considerations, and sometimes also deeply entrenched class structures. It is perhaps more helpful to explore the spectrum of Muslim women's roles and rights in South Asia, which spans from complete sequestration from public spaces to full and active participation in political, professional, and social areas. In the two "Muslim" countries of South Asia, for example, three different women have served as democratic leaders of their respective nations. Benazir Bhutto (d. 2007) was twice elected to Pakistan's highest office, from 1988 to 1990 and from 1993 to 1996. In Bangladesh, Khalida Zia served as prime minister from 1991 to 1996 and from 2001 to 2006; and Sheikh Hasina has occupied that post from 1996 to 2001, and again since 2009. Although there has been some opposition to their election in both Pakistan and Bangladesh on the basis of the conceit that women cannot and should not govern an Islamic state, such a view has not gained significant currency among members of the public, which does not consider gender to be a disqualifying factor or an anathema.

While the election of women to the highest political office in Pakistan and Bangladesh may indicate a promising atmosphere for gender politics in South Asia, there are some glaring challenges facing large numbers of Muslim women in the region. Clearly there are people who exploit the lack of education of significant segments of society by finding Islamic rationales to suppress women; their views take advantage of people's ignorance about Islam and are enforced through cultural and tribal modalities of social control. The marginalization of women by restricting access to education and employment opportunities occurs in both urban and rural settings, where resources may be limited and generations of patriarchal social custom militate against change. While Muslim women may be entitled to the protection of their civil rights through state action, familial, communal, tribal, and sometimes even feudal norms intervene to deny them access to, and to deprive them of, improved lives and livelihoods. This phenomenon occurs everywhere, be it in politically fluid countries such as Pakistan and Bangladesh or in stable democracies like India.

In addition to cultural considerations, gender politics in the Muslim communities of South Asia exists within the context of equally entrenched fissures that are based on class distinction; this creates situations where wealthy women enjoy more rights in society than indigent men. Moreover, sectarian conflicts among the various factions comprising the Islamic landscape of South Asia destabilize civil society to such an extent that an otherwise naturally occurring progression toward greater enfranchisement of women is impeded. While conditions for women in these Muslim societies may be far from optimal, it is important, however, to assess whether mechanisms for improvement are available. Through local social and political movements involving both men and women, the issue of women's rights remains a highly visible topic in the public debate.

Conclusion

Islam has maintained a historical presence in South Asia since its very inception. Adapted to local demographic, social, and cultural realities, the form of Islam that is practiced in modern-day India, Pakistan, and Bangladesh attests to the vibrant and at times volatile interaction of this faith with other religious traditions of the region, as well as contesting and negotiating its own internal tectonic plates. Home to nearly one in every three Muslims in the world, South Asia possesses a variety of Islamic expressions that speak to the ideological, political, and cultural complexities of a multi-faith, multilingual, and multicultural space.

The manner in which Islam has emerged and evolved in South Asia over the centuries serves as a model of great interest for Muslims in other parts of the world who contend with religious, cultural, and political diversity. Consequently many South Asian Muslims have had an immense influence on other Muslim societies through their scholarship and writings. Whether by playing a role in outside movements such as the Muslim Brotherhood in Egypt, as happened through Mawdudi's work with the Jamaat-e-Islami, or by producing intellectuals like Muhammad Iqbal (d. 1938) or Fazlur Rahman (d. 1988), South Asian Muslims have made profound contributions to Islamic discourse both regionally and beyond.

The variety among the region's Muslims makes it impossible to define a single, monolithic South Asian Islam. Whether Islam in South Asia is taken as a microcosm of the global Muslim world or as a highly specialized manifestation of the faith and its adherents, its organic nature becomes evident to anyone who examines its history: a 14-century-long history of interaction that has embraced conflict and cooperation and has forged a local typology of Islam unlike anything visible elsewhere in the world.

Notes

1   Similarly, many South Asians, irrespective of their religious affiliation, enjoy Islamic culture: its art and architecture, its poetry, represented by such masters as Amir Khusro and Mirza Ghalib, and its music, represented by the devotional Qawaali of the late Nusrat Fateh ʿAli Khan and the Sabri Brothers.

2   Hyderabad remained an independent princely state with its own currency and postal service until September 1948, when it was invaded and absorbed by India.

3   The destruction in 1992 of the 16th-century Babri Mosque by Hindu extremists and the ensuing communal violence were seen to be the result of political exploitation related to the introduction of Hindu nationalism into India's political equation by way of the Bharatiya Janata Party (BJP) and its rise to power in the early 1990s.

4   The four recognized Sunni schools of thought are Hanafi, Maliki, Shafiʿi, and Hanbali.

5   Mawdudi's disdain for the *ulamā* may appear ironic, given his own lack of formal education in the Islamic disciplines. He was a professional journalist and considered journalism to be his principal vocation, despite his political activism.

Discussion Questions

1   What influence did Islam's contact with the Indian subcontinent's other religions – for instance Hinduism, Sikhism, Jainism, or Buddhism – have on the form of Islam in South Asia?

2　How did British colonial rule impact Islam in South Asia?

3　Nearly one out of three Muslims in the world is from South Asia. How does this fact affect the expression of global Islam?

4　What role has Muslim culture played in shaping South Asian society?

Suggested Further Reading

Ahmad, Imtiaz and Helmut Reifeld (2004). *Lived Islam in South Asia*. New Delhi: Social Science Press.

Ahmed, Akbar S. (1997). *Jinnah, Pakistan and Islamic Identity*. London: Routledge.

Eaton, Richard M. (2000). *Essays on Islam and Indian History*. New Delhi: Oxford University Press.

Hardy, P. (1972). *The Muslims of British India*. London: Cambridge University Press.

Malik, Hafeez (1988). *Sir Sayyid Ahmad Khan and Muslim Modernization in India and Pakistan*. Karachi: Royal Book Company.

Malik, Jamal (1996). *Colonialization of Islam*. Lahore: Vanguard Books.

Metcalf, Barbara (2009). *Islam in South Asia in Practice*. Princeton, NJ: Princeton University Press.

Nasr, S. V. R. (1996). *Mawdudi and the Making of Islamic Revivalism*. New York, NY: Oxford University Press.

Pew Research Center (2010). *The Future of the Global Muslim Population*. The Pew Forum on Religion and Public Life. At http://www.pewforum.org/The-Future-of-the-Global-Muslim-Population.aspx (accessed September 11, 2012).

Raja, Masood Ashraf (2010). *Constructing Pakistan*. Oxford: Oxford University Press.

Richards, John F. (1995). *The Mughal Empire*. Cambridge: Cambridge University Press.

Robinson, Francis (2000). *Islam and Muslim History in South Asia*. New Delhi: Oxford University Press.

Robinson, Francis (2007). *Islam, South Asia, and the West*. New Delhi: Oxford University Press.

11

Islam in Central Asia

Maria Louw

Introduction

Central Asia (see Map 11.1) – here understood as the former Soviet republics of Kazakhstan, Kyrgyzstan, Tajikistan, Turkmenistan, and Uzbekistan – is a rather understudied part of the Islamic world. Up until the dissolution of the Soviet Union, its Muslim citizens – around 50 million people, most of them living in Central Asia – had only been of interest to a small group of dedicated scholars in the West. Two of the most prominent among them, Alexandre Bennigsen and

An Introduction to Islam in the 21st Century, First Edition. Edited by Aminah Beverly McCloud,
Scott W. Hibbard, and Laith Saud.
© 2013 Blackwell Publishing Ltd. Published 2013 by Blackwell Publishing Ltd.

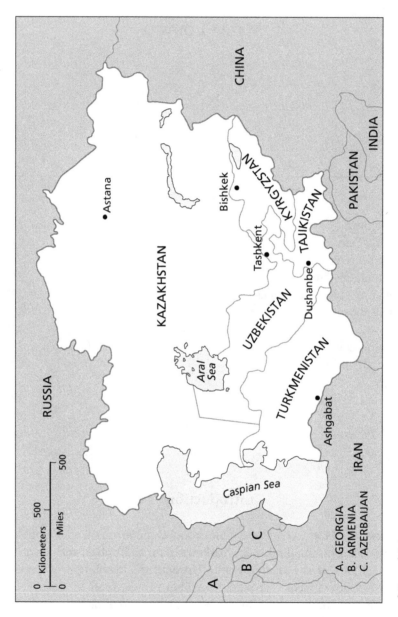

Map 11.1 Map of Central Asia.

Chantal Lemercier-Quelquejay, called their subject of study *les musulmans oubliés*, in a book of this very title (1981). Although this state of things is now in the process of changing, there is still a tendency for the region to be treated "as an Islamic periphery to be measured against the Middle Eastern heartland," as Morgan Liu (2011) has formulated it in a recent review of the anthropology of Central Asia. Thus, at the beginning of the 1990s, when the first fieldwork-based publications dealing with Islam in post-Soviet Central Asia started to appear, they were often more concerned with how people there were *not* Muslims – how their ideas and practices differed from a perceived Islamic orthodoxy – than with the meanings that Islam and Muslimness actually had for them. A common theme was the eradication of knowledge about Islam: it was pointed out that, although ritual practices such as those connected with life-cycle ceremonies and the veneration of saints continued to be observed throughout the Soviet period, the result of the onslaught on religion was that knowledge of orthodox Islam was reduced to a minimum.

During recent years, however, we have seen an increasing number of studies undertaken by scholars, foreign and local, who attempt to study the meanings of Islam in Central Asia as more than mere derivations from some "proper" Islam and to understand the complex ways in which people living there explore and negotiate what it actually means to be Muslim.

The Early Years of Independence

The years surrounding the breakup of the Soviet Union and the independence of Central Asian states were turbulent ones for the people who lived in the region: it was a time when the world as they knew it was replaced by something yet to come into being, and when all sorts of hopes and fears for the future proliferated. Many of these hopes and fears had to do with religion. In the Soviet Union religion was seen in Marxist terms, as a form of false consciousness that inhibited people, preventing them from acting in and on the real, material world and from realizing their true humanity. Restrictions against religious practice had been a central aspect of government policies since the revolution, and the Sovietization of Central Asia involved a massive assault on Islam. Anti-religious campaigns were launched; these included mass rallies where women were encouraged to burn their veils, which for the Bolsheviks were icons of Islamic tradition associated with repression, ignorance, and religious fanaticism. Religious property was confiscated, mosques and *madāris* (religious schools – the plural of *madrasah*) were destroyed, members of the *ulamā* were persecuted, and Soviet Muslims were isolated from contact with the rest of the world. The number of mosques permitted to operate was relatively small and people were discouraged from attending them. As a result, for many Muslims the practice of Islam was largely confined to the performance of life-cycle rituals such as weddings, circumcisions, and funerals; to some extent Islam was rendered synonymous with tradition – a marker of national identity.

When the Soviet Union dissolved, there was a sense among large parts of the population in the region that the 70 years of Soviet rule had made them forget what it meant to be Muslim, and, correspondingly, there was widespread hope that people would soon be able to recover that lost knowledge. But people equally feared that social and economic instability – and what many, in particular the intelligentsia, considered to be an "ideological vacuum" – could make a fertile soil for religious extremism. Most studies and reports dealing with Islam in Central Asia that were published throughout the 1990s and early 2000s were also concerned with the threat that Islam might pose to secular governments and regional stability: the appearance of radical Islamist groups, together with the risk that such groups might appeal to the broader population in societies haunted by economic despair, ethnic tensions, social injustice, and (in some cases) authoritarianism. While this tended to give a somewhat skewed picture of the meanings of Islam among people in the region, it reflected a growing concern among the governments of the newly independent states as well as among ordinary people living there; this concern, as we shall see, has very much influenced – and continues to influence – the way people think about, and practice, their religion.

During this period many commentators talked about an Islamic "resurgence" taking place, which would be evidenced by the increase in the number of mosques, the formation of Islamic political parties, and the activities of missionaries from other Muslim countries. While many citizens continued to lead a rather secular life, others began to observe rituals such as the five daily prayers or the fast of the Ramadan month openly, or – in the case of women – to adopt the hijab. Some began to claim a greater role for Islam in social and political life. For example, a Tajik branch of the Islamic Rebirth Party (IRP) was registered in Tajikistan in October 1991 and came to head a diverse coalition, which was opposed to the government and included liberal reformists as well as Islamists. The government's and the opposition's failure to reach any compromise eventually led to the outbreak of a civil war in mid-1992. Although a complex range of interests was involved, including regional interests,[1] the defenders of the old order were largely successful in portraying the opposition coalition as Islamic extremists. The conflict was formally brought to a close in June 1997, when a peace treaty was signed. The IRP, which had been outlawed in Tajikistan in 1993, was made legal again in the run-up to the 1999 parliamentary elections.

At the beginning of the 1990s other non-official Islamic groups surfaced from the underground; new ones emerged, too – partly under the influence of ties that were forged with other parts of the Islamic world. Religious literature became increasingly available and programs on Islam were broadcast on radio and television. Also Central Asia's Sufi orders re-emerged as networks with increasing numbers of followers. These orders had been very influential in the pre-Soviet past, but they were severely reduced during the Soviet period, when they became prime targets of the campaigns against Islam, being seen as clandestine anti-Soviet organizations made up of Muslim fanatics. Now their networks started re-establishing links with Sufis in other parts of the world. This was partially encouraged by post-Soviet Central Asian governments, which adopted aspects of Sufism in their nation-building project and in their efforts to control Islam (see below).

Large parts of the population in the whole of Central Asia – just like the post-Soviet governments in the area – continued to subordinate Islam to nationalist discourses, treating the revival of Islam as merely one aspect in a broader process of reclaiming national cultural patrimonies. These people argued that what needed to be revived in the first place were local and customary ways of being Muslim. Others, on the contrary, argued that what was needed was the revival of an Islam cleansed of local customary practice. In Kyrgyzstan and Kazakhstan, groups of intellectuals rehashed the old idea that the region's nomads had never really been Muslim: they would have been only superficially Islamized. These intellectuals started promoting Tengrism as a native alternative to Islam. Tengrism was an arguably more genuinely nomadic worldview, of Turkic origin and centered around Tengri, "the Sky-Father." Other new religious movements also appeared: some of them took on a distinctly Muslim cast, for example the Aq Jol (Pure Way) movement in Kazakhstan, which centered on local traditions of healing and visitation of the shrines of Muslim saints and accentuated the importance of spiritual purity. But missionaries who represented other religions, mostly from the US, Europe, and South Korea – notably Protestant evangelism and Pentecostalism – also started practicing in the region; and these succeeded in converting mainly young people and newly urban parts of the population, in particular in Kyrgyzstan and Kazakhstan, thus challenging the close link between religious and ethnic identity that had been largely upheld up until then.

Although the more radical groups that emerged on the public scene during these years were not really popular among the broader population, they are the ones that caught the eye of outside observers and came to influence state policies toward religion. They were radical in the sense that they called for a radical change to the social, political, and moral order – and this was meant to include the secular nature of the Central Asian states. One of the more radical groups that appeared in Central Asia was Adolat (Justice), which portrayed itself as an organization created in response to moral decay, corruption, and social injustice and demanded an Islamic revolution. In 1990, with Saudi funds and some 5,000 young followers, the movement started building a new mosque and a *madrasah* in the city of Namangan, in the Ferghana Valley, and its leaders began to impose on people elements of the *sharia* such as making them read the *namoz* (prescribed prayer) regularly and insisting that women wear the hijab. In December 1991 Adolat members seized the headquarters of the Communist Party in Namangan and started a movement that, they claimed, was a jihad designed to remove President Karimov. In March 1992 the government cracked down: Adolat was banned and 27 members were arrested. Adolat leaders Tohir Yo'ldoshev and Juma Namangani fled to Tajikistan, where they joined the Tajikistan Islamic Renaissance Party. Later on they moved to Afghanistan; there they would make up the core of the Islamic Movement of Uzbekistan (*O'zbekiston Islom Harakati*) – another central Islamic opposition movement, but a more militant one, which was established in the course of the

1990s. In their exile they developed close relations with Islamic militants in those places and in other parts of the Islamic world, and they came under the patronage of the Taliban and al-Qaeda. In August 1999 Yo'ldoshev and Namangani issued an official communiqué that declared jihad on the Karimov regime and called for its overthrow. Shortly after, around 1,000 fighters from the movement succeeded in entering southern Kyrgyzstan. Confrontations between the insurgents and the Kyrgyz military continued for two months, until the Uzbek air force bombed the territory. The incursions began anew in August 2000, this time initially in Uzbekistan's southern province of Surxondaryo, in a mountainous area on the border with Tajikistan. Within a week separate incursions had begun in several places in southern Kyrgyzstan, as well as in the mountains just to the east of the Uzbek capital Tashkent. Over a month passed before the military drove the fighters out of Uzbekistan's territory. The forces of the Islamic Movement of Uzbekistan were scattered by the US-led military intervention in Afghanistan that started in 2001. Since then there have been occasional proclamations from Yo'ldoshev and rumors of a re-emergence under the name "the Islamic Movement of Turkestan."

In the mid-1990s Hizb ut-Tahrir al-Islami (the Islamic Freedom Party), which has branches in large parts of the world and whose goal is to re-establish the historical caliphate, was introduced into Central Asia. It has since become the most popular and widespread underground movement in the region. However, as it is an underground movement, little can be said with certainty about its number of followers and influence, and a lot of what is known about it is based on secondary sources, rumors, and guesswork.

State Policies: From Soviet Aggressive Secularism to Emergent Ambiguous Secularisms

The Central Asian states responded in different ways to this boom in religion and to the appearance of new religious movements and interpretations of Islam. In all these states religion continues to be regulated through quasi-statal administrations. In the Soviet Union four regional Muslim "spiritual administrations" were already in place; they were responsible for controlling a limited number of mosques, *madāris*, and clerics, for appointing imams, and for monitoring religious practice. After independence these administrations were "nationalized," each republic forming its own independent administration – "muftiate." While they all are formally non-governmental institutions, in practice they remain very much under the control of state authorities, in particular in Turkmenistan and Uzbekistan, which remain the most authoritarian of the Central Asian states.

Uzbekistan has often been the main point of attention in discussions about Islam in post-Soviet Central Asia, being seen as the regional epicenter of struggles over the kind of Islam that should be revived and the role that Islam should play in the region. President Islam Karimov has lead an authoritarian government since Uzbekistan's independence, crushing dissents, banning all serious political opposition, and exerting complete control over the media. Most notably, the government has launched repeated crackdowns on Islamic activism, in an attempt to limit the influence of unofficial Islamic movements and groups.[2] Measures against the latter reached a peak in the aftermath of a series of bombings in Tashkent in 1999 that were attributed to Islamic extremists. Later, on May 13, 2005, hundreds of protesters were killed in the city of Andijan: according to the Uzbek government they were armed extremists, but according to international human right groups the majority were unarmed civilians who had gathered to protest against economic hardship and authoritarian rule.

In the official discourses of the Uzbek government no significant distinctions are made between the various unwanted Islamic movements and ideologies. Most often they are all referred to as "extremists" or "Wahhabis." Throughout the whole of the former Soviet Union, including Uzbekistan, the term "Wahhabi" is widely used – in what Muriel Atkin (2000) has aptly called the "rhetoric of Islamophobia" – as a shorthand for the general idea of Islamic menace and as an umbrella desig-nator for Muslims considered to be a threat to the established system.

In contrast, Kyrgyzstan became known as the most liberal of the Central Asian states – and this in relation to religion, too. To begin with, the post-Soviet Kyrgyz largely preferred to stay away from religious affairs, and people were relatively free to explore and discuss different understandings of Islam and of the proper domain of religion. However, as the religious landscape started to change – missionaries entering the country; *davatchis* (Muslims who call others to Islam) knocking at people's doors; mosques continuing to grow in number; more and more people displaying a "religious" identity in public through dress and behavior – many state authorities as well as ordinary people grew concerned and issued warnings to the effect that policies of non-interference in religion had allowed fundamentalist trends to flourish and missionaries to split up communities and families, threat-ening the integrity of society (see Figure 11.1).

Debates began in government circles about how to control religious activities and about what it actually meant that Kyrgyzstan was a secular state. Laissez-faire policies were now being gradually replaced by a more ambiguous approach, which engaged with "religion" as a site of ideas and forces that could be mobilized for the good of society but were also potentially dangerous. The laws remained relatively liberal, while the state sought to control religious organizations through direct interference with the muftiate and the mosques.

Central Asian governments, however, sought not only to control Islam, but also to co-opt it as an element in their state-building projects and as a source of legiti-macy. The situation in Turkmenistan has been the most odd. There President Saparmurat Niyasov, who ruled the country until his sudden death in 2006, combined a repression of independent religious activity with the creation and promotion of a spiritual creed centered on his own person. In 2001 he published the book *Ruhnama* (*Book of the Soul*), which contained a mixture of folk sayings, references to Islam, personal history and Turkmen history, philosophy, and tradition as interpreted by himself: a book that every Turkmen is supposed to use as a guide for his or her life.

Figure 11.1   Praying at a sacred place.

Not only is it, to date, recommended reading for schoolchildren and university students, it is also read in mosques and in some ways treated on a par with the Qur'an.

In Uzbekistan Islam Karimov has regularly referred to Islam in political speeches and interviews, lamenting the destruction of Islamic culture and of ancient moral principles – or more precisely of Uzbek's *Musulmonchilik*, "Muslimness" – during the Soviet years. The form of Islam that is promoted by the government in Uzbekistan – and indeed by all post-Soviet Central Asian governments – is formally based on the Sunni Islam of the Hanafi School. In practice, however, the most diverse thinkers and mystics who have a connection with the present territory of Uzbekistan have been co-opted to the ideology of national independence as progenitors of official nationalist ideology, as if their views were mere manifestations of a single spiritual thread running through history. Aspects of the Sufi tradition, notably, are pictured as expressions of a kind of Islam that developed in harmony with the Uzbek national character and that is compatible with a modern secular state – in an ironic contrast to the way Islam was pictured in Soviet research and propaganda. A distinction is made, then, between "good" Uzbek Islam, which is portrayed as indigenous, tolerant, and non-political, and "bad," "extremist," or "Wahhabi" Islam, which is characterized as alien, antithetical to national spiritual values, intolerant, and politically motivated. The interpretations of Islam that are seen to be in accordance with the ideology of national independence are promoted through the muftiate, which issues outlines for the sermons to be held during the Friday prayer.

Figure 11.2   A perilous pilgrimage.

The attitude toward sacred places – the restoration of shrines, the patronage exerted over them, and the nationwide celebrations of the saints and scholars associated with them – is perhaps the most important aspect of the Central Asian governments' co-optation of Islam. In Kazakhstan, for example, the rehabilitation of the Sufi mystic Ahmad Yasavi was marked by the restoration of the Ahmad Yasavi shrine complex in the city of Turkistan. In Turkmenistan, pilgrimages to sacred places are a rare case of a religious practice that is not strictly controlled by the government – in fact the government seems even to encourage it by providing free accommodation for pilgrims. In Uzbekistan, patronage of shrines has been one of President Karimov's most common reference points for the argument that his government has worked toward the rehabilitation of the nation's Islamic tradition. Not least, the shrine of the Sufi Saint Bahouddin Naqshband, who lent his name to Naqshbandiyya – one of the region's (and indeed the world's) main Sufi orders – became a primary focus for the state's effort to co-opt Islam in its nation-building project (see Figure 11.2).

Sidebar 11.1   Naqshbandiyya

Naqshbandiyya is one of the world's most widespread Sufi *turuq* (the plural of *tariqa*) – "ways" or "orders." It is named after Bahouddin Naqshband (or Baha' al-Din Naqshband, 1318–1389), who was born, and later buried, near Bukhara. Naqshbandiyya is known for its sobriety in devotional practice – in contrast to other Sufi orders, which have developed more ecstatic forms of worship. This sobriety is expressed in the order's preference for the silent, unspoken *dhikr* – the recollection of God that is characteristic of Sufi worship. The Naqshbandiyya *tariqa* has played a very important role in Central Asia throughout history: leading Naqshbandis had most major post-medieval rulers as their patrons, served as their spiritual and political advisors, and drew legitimacy from their rule.

In 1989 the mosque was officially reopened, and in 1993 Bahouddin Naqshband's 675th birthday was celebrated through the inauguration of his newly restored shrine complex. The event was closely followed by the state media and several notable figures participated in it, including the mufti Hajji Muxtar Abdullaev, President Karimov, and numerous Sufi sheikhs from all over the Muslim world. An international conference on Bahouddin Naqshband, Naqshbandiyya, and Sufism in general was also held, at which scholars discussed the relevance of Naqshbandiyya's teachings for present-day Uzbekistan; souvenirs were produced to commemorate the event; billboards featuring the sayings of central Naqshbandi saints were erected; and Bukhara's main street, once named after Vladimir Lenin, was renamed after Bahouddin Naqshband.

There is good reason for this co-optation of sacred places: the veneration of saints and sacred places is a very – perhaps *the* – most important aspect of popular Islam in the region. The belief that sacred places embody the divine and are thus endowed with some kind of contagious blessedness has been rejected and condemned as *shirk*, idolatry, by many of the more scripturally oriented Muslims, but it is nevertheless widespread among Muslim believers who come to the places in order to perform what they consider to be their duty as Muslims: to search for blessings on the occasion of rites of passage or in more individual situations characterized by illness, misfortune, and uncertainty; to pray; to reflect; or to find moments of peace. The saints who are associated with many of these places are commonly thought of as persons who, through the grace of God and through their exemplary lives, hold a special relationship with God and possess *Baraka*, "blessing power"; and this power may affect the lives of ordinary people in various ways, as evidenced by the numerous miracle stories that are often connected with the places (see Figure 11.3).

Sidebar 11.2   Wali

Wali is commonly translated as "saint." During the early centuries of Sufism the concept of *wilaya* (saintship) developed on the basis of the relation between the *sheikh* (master, guide) and the *murid* (disciple, aspirant), and theories developed about a whole hierarchy of saints – those who had indeed achieved mystical union in God. While some Muslims consider the practice of saint veneration to be *bid'a* – that is, a heretical innovation not conforming to the *sunna* – or *shirk* (idolatry), it is popularly believed that because a saint is someone close to God, he or she is able to intercede with God on behalf of ordinary people.

Sidebar 11.3   Baraka

Baraka means "blessing," "abundance." The concept is often used to describe a spiritual power believed to be possessed by certain persons and objects – for example by saints, by their burial places, and by other places and objects related to them.

Often no verbal distinction is made between the saint as a (living or dead) person and the (saint as a) sacred place – which points to the fact that the physical materials associated with the saints are commonly regarded as extensions of them, as somehow embodying their powers. However, many hold ambiguous ideas about the powers of sacred places. On the one hand, people may express the belief that a place is not something of importance, since God is everywhere and can be praised every-

Figure 11.3   Public prayers.

where, and since the most important thing for one's prayers to be met is faith; on the other hand, they may have experienced unusual things at such places – for instance they may have felt the presence of powers and feelings they are unable to explain. These feelings surround the places in a special atmosphere, which the post-Soviet Central Asian states sought to assimilate to various degrees and to link with the new nationalist ideas and the new patterns of power.

To sum up, the aggressive secularism that dominated during the Soviet period has been replaced by more ambiguous forms of state secularism, which distinguish between "good" and "bad" versions of Islam – between versions that support and express societal values and integrity on the one hand, and versions that undermine them on the other. In the remaining part of this chapter I will discuss how people navigate these ambiguous secularisms on the ground, articulating and negotiating what it means to be Muslim.

Negotiating Good Muslimness

The situation among Muslims in Central Asia today has most often been described as a clash between Muslims promoting "universalist" or "scriptural" interpretations of Islam, "traditionalists" who practice and advocate local forms of Islam, and "secularists" who may identify themselves as Muslims but have little interest in religion. The scripturally oriented Muslims typically criticize traditional popular practices such as the visit to and veneration of saints and sacred places, the consultation of clairvoyants, various customs related to funerals, and the belief in and practices related to ancestor spirits. Instead they emphasize the unity of God (*tawhīd*), daily prayer and supplication, and modest dress, including veiling for women. And, like the adherents to the "revivalist" or piety movement in other parts of the Muslim world, they attack their fellow countrymen and country-women for embracing Muslim ritual practices unreflectedly and merely out of custom rather than out of personal piety. The "traditionalists," on the other hand, tend to conceive of these "new" Muslims as brainwashed extremists who promote versions of Islam that are foreign to Central Asia. They advocate instead forms of Islam grounded in local practice. In Kyrgyzstan, for example, there is a widespread belief that the ancestor spirits, or *arbak*, follow the lives of their relatives and often seek to interfere in them. The ancestor spirits also play a central role in the way many understand and practice Islam: often Kyrgyz peoples' relationship with the Qur'an, for example, is limited to the verses that are recited on their ancestors' memorial days, or that they might themselves recite when their ancestors, as it is believed, visit them in their homes on Thursdays or Fridays, to see how they are doing. The beliefs and practices related to *arbak* have increasingly come under attack from people who adopt a more scripturalist version of Islam; nevertheless, they continue to be of major importance to others, who consider the critique launched by their more scripturally oriented countrymen and countrywomen to be disrespectful toward the Kyrgyz tradition as well as toward the ancestor spirits themselves.

This clash between traditional and scripturally oriented Muslims also manifests itself as a clash between traditional religious specialists on the one hand – men and women who serve at religious rituals and provide Islamic education for boys and girls in the neighborhood without having a formal religious education – and, on the other, graduates from religious educational institutions who have started to compete with them and often question their knowledge and interpretation of Islam.

Sometimes the clash expresses itself as a generational one. Anthropologist Manja Stephans has described how, in Dushanbe, the capital of Tajikistan, private religious lessons for boys and girls enjoy considerable popularity. The secular educational system being insufficient in the eyes of many, numerous Muslim families fall back on religious authorities and institutions when it comes to the upbringing of their offspring. Parents generally prefer to entrust their children to traditional local religious authorities who acquired their religious knowledge during the Soviet era, as these figures represent an extension of parental authority and create continuity and a sense of homogeneity between instruction at school and upbringing at home. In contrast, many adolescent Muslims are more interested in lessons given by younger religious teachers, who have a formal religious education, are more versed in Arabic and foreign languages and in recent Islamic literature, and are sometimes educated abroad. These younger teachers usually stand for a more scripturally oriented interpretation of Islam, which challenges the traditional understanding dominant among older generations.

In Kyrgyzstan and Kazakhstan in particular there is a high degree of anxiety surrounding Islam, which reflects recent concerns in government circles. It has long been orthodoxy in scholarly discourses on Islam in Kyrgyzstan, Kazakhstan, and Turkmenistan that Kyrgyz, Kazakh, and Turkmen people are not "real" Muslims; that their Muslim identity has always been shallow; that their way of practicing Islam is "mixed" with pagan, pre-Islamic, animistic or shamanistic elements shared with the indigenous people of Siberia and Mongolia. Such ideas have their roots back in European colonial discourses about the "decay" of the Islamic world – discourses that fragmented Muslim life into parts, some of which could be labelled "real Islam" while others were considered either "pre-Islamic survivals" or "degenerate" / "popular" Islam. The Russians, who expanded in Central Asia in the 18th and 19th centuries, saw the sedentary populations as more "Islamic" than the nomadic ones. The latter seemed to lack what officials, ethnographers, and orientalists alike took to be the markers of Islamic orthodoxy – mosques, Islamic educational institutions, and clerics; on the other hand, they engaged with "spirits," "sorcerers," and "fortune-tellers," who were perceived as fundamentally un-Islamic. The idea was consolidated during the Soviet period: because they were perceived to be less "religious" or "Muslim" than sedentary people like the Uzbeks, nomadic people were less targeted and hence less affected by the anti-religious campaigns of the 1920s and 1930s.

This view has recently been criticized as being essentialist. However, it seems that the idea that the inhabitants of these areas have never been "real" Muslims has come to be increasingly compelling for many local Kyrgyz and Kazakhs in recent years, as religion has become more and more of an issue, both in public debates and in the context of everyday life. Many connect the booming interest in religion with hypocrisy and radicalism and prefer to call themselves secular or atheists in spite of the fact that they may believe in, experience signs from, and occasionally pray to, God.

Such ideas, however, do not stand uncontested, and it is not merely in religious institutions such as mosques and *madāris* that the kind of Islam to be pursued by the not so "real" Muslims is debated. In a recent article Julie McBrien (2006) has demonstrated how wedding feasts in southern Kyrgyzstan have become an important arena for debates and negotiations about what constitutes "real" Islam and what kind of Islam is suitable for the Kyrgyz. McBrien describes how people explore alternative ways of living a Muslim life through attendance at "new" wedding feasts, held in some households, which are characterized by gender segregation, religious sermons, and the lack of alcohol, music, and dancing (which is typical of more "traditional" Kyrgyz weddings); and she explains how such ceremonies provide a focus in discussions about what it means to be a "real" Muslim.

Most people, however, do not position themselves unambiguously on one side or the other of the divide between scripturally oriented and "traditional" Muslims. In Kyrgyzstan, many surround Islam with an ambiguous attitude. They associate the perceived increase in "religiousness" in society with all sorts of post-Soviet – and indeed global – excesses, yet at the same time they see "religion" as a source of ideas through which people might find the resources for a purposeful and morally righteous life, which could be mobilized for the good of society. In Uzbekistan, as Johan Rasanayagam (2011) has demonstrated in a recent book, traditional healers who interact with spirits – and for that reason are accused of being "shamans" (*bakshi, folbin*) working with *jinn* (genies) – tend to locate themselves firmly within Islam, insisting that their healing power and the spirits they communicate with come from God, presenting themselves as devout Muslims, and incorporating the recitation of Qur'anic verses. (Quite often they exclude other healers from genuine Islam, accusing them of the same things they are accused of themselves.) More generally, in their efforts to explore Islam and to constitute themselves as good Muslims, people may draw on various ideas and practices that would seem contradictory to an external observer: Islam's scriptural sources or new ways of dressing and acting piously, but also spirit encounters in dreams, visions, visits to the tombs of saints, and experiences of illness and healing. As Johan Rasanayagam has pointed out, the sociality of interacting with others in networks of obligation and reciprocity is also central to many people's understanding of Muslimness.

Furthermore, as has been noted by many researchers, people in Uzbekistan have to tread a very fine line when striving to constitute themselves as good Muslims. While in governmental rhetoric the distinction between "good" and "bad" Islam seems unproblematic, in practice it is not at all clear which ways of expressing piety are acceptable – and indeed highly valued – expressions of Uzbek "Muslimness" and which are signs of "Wahhabism." In the current atmosphere of fear and vulnerability, the label "Wahhabi" has come to apply to any religious expression that people are uncertain about – for example to religious expressions related to Christianity. This means that the practice of Islam is generally surrounded by a great deal of paranoia. Even Sufis, who practice a form of Islam that has been promoted as belonging in the national spiritual heritage, often experience harassment from local officials who regard their strong religious devotion with suspicion.

This also means that religious authorities who may be critical of popular practices such as shrine visitation feel nonetheless compelled to accommodate them. Anthropologist Krisztina Kehl-Bodrogi (2006b) has demonstrated how officially appointed imams at a major shrine in Khorezm are caught in a dilemma between their conviction that the worship of a saint's shrine is a form of idolatry and the need to conform to state policies that encourage the visitation of shrines as a manifestation of "good" Uzbek Islam.

Future Prospects

A lot has been written on Islam in Central Asia around the question of whether it is likely that militant Islamist movements will gain a stronger foothold in the region. This is an important discussion indeed – and I fully agree with the analysts who have pointed out that the post-Soviet Uzbek government's general authoritarianism, and especially its repression of religious freedom, are counterproductive, may lead to growing discontent among the broader population, and could make more people feel that the only means of resistance is violent protest. But it is also important to point out – and it has indeed been demonstrated in several of the recent fieldwork-based and fine-grained studies of Islam in the region – that, in spite of economic hardship, in spite of the experience of all sorts of social injustice, and (in some parts of the region) in spite of state authoritarianism and the repression of religious freedom, the highest priority for most people on the ground is peace. Contrary to the prevalent idea that Muslim piety equals radicalism and should be seen by definition as a threat to the secular order,[3] for most Muslims in the region engagement in Islam appears to have more to do with the cultivation of moral selfhood in a broader social context, where radical social change has challenged received ideas about accountability, community, and justice and where people can choose from a rich variety of ideas about what it takes to be a good Muslim.

Notes

1   Whereas the government was dominated by people from the Leninabad region (who had also made up most of the ruling elite during the entire Soviet period), the opposition was dominated by people from Garm and Gorno-Badakshan.

2   Independent human rights and crisis watch organizations have regularly documented how these crackdowns have hit not only Islamic radicals or militants but also their families, as well as thousands of ordinary pious practicing Muslims, who have been exiled, jailed, tortured, and sentenced to long prison terms for anti-state activities and alleged links with Islamic fundamentalists.

3   As David Abramson (2010) has demonstrated in a recent report on foreign religious education among Central Asian Muslims, notably Muslims who travel abroad in order to study Islam are likely to be suspected of being politically motivated, although the vast majority pursue their studies for a wide range of non-violent and not radical reasons.

Discussion Questions

1   Does the Soviet past still influence the way Islam is understood and practiced in Central Asia today?

2   What is the relationship between state policies toward Islam and the ways in which people in the region are able to explore what it means to be Muslim?

3   Which beliefs and practices are contested among Muslims in Central Asia, and why?

Suggested Further Reading

Abashin, Sergei (2006). The logic of Islamic practice: A religious conflict in Central Asia. *Central Asian Survey*, 25(3): 267–286.

Abramson, David M. (2010, March). Foreign religious education and the Central Asian Islamic revival: Impact and prospects for stability. Silk Road Paper published by the Central Asia-Caucasus Institute and Silk Road Studies Program.

Atkin, Muriel (1995). Islam as faith, politics and bogeyman in Tajikistan. In M. Bourdeaux (ed.), *The Politics of Religion in Russia and the New States of Eurasia*. Armonk, NY: M. E. Sharpe, pp. 247–272.

Atkin, Muriel (2000). The rhetoric of Islamophobia. *Central Asia and Caucasus Journal*, 1: 123–132.

Bennigsen, Alexandre and Chantal Lemercier-Quelquejay (1981). *Les Musulmans oubliés: L'Islam en Union soviétique*. Paris: Maspéro.

Hilgers, Irene (2009). *Why Do Uzbeks Have to Be Muslims? Exploring Religiosity in the Ferghana Valley*. Münster: Lit Verlag.

Jessa, Pawel (2006). Aq Jol soul healers: Religious pluralism and a contemporary Muslim movement in Kazakhstan. *Central Asian Survey*, 25(3): 359–371.

Kamp, Marianne (2006). *The New Woman in Uzbekistan: Islam, Modernity, and Unveiling under Communism*. Seattle, WA: University of Washington Press.

Kehl-Bodrogi, Krisztina (2006a). Islam contested: Nation, religion, and tradition in post-Soviet Turkmenistan. In Chris Hann and the Civil Religion Group (eds.), *The Postsocialist Religious Question: Faith and Power in Central Asia and East-Central Europe*. Münster: Lit Verlag, pp. 125–146.

Kehl-Bodrogi, Krisztina (2006b). Who owns the shrine? Competing meanings and authorities at a Pilgrimage site in Khorezm. *Central Asian Survey*, 25(3): 235–250.

Khalid, Adeeb (2007). *Islam after Communism: Religion and Politics in Central Asia*. Berkeley, CA: University of California Press.

Larouelle, Marlene (2007). Religious revival, nationalism and the "invention of tradition": Political Tengrism in Central Asia and Tatarstan. *Central Asian Survey*, 26(2): 203–216.

Liu, Morgan (2011). Central Asia in the post-Cold War world. *Annual Review of Anthropology*, 40: 115–131.

Louw, Maria (2007). *Everyday Islam in Post-Soviet Central Asia*. London: Routledge.

Louw, Maria (2010). Dreaming up futures: Dream omens and magic in Bishkek. *History and Anthropology*, 21(3): 277–292.

Louw, Maria (2011). Being Muslim the ironic way: Secularism, religion and irony in post-Soviet Kyrgyzstan. In Nils Bubandt and Martijn van Beek (eds.), *Varieties of Secularism in Asia: Anthropological explorations of religion, politics and the spiritual*. London: Routledge, pp. 143–162.

McBrien, Julie (2006). Listening to the wedding Speaker: Discussing religion and culture in southern Kyrgyzstan. *Central Asian Survey*, 25(3): 341–358.

Northrop, Douglas (2004). *Veiled Empire: Gender and Power in Stalinist Central Asia*. Ithaca, NY: Cornell University Press.

Pelkmans, Mathijs (2006). Asymmetries on the "religious market" in Kyrgyzstan. In Chris Hann and the Civil Religion Group (eds.), *The Postsocialist Religious Question: Faith and Power in Central Asia and East-Central Europe*. Münster: Lit Verlag, pp. 29–46.

Rasanayagam, Johan (2011). *Islam in Post-Soviet Uzbekistan: The Morality of Experience*. Cambridge: Cambridge University Press.

Sahadeo, Jeff, and Russell Zanca (eds.) (2007). *Everyday Life in Central Asia: Past and Present*. Bloomington, IN: Indiana University Press.

Stephan, Manja (2010). Education, youth and Islam: The growing popularity of private religious lessons in Dushanbe, Tajikistan. *Central Asian Survey*, 29(4): 469–483.

12

Islam in Indonesia and Malaysia

AMINAH BEVERLY MCCLOUD

Introduction

Indonesia (see Map 12.1) is the world's largest Islamic country: almost 90 percent of its 238 million people are officially identified as Muslim. The remaining 10 percent are Christian, Hindu, Buddhist, Confucian, and animist. Indonesian Muslims are almost all Sunni. The country has not, however, been plagued by the

An Introduction to Islam in the 21st Century, First Edition. Edited by Aminah Beverly McCloud, Scott W. Hibbard, and Laith Saud.

kind of intolerance, extremism, and religious violence that has characterized other parts of the Muslim world. On the contrary, until 1998, the government based its legitimacy on the twin pillars of national unity and religious pluralism. Even if President Suharto, a long-time ruler, relied upon repression and military rule to stay in power, the government's policies toward religion encouraged an inclusive and tolerant interpretation of the Islamic tradition, which could thus at least survive, if not thrive. Moreover, since Suharto's resignation in 1998, the country has been governed by democratic institutions, which include a popularly elected president and a parliament, as well as an independent judiciary. Remarkably, though, this open political system has nonetheless provided space for the emergence of some anti-democratic groups – such as Laskar Jihad, which has targeted the Christian population with violence. However, the pluralist nature of the general population's beliefs has secured a strong resistance to these kinds of incursions into a progressive society.

Arab Muslim traders made their first contact with Indonesians in the 8th century. This assertion is based on evidence in the form of gravesites, which have been preserved over the centuries by generations of indigenous villagers. But the population remained predominantly Hindu, Buddhist, and animist until the end of the 13th century, when accounts of the spread of Islam began to be made. Then came Muslim traders, mostly from Gujarat in India, who helped spread Islam through marriage; they also introduced it into the royal houses of the principal ruling families of the islands' kingdoms. By the end of the 13th century Islam was firmly established in North Sumatra; by the end of the 14th it had spread in northeast Malaya, Brunei, the southwestern Philippines, and some of the countries of East Java; by the fifteenth century it reached Malacca and other areas of the Malay Peninsula. Again, the spread of Islam was not associated with military conquest; rather it was done mainly through assimilation and marriage. Islam subsequently supplanted Hinduism and Buddhism as the dominant religion; this happened in the 17th century. Bali adopted both Islam and Christianity throughout the 17th and 18th centuries. During this process of acculturation influences from Hinduism and Buddhism were tolerated and some practices were Islamized.

Sidebar 12.1   Islam in Indonesia

8th century	The Arabs make initial contact
13–17th centuries	Muslim traders arrive from India and spread Islam across the islands
15th century	The Portuguese invade Indonesia
16th century	The Spanish Inquisition is introduced in the Philippines; Indonesia is divided between a Spanish north and a Muslim Malay south
17th century	The Dutch displace the Portuguese as principal colonial power
Late 17th century	The British invade Indonesia
Late 19th century	The Dutch re-invade Indonesia
1942	The Japanese invade and occupy Indonesia
August 17, 1945	Indonesia becomes independent
1946	The British withdraw
1948	The Dutch attempt a re-invasion
1950	Indonesia becomes the Federal Republic of the United States of Indonesia

There are a few scholarly accounts of conversion narratives and changes in governmental or societal structures from which more details about the engagement of Islam can be drawn. From this fragmentary evidence research can conclude that the spread of Islam was slow; the process was still incomplete by the time of European colonization. What really defines Indonesian Islam is its pluralism, its tolerance, and its syncretism. This is due in large measure to its early history and to the extreme diversity of indigenous cultures that inhabit the 16,000 islands comprising modern-day Indonesia. As Islam spread, it merged with these indigenous cultures, beliefs, and practices, often retaining elements of the Hindu tradition it displaced. Although a more orthodox interpretation of Islam came to be more pronounced in the 18th and 19th centuries, the syncretistic Islam – along with a strong Sufi tradition – has continued to be influential. This diversity of religious practice, allied to the ethnic makeup of the country, has created the basis for a relatively high degree of religious and political tolerance in the whole society.

The Colonial Encounter

The Portuguese arrived in the region first, capturing and then occupying the commercially important Straits of Malacca in 1512. Local Islamic scholars migrated, along with traders, to other islands, spreading Islam in the places where they landed. Ottoman forces were able to halt much of the Portuguese aggression and created a balance of power between Portugal and the rulers of the region, but only for a short time. The Spanish came next, and they were militarily more powerful than the Portuguese. Magellan arrived in 1521, just around the time when the sultan of Manila accepted Islam. In 1564 the Philippines fell to the Spanish, who then introduced what Malay scholars refer to as an "Inquisition": there were forced conversions to Catholicism, the alternative being death. The Portuguese and Spanish invasions halted the northern spread of Islam and prevented its spread into Vietnam and Indochina. Political resistance to the Europeans from indigenous populations was widespread, and a stalemate was eventually reached in the 16th century when a boundary was drawn between the Spanish possessions in the north and Muslim Malay territories to the south.

In the 17th century the Dutch colonized the region, displacing the Portuguese as the principal colonial power in the Far East. By this time the region was known in the world for its immense natural resources and opportunities for trade. Spices such as nutmeg, pepper, clove, as well as sandalwood, rubber, and teak were highly prized in Europe as items for trade. The aims of the Dutch included creating a monopoly of trading ports; in this way they inadvertently helped facilitate the spread of Islam into rural areas, as Muslim traders were forced to relocate. The Dutch captured and indentured large numbers of Malays, then transported them to other possessions such as South Africa, again, inadvertently

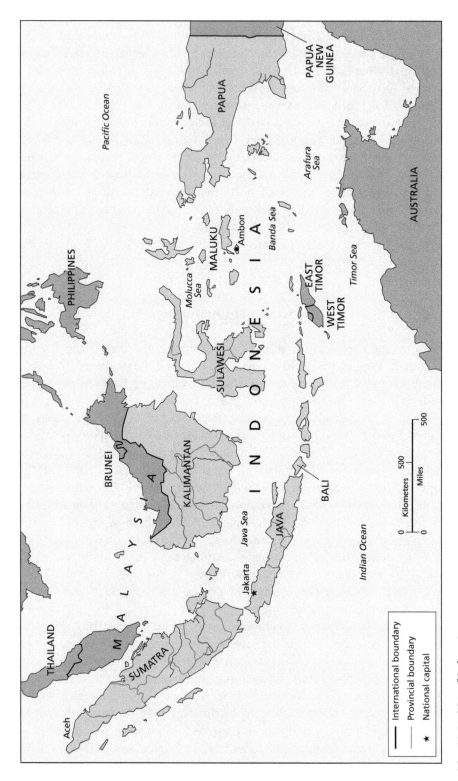

Map 12.1 Map of Indonesia.

introducing and spreading Islam there. The British, after consolidating their holdings in India, proceeded to occupy the Straits of Malacca in 1812. In the second half of the 19th century the states of the archipelago fell like domino pieces to the Dutch and the British.

In the ensuing struggle for independence, the Malay language provided a common bond for the population, while Islam was a primary vehicle for the expression of their demands for freedom. The struggle for independence gave impetus to the consolidation of Islamic influence. The faith of Islam spread, and by the turn of the 20th century the entire archipelago had become Muslim, except for the Island of Bali and Singapore.

An important part of this history is the migration of Chinese to the region. In pre-Islamic Asia, China had the greater political–military–technological influence on the continent's eastern civilizations, while India had the greater religious–cultural influence. During the 19th century, however, many Chinese were brought to work on plantations in Malaysia and Indonesia, while others came as merchants and stayed. By the end of the century the Chinese formed a third of the population of Malaysia and a small but extremely influential minority of the population of Indonesia. Most of the Chinese migrants did not become Muslim, as many had converted to Christianity; this reflects the importance of European influence at that time. They also established themselves as economic elites in these areas, in part because of their connections to the Chinese mainland and in part due to the favoritism they enjoyed under European colonial rule. But this would cause considerable problems for them in the postcolonial period, when the nationalist agitation was to take on anti-Christian and anti-Chinese overtones.

Indonesia in the 20th Century

Politics and Economics

In the 20th century the Dutch introduced the Ethical Policy, under which farming and limited health and educational services were developed for Indonesia. Railways, roads, and inter-island shipping were expanded. The policy helped create two new social elements: a Western-educated class of Indonesians; and a smaller group of Indonesian entrepreneurs, who began to compete with a predominantly Chinese commercial class. Nevertheless, social movements at the beginning of the 20th century were aimed at ridding the country of foreign occupation.

The first important vehicle for the anti-Dutch nationalist movement was the Sarekat Islam (Islamic Union) established in 1912. This movement grew from an association designed to protect batik merchants, and it found in Islam a useful language for political mobilization. Six years later the organization had more than 2 million members from all over the archipelago. The Dutch were initially tolerant of nationalist organizations and in 1916 created the People's Council, where representatives from various groups could debate and advise the government on policy. This policy of inclusion proved to be too little given too late. After World War I, the Dutch government became more repressive in the face of a more assertive nationalist opposition, and the rise of communism was even more problematic. In the 1920s, men whose first priority was not the re-establishment of Islamic states but freedom from oppression headed the Indonesian nationalist movement. The first chief of state of postcolonial Indonesia, President Sukarno, was one of the leaders of this independence movement. Despite repeated arrests by the Dutch administrators, he and his co-conspirators were able to sustain its momentum and the spirit of democracy well into the years preceding World War II.

In 1942 the Japanese invaded and occupied Indonesia. Key Japanese priorities in the war were gaining Indonesian support for their regime and, even more importantly, gaining access to Indonesia's strategic petroleum reserves. The Japanese gave symbolic political freedom to leaders of the Indonesian Nationalist Party on the one hand, although on the other they forced tens of thousands of Indonesians into conscripted labor. Consequently the Japanese were not welcomed as liberators from the Dutch. On August 17, 1945, two days after the Japanese surrendered to the Allies, the Nationalist Party declared an independent Republic of Indonesia. When the British landed to take advantage of the Japanese retreat a month later, a functioning republican administration had been established in Java and Sumatra. Subsequently the British were forced to withdraw in 1946, and the Linggajati Agreement was signed between British, Dutch, and Indonesian authorities: it was designed to give authority to the Republic in Java and Sumatra, which had plans for a federal Indonesia.

The Dutch, reluctant to let go of lucrative holdings, launched missile attacks on Indonesian forces in 1947, claiming that the Indonesians had violated the Linggajati Agreement. They defied a UN cease-fire in December 1948 and attacked the Republic again, undeterred. They immediately arrested the Indonesian leaders and sent them into exile. However, resistance from Indonesians, along with protests from the international community, produced a cease-fire. In 1949 the Dutch finally agreed to relinquish sovereignty to the Federal Republic of the United States of Indonesia – the formal name of the republic since 1950. At this point the Indonesian government had the incredible task of creating a viable state from the many peoples and cultures of the islands and to quell various uprisings and staunch remnants of Dutch-led resistance movements on small islands.

Despite an early commitment to democratic rule, President Sukarno sought to reform the party system and to replace liberal democracy with what was referred to as a "guided democracy." His localization of power and its benefits in the central government, with little attention paid to the smaller islands, led to further uprisings inspired by a group that received covert aid from the US and Taiwan. Meanwhile Sukarno pursued an active foreign policy and a policy of suppressing dissent at home, thus killing hundreds of thousands of citizens. During his regime all elections were tightly controlled, and all enterprises were owned by the state. Sukarno did, however, institutionalize a secular vision of national development – one premised upon the so-called Pancasila ("five principles"): (1) a non-sectarian belief in God; (2) an emphasis upon national unity; (3) consensus through deliberation; (4) humanitarianism; and (5) social justice. This understanding of secular nationalism is reflective of the era and of other countries pursuing similar policies (these are described in Chapter 6). Secularism in this sense meant non-discrimination in matters of belief and reflected the religious and ethnic diversity of the country.

When Sukarno was forced out by the Indonesian military in 1968, his successor and a former general, the new President Suharto, followed largely similar policies. Suharto's two fears were political mobilization on the left, from the Communist Party (which had tried to overthrow Sukarno earlier) and political mobilization on the right, from right-wing Islamic activists. Suharto's "New Order," which governed from the mid-1960s until 1998, subsequently used the various institutions of the state to dominate both of these opposition groups, while continuing to promote a depoliticized Islam in the state schools. Atheism was banned (tied as it was to communism), and religion highly regulated by the state. Economically, Suharto used his dominance of the political system to regulate access to resources in the country. By the 1990s a large portion of Indonesia's wealth was concentrated in the hands of the president's family and associates.

Culture

Muslim women leaders arose from networks of two central Muslim organizations: Muhammadiyah – founded in 1912, with 20 million followers, and considered modernist – and the more traditional Nahdlatul Ulama (NU) – founded in 1926, with around 30 million followers. These groups have guided and influenced Indonesian Muslims since the beginning of the 20th century. Both have branches for women and offer their female members opportunities to be active religious leaders and teachers. The primary differences between them are in their methods of interpreting the sources of Islam and in their tolerance for local cultural norms.

Modernists/reformists encourage the direct reading of the Qur'an and of various hadith. Rather than relying on the perceived wisdom of classical scholarship, they are in favor of the use of independent reasoning, and thus opinions, in shaping interpretation. They are less tolerant of local cultural idioms and feel that these artifacts must be removed from Islamic belief and practices, wherever they may be found. Traditionalists, on the other hand, rely on the Qur'an, hadith, and jurisprudence along with classical works for guidance and interpretation. They are much more tolerant of local cultural expressions, as long as these do not contradict Islam.

In Indonesia the predominant branch of Islam is Sunni, and within it the predominant legal school is Shafi'i. Both Muhammadiyah and NU promote a moderate version of Islam over and against more conservative or politically traditional versions. Muhammadiyah's 'Aisyiyah was set up in 1917, whereas the

NU did not allow its women to start the Muslimat until 1946. In each group there are organizations for girls and young women to guarantee the transmission of knowledge and legacy. Undoubtedly these organizations had to adjust to Dutch colonization and to the struggle for independence along with having discussions on women's roles in the Muslim world.

Within these networks, women have had to convince male leadership that the issues women raise are serious and that sometimes there is a need for reinterpretation when these issues are not addressed in traditional – or even in modern – scholarship. Women in these organizations consider themselves grassroots organizers and are committed to the education of women. Before the country's independence many of the women "preachers" were informally educated, but afterwards the government opened state sponsored institutes for Islamic higher learning where men and women could study to become leaders in the Muslim community. From the 1990s on female scholars could be full members of the main male organizations and members of the committees that produce fatwas (advisories) and interpretations of the Qur'an and hadith. Indonesia is unique in that it counts large numbers of women who, officially and unofficially, participate in the interpretation of the sources of Islam. Readers should note that this accomplishment is not without resistance from men, as women still struggle for a piece of the discourse action.

After independence, Muslimat NU women became active in politics by serving their organization and participating in the formation of the governmental system. Five of the 45 seats in parliament were given to them in the 1955 election, along with five seats to women in the Communist Party and three seats to women in the Reformist Party.

In the 20th century, after independence, Indonesia began the difficult process of carving a national ethos and identifying elements of a common identity for the hundreds of ethnic and linguistic groups living within the country's territorial boundaries. A common identity developed largely in opposition to colonialism and the struggle against European imperialism. Although at the end of the 20th century the Republic of Indonesia was only 50 years old, its multicultural experiences clocked up at least 16 centuries. Indonesia's sheer size and ethnic diversity has made national identity problematic and sometimes hotly contested. Scholars of the region assert that identity is defined at many levels: through Indonesian citizenship; through the flag, the national anthem, and certain other songs; through recognition of national holidays; and through an education that includes Indonesia's history and the five principles on which the nation is based.

For much of the 1950s and 1960s the nation was held together by military force. This was due primarily to the real and potential danger of ethnic and regional separation. As mentioned earlier, the relationships between native Indonesians and migrant Chinese have been greatly influenced by government policies – first Dutch, then Indonesian. While the Chinese only number 4 to 6 million or about 3 percent of the population, they are said to control "as much as 60 percent of the nation's wealth."

Ethnic and religious differences may be related. Indonesia has the largest Muslim population in the world, and many ethnic groups are exclusively Muslim. Dutch policy permitted proselytization to Protestants and Catholics among the non-Muslim groups who followed traditional religions; ethnic communities that are exclusively Protestant or Roman Catholic were created. Tensions arise when communities of one religion migrate to a place where a different religion is already established. Political and economic power becomes linked to both ethnicity and religion, as groups favor their own family and ethnic group for jobs and other benefits.

The basic economy revolves around subsistence farming, which produces market crops. Plantations are devoted to oil palm, rubber, sugar, and diesel, which underscore the richness of the region. One important change during Suharto's "New Order" regime (1968–1998) was the rapid urbanization and industrialization of Java, where the production of goods for domestic import and export expanded exponentially. Though this economic development benefitted most people, it also widened the gap between rich and poor, urban and rural. The severe economic downturn in the nation after 1997 and the political instability that followed the fall of Suharto drastically reduced foreign investment.

Indonesia in the 21st Century

Throughout 2000 Indonesia experienced deep governmental crises, and thus many institutions were redesigned. Since the 1945 Constitution, there are six mandated organs of the state: the People's Consultative Assembly, the presidency, the People's Representative Council, the Supreme Advisory Council, the State Audit board, and the Supreme Court. The president is elected every five years by the People's Consultative Assembly, which has 1,000 members elected from the provinces. Even with all of these stopgap organs, Suharto had managed to make Indonesia his own reserve.

Although the country's government leaders managed to forgive Suharto's massacres and the Western support he enjoyed, the region is reeling in the aftermath. Researchers report that, after a decade of democracy, secular political parties dominate Muslim-majority Indonesia. New Islamist parties have thus far found that they only receive a fraction of the vote in elections, which minimizes their influence on government, but their numbers have increased their influence among the people. For example, new masajid are being built everywhere, and more women wear the veil. However, this popular influence has not yet made its mark on the political scene.

Elites remain in control of the wealth and, as poverty continues to increase, the gap between rich and poor grows exponentially. According to the World Bank Report (2010), 49 percent of Indonesians survive on less than $2 a day. Post-Suharto Indonesia is now known as Asia's least well-educated country; it is a supplier of raw materials and an assembly line for multi-national companies. Also, according to the UN Report, in 2006 Indonesia became the world's most natural disaster-prone nation.

Indonesia is experiencing some small-scale religious tensions and intolerance, undoubtedly due to economic conditions and recent climate disasters. Yet according to *The Asia Times* (2006) Islam maintains a more visible place in a secular Indonesia. The democracy that seems to be in the process of consolidating there is one in which Muslim parties of all kinds – Muslim brotherhood-inspired urban parties, rural patron–client parties, programmatically secular parties with Muslim organizations as their mass bases – have lost support to fully secular parties. The picture in the 21st century thus far is one of a majority Muslim population in a secular Indonesia struggling over its natural resources with multi-nationals supported by the West.

Malaysia

History

Initially the history of Islam in Malaysia is the same as the history of Islam in Indonesia. The differences lie in geography. The spread of Islam is more continuous. Lying midway between India and China, Malaysia's monsoons were instrumental in the development of commerce and trade, and thus Islam, ironically, followed the monsoons. Adventurers and merchants recount their visits to the country as early as 1292, when Marco Polo sailed through the Strait of Malacca, between Malaya and Sumatra. Malacca, a fishing village, was the initial contact for Islam. From there Islam spread to Malaysia when Muzaffar Shah, an Indian Muslim, converted his people to Islam. This extraordinarily rich island also attracted the Europeans – the Portuguese, the Dutch, and the British – and later the Japanese.

After each of the military incursions of these people the wealth of the country was directed to the colonial home; the indigenous populations had little idea of the wealth extracted from their labor and land. Colonizers found themselves in control of unimaginable riches and had few constraints over their actions. Toward the end of the 18th century the Dutch, like the Portuguese before them, were overextended in protecting their land holdings and found themselves subjugated by British military power. The British extended their control (and sovereignty) over the Straits and created an exclusive sphere of influence in most of the Malay Peninsula by 1824. Due to the new industrial innovations in mass production and to the demand for tinned meats and fish during the Civil War in the United States, enterprising Chinese merchants in Malaysia expanded their mines and their commercial activities. They also imported to Malaysia tens of thousands of indentured Chinese workers. This was the major (though inauspicious) beginning of a significant Chinese presence in this country. The British brought prosperity to themselves, and indirectly to Malaysia, along with a large Chinese population and a Western understanding of the rule of law. Malays, of course, survived the occupation and usurpation of their wealth but incurred the enduring challenges and racial and class struggles that colonization left in its wake.

The population of indentured Chinese workers remained and grew (currently it represents 23.7 percent of the population), and its wealth increased as the British nurtured and favored it over native Malays. In 1957, the year of independence from British rule, the population of Malaysia was about 12 million. The constitution created a federation of 13 states across two regions – peninsular Malaysia and east Malaysia. The government is set up in such a way that the head of state is the king – a monarch elected every five years, who is chosen from the hereditary rulers of the nine Malay states. The head of government is the prime minister, whose office also rotates among the states. The federal constitution of 1957 made Islam the official religion and affirmed religious freedom, on condition that others should not proselytize Muslims. Citizenship was also regulated. Citizenship is not automatically granted to those born in Malaysia, but it is granted to any child born of two Malaysian parents outside of the country. Dual citizenship is not permitted. All ethnic Malays are considered Muslim by law and obliged to follow the decisions of *sharia* courts in matters of religion such as marriage, inheritance, divorce, apostasy, religious conversion, or custody. No criminal or civil offences are under the jurisdiction of the *sharia* courts; civil courts handle such offences.

The Education Act of 1961 sought to restore native Malays to a position of control over their country through a series of initiatives resembling affirmative action. For example, state primary schools could teach in Malay, English, Chinese, or Tamil, but secondary schools could teach only in Malay or English. Native Malays were given tuition, free secondary education, economic privileges, special quotas for land grants, educational grants, and so on. Needless to say, the inter-ethnic tensions caused by this Act were intense. Not only did the educational reforms favor Malays, but there were other reforms and initiatives that put Malays in firm control of their land, often at the expense of the Chinese Christian minority elite. Similarly, in 1965 the government founded the Bank Bumiputra ("Son of Soil"), which offered credit, banking services, and technical assistance to Malay individuals and businesses. Companies receiving government assistance were encouraged to hire Malays where their preference had been Chinese. In 1969 the tensions caused by this preferential treatment were boiling, and the elections of that year, which saw a backlash against Malay parties, resulted in race riots in the capital and elsewhere in the country.

As a result, the government began a series of new economic plans. In 1970 a new economic policy was especially designed to implement an economic restructuring intended to correct imbalances between Malays and the Chinese workers. This plan stressed national harmony and saw economic growth as key to minimizing ethnic and religious tensions. The second, third, and fourth plans (1971–1985) continued the emphasis on rural development, education, and employment under a constitutional amendment that forbade public discussion of special rights for Malays. The infrastructure of Malaysia is one of the most developed in Asia; its telecommunications are second only to those of Singapore. The country has seven international ports, along with 200 industrial parks. Fresh water is available to over 95 percent of the population. Malaysia has 118 airports, state-run railways, and news systems. These statistics are what keeps the general population relatively moderate in its tastes, politics, and religion. Nevertheless, even though the economic record has been impressive, ethnic tensions remain. Still, these tensions have not yet derailed the economic success.

Women, Islam, and Transnational Movements

In 1987 a group of women lawyers, activists, academics, and journalists began to discern challenges that women were facing in their treatment in *sharia* courts. In 1990 Sisters in Islam (SIS) was born, a women's organization aiming to challenge laws and policy made in the name of Islam that discriminate against women. Later their work expanded to include issues emerging around democracy, human rights, and constitutionalism. Like women's groups in Indonesia, SIS was not without its detractors. Its most ardent attack was on the institution of polygyny and on the government's defense of it. Islamist groups have consistently attacked the organization, even contesting its use of the word "Islam" in the name. SIS is vigilant about any real or potential breach of women's rights, regardless of whether the women concerned know their rights or not. This in many ways is a first in the Muslim world – just like the two women's groups in Indonesia that are promoting the need for the education of women into the ranks of Muslim authority. Added to these internal instances of growth and development are links to the outside Muslim and non-Muslim world.

Non-state Islamist movements that are fluid and dynamic in their organization, in their innovative techniques, have a wide pool of potential transnational partners. Questions arise as to what to do proactively to prevent chaos. One suggestion is that the Malaysian government could integrate the Islamists' transnational contracts into the mainstream. They should not be regarded as a challenge. Friendly governments such the United States could assist the government by not associating these Islamists groups with terrorist threats, though there is a rising anti-American sentiment caused by US intrusiveness into government affairs.

Ties between Malaysians and other Muslims in Southeast Asia and in the Arab world have their origins in the 7th and 8th centuries. These links pre-date by far those formed in the 18th century, when Malaysians were already traveling to the Middle East for the obligatory pilgrimage to Mecca and to seek religious education in places like Egypt. As in Indonesia, Arab and Indian reformist thinkers influenced some of these Malaysian students, both during and immediately after the colonial era. Many of them were part of the Islamist movement and led the ideological fight against colonialism. Later on, these same activists were very influential in shaping a more overt Islamic identity in Malaysia. Global Muslim identity is not a new development, but the connections had previously been limited to elites. The current generation of Islamists, like their brethren, want to implement Islamic law in every aspect of life, as in Saudi Arabia. Their ideology, though challenged on many fronts, is making headway regarding outward manifestations of Islam such as dress and gender separation.

There is, however, fierce non-European competition for influence in the region as Iran and Saudi Arabia vie with each other. The 1979 Iranian Revolution caught the attention of many Muslims throughout the world. The admiration for the Iranians, researchers assert, had more to do with the regime's stance against the West than with any ideological affiliation. Some youth groups adopted the political slogans of Ayatollah Ruhollah Khomeini, and some of their leaders went to Iran to support the success of the revolution. Youth from some of these groups sought to establish an Islamist state *à la* Iran in Malaysia. The Iranian government and its revolution were of major concern to many Muslim governments in the 1980s, as they feared that they would predispose their people to revolution. Iran's overtures to the Indonesian people did lead to the emergence of a small Shi'i community there. Saudi Arabia used other strategies.

Saudi Arabia provided Malaysia with scholarships for Islamic training and learning in its universities and assisted students in the formation of "study groups" whose job was to push the Islamist agenda. As mentioned earlier in the section on Indonesia, not all Malaysian and Indonesian students were influenced by Salafi or brotherhood ideologies. Many of them have supported the government against the onslaught of Islamists in their countries. Yet these Islamist groups did have an impact on thinking in the region.

Wahhabi and brotherhood movements have provided platforms on which Islamists throughout the Muslim world interact and exchange ideas. One infamous case, in 1973, was that of Anwar Ibrahim, one of the leaders of an Islamist student group who had become a very influential political leader both at home and abroad. Ibrahim was subsequently brought into the government under Prime Minister Mahathir Bin Muhammad, who sought to use religion as a means of sanctioning authoritarian rule. In the early 1990s, however, Ibrahim and Mahathir had a conflict of interests and agendas. Ibrahim was subsequently jailed by the government on charges that, on the surface, had little to do with his political affiliations but everything to do with defaming him and his ideology. Muslims all over the world protested against his arrest, regardless of whether they agreed with him or not, as they saw here the beginning of Malaysia becoming a repressive state. While Ibrahim is now a free man who continues with his international connections, researchers speculate on whether the ensuing chaos could not have been avoided by simply allowing freedom of speech and thus dissent – a perfectly Islamic thing to do. There are myriad instances where the brotherhood has served a mediating role between Muslims, Muslims and non-Muslims, thus affirming the Islamic obligation of mediation.

When the 1990 war in Kuwait broke out, Islamist parties and groups coordinated their efforts to resolve the conflict. While the mission was unsuccessful, it led to the formation of a formal conference called the International Gathering of Islamic

Groups, held in London in 1991. Malaysia was well represented at this conference. Throughout the 1990s the group tackled issues that represented a challenge for Muslims, such as the conflicts in Bosnia, Kashmir, and Chechnya. Malaysia's government has not prevented Jamaat leaders from coming to Malaysia to hold study trips, so perhaps the government has reconsidered its stance on free speech and dissent.

Conclusion

After the September 11, 2001 terrorist attacks and the subsequent ones in London and Italy, which culminated in a global war on terror, the arbitrariness of military actions caused shock and awe in the entire Muslim world. Most Southeast Asian Muslims considered all of the attacks inhumane and condemned the actions of those involved. But in 2003 they began to see the war on terror as a war against Islam. In Indonesia, surveys conducted by the Center for the Study of Islam and Society in Jakarta (Indonesia) in 2003 found that the majority of those surveyed felt that Indonesia should have an Islamic government based on the Qur'an and that all Muslims should be required to abide by Islamic law. In 2004 a Malaysian survey that is no longer available, conducted by the Merdeka Center, found that 50 percent of the Muslim respondents believed that the implementation of Islamic criminal laws would lead to a lower crime rate, and 91 percent supported Malaysia as an Islamic state. Yet the geography and pluralist heritage of these countries prevented the Islamists from capitalizing on anti-American sentiments wholesale. In both cases ethnic diversity has fostered a greater degree of political and religious pluralism.

What Islamist groups did was to encourage Muslim activism rather than anti-American sentiments. Nevertheless, the Western obsession with terrorists – treated as actors to be pursued with or without government's knowledge and to be killed regardless of states' sovereignty and the rule of law – has led in recent years to a new discourse, which departs from the previous narrative of Malaysia and Indonesia as bedrocks of peaceful and tolerant Islam. These countries continue to "keep the peace" between ethnic and religious groups, but Western military actions against Muslims in South Asia, the Middle East, and the Horn of Africa have fostered a greater degree of anti-Western sentiment. Reports that Malaysia facilitated movements of al-Qaeda operatives and provided a haven for meetings, illegal transfers of funds, and training have put Malaysia near the front in the minds of Western strategists where terrorism is concerned.

The Malaysian government's response in 2002 was to work on its own anti-terrorist credentials, which it did by allowing the United States to operate the Southeast Asian Regional Centre for Counter-Terrorism. While most Malays see the immediate benefits of such an alliance with the US (since it brings greater security and defense capacity), the backlash in some quarters of the community grows as this "mutual cooperation" progresses. Some Malays fear that the US will attack without provocation, as it did in Iraq, Afghanistan, and Pakistan. The Malay government's move toward cooperation with a Western power was also an attempt to thwart the ongoing efforts of Islamist groups. Western alliances, however, muddy the water in other ways. Westerners do not distinguish between activists, preachers, and terrorists. There is little discernment of legitimate dissent; consequently, the highly intrusive information gathering and surveillance of religious activities extends widely into a variety of communities. The US military and security services have little understanding of a truly multicultural, multi-religious society (particularly one that is an Islamic state); nor are the strategists able to understand the relationship of Muslim lands on the periphery with the Muslim center in the Arab world. There is, in short, little understanding of the diverse ways in which Islam operates in public life.

These highly diverse societies of Malaysia and Indonesia defy superficial stereotyping. Southeast Asian Muslims have lived in relatively healthy pluralist societies and are at home with their numerical majority, though non-natives control the wealth in both countries. Both countries have invested in their heterogeneity and have absorbed much of the Islamist rhetoric. This rhetoric has predominated not because it threatens the society, but rather because it vacillates dramatically from moderate to radical to quietist. Both countries felt the effects of the Asian economic crash. Malaysia survived better than Indonesia, but, after centuries of colonial exploitation, both countries have limited supplies of resources. Luckily the Suharto reign hardly left any legacy in Malaysia; as for Indonesians, it is fortunate that they survived.

Rulers in both countries have attempted to build a kind of nationalism that transcends ethnic and religious differences between peoples. They have done so in a manner that emphasizes a vibrant and tolerant Islam. Consequently the success of these nationalist endeavors is evident in the two countries' ability to remain cohesive in the face of economic crisis and to avoid the pitfalls of religious and ethnic chauvinism. What can be learned is that there are several kinds of political Islam; one kind seeks the homogeneity of ideology, another rules a country that is heterogeneous. Malaysia and Indonesia are prime examples of the diversity of the Muslim experience in the 21st century.

Discussion Questions

1   How does the experience of Indonesia and Malaysia differ from that of other regions discussed in this volume? How is it similar?
2   How do historical context, ethnic diversity, and geographical location affect the dominant understanding of the religious tradition? How might a different historical experience produce a different outcome?
3   How do the two cases differ from each other? In what respects are they most similar?

Suggested Further Reading

Azra, Azyumardi (2006). *Indonesia, Islam and Democracy: Dynamics in Global Context*. Solstice Publishing. At www.solsticepublishing.com.

Geertz, Clifford (1971). *Islam Observed: Religious Development in Morocco and Indonesia*. Chicago, IL: University of Chicago Press.

Laffan, Michael Francis (2007). *Islamic Nationhood and Colonial Indonesia*. New York, NY: Routledge.

Laffan, Michael Francis (2011). *The Makings of Indonesian Islam: Orientalism and the Narration of a Sufi Past*. Princeton, NJ: Princeton University Press.

Owen, Norman (ed.) (2004). *The Emergence of Modern Southeast Asia: A New History*. Honolulu, Hawaii: University of Hawaii Press.

Pringle, Robert (2004). *Understanding Islam in Indonesia: Politics and Diversity*. Honolulu, Hawaii: University of Hawaii Press.

Ricklefs, M. C. (2008). *A History of Modern Indonesia Since 1200*. Palo Alto, CA: Stanford University Press.

Tanthowi, Pramono (2008). *Muslims and Tolerance: Non-Muslim Minorities under Shariah in Indonesia*. Chiang Mai, Thailand: Silkworm Books.

Weintraub, Andrew (2011). *Islam and Popular Culture in Indonesia and Malaysia*. New York, NY: Routledge.

13

Muslim Histories in Latin America and the Caribbean

John Tofik Karam

Introduction

Muslims inhabit the more than 500-year history of Latin America and the Caribbean. In the 16th century Iberians and North Africans with Muslim ancestry, often labeled *moros* (Moors) or *moriscos* (Moorish descendents), were implicated in the Spanish colonization of the New World. From that time until

An Introduction to Islam in the 21st Century, First Edition. Edited by Aminah Beverly McCloud, Scott W. Hibbard, and Laith Saud.

© 2013 Blackwell Publishing Ltd. Published 2013 by Blackwell Publishing Ltd.

the mid-19th century, enslaved Muslims from West Africa were brought to both Spanish and Portuguese colonies. They even organized the 1835 slave rebellion in Brazil. Beginning a decade later, British imperial interests contracted Muslims, mostly from northern India, as indentured laborers to toil in the Caribbean. From the late 19th century until today, Muslims from the Arab lands known as As-Sham (present-day Lebanon, Palestine, and Syria) migrated to Amirka (the Americas). These flows intersect with those of Latin American and Caribbean converts – or "reverts" – today.

In drawing together the history of Muslims in the Americas, this chapter has two aims: first, to trace how Latin American and Caribbean Islam stemmed from distinct regions around the world such as Iberia, West Africa, South Asia, the Middle East, as well as the Americas themselves; and, second, to map these geographies of Islam within key Latin American and Caribbean historical processes and experiences, namely colonialism, slavery, creolization, civil society, and counter-terrorism. In a nutshell, my point is that Islam was shaped by, and in turn it helped to shape, Latin American and Caribbean histories since the late 15th century up until today. By situating in the same frame of analysis Iberian colonial subjects, enslaved Africans, indentured South Asians, migrant Arabs, and Latin American and Caribbean converts, this chapter reveals the global breadth of Islam and its indelible but often overlooked role in the making of Latin America and the Caribbean (see Map 13.1).

Sidebar 13.1   *Reconquista*

Reconquista ("Reconquest") is a term coined in the 1700s by Christian Spaniards. It refers to their political and military campaign, conducted from 711 to 1492, to "take back" lands governed or populated by Muslims Spaniards. During this 700-year period, the term *Reconquista* was never used by Christians waging war against Muslims, but it came in to usage among 18th-century Spanish writers and intellectuals who claimed that Christianity was at the core of Spanish identity.

It must be stated from the outset that the study of Islam in Latin America and in the Caribbean is of key importance not because of demographics. According to a recent estimate, there are 1,486,000 Muslims in Latin America and the Caribbean (Pew Research Center 2009: 32; see Table 13.1). This corresponds to less than 0.003 percent of the region's total population. Despite such a low number, Islam has run through the "open veins" of Latin America for five centuries (Galeano 1971), sustaining the status quo as well as nourishing resistance to it, reaching not only outward, in the public realm of power, but also inward, around the self and subjective being. The point is that Muslims from five distinct places of origin have shaped and have been shaped by a region of the world in which they seem to be demographically insignificant. By studying *la longue durée* of Muslims from Iberia, West Africa, South Asia, and the Middle East in Latin America and the Caribbean we globalize our view of what constitutes the "Islamic world" itself.

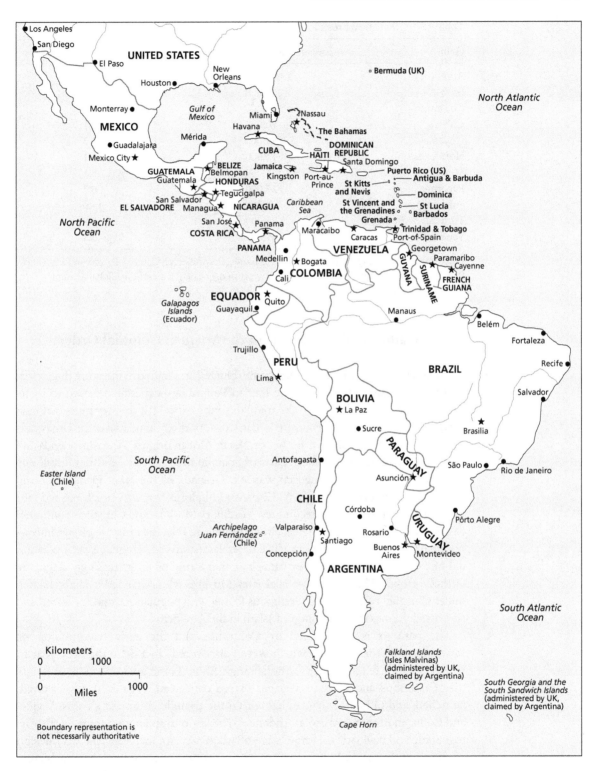

Map 13.1 Map of Latin America.

Table 13.1   Statistical breakdown of the Latin American Muslim population

Country	Estimated Muslim Population	Percentage Muslim Population
Argentina	1,000,000	2.5
Brazil	204,000	0.1
Colombia	14,000	< 0.1
Cuba	10,000	0.1
Guyana	55,000	7.2
Honduras	11,000	0.1
Mexico	111,000	0.1
Panama	25,000	0.7
Suriname	84,000	15.9
Trinidad & Tobago	78,000	5.8
Venezuela	95,000	0.3

Data from: *The Future of the Global Muslim Population*, Pew Research Center's Forum on Religion & Public Life, January 2011. At http://www.pewforum.org/The-Future-of-the-Global-Muslim-Population.aspx.

Shadows of al-Andalus in the Spanish Colonial Order

Boundaries between Islam and Christianity blurred and shifted in the more than seven centuries of Muslim polities on the Iberian Peninsula – generally referred to by its Arabic name, al-Andalus. From the mid-8th to the early 11th century most of Iberia was governed by a Muslim dynasty based in Córdoba that was related to the Umayyads of Damascus. Other rulers of Berber or North African origins – the Almoravids and Almohades – took over southern parts of Spain in the next two centuries, until only one last Muslim Spanish kingdom was left: Granada of the Nasir Dynasty, on the peninsula's southernmost edge. As Christian kingdoms from the north pushed into Muslim Iberia in an alleged "reconquest," ordinary Muslims and Christians continued to borrow and blend each other's cultural practices. Take the example of *mozárabes* – nominal Christians who adopted Muslim/Arab customs and language: their position did not end abruptly when they came under the rule of an increasingly dogmatic Catholic crown. There were also *mudéjares*, Muslims who remained in lands that fell under Christian rule. This multi-religious Iberia, with populations that conflicted and co-existed, frames the beginnings of Islam in the Americas.

The paradox is exemplified by Columbus and the early transmission of Muslimness to the "Indies," which were "discovered" in 1492 – the very year in which Granada fell to Spain's Catholic kings. Abbas Hamdani (1992: 273) recounts that Columbus and his four voyages "were conceived, organised, provisioned, launched, and ultimately concluded within the triangle comprising Palos, Seville, and Cádiz, in other words, in al-Andalus." These Columbian voyages used the cartographic and navigational knowledge of Islamic Spain, including the very design of the ships that set sail (ibid., pp. 278–279, 289–290). Moreover, Columbus's crew included an Arabic-speaking Jew who had converted to Christianity (Fuentes

1992). Notwithstanding this Arabic background to the Columbian voyages, the venture financed by Spain's Catholic kings developed out of a "medieval crusading milieu obsessed with the Muslim presence in Europe and the Holy Land" (ibid., p. 273). Columbus and his son imagined that the "discovery" of a new western trade route to the Indies would better Christendom's chances of "conquering" Jerusalem by circumventing the Muslim Arab lands that lay between Europe and the East. In other words, Columbus used Islamic technologies to serve a Christian fixation against the Islamic world.

Catholic Spain's so-called "reconquest" of the Iberian Peninsula fed into its alleged "conquest" of the New World. Though such terms were created in the 18th century (Gibson 1977: 21), Catholic Spaniards living at the time, in the 16th century, referenced the relationship between their wars in Iberia and the New World. Hernando Cortés, the conquistador who caused the defeat of the Aztec or Mexican Empire in 1521, "referred to Mexican Indian temples as *mezquitas* (mosques)" in his letters to the Spanish King Carlos V (Cortés 1991: 68; Gibson 1977: 19). In 1535 a historian of the period even claimed that the New World – like al-Andalus – had been the possession of Spain for several millennia before. Meanwhile the *morisco* moniker, which was once used to label Christians with Moorish ancestry in Spain, came to designate, for the next two centuries, offspring of "mixed" parentage in the New World. In these instances the image of the Muslim Other that Christian Spaniards cultivated in Iberia until 1492 served as a template for imagining the Indian Other, whom they would also fight and mix with from 1492 onwards. An orientalist version of "Islam" helped shape Spain's colonization of the New World (Said 1978).

Although facing exclusionary policies during the 16th century, many Muslims remained in southern Spain. But between 1609 and 1614 the Spanish Crown expelled these *moriscos*. Most fled to North Africa, but some, who suffered earlier discrimination or actual expulsion, allegedly headed to Latin America and the Caribbean. For a number of reasons, only slight evidence of this trajectory exists. After the "discovery" of the New World, the Spanish Crown instituted lax decrees forbidding anyone with Muslim ancestry from moving there (Cook 2008a). Far more deadly was the Inquisition. Charged to punish any deviation from a strict version of Roman Apostolic Catholicism, the Inquisition persecuted *moriscos* in Spanish dominions, and this led to a 16th-century fatwa (legal pronouncement) of the Mufti of Oran (Cardiallac 1979; Longas 1990) that encouraged *moriscos* to practice *taqiyya* (dissimulation) – hiding one's faith under duress. This fatwa promoting *taqiyya* not only explains the little textual evidence of Muslims in the New World, but also points to how Islam was shaped by the Spanish colonial order.

Whether of Iberian or North African origin, some *moriscos* turned themselves in to the Inquisition in the New World (see Cook 2008b; Fadda-Conrey 2006; García 2007). In 1594 "María Ruiz, a Morisca born in the town of Albolot in the Alpujarras mountains of Granada, denounced herself before Mexican inquisitors" (Cook 2008b: 78). Having lived in Mexico City for more than a decade as the wife of an "old Christian," Ruiz confessed to praying in Arabic and calling out the name of Muhammad. In 1660 a slave named Cristóbal de la Cruz denounced himself and testified before the Inquisition in the Mexican port city of Veracruz (ibid., p. 63). Born in Algiers but captured and taken to Spain at a young age, de la Cruz alleged to have met other *moriscos* on his way to the New World, including one Abderhaman who worked as a cook on a ship docked at Santo Domingo (ibid., pp. 67–68).

Confessing that he wavered between Islam and Christianity, de la Cruz recited Qur'anic verses and the *shahada* to show his sincere yearning for personal salvation in front of the Inquisitors. In adopting the practice of other subalterns who shielded themselves from their husbands or masters by turning themselves in to the Inquisition (McKnight 1999; Villa-Flores 2002), Iberian and North African Muslims left their mark on one of the most powerful instruments of the Spanish colonial order.

The most enduring Iberian "shadow of Islam in the conquest of America" (Taboada 2004) was an aesthetic and architectural genre called in Spanish *mudéjar*. This style developed out of the nearly 1,000-year presence of Muslims and inter-religious exchange on the Iberian Peninsula. Its distinctive, interlaced patterns and arabesques adorned many Latin American and Caribbean colonial churches and government buildings erected in the 16th and 17th centuries. Art historian Manuel Toussaint points out that the chapel of San José de los Naturales in Mexico City – built in the 16th century and destroyed not long after – shared many characteristics with one of the most famous *mudéjar* structures in southern Spain, the Mesquita-Catedral of Córdoba. Likewise, the Royal Chapel of Cholula, Puebla appears to have been based on the design of a hypostyle mosque – a mosque centered around the quibla and without a dome – which was characteristic of the early years of Islam (Ledesma 2010: 91). That these symbolic and material contours of al-Andalus were transferred to the New World suggests both the role of Islamic Iberia and its erasure in the making of the Spanish colonial order.

Sidebar 13.2   Mudéjar

Mudéjar is a Spanish term said to derive from the Arabic *mudajjan* ("permitted to stay"). It was used to label Muslim subjects who lived under the rule of Christians in Spain, and it came to refer to a style of architecture prevalent in Spain from the 11th to the 15th century that is today often glossed as "Islamic" but represents a blending of Arab, Gothic, and North African architectural traditions.

African Rebellion and Refuge in a Slavocrat Society

Islam entered sub-Saharan Africa in the 9th century, just as it did the Iberian Peninsula. There were two Muslim African waves reaching Latin America and the Caribbean. During the first, from the late 1400s to the late 1700s, Islam became "the religion of merchants and rulers." It was also part of the religio-cultural practices of subalterns in the region they left behind – Senegambia or Upper Guinea (Gomez 2005: 11; Sweet 2003: 18–19). Distinguished from other Africans in Iberian colonies, these

Muslims were called *mandingos* but belonged to distinct ethno-linguistic groups – such as the Jolof, the Fula, or the Mandinga. At the turn of the 19th century another wave of Muslim Africans arrived from Lower Guinea, namely through the Bight of Benin; it was comprised of Hausa, Yoruba, and Nupe. These Muslim Africans were generally labeled *males* in Brazil. They were coming from an area where Islam had served as the religion of competing empires and of subjugated peoples alike. The two waves represented only a small part of the over 12 million Africans enslaved and brought to the New World, but many in the non-Muslim majority would have been familiar with Islam. As "an ally of power" used to justify territorial expansion and as a "refuge for the poor" that lent "spiritual and moral strength," Islam brought into the fold African-born believers and non-believers, who were to confront (or at least endure) chattel slavery in the New World (Reis 1993: 95–96).

Situated between the Senegal River to the north and Cape Mount to the south (Sweet 2003: 19), Senegambia and the Upper Guinea region had been home to the Jolof Empire, whose elites incorporated Islam as one source of indigenous religio-cultural practices from the very inception of the empire in 1360. As the empire broke down after the mid-15th century, the Spanish bought and enslaved many of its subjects, who were often called *jalof* or *geolof*, and eventually brought them to their colonial dominions, in the Caribbean and elsewhere. In 1522 "negros of jalof" led one of the first slave rebellions in the New World (Gomez 2005: 1–2, 8–9). They rose up on the island of Hispaniola, then governed by Columbus' own son, Diego. For three days beginning on early Christmas morning, 20 captives took up machetes and marched for some 30 miles, putting into practice warfare skills that they had perhaps learned in the waning years of Jolof rule. As a result, the Spanish crown tried to exclude from the New World "slaves suspected of Islamic leanings, such as the notorious *esclavos Gelofes* (Jolofs) of the Guinea area, many of whom not only were infidels but were prone to insubordination as well" (Bowser 1974: 28).

Nonetheless, in 1627, the Spanish Jesuit missionary Alonso de Sandoval (1956: 75, 91) detected the presence of these "Mohamaden" slaves in the Columbian port town of Cartagena. In endeavoring to convert the non-Christian masses, Sandoval occasionally fretted about Muslims. He identified some "orators who have the duty [...] to refer to the victories of their ancestors [...] finishing their prayers with the greatest one of all, which is to annihilate our holy faith and enhance the cursed sect of Mahoma, persuading others to persevere and not become Christians." Later on in his account, he remarked that "iolofes [Jolofs], berbesies, mandingas, and fulos tend ordinarily to understand one another, despite their distinct languages and castes, because the greatest communication that they have is due to all these nations having commonly received the evil sect of Mahoma." Apart from transmitting his anti-Islamic zeal, Sandoval's observations imply that African Muslims commiserated and prayed together as well. Muslims from Upper Guinea, in this light, both fought outwardly against the slavocrat regime and turned inwardly against it.

Such dynamics continued in the second wave of enslaved Muslims from Lower Guinea, the one initiated in the early 1800s. Located between Cape Palma and the Bight of Biafra (Sweet 2003: 19), Lower Guinea (namely northern Nigeria) served as the setting of the jihad declared by Usuman dan Fodio in the early 1800s. As one of several Islamic reformist movements, this jihad changed the "ethnic background" of Africans who entered Bahia in the 1800s (Lovejoy 1994: 178). During the warfare that ensued in Lower Guinea many Muslims were taken captive and shipped to Bahia in northeastern Brazil. Stressing this transatlantic connection, some authors have argued that the jihad carried out in northern Nigeria reached across the Atlantic to northeastern Brazil (Bastide 1978; Goody 1986; Lovejoy 1994; Luna 1967). They suggest that Usuman dan Fodio's jihad fed into several slave rebellions that took place in Bahia during the first three decades of the 19th century and culminated in the 1835 *male* slave rebellion.

This "jihadist thesis," however, has been critiqued by João Jose Reis (1995). Rather than argue for a "continuation" or "reproduction" of the jihad on Brazilian soil, Reis contends that the 1835 slave rebellion was an *African* uprising, which was led by Muslims and at the same time appealed to non-Muslims across ethnic and religious lines. Based on the police and court records that investigated the Muslim and non-Muslim African insurgents who attacked Portuguese military and political outposts in the Bahian capital of Salvador, Reis (1995: 175) concluded that Islam furnished "the predominant ideology and language" of the 1835 rebellion that attracted Africans of multiple ethnic and religious backgrounds. The most powerful and visible cultural markers of this Islamic mold of the uprising were charms called *mandingas*, which were small cloth pieces containing a paper with one or two Qur'anic verses written in Arabic. They were prepared by educated African Muslims (as was common in Lower Guinea) and identified with Islam; Muslim and non-Muslim Africans alike used them for protection. By serving as the "glue" of African "ethnic solidarity" against a highly unequal Luso-Brazilian slavocracy, Islam shaped one of the most important slave uprisings in the Americas (second only to the Haitian Revolution). In response, Brazilian authorities expelled the Muslim insurgents to Africa, using the 1835 rebellion to claim Christianity as Brazil's native religion and Islam as "foreign."

Muslim Africans, however, continued to congregate and pray together in Rio de Janeiro, Salvador, and other Brazilian coastal cities through to the late 19th century (see al-Baghdadi 2001; Rio 1906). This traditional aspect of Islam – that of being a "refuge" – was hardly limited to what had become the Republic of Brazil (1889–1930); one can also find it in a contemporaneous manuscript, authored by a certain Sheikh Sana See in Panama. Probably a Fula from Senegambia who would have been aware of Fodio's declaration of jihad, Sana See most likely passed through the Caribbean before arriving to help build the Panama railroad in the early 1850s (Bayoumi 2003: 71, 74). While he worked on the Panama railroad, he composed a six-page manuscript that was "essentially an interior version of Islam," speaking not "of revolt but of remembering." Instead of making any critique of, or reference to, the near-slavery conditions that he probably toiled under during the second half of the 19th century, Sana See's text "promotes the idea that the proper remembrance of Allah will assist and protect the believer." This suggests that, long after the defeat of Muslim rebels in the public sphere, the inward-looking practices central to Islam continued.

From Muharram to Hosay in Caribbean Creolization

Just as in Iberia and Africa, Islam began its history in South Asia not long after the death of Prophet himself. There it reached its political apex in the 16th century, with the Mughal Empire, which came to rule over much of the subcontinent. As nominal Muslims, Mughals governed over a religiously diverse India that embraced Hindus, Sikhs, Buddists, and Christians – as well as Sunnis and Shi'as, who were numerically significant in the northeastern regions. As the British Empire took effective control over significant parts of the Mughal territory in the early 19th century, the seemingly distant British colonists based in the Caribbean arranged to contract Indian laborers for their plantations, which could no longer rely on African captives after the imminent abolition of slavery. Between the 1840s and the 1910s, the overwhelming majority of Indian laborers indentured to British planters were coming from the northeastern provinces of Oudh and Bihar. Though only an estimated 15 percent of them were Muslim (Prorok and Hemmasi 1993), most Hindus would probably have been familiar with Islam, since they came from an area with a significant Muslim presence. As in the case of earlier Muslim waves to the Americas, this multi-religious setting is essential for grasping how elements of Islamic culture were transferred and took root among Muslims and non-Muslims in the Caribbean.

Through the British-controlled port of Calcutta on the northeastern Indian coast, waves of indentured migrants were sent to the Caribbean – first to Guyana, in 1838, then to Trinidad and Tobago, after 1845. Smaller numbers of Indians were also brought to other British colonies such as Belize and Jamaica until 1920. Though most of Spanish-ruled Latin America and the Caribbean had gained independence by then, these and other circum-Caribbean countries had been wrested by the British from the Spanish more than a century before. With a lucrative sugar economy, British planters intended to use east Indians to flood the market with cheap labor, so that freed blacks would lose whatever leverage they might gain with the abolition of slavery (Kale 1995). In exercising this "divide-and-rule" policy, the British planters spoke of Indians as "servile" and "industrious" while they construed blacks as "insubordinate" and "lazy" (Munasinghe 2001). Although these colonial categories were subsequently taken up by Indians and blacks themselves, both groups came to labor together on sugar plantations, and their early attempt at collective "self-definition" at a popular event that had been dubbed "Hosay" in the 1880s was met with violent responses by British colonial authorities (Kale 1995).

"Hosay" was the novel moniker given to the observance of Muharram, a set of rituals held in the month of Muharram (the first month of the Islamic year), which mourn the massacre of Husayn near Karbala in 680 CE. This is considered to be the most important date in the Shi'a religious calendar and is likened to the "passion of Christ" for Catholics (Korom 2003: 56; Mottahedeh 1985: 147–148). Being one of the most visible Islamic practices carried out by South Asian migrants to the

Caribbean, Muharram became known as Hosay, probably because of the shouts and cries of "Ḥusayn" made by ritual participants in the early years. The first recorded observance of Muharram – or Hosay – in Trinidad can be traced back to 1854, just a decade after the arrival of the first Indian laborers (Korom 2003: 107). According to the contemporaneous account of Kenneth Grant, a Christian missionary, the main observance of Hosay was a public procession of no less than 80 floats called *tadjahs*, which symbolized the tomb of Husayn; during that procession participants mourned his massacre. Other important elements, then and now, were drumming and two standards in the form of a crescent moon, imagined to represent "the two brothers" Husayn and Hasan. Each *tadjah* float, from construction to circulation, was led by Indians from the plantation where they were indentured. Though caste and region were key markers in *tadjah* building and display in India, in the Caribbean the organizing logic of these processes was dictated by the plantation the Indians were indentured on. The Islamic performance of Muharram was thus shaped by the context of Caribbean plantocracy.

Afro-Trinidadians and other non-Indians took part in the observance of Hosay throughout the British-ruled Caribbean in the second half of the 19th century. They were paid to play the drums during the procession and occasionally carried the *tadjah* floats themselves. Frank Korom (ibid., p. 108) points out that Afro-Trinidadians did not likely share the ethnic or religious sentiment of non-Muslim or Muslim Indians, but co-opted the event for their own carnivalesque purposes. Varied religious and ethnic groups thus came to participate in Hosay early on, and there was as much "mixing" or "creolization" as there was rioting. A number of popular disturbances marked the Hosay celebration in the 1850s, 1860s, and 1870s; they were escalated by British colonial authorities and culminated in what many still call the 1884 Hosay massacre in Trinidad (mentioned earlier). In a related vein, in British-ruled Guiana, "the *tadjah* became a symbol of defiance for sugarcane plantation laborers against their British overlords" (ibid., p. 109). Though colonial authorities endeavored to "divide and conquer" their subjects in the Caribbean, the Islamic ritual of Muharram came to serve as an arena for East Indian and African descendants to come together in ways that disrupted British rule there.

But the colonialist division between "Indians" and "blacks" remained, even in the anti-colonial movements that emerged in the mid-20th century. In the creole ideology that became identified with Afro-Trinidadians and with Eric Williams, the founder of the People's National Movement (PNM), Indians were "bearers of culture" (such as "Hosay"), while blacks were construed as "producers of culture" – a creole national culture (Munasinghe 1994). East Indians were thus left at the margins of the "creole nation" of Trinidad and Tobago when it attained its independence in 1962. This, however, began to change in 1971, when the then Prime Minister Eric Williams visited four *tadjah* building yards in the district of St. James in the capital of Port of Spain, in ostensible efforts to gain the support not only of the Shiʿa Muslim families who still sponsored the building of the *tadjahs*, but also of their non-Muslim and even non-Indian collaborators. Williams endeavored to make Hosay into a showpiece of national culture for international tourist consumption (Korom 2003: 122). In fact Trinidad's "Tourism Development Authority" began to advertise Hosay in this manner around that time. In this post-colonial present, Hosay has come to serve as a multivalent affair whereby Shi'a Muslim families still organize the *tadjahs* and other ritual elements of a religious passion play, non-Muslim Indians participate in what they construe to be part of an Indian ethnic heritage, and non-Muslims as well as non-Indians join in what is glossed as a carnivalesque event.

Institutionalizing Islam in an Emergent Civil Society

The dawn of Islam is contiguous with its presence in the area known as Bilad al-Sham (present-day Lebanon, Palestine, and Syria). Coming under the rule of the Sunni Muslim-led Ottoman Empire by the 16th century, these Arab lands had been home to several Islamic and Christian religious minorities, including 'Alawīs, Assyrians, Druze, Maronites, Melquites, and Shi'as. As in earlier Muslim flows, this multi-religious point of origin is the key to grasping how Islam took shape in Latin American and Caribbean settings. Since Muslims made up roughly 15 percent of the migrants from the Arab world (Karam 2007), 'Alawīs, Druze, and Shi'as were as visible as Sunnis in setting up community associations in their countries of settlement. Unlike their predecessors, however, Muslim Arabs were not forced or coerced into migration. Due to a downturn in the region's economy and improved means of transportation, many began to travel because they both "could" and "wanted" to do so from the 1870s onward (Khater 2001). Though radiating out across the Americas, Muslim Arabs settled in equally high numbers in Argentina and Brazil (as well as in the United States) in pre-World War II times.

During the first half of the 20th century, Muslim Arabs participated in founding hundreds of charity or civic associations and established dozens of institutions with explicitly Islamic names throughout Latin America and the Caribbean. In Argentina, specifically in Buenos Aires, they inaugurated the Sociedad Árabe Islámica Alauita de la Angelita in 1926 (Montenegro 2009 81), the Sociedad Drusa de Beneficencia in 1927 (Devoto and Míguez 1992: 119), and the Sociedad Yabrudense Musulmana in 1932 (Cazorla 2003: 37, 44), and, in the city of Córdoba, the Sociedad de Socorros Mutuos y Ayuda Social Arabe Musulmana de Córdoba in 1928 (Martos 2007: 142). Likewise, in Greater São Paulo, Brazil, they established the Sociedade Alauíta de Beneficencia in 1922 (Safady 1966: 313), the Associação Druza Beneficente in 1927 (ibid., p. 310), as well as the Sociedade Beneficente Muçulmana de São Paulo in 1929 (Duoun 1944: 223). The last institution brought together Arabs from varied Christian and Islamic denominations to lay the cornerstone of the Mesquita do Brasil (Mosque of Brazil) near the city center (Karam 2007). Such inter-religious collaboration caught the attention of an Egyptian newspaper in 1930, which declared that Muslims and Christians in the Arab world should follow the example of the allegedly "harmonious coopera-tion between Muslim and Christian Syrians in Brazil" (Philipp 1985: 113).

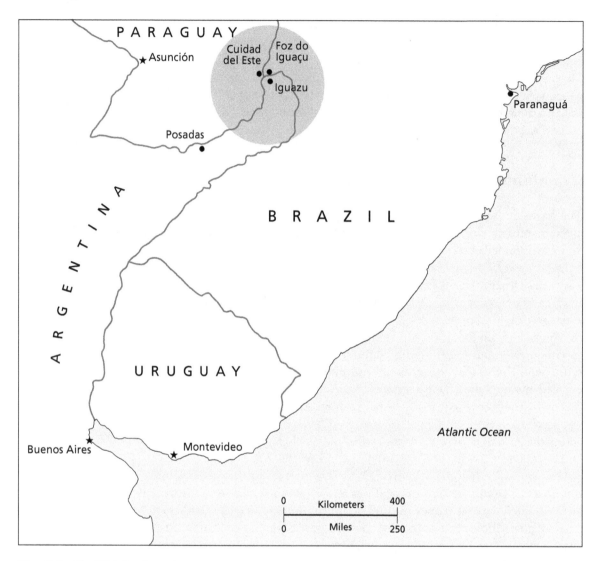

Map 13.2   The Triple Border region.

Notwithstanding the romanticized tone, this shows that Muslims' interactions with Christian Arabs in South America were evoked as a model for Islamic-majority societies in the Arab world. In other words, diasporic civics from South America could shape Islam too.

Although Arab migration to Latin America and the Caribbean slowed considerably after World War II, it still continues to the present day. Since the mid-20th century until today, mostly Muslim Lebanese have been attracted to a region called Triple Frontera (the Triple Border) between Brazil, Paraguay, and Argentina (see Map 13.2). This region is populated by migrants from the Bekaa Valley and South Lebanon. Sunni and Shi'a set up their businesses and homes in the two main cities of the border zone, Foz do Iguaçu in Brazil and Ciudad del Este in Paraguay. In the late 1970s, they established the region's first Muslim charity association on the Brazilian side of the border – the Sociedade Beneficente Islamica (Islamic Benevolent Society). But the founders were not much interested in religious piety. According to an early migrant, it was hoped that an explicitly Islamic organization in Brazil could better attract donations from Muslim-majority Arab states associated with OPEC (Organization for Petroleum Exporting Countries), which were then flush with capital from oil price hikes. In order to gain official recognition as a non-profit organization, the group came up with its first charter by copying one of the Sociedade Beneficente Muçulmana from São Paulo (mentioned before). At the time of its creation in the late 1970s, this Islamic Benevolent Society of Foz do Iguaçu drew upon and continued the then half-century-old Muslim Arab civic history of South America itself.

By the early 1980s, Sunnis and Shiʻas (and many non-Muslims) began mobilizing in order to build the first mosque in Foz do Iguaçu. In 1981 a city councilor of non-Arab origins helped propose the bill that donated a sizeable plot of public land to the Centro Cultural Beneficente Islamico (Muslim Benevolent Cultural Center), the organization established to spearhead the construction of the mosque and an adjacent community center. The city councilor – then married to a career Brazilian military officer critical of the 1964 military coup, which came to an end with the 1985 return of civilian rule – participated in the groundbreaking ceremony that laid the future mosque's head cornerstone in March 1983 as well as in the event that celebrated the actual opening of the mosque in May 1987. In collaboration with pro-democracy leaders at the twilight of military rule in the South American borderland, the opening of the mosque epitomized the return of democratic rule and civil society to the Brazilian side of the border.

When the time came to name this mosque and its adjacent community center, however, a handful of the most wealthy Sunnis insisted on the name "Omar Ibn Al-Khattab." By so doing they intended to estrange Shiʻas, because, in the theological imaginary, this "Omar" – a caliph of the *ummah* (Muslim community) – is considered to have usurped the power from ʻAli, whom Shiʻas believed to be the true heir to the *ummah*. "Rich Sunnis," it was stated by a politically liberal Sunni, chose this designation for the mosque so that "no Shiʻa would want to go (to the mosque)." In turn, most Shiʻa were relegated to the building that had housed the Sociedade Beneficente Islamica, the association founded in the previous decade. Disaffected Shiʻa as well as middle-class, more politically progressive Sunni changed its name to Ayatollah Khomeini (and often referred to it as "the Huseiniya," after ʻAli's martyred son). Consequently, by the early 1990s, a historically overlapping relationship gave way to greater divisions between wealthy Sunnis partial to pan-Arab nationalism and Shiʻas sympathetic to the Iranian revolution. Rather than be construed as sectarian or derivative of Middle East conflicts, this tension is better grasped in terms of the proliferation of civic associations and social movements that characterized much of South America at the dawn of democracy in the 1980s. Islam helped to shape, and was shaped by, the post-authoritarian emergence of civil society in South America.

Conversion (or Reversion) at a Time of Counter-Terrorism

Ibrahim Gonzalez, a Puerto Rican in the Bronx and co-founder of the Alianza Islámica, selected two important moments from this Muslim history of Latin America and the Caribbean when he explained his reversion to Islam nearly four decades ago: "I was inspired by the history of Andalusia, the kingdoms of Muslim Spain, and our African ancestry also has elements of Islam – the Wolof [Jolof] and Fulani brought the faith…" (cited in Weinberg 2003: 25). Not long after the first attack on the World Trade Center in 1994, however, Gonzalez was paid a visit by FBI agents who were "looking for terrorists." This experience speaks to the paradox of a growing number of Muslims in the Americas – they are well aware of their long history there – during an increasingly repressive governmental apparatus, which attempts to erase that history in order to construe them as a threat. On the one hand, conversion to Islam – or what believers consider to be a return, and hence a reversion to their rightful faith – gained momentum across the Americas from the late 20th century until today. Yet on the other hand, counter-terrorist modes of surveillance that unduly targeted Islamic institutions and individuals expanded from the 1990s onward.

Though converts come from all backgrounds and give many reasons for their conversion, people of color in Latin America and the Caribbean are especially attracted to Islam, not because of the influence of Arab or South Asian Muslims, but rather because of the popular portrayals of African American Islam and of African American Muslims (Oliveira and Mariz 2006: 107–108). Some Afro-Brazilians explained that their journey to Islam began after watching the movie *Malcom X*. Another long-time black Brazilian activist stated: "I didn't arrive at Islam through the Arabs, but rather through the struggle of the black people of North America." The Islamic contours of the Black Power movement of the 1960s and 1970s have been equally influential among Afro-Trinidadians and Afro-Guyanese. Latin American and Caribbean people of color, who often are working-class people or live in shantytowns, find resonance with the not dissimilar inequalities faced by African American Muslims. At the same time, however, recent Latin American and Caribbean converts also discover and identify with the older histories of Andalusian or African Muslims, which extend beyond the United States' borders, into the Americas.

In these counter-terrorist times, however, the attraction that many Latin American and Caribbean people of color feel for Islam is often construed as a threat by counter-terrorist analysts, who usually take one token example of Muslim extremism to generalize about a far broader and growing Muslim public "south of the Rio Grande." Cited again and again in the field of hemispheric security studies is the unique case of Yasin Abu Bakr and his group, the Jamaat al-Muslimeen, which led an attempted government coup in Trinidad and Tobago in 1990. Held at a distance by Indo-Trinidadian Muslims, Abu Bakr is an Afro-Trinidadian who converted to Islam some time in the early 1970s. After a series of confrontations with the local government and military in the 1980s, Abu Bakr had his movement's headquarters occupied by the army and lost his appeal in the courts to regain them. Though representing only a handful of Muslim converts, Abu Bakr and the Jamaat al-Muslimeen are often used by security analysts to paint a picture of an Islam threatening the hemispheric order of the Americas.

Rather than view this counter-terrorist moment as only an impediment to raising critical awareness about Islam, many converts see it as an opportunity. One thirty-something woman in Quito remarked: "Since 9/11 people in Ecuador have been trying to learn more about Muslims and what we are about. We as Muslims should be the ones that reach out to other faiths or no faith in a way that is not preachy or lecturing" (Rahman 2010). She and many other Latin American and Caribbean Muslims converted after September 11, 2001, not unlike their counterparts across North America and Europe. These and other recent converts are frequently the most active ones where *dawa* (proselytizing and raising awareness about Islam) is concerned, whether they do it through pamphlets in Mexico City (Alfaro Velcamp 2002) or through internet chat rooms in Brazil (Oliveira 2006). This *dawa* zeal, specifically among non-Arab and non-Indian converts, is an attempt to create a community of believers that will ostensibly strengthen the converts' own journey to Islam.

These community-building efforts of Latin American and Caribbean Muslim converts, often but not always of color and from the working class, serve as a response to their lack of interaction with immigrant or second-generation Arabs or South Asians. Asked whether he engaged in *dawa* at the aforementioned trinational border between Brazil, Paraguay, and Argentina, the Arab sheikh of the Omar Ibn Al-Khattab mosque remarked that his goal is to maintain the religion in the mosque's second and third generations. In Trinidad and Tobago, the mosques established by South Asian Muslims also seem primarily concerned with their own descendents, maintaining some distance from non-Indian and Afro-Trinidadian converts. While Islam is being "ethnicized" by Arabs in Brazil (Pinto 2005), Muslims in the Caribbean define themselves by their ethnic affiliation, and not by their religious one (Voll 1992). This implies that, as Latin American and Caribbean converts identify with the Andalusian or African Muslim past of the region, they are ignored or marginalized by present-day Arab and South Asian Muslims.

In this regard, an Arab Brazilian Muslim who lives and works between Foz do Iguaçu and Ciudad del Este once commented to me that converts will be one of the future problems faced by Islam in South America because of their alleged affinity with radical politics. Ironically, however, this Arab Brazilian's own community at the Triple Border has suffered profiling, house raids, and violent operations at the hands of multi-governmental forces after the respective 1992 and 1994 bombings of the Israeli embassy and a Jewish community association in Buenos Aires, Argentina (Karam 2011). Though the perpetrators of those attacks are still unknown, all Arabs at the Triple Border have been unduly blamed and have witnessed their own political disenfranchisement since the mid-1990s. Though descendants view converts with suspicion, all Muslims are being framed in similar ways by the counter-terrorist order of the Americas.

Conclusion

The over 500-year Muslim history of Latin America and the Caribbean narrated in this chapter holds the key to counteracting the idea that Islam is something new or foreign to the Americas. Transmitted through Iberian colonial subjects, enslaved Africans, indentured South Asians, migrant Arabs, and converts in Latin America and the Caribbean, Islam has both reflected and shaped the historical course of colonial and slavocrat societies as well as their creole ideologies, civic practices, and counter-terrorist politics. By studying this Muslim history of the Latin America and the Caribbean, we learn about the formative role played by Islam in a region of the world that, at first glance, appears to have a negligible Muslim population. Today a Latin American and Caribbean framing of Islamic world history is more important than ever, as counter-terrorist logics are attempting to construe Islam as a foreign threat to the hemisphere and ultimately to erase its influence.

Discussion Questions

1   Who are the *moriscos*? What does their presence in inquisitions of the Old and New World tell us? How does their presence in Spain and in the Spanish Americas change our view of Spanish colonization?
2   Do African Muslims' participation in rebellions against their enslavement in the Caribbean and South America speak to the paranoia of their masters, as well as to the political and military conflicts that occurred both in New World contexts and in African points of origin?
3   How are South Asian and Arab Muslim migration histories similar to and distinct from previous Iberian and African Muslim waves?
4   Is it possible to speak of a 500-year presence of Muslims in this hemisphere? Why or why not? How are their histories being erased in the late 20th century and in the early 21st century?

Suggested Further Reading

Al-Baghdadi, Abd al-Rahman (2001). *The Amusement of the Foreigner*, trans. Yacine Daddi Addoun and Renée Soulodre-La France. Toronto: York University.

Alfaro Velcamp, Theresa (2002). Mexican Muslims in the twentieth century: Challenging stereotypes and negotiating space. In Yvonne Haddad (ed.),

Muslims in the West: From sojourners to citizens. New York, NY: Oxford University Press, pp. 278–290.

Bastide, Roger (1978). Black Islam in Brazil. In Roger Bastide, *The African Religions of Brazil*. Baltimore, MD: Johns Hopkins University Press, pp. 143–154.

Bayoumi, Moustafa (2003). Moving beliefs: The Panama manuscript of Sheikh Sana See and African diasporic Islam. *Interventions*, 5(1): 58–81.

Bowser, Frederick (1974). *The African Slave in Colonial Peru, 1524–1650*. Stanford, CA: Stanford University Press.

Cardaillac (1979). *Moriscos y cristianos: Un enfrentamiento polémico, 1492–1640*. Madrid: Fondo de Cultura Económica.

Cazorla, Liliana (2003). *Presencia de inmigrantes sirios y libaneses en el desarrollo industrial argentino*. Buenos Aires: Fundación Los Cedros.

Collihan, Kathleen M. and Constantine P. Danopoulos (1993). Coup d'état attempt in Trinidad: Its causes and failure. *Armed Forces and Society*, 19(3): 435–450.

Cook, Karoline (2008a). Forbidden crossings: Morisco emigration to Spanish America, 1492–1650. PhD Dissertation, Princeton University, Princeton, New Jersey.

Connell, Curtis C. (2004). *Understanding Islam and its Impact on Latin America*. Montgomery, AL: Maxwell Air Force Base.

Cook, Karoline (2008b). Navigating identities: The case of a Morisco slave in seventeenth-century New Spain. *Americas*, 65(1): 63–79.

Cortés, Hernando (1991). The Second Letter. In *Hernando Cortés: Five Letters, 1519–1526* [1520], trans. Morris, J. Bayard. New York, NY: W. W. Norton.

Delval, Raymond (1992). *Les Musulmans en Amérique latine et aux Caraïbes*. Paris: Dominique Guéniot.

Devoto, Fernando and Eduardo José Míguez (1992). *Asociacionismo, trabajo y identidad étnica*. Buenos Aires: Centro de Estudios Migratórios Latinoamericanos.

Duoun, Taufik (1944). *A emigração siriolibanesa às terras de promissão*. São Paulo: Tipografia Editora Árabe.

Fadda-Conrey, Carol (2006). The passage from west to south: Arabs between the Old and New World. In Darcy Zabel (ed.), *Arabs in the Americas: Interdisciplinary Essays on the Arab Diaspora*. New York, NY: Peter Lang, pp. 29–44.

Fuentes, Carlos (1992). *El espejo enterrado*. Mexico City: Fondo de Cultura Economica.

Galeano, Eduardo (1971). *Las venas abiertas de América Latina*. Montevideo: Universidad de la República.

García, María del Rosario (2007). *Identidad y minorías musulmanas en Colombia*. Rosario: Centro de Estudios Politicos e Internacionales/Editorial Universidad del Rosario.

Gibson, Charles (1977). Reconquista and conquista. In Raquel Chang-Rodríguez, and Donald A. Yates (eds.), *Homage to Irving A. Leonard: Essays on Hispanic Art, History and Literature*. East Lansing, MI: Latin American Studies Center at Michigan State University, pp. 19–28.

Gomez, Michael A. (2005). *Black Crescent: The Experience and Legacy of African Muslims in the Americas*. Cambridge: Cambridge University Press.

Goody, Jack (1986). Writing, religion, and revolt in Bahia. *Visible Language*, 20(3): 318–343.

Griffith, Ivelaw (2002). Security, sovereigny, and public order in the Caribbean. *Security and Defense Studies Review*, 2: 1–18.

Hamdani, Abbas (1992). An Islamic background to the voyages of discovery. In Salma Khadra Jayyusi and Manuela Marín (eds.), *The Legacy of Muslim Spain*. Leiden: Brill, pp. 273–304.

Kale, Madhavi (1995). Projecting identities: Empire and indentured labor migration from India to Trinidad and British Guiana, 1836–1885. In P. van der Veer (ed.), *Nation and Migration: The Politics of Space in the South Asian Diaspora*. Philadelphia, PA: University of Pennsylvania, pp. 73–92.

Karam, John Tofik (2011). Anti-Semitism from the standpoint of its Arab victims in a south American frontier zone. *Latin American and Caribbean Ethnic Studies*, 6(2): 139–165.

Karam, John Tofik (2007). *Another Arabesque: Syrian–Lebanese Ethnicity in Neoliberal Brazil*. Philadelphia, PA: Temple University Press.

Kephart, Janice (2006, June 8). Western hemisphere travel initiative. Testimony before the House Judiciary Committee. Committee on House Judiciary Subcomittee on Immigration, Border Security, and Claims.

Khater, Akram Fouad (2001). *Inventing Home: Emigration, Gender, and the Middle Class in Lebanon, 1870–1920*. Berkeley, CA: University of California Press.

Korom, Frank (2003). *Hosay Trinidad: Muharram Performances in an Indo-Caribbean Diaspora*. Philadelphia, PA: University of Pennsylvania Press.

Ledesma, Isabel (2010). El espacio religioso en el Islam. In Zidane En Zeraoui (ed.), *El Islam en América Latina*. Monterrey: Editorial Limusa, pp. 67–94.

Longás, Pedro (1990). *La vida religiosa de los Moriscos*. Granada: Universidad de Granada.

Lovejoy, Paul (1994). Background to rebellion: The origins of Muslim slaves in Bahia. *Slavery and Abolition*, 15: 151–180.

Luna, Luís (1967). *O negro na luta contar escravidão* [1976], 2nd ed. Rio de Janeiro: Editora Lectura.

Martos, Sofia (2007). The balancing act: Ethnicity, commerce, and politics among Syrian and Lebanese immigrants in Argentina, 1890–1955. PhD dissertation, University of California, Los Angeles.

McKnight, Kathryn Joy (1999). Blasphemy as resistance: An African slave woman before the Mexican Inquisition. In Mary E. Giles (ed.), *Women in the Inquisition: Spain and the New World*. Baltimore, MD: The Johns Hopkins University Press, pp. 229–253.

Montenegro, Silvia (2009). Panorama sobre la inmigración árabe en Argentina. In Abdeluahed Akmir (ed.), *Los árabes en América Latina: Historia de una emigración*. Madrid: Siglo XXI, pp. 60–98.

Mottahedeh, Roy (1985). *The Mantle of the Prophet: Religion and Politics in Iran*. New York, NY: Simon & Schuster.

Munasinghe, Viranjini P. (2001). *Callalo or Tossed Salad? East Indians and the Cultural Politics of Identity in Trinidad*. Ithaca, NY: Cornell University Press.

Novakoff, Renee (2008, July). Islamic terrorist activities in Latin America. *Air and Space Power*. At http://www.airpower.au.af.mil/apjinternational/apj-s/2008/2tri08/novakoffeng.htm (accessed May 1, 2011).

Oliveira, Vitória Peres de, and Cecília L. Mariz (2006). Conversion to Islam in contemporary Brazil. *Exchange*, 35(1): 102–115.

Oliveira, Vitória Peres de (2006). Islã no Brasil ou Islã do Brasil. *Religião e Sociedade*, 2: 1–23.

Pew Research Center (2009). *Mapping the Global Muslim Population: A Report on the Size and Distribution of the World's Muslim Population*. Washington, DC: Pew Forum on Religion and Public Life.

Philipp, Thomas (1985). *The Syrians in Egypt, 1725–1975*. Stuttgart: Steiner-Verlag.

Pinto, Paulo Gabriel Hilu da Rocha (2005). Ritual, etnicidade e identidade religiosa nas comunidades muçulmanas no Brasil. *Revista USP*, 67: 228–250.

Prorok, Carolyn V. and Mohammad Hemmasi (1993). East Indian Muslims and their mosques in Trinidad: A geography of religious structures and the politics of ethnic identity. *Caribbean Geography.* 4(1): 28–48.

Rahman, Samia (2010, *March 23*). Young and Muslim in Ecuador. *The Guardian.*

Reis, João José (1995). *Slave Rebellion in Brazil: The Muslim Uprising of 1835 in Bahia.* Baltimore, MD: Johns Hopkins University Press.

Rio, João do Paulo Barreto (1906). *As religiões do Rio* [1928]. Rio de Janeiro: Editora Companhia Nacional.

Safady, Wadih (1966). *Cenas e cenários dos caminhos da minha vida.* São Paulo: Penna Editora.

Said, Edward (1978). *Orientalism.* New York, NY: Pantheon.

Said, Edward (1981). *Covering Islam.* New York, NY: Pantheon.

Sandoval, Alonso (1956). *De instauranda aethiopum salute: El mundo de la esclavitud negra en América* [1627]. Bogotá: Empresa Nacional de Publicaciones.

Sweet, James H. (2003). *Recreating Africa: Culture, Kinship, and Religion in the African–Portuguese World, 1440–1770.* Chapel Hill, NC: University of North Carolina Press.

Taboada, Hernán G. H. (1994). El golpe de estado Islámico en Trinidad. *Cuardernos Americanos,* 8(5): 205–216.

Taboada, Hernán G. H. (2004). *La sombra del Islam en la conquista de América.* Mexico City: Universidad Nacional Autónoma de México.

Toussaint, Manuel (1967). *Colonial Art in Mexico.* Austin, TX: University of Texas Press.

Villa-Flores, Javier (2002). "To lose one's soul": Blasphemy and slavery in New Spain, 1596–1669. *Hispanic American Historical Review,* 82(3): 435–468.

Voll, John (1992). Muslims in the Caribbean: Ethnic sojourners and citizens. In Yvonne Haddad (ed.), *Muslim Minorities in the West: Visible and Invisible.* New York, NY: Altamira, 265–277.

Weinberg, Bill (2005, May/June). Muslims in the Americas face scrutiny. *NACLA Report on the Americas,* pp. 25–27.

Zeraoui, Zidane (ed.) (2010). *El Islam en América Latina.* Monterrey: Editorial Limusa.

14

The Ecology of Teaching about Islam and Muslims in the 21st Century

Aminah Beverly McCloud

Introduction

The teaching about Islam and Muslims in the 21st century is necessarily different from the one in previous centuries. Wars, insurgencies, issues over occupations and nuclear proliferations, along with the specific American "war on terrorism" in the Muslim world have challenged teachers to research new pedagogies and information caches. This state of affairs also demands the engagement of a series of new inquiries – such as: Who teaches about Islam and Muslims? What are the debates in academe over content? Should Islam be taught solely as a religious studies course, or ought Islamic studies to be more broadly conceived? First, a historical note.

An Introduction to Islam in the 21st Century, First Edition. Edited by Aminah Beverly McCloud, Scott W. Hibbard, and Laith Saud.
© 2013 Blackwell Publishing Ltd. Published 2013 by Blackwell Publishing Ltd.

By the middle of the 20th century a series of fragile ecosystems of Muslim cultures remained all over the world, after various wars and negotiations of independence. Whether one examines Muslim cultures in former Soviet states or in former British or French colonies, repair of culture and religious life is underway; the background for explorations of Muslim cultures in postcolonial states is provided. Researchers have often seen "postcolonial" societies as being in the throes of chaos and as attended by various levels of violence. An alternative lens, however, offers more complex interpretations. Colonization and its destruction of infrastructures and civil life have to remain one aspect of interest to any investigation of Islam and Muslim cultures in the 21st century.

World events, changes in ideologies, and even changes in enemies, all threaten the balance of the ecosystem of the Islamic world and its relations to other world systems, making accurate and factual knowledge an imperative. One immediate challenge for the 21st century Western classroom is an Enlightenment heritage of what can and cannot be taught about religion. As discussed in earlier chapters, centuries ago Europeans and their cousins in the United States, in their church-versus-state wars, debated and agonized over how and what the state could support in the teaching of religion, and ultimately if the state should support the teaching of religion at all, even in private institutions. The outcome continues to be a matter of debate. Freedom of religious belief and practice is understood as a highly cherished value and particular beliefs and practices are best taught privately, though parochial schools have perennially sought government assistance with teachers' salaries, texts, transportation, or supplies. In the sphere of state schools and universities challenges have been ongoing, and they took a particular form in the case of Muslims and Islam, which have always been portrayed either as an incident in history or as a religion of barbarians.

In Western universities apart from seminaries, a typical rubric in the teaching of religion has always been the distinction between the academic study of religion from its devotional counterpart. In other words, Western educators expose students to religious teachings without intimating which one is acceptable. Students are consequently asked to study, not to practice; and religious studies courses are designed to educate, not to proselytize or denigrate. Teachers generally agree that knowledge of religions is not only the characteristic of an educated person, but also something absolutely necessary for understanding a world of diversity and for living in it. They also know that almost all of history, art, music, literature, and contemporary life are unintelligible without an understanding of the major religious ideas and influences that have shaped history and culture. What teachers *know* about the teaching of various worldviews is essential – or at least should be at the heart of their pedagogy; but in the case of Islam and Muslims we have a different set of circumstances to consider. As the *teaching* profession has extended its membership beyond normal boundaries and the contents of teaching vary according to the political discourses and temperaments of its *experts*, the way in which Islam is being taught has changed. In the present chapter we will examine these issues and explore several aspects of the ecology.

Teaching about Islam and Muslims in the 21st century has to be considered, to begin with, in the light of prevailing relationships: between the *teachers* of Islamic studies, their training, and the world of events; between teachers, administrators, colleagues, and the Muslim community in the United States and Europe; between teachers and the 21st century student; and among members of the Muslim community. The organizing concept is, thus, ecology.

Ecology in its most basic sense provides a broader lens, as a study that includes exploring adaptations, movements, and relations of humans along with their interactions in and with a common environment (in this case, Islam). This chapter will discuss some of these inter-relations.

Who Teaches? An Ecosystem on the Brink

Brannon M. Wheeler asserted in 2003 that "there are currently only about 100 scholars trained in Islamic studies and religious studies in North America" (Wheeler 2003: v). The expertise of many of these scholars lay in ancient languages and historical studies, which decreases still further the number of those who are actively engaged in teaching anything about the religious, political, or spiritual circumstances of modern or contemporary life. According to an issue of *Religious Studies News* from the same year, only 26 percent of religious studies departments offered courses on Islam to their undergraduate students, while 30 percent offered course in Judaism and 96 percent offered courses in Christianity. Most professors of Islamic studies are specialists with little (if any) training in the study of various religious traditions or in the study of Islam as a "religion." It is important to note that "religious studies" is a relatively new field, created in the West to study various world systems of spiritual/cultural traditions. These world systems – especially Hinduism, Buddhism, Taoism, Confucianism, Judaism, and Islam – do not readily fit the restrictions of "religious studies." When we say that someone is trained in "Islamic studies," we are not referring to religious studies, but rather to the Islamic sciences, which include Qur'anic studies, hadith and sira studies, Islamic law and its methodologies, along with Islamic history. Middle and Near Eastern studies are 20th-century academic fields that focus on particular regions' languages, cultures, and history. So *who* is teaching about Islam and Muslims today? Here are several and sometimes overlapping categories identified. The distinctions made here are by no means fixed or definitive, yet they are useful for understanding *who* is teaching about Islam and Muslims.

Scholars of Islamic studies are trained across the whole spectrum of Islamic sciences: Qur'anic studies, hadith and sira literatures, law, and history. Since 1958, scholars of Middle and Near Eastern studies were trained to have

---

Sidebar 14.1   Why explain the Muslim world?

The 1960s was the decade when most of the Arab-speaking world was experiencing a new kind of colonialism. Many states either had been given their independence through various agreements that stipulated dependence on former colonists or had fought and won their independence. As the United States had become the major world power and the arbiter of relations, it became imperative to explain the Muslim world in social studies classes in United States universities.

specialized knowledge and broad understanding of these crucial parts of the world, in preparation for leadership roles in journalism, translation, business, and international law and for careers as scholars and teachers in institutions of higher education. This training is generally done through the disciplinary approaches of history, anthropology, and sociology. As a rule, such scholars are not trained in Islamic sciences.

Scholars of religious studies, especially those who enroll in history of religion programs, claim expertise in all the religions they study; and one of these religions is sometimes Islam. Though all of these scholars have equal credentials once they become professors, their training is significantly different when it comes to expertise in Islamic studies. Their lack of expertise creates problems in the transmission of accurate knowledge to students and an accumulation of misinformation.

Lay Muslim thinkers and teachers actively engage in a variety of inter-religious dialogues about Islam and/or Muslims but are not necessarily trained academically in Islamic studies or in Middle Eastern studies. Their credentials are often in other areas of study, but these can include what we call seminary training. In the United States (but not in Europe), these lay scholars are sometimes recruited to teach religious studies in history faculties by virtue of their language proficiency and national origin, although they do not have credentials in Islamic or Middle Eastern studies. Their personal knowledge as Muslims is often limited and sometimes confusing to media and inter-faith dialogues, especially when the audience has heard scholars on the same issues.

A peculiar group has emerged in the 21st century: the *opportunist* teachers of Islam. This category includes *the experts*, former Muslims, Muslims, non-Muslim religious clergy, talk-show hosts, editorial writers, and radio pundits. They are economic and political opportunists. Here there is overlap, as some of them are trained in Middle and Near Eastern studies, along with *lay* Muslim thinkers. This category is characterized by high-profile, nationally and sometimes internationally acclaimed respondents to "everything about Islam and Muslims at every point in history and in all places on the globe." They frequently claim to know – which they do with remarkable inaccuracy – the inner thoughts, the potential trajectories of those thoughts, and the subsequent actions of any Muslim, anywhere, at any time. What marks this category is the breadth of its influence on all things about Islam and Muslims in the United States and Europe. Teachers from this category have proliferated after September 11, 2001. Many have come with vicious anti-Islamic/anti-Muslim narratives aimed at inciting violence of one sort or another, or at winning support for the euphemistic war on terror aimed at Muslims and Islam. "Teachers" in this category have become familiar TV and radio personalities, along with best-selling authors. Their denigration of Islam and condemnation of any Muslim presence in the West (beside that of "moderate" Muslims sanctioned as such) has earned them considerable wealth.

Unlike most subjects in university teaching, the teaching of religion requires self-disclosure regarding one's religious affiliation and attitude toward religion – which is a modern result of post-Enlightenment ideals. Depending on the religious persuasion of students, self-disclosure fixes the environment in which they learn about Islam. Generally speaking, if the teacher is Muslim, students expect a bias in teaching, whereas if the teacher is not Muslim, they expect objectivity. In the 21st century Muslim teachers in all disciplines are under the cloud of suspicion owing to the legacy of 9/11, and this state of affairs can compromise their ability to teach their subject in an objective manner (especially if their specialty is something to do with Islam and politics). Also, anyone with little or no training can (and does) teach about Islam and other world systems – apart from Judaism or Christianity. This is due in part to a shortage of qualified teachers, coupled with a high demand for instruction in this field. Whatever the reason, the ecosystem of religious studies has been endangered since its beginning, as it values learning and credentials in several areas and is lax in other areas. In the 21st century many departments of religious studies found that they not only did not teach about Islam (a major world tradition), but had few interested members among the teaching staff.

Additionally, the ecosystem – an aspect of which consists in the relationships between the actual content of Islamic studies and those who *teach* it – is in flux and is contentious. There is always the potential danger of Islamic studies having its content rearranged or eclipsed through pseudo-knowledge, as signaled by some teachers in the categories listed above. The "opportunistic" teachers' uses of language in teaching about Islam and Muslims "are typical of the policing languages of mastery, and cannot, do not permit new knowledge or encourage the mutual exchange of ideas" (Morrison 1993). While this may not reflect the sentiments of the majority populations, it is extremely difficult to contain the influence of hate speech in an open society.

Sentiments since 9/11

Professors of Islamic studies (in all of its variety of names) have felt enormous pressure to expand their roles as scholars in American and European universities since the 1960s, and especially after 9/11. For most, the aftermath of 9/11 has been a time of reflection, anger, fear, and resolve. One widely held set of opinions was quite articulately expressed by Tazim Kassam (2003), who reflects on the intellectual joy that study in a history of religions program brought him and on his immediate dismay at the decline in civil discourse after the tragic events of September 11, 2001. Particularly for scholars of immigrant descent, there is an invaluable set of benefits to living and working in the United States, Canada, or Europe, which include "an environment of civil discourse that encourages the peaceful co-existence of a plurality of beliefs, ethnic backgrounds, and lifestyles […]" (Kassam 2003: 128). Though in short supply, before 9/11 there certainly were opportunities for, and relatively reasonable access to venues for, self-expression and creativity rarely available in Muslim-majority countries. There is also, in Western societies, "the orderly exchange of materials, cultural and intellectual goods" (ibid.), which is rarely in evidence in the Muslim world. All of this comfort was and continues to be threatened by ongoing detainments and arrests for potential and actual criminal activity. The widespread surveillance, by government authorities and news reporters/journalists, of conversations, associations, and actions, job loss for some, fear of colleagues, administrators, and students, along with the loss of academic freedoms such as the right to air "dissenting opinions" – all these are crippling intellectually, professionally, and spiritually. Even now scholarship is called into question as adversaries ask, "Who speaks for Islam?" and "Who is teaching about Islam and Muslims?"

These reflections are critical in a brief exploration of the teaching of Islam. The nature and content of the rhetoric unleashed in President Bush's speeches after 9/11 and reiterated in endless varieties by various *opportunistic* teachers of Islam, along with the arrests of suspects in declared plots against Americans, have rendered all Muslims in the West suspect. Their non-Muslim colleagues who teach about Islam and Muslims in any form have also been put under the same kind of close scrutiny for their associations and conversations with Muslims.

In ways largely unknown in teaching about a worldview, scholars of Islam are now requested to answer questions about *why* and *who* the Muslim terrorists out to destroy the Western world were – or else they would be put under the umbrella of the seditious or unpatriotic. Teachers of Islamic studies are expected to become "teacher, scholar, critic, advocate, public intellectual, media expert, policy advisor" and so on: all this overnight and on the "us" side of the "us-versus-them" scenario. What these teachers have been stressing over in the teaching of 15 centuries of history and culture in one single semester is now to be further condensed, presented quickly, put "in a nutshell" for TV and radio – and all this should be done under close scrutiny. This set of factors was added to what, for Brannon Wheeler, was an already delicate situation – one in which "many scholars of Islamic studies find themselves as the only or the *token* Islamicist on campus, responsible for all aspects of Islam, the history of Islamic civilization, and the worldwide distribution of Muslim societies" (Wheeler 2003: vi).

Indigenous Muslim scholars of Islam, who were often ignored and marginalized because they are American or European, have had their fair share of challenges too. Though these scholars have had to spend their time in the Muslim world as part of their training, the very fact that they are Western and lacking in Islamic heritage makes their scholarship suspect. They are battling issues of authenticity, expertise, and identity on several "fronts." Despite years of training, the absence of an Islamic heritage and the presence of an American or European heritage grant them tolerance in the Muslim world, but not authenticity. Their choice of Islam as a worldview is applauded in the Muslim world but looks suspicious in the Western world. It is often perceived that, since they have taken the study of Islam as a profession along with adopting Islam as a faith, their choice renders them "sympathetic" to Muslim points of view on all matters involving Islam and/or Muslims. Given the fact that "all the Muslims are from over there," indigenous Muslim scholars of Islam are rarely consulted about any social or political unrest in the Muslim world – or even in the West. Amina Wadud (2003: 273) maintains that, "in some cases, this was done specifically because they were Americans and therefore could not assist in the nagging questions about the loyalty of Muslims in America to American interests over and above foreign interests."

Nevertheless, scholars of Islam, regardless of personal religious affiliation or opinion, all feel the pressure of events beyond their control. For some, their expertise is either not broad enough or in the right area, while for others it is not deep enough. Still others have little or no acquaintance with the contemporary world in a scholarly sense. Few scholars were prepared for the media and its "nutshell" thinking, or for close surveillance from colleagues, students, administrators, and the general American community; and thus the "experts" have become the teachers. But there are other debates about the content of teaching.

Debates: How to Describe Islam

Scholars of religion have always had difficulty with the term *religion*, whether it is used to speak of an academic discipline or more expansively, as in the phrase *world religions*. Peter Beyer reminds us "that both the categories of 'religion' and 'religions' are derived from Christian, or at least Western experience, and are thus unsuitable for understanding the religious aspects of non-Western cultures: constructing the discipline with these concepts amounts, one often hears, to the mistaken or imperialistic imposition of 'our' culture on 'them'" (Beyer 1998: 1). The academic study of religion is also restrictive. Along with privileging the study of some traditions over others, a clear hierarchy is imposed among those traditions. Yet in American colleges and universities, the discipline continues to exert a presence. When scholars attempt to define Islam solely as religion, all of the concerns with this category come forth.

John Voll asserts: "confusion is also created by attributing to Islam the characteristics of terms that are thought to be generic but in fact have distinctive cultural or historical referents." (Voll 1994: 213). Readers have undoubtedly heard of Islam described as a religion, as culture, as civilization, as a way of life, and as an Abrahamic tradition. These are just some efforts to get beyond the limitations of any single descriptor. Let us look at all of the terms used to describe Islam. Immediately the term "religion" reduces patterns of understanding and relationship among people to categories of belief

> ### Sidebar 14.2   Standard definitions
>
> Religion is a set of beliefs concerning the cause, the nature, and the purpose of the universe, especially when considered as the creation of a supernatural agency or agencies, usually involving devotional and ritual observances, and often containing a moral code that governs the conduct of human affairs.
>
> Culture is the cumulative deposit of knowledge, experience, beliefs, values, attitudes, meanings, hierarchies, religions, notions of time, roles, spatial relations, concepts of the universe, and material objects and possessions acquired by a group of people in the course of generations, through individual and group striving.
>
> Civilization is a relatively high level of cultural and technological development – *specifically*, the stage of cultural development at which writing and the keeping of written records is attained.

and practice, makes them comprehensive, and thus marginalizes other, not so easily defined attitudes and/or dispositions, such as spirituality. What is the referent? Is it unique institutions, or discernible ways of speaking about matters of individual conscience? What happens when beliefs and practices in a tradition do not fit? Some Muslims and many non-Muslim scholars of Islam have attempted to define Islam in "cultural" terms, in order to avoid this problem.

In much of Western popular culture, Islam is directly and perennially associated with the Arabs, despite plenty of evidence to the contrary, yet this is also perceived by Muslims and others as the major seat of authority. For the better part of 15 centuries, Sunni Arab thought has been authoritative beyond its actual quality. The Qur'an is read, memorized, recited, and written in Arabic. Thus it is quite natural for Islam to be identified with Arab culture; and, unless the center of authority changes, this will continue to be the case. Yet in reality – and despite that portion of reality – Islam is a trans-ethnic, transnational, trans-racial idiom. It is also true that other Muslim ethnic groups contribute to the ongoing Islamic discourse. Given these at least parallel realities, defining Islam as Arab culture, as anything but an extremely hegemonic culture in the world of Islam, still does not provide an insight into the world community of Islam, but just a narrow exploration. That leaves us with the rest of our descriptors still to be explored.

If we think of Islam as the youngest of the three Abrahamic traditions, then at best we obscure, and at worst we deny a central portion of the message of Islam. Islam, the Qur'an states, is primordial, and the Qur'an is not the only, but the last message to humankind about its obligation to worship the one and only one God. To reduce Islam to a short historical lifespan (beginning in 7th-century Arabia) and to make it the last in a short continuous line is very restrictive. The phrase "Abrahamic tradition" is used most often to demonstrate the continuity of monotheism in human history. Muslims also describe Islam as a way of life, with the inclusion of legal aspects. The general idea here is the inadequacy of defining Islam as a religion or culture, and the need to include more dimensions. Islamic legal scholars lean toward including Islamic jurisprudence as a central aspect of their definition of Islam. Since the law governs a great deal of everyday life, it becomes a critical portal for any examination of Islam and Muslims. Other scholars insist on the addition of Sufism as an interpretive lens in the definition of Islam as a way of life, as they seek to identify critical aspects of that way of life. Some of these deliberations have led to the use of the term "civilization."

The history of the world, from a Western point of view, is taught largely as a history of civilizations that emerged long ago, reached their peak, declined, and died. Some of these civilizations' philosophies and artistic efforts have been privileged (their memory is celebrated through literature and artifacts), while others have been deemed either unremarkable or worthy only of footnotes or exotic movies. The hallmarks of cultures that can be described as "civilizations" are other terms, such as "advanced" and "high" (as in "high level of cultural and technological development" or "advanced levels of technological development"). Hence the problem! What are the criteria for the terms "advanced" and "high?" These are entirely subjective designations. There is also a problem with the suggestion that history is of no real value to us in the present, because it is "in the past." As William Faulkner famously wrote, "the past is never dead, it is not past". The linear view of time and history is one legacy of the Enlightenment. The notion of progress – and of the present being an improvement of the past – has become part of the measure of civilization. In this formulation, history is an artifact rather than a guide for the literate and well educated. The masses however, remain attached to history even when this means forgoing progress. The concept of civilization also has connotations of a timeline and shares boundaries with chosen watershed events happening outside of the civilization. What comprises Islam has only one short period – 23 years – of fixed events and a minimal number of actors, while the subsequent 14 centuries are filled with dynasties, intrigue, philosophies, arts, and so on, spanning continents and dozens of cultures that continue to morph with world events. Islamic civilization is in some ways a closer definition, but still not an adequate one.

John Voll attempts to avoid some of the most obvious pitfalls of definitions by gauging the core thought of Immanuel Wallerstein's concept of moral systems, William McNeill's mega formulations of Islamic history, and Robert Wuthnow's ideas about discourse; and he does this in order to explain what, he concludes, is a double-level of world system operation. If we combine the efforts of all of these labors and are mindful of the potential pitfalls, perhaps we can describe Islam rather than define it, even though this attempt, too, is unlikely to end the debate. The stakes are extremely high, since, as Kassam reminds us, "the framework of inquiry [into Islam] [...] is locked into questions of violent conflict, national defense and security, access to oil reserves, geopolitical and economic interests, human rights abuses, and so on, even genuine efforts to understand the world's Muslims is doomed to failure" (2003: 132).

A promising tool for a description of Islam could possibly lie in thinking of it as a moral world system's operation that has a distinctive moral discourse centered on the revelation of the Qur'an and of the life of Prophet Muhammad ibn Abdullah. This includes our various discourses on religion, culture, and civilization and allows us to expand our understanding into the political and economic spheres. With this basic description in mind, perhaps we can then turn our attention to teaching about the more contentious events that have occurred and are occurring in modern and contemporary times. I think this is an appropriate place for revisiting some of Tazim Kassam's reflections on teaching religion.

The quest for knowledge and the thrill of research and discovery is not to be belittled. But in our enthusiasm for our subjects, legitimate and proper in one context, we develop what M. Robert Gardner has aptly termed the "furor to teach." Ironically he says: "true teachers want too much to teach, want to teach too much, I want too much to teach what they want to teach whenever, however, and to whomever they want." So keen and earnest is our desire to convey to students what we think they ought to know, that we forget the pedagogical necessity to find a fit between what teachers want to teach and what students want to and are ready to learn. We overlook the educational imperative that scholarship and learning needs [*sic*] to be meaningfully connected to the realities of our students. (Kassam 2003: 193)

This is especially true in the case of the teaching about Islam and Muslims in the 21st century. Teachers of Islamic studies and of Middle Eastern studies are not only faced with the perennial problems of shrinking 15 centuries of system operations into a quarter or a semester and into the discourses generated by those other *teachers* of Islam, but also with the everyday need to address emerging conflicts and announced terrorist threats.

Debates: Questions of Violence

As previously mentioned, the legacy of the European Enlightenment continues in the 21st century, being fortified by military might and by some good intentions. Western ideas and ideals determine the markers of modernity and the standards of progress, as they stand as sentries along borders between Western nations and others. Along with colonizations and invasions, Western scholarship has served various empires in its coinage of vocabularies to represent an appropriate history, to enable its populace to make sense of the present and to speculate on the future. One task of the person who teaches about Islam and Muslims in their varying relations with the West in the 21st century is to decode, demystify, and correct the historical record, especially regarding issues such as violence and Islam.

Jonathan Lyons (2012: 112) traces the Western discourse on "Islamic violence" to older texts; in his opinion the war on terrorism has "been presented as part of a never-ending struggle in defense of Western civilization and values against fanatical, nihilist Muslims who hate modernity, democracy, and the very notion of freedom." This conversation began not a few decades ago, as a defense of why, during the Crusades, Christians had to rise to take back the Holy Land of Jerusalem. It was part of wider conversations on modernity and freedom.

One typical Western tendency is to introduce inaccurate terminology about Islam and Muslims into the field of discourse and afterwards to argue that it is there and it is being used, so we must deal with it. Another Western inclination is to problematize the terminology as if it represented something real and accurate, and then to have debates about it. The use of terms such as Islamist, Islamicist, Islamicism, and Islamist – as articulated by some authors in Martin and Barzegar's *Islamism* (2009) – are cases in point. Thus we must deal with the forging of the phrase "Islam and violence" and its handmaidens. But let us begin with the Western notion that religion is inherently violent and that Islam is the primary example of this fact.

As the Middle ("Dark") Ages receded, the haste to bury the fear, violence, excesses, and general misery of the masses during this period demanded that it become a footnote in history books, so as to make space for the only history that matters. The ethical/moral consequences of this strategy are considerable. Ideals and ideas of justice, mercy, integrity, moral accountability, and responsibility became estranged from their meanings and contorted in their applications; they fell by the wayside, as archaic notions that impeded progress. Only that which served the steady march of progress and Western hegemony was permitted. This is the way of all empires, not just the newest ones.

Enlightenment philosophers, artists, and others could not but associate violence with religious zeal and its handmaidens – superstition and fanaticism. This is what their own lives and those of their fathers had experienced. Without a system of checks and balances, the control that the church exerted over society and the lives of people makes these conclusions entirely reasonable. Some scholars assert that the Christian religion became so closely associated with violence that later thinkers saw religion in general as inherently violent. After all, two of the reasons why pilgrims and others came to the "New World" were Christian violence and persecution – the attitudes and actions of which were carried out on them.

The link between Islam and violence is unfortunately unavoidable when one teaches about Islam and Muslims, though there is no necessary correlation here. Islam has been closely associated with violence, particularly within the context of the so-called war on terror and through various media. Western scholars now subsume phrases like Islamic radicalism, Islamic fundamentalism, and political Islam – all concepts associated with violence – under Islamism, an awkward term whose meaning changes with the speaker. Most non-Muslim Westerners have been taught, curiously, that Islam is a religion of violence, while Muslims have been taught that they must provide a counterpoint to this rhetoric. For many Muslims, Western Christian violence against them has changed the nature of wars of rebellion against corrupt Muslim governments and against Western capitalist incursions: bullets with references to biblical verses were used on them, prisoners were taunted and tortured about their religion. Charging Muslims with Islamic violence seems strange to Muslims when members of the US military use bullets with biblical inscriptions to kill Muslims.

European modernity fostered and continues to foster the technologies that have built lives of convenience and considerable material wealth for those living within its borders. We cannot deny the legacy of European colonialism in the Muslim world, and this legacy is twofold: first, colonialism contributed to some material progress and to an appetite for more; second, for the colonized, colonialism facilitated a comprehensive alienation between peoples and their lands, resources, and, most importantly for our purposes, institutions: extreme cultural intervention. The legacy also enabled understandings and vocabularies that make present conversations on Islam and Muslims confusing and the future challenging.

Enlightenment philosophies and their students associated violence with religious zeal and its handmaidens – superstition and fanaticism. Europeans had witnessed their misery, hedonism, and fear. The absence of reason and the control exercised by the church officials over the lives of the masses of people and over the state itself made these conclusions (we repeat) entirely reasonable. Some scholars assert that Christianity became so closely associated with violence of all kinds that later thinkers saw religion as a whole as the most potent instigator of violence. They disseminated these notions throughout the world as ancient fact and universal knowledge, making the inherent violence of religion the source of all violence. Former Prime Minister Tony Blair recently proclaimed that the greatest threat to the world is radical Islam. This is an especially obvious political stratagem, given that most of the world considers corporate greed, hunger, and natural disasters the greatest threats to the world. Making such a claim is akin to throwing toxic waste onto global discourses.

In Islamic history, Muslims engaged knowledge as life's blood very early on, and interpretations of the Qur'an flourished along with debates over legal issues. By the 1500s there were dozens of legal schools. A few centuries later this energetic intellectual activity ceased and was replaced by a small corpus of interpretations of the Qur'an; a fraction of legal thought (five schools survive) became hege-monic–authoritative. Those who mastered this corpus also became authorities who could determine what is Islamic and what is not. The center of authority has always been Saudi Arabia and Egypt. Despite their Muslim numerical insignifi-cance, centers of Arabic learning are the controlling element, as mentioned ear-lier. Mirroring the dispersion of Enlightenment ideals, the authoritative is dispersed in the Muslim world too, but it is wedded in this case to particular Qur'anic inter-pretations.

Modern Islamic history was fashioned by modern Sunni historians like Tahtawi to affirm Arab dominance, and the histories of other theological and/or political positions, from other (or even from the same) countries, were billed as untenable or too insignificant to mention. As the populace learned what the Qur'an said through interpreters (*ulamā*), the intellectual effort demanded even by the Qur'an was lost and the interpreters gained in power. A rich and varied intellectual tradition was shrunk to a fraction of its size, and its growth was largely stunted. But it is the welding of all that is Islam simply to religious obligation that distorts it. Formulaic interpretations riddled with biblical explanations and with Arab and South Asian folklore become controlling over essential aspects of life. For example, what the Qur'an says about the treatment of women is interpreted in such a way that women can be beaten, thrown out, and otherwise disenfranchised. Another example is the preference for a few inter-religious exclusionary discourses over those (and there are many of them) that facilitate cooperation. A study of the ecology of various Muslim cultures would reveal disconnections from the Qur'an and from each other.

As mentioned in Chapter 8, circumstances enable the growth and development of two different types individuals inside two different worldviews. The vocabulary that develops in the Muslim world is one of restriction, with terms that have Qur'anic origins but not Qur'anic intent. Anything unknown is to be examined but becomes *bida'* (unsanctioned innovation) in the new formulation – to be shunned with the threat of hellfire for any engagement.

Thus, after formal colonialism ended, anything associated with capitalism – industrialization, the freedom of press, the freedom of speech, private economic growth, women's rights, and so on – was explicitly linked to the West and labeled as un-Islamic. What remains is, by and large, failing societies without the infrastructures necessary for growth and well-being.

For the practicing Muslim and for most non-practicing Muslims born and raised in Muslim cultures, the ayat (signs) of the Qur'an and of selected hadith are memorized early. This combination of knowledge is repeated daily in multiple forums, until it is one with the psyche. Any issue is responded to with a reference to the Qur'an and to an appropriate hadith, either to facilitate or to thwart a thought or an action. Though in the country there may be a superficial separation between the ruler and the religious authority, the hearts and minds of the believers are filled with ayat and hadith, learned correctly or otherwise. Since there are no courses on critical theory or analysis, correlations, contextualizations, or even historical instructors, imams and others (who have the ears of the people) control what is learned as matter of fact. Concepts such as critical thinking, critical analysis, or questioning authority are alien. When Western societies demand that second-generation Muslims accept what they are taught and adopt Western ways of understanding, there is an uphill battle, just as when Western students are asked to problematize the stereotypes of Muslims to understand them.

The task of the instructor is to focus not on changing minds, but rather on informing them. Wrestling with the events of history will, of course, engender resistance. The resistance will be bolder and more vocal when there is, on both sides, a feeling of being terrorized. The ecology of teaching about Islam and Muslims is a fragile one, as the history and the civilizational contributions of Islam and of Muslims continue to be maligned in ways from which there is no apparent recovery. The efforts to remove Islam from history as a world religion whose adherents have made contributions to societies across the globe continue. Recently, in the United States, some instructors in world religions have felt the need to advocate their Christian faith in classrooms and, when Muslim students complain, these teachers feel themselves victims of terrorist jihads. The waters are not only muddied, but also at times poisoned. As of this writing, the few institutions that hired Muslim scholars to teach about Islam and Muslims are appointing either people with a deep-seated animus toward Islam or people who are Christian or Jewish only. While this is a travesty in academe, the closing of the American mind progresses without intervention.

Discussion Questions

1   What is meant by the term "ecology" in this chapter?
2   How have historical events influenced teaching about Islam and Muslims?
3   What are the categories of teachers of Islam and about Muslims?

Suggested Further Reading

Beyer, Peter (1998). The religious system of global society: A sociological look at contemporary religion and religions. *Numen*, 45(1): 1–29.

Kassam, Tazim (2003). On being a scholar of Islam: Risks and responsibilities. In Omid Safi (ed.), *Progressive Muslims: On Gender, Justice and Pluralism*. Oxford: OneWorld, pp. 191–215.

Lyons, Jonathan (2012). *Islam through Western Eyes*. New York, NY: Columbia University Press.

Martin, Richard and Abbas Barzegar (eds.) (2009). *Islamism*. Palo Alto, California: Stanford University Press, 2009.

Morrison, Toni (1993). Nobel Prize Acceptance Speech. At http://www.nobelprize.org/nobel_prizes/literature/laureates/1993/morrison-lecture.html (accessed September 21, 2012).

Voll, John (1994). Islam as a special world-system. *Journal of World History*, 5(2): 213–226.

Wadud, Amina (2003). American Muslim identity: Race and ethnicity in progressive Islam. In Omid Safi (ed.), *Progressive Muslims: On Gender, Justice and Pluralism*. Oxford: OneWorld, pp. 270–285.

Wheeler, Brannon M. (ed.) (2003). *Teaching Islam*. New York, NY: Oxford University Press, 2003.

Part IV

Islam in a Globalized World

15

Terrorism, Islamophobia, and the Media

SCOTT W. HIBBARD

Outline

An Introduction to Islam in the 21st Century, First Edition. Edited by Aminah Beverly McCloud, Scott W. Hibbard, and Laith Saud.
© 2013 Blackwell Publishing Ltd. Published 2013 by Blackwell Publishing Ltd.

Introduction

As we saw in Chapters 6 and 7, the Islamist movement that emerged in the early 20th century was both anti-colonial and anti-secular. The early Islamists perceived the weakness of Muslim countries in the Middle East and in South Asia as being rooted in their societies' loss of religious faith. From the Islamist perspective, this was nowhere more apparent than in the effort of political leaders to emulate the West. From their point of view, the creation of secular European political structures in places such as Turkey, Egypt, and Iran entailed replacing God's rule (*hakimīyyat Allah*) with the rule of man. Not only was this seen as an affront to God, it was also perceived as hastening the demise of Muslim society. While this message may have been articulated in religious terms, the goals (and methods) of the early Islamists were distinctly political. This was particularly evident in the example of the Muslim Brotherhood in Egypt and of the Jamaat-e-Islami in Pakistan, which created political parties, organized at the grassroots, and set up mechanisms to provide basic social services within the communities in which they lived. In certain cases, this type of political activism also entailed the creation of a military apparatus and the use of violence.

It is this connection between religion and violence that has shaped contemporary perceptions of the Islamist movement and, increasingly, of Islam writ large. As numerous commentators have noted, however, not all Muslims are "fundamentalists," and not all "fundamentalists" are terrorists. On the contrary, the militant fringe is a distinct minority, and its understanding of tradition is rejected by the majority of Muslims, who do not see violence as being consistent with the Islamic commandments to treat fellow human beings with compassion and justice. Nonetheless, in post-9/11 America there is a widespread perception that Islam is violent and that expressions of Muslim identity are a legitimate source of suspicion. This chapter seeks to explore such misconceptions as well as the basis for the beliefs that generated them. It is important to note from the outset that the association of religion and violence is not unique to Islam. On the contrary, all religious traditions have a complex – and often paradoxical – relationship to violence and the use of force. This is what Scott Appleby has referred to as the "ambiguity of the sacred" (Appleby 2000: 27). While religion can give a justification for violence, hatred, and xenophobia, it also has a mandate for peacemaking and tolerance. The key factor is how one interprets his or her tradition.

The first part of this chapter will explore the connection between religion and violence in general and in the Islamic tradition in particular. To this end, we will examine the ideology associated with Islamist militancy – including the religious sanction of the use of violence – as well as the historical trends that bred the rise of an international militant network. This examination will include a review of the ideas associated with Sayyid Qutb, an influential member of the Egyptian Muslim Brotherhood, and with other thinkers who issued religious justifications for political rebellion and violence. We will also examine the phenomenon of terrorism, by which we mean the targeting of civilian populations for political ends, and we will look at how these trends came together in the events of 9/11. The second part of the chapter will examine the context in which these trends emerged and how they were subsequently transformed. Islamist militancy did not occur in a vacuum. On the contrary, it is very much the legacy of Western intervention in the Middle East and South Asia. As we will see, the emergence of a transnational militant (or "jihadist") movement was an unintended consequence of the United States' support for the *mujahidin* in Afghanistan during the 1980s. Moreover, the contemporary manifestation of this jihadist movement is very much a reaction to the continuing intervention of Western powers that is discussed below. In this respect, the global networks of "militant Islam" are a byproduct – or a corollary, if you will – of the international security order constructed by the United States.

Finally, the last part of the chapter will examine how this legacy has informed Western perceptions of Islam as a religion. While it is clearly misguided to "blame Islam" for terrorism or for the events of 9/11, many do. As one commentator has noted, not only is this "wrongheaded, it is ultimately self-defeating" (Habeck 2006: 3). Nonetheless, there is a tendency among Western commentators to conflate the ideology of Islamist militancy with the religion of Islam as a whole. In doing so, they promote an image of a religion that is violent and implacably hostile to Western values. Aside from being incorrect, this politicization of Islam is commonly generated by base motives and the pursuit of partisan gain. In other words, the denigration of Islam is done by politicians and political commentators in order to help get particular individuals elected to public office, influence government policy, or silence critics of American foreign policy. This type of politicization has also helped to create a virulent "Islamophobia" – by which we mean the fear (or hatred) of Islam. Although the depiction of Arabs and Muslims as subversive – and often subhuman – is not new, the willingness to stigmatize them as a community in the post-9/11 period represents a new and disturbing trend. Such fear-mongering is reminiscent of the anti-communist hysteria of the 1950s and has had a disturbing influence on public discourse, let alone the treatment of minority populations in the West. It is ironic (and paradoxical) that some of the most hateful of these commentators commonly claim to speak on behalf of a loving God.

Religion and the Question of Violence

The religious sanctioning of violence is not unique to Islam. On the contrary, all religions have an ambiguous relationship with war, violence, and militancy. Pacifist interpretations of religion prohibit recourse to violence in any context. While individuals such as Mahatma Gandhi, the Dalai Lama, or Martin Luther King have come to embody the religious ethics of non-violence, this ethics is not unique to such individuals or to the traditions they represent. More common, perhaps, is the presence, in almost all faith traditions, of the "just war" (*justum bellum*) tradition, which recognizes the reality – and often the necessity – of war and violence in the world. In this context, however, coercion and bloodshed are perceived as necessary evils that need to be confined and strictly limited. Although the just war tradition is typically associated with Western and Christian thinkers, there is a corresponding and well-developed tradition within Islam (see Kelsay 2009). In this tradition violence is almost universally understood to be legitimate only when it is used in defense of the *ummah* (the Muslim community) and against those who wage war against, or otherwise threaten, Muslims. Finally, in all religions there is a "holy war" tradition that provides a warrant for militancy and is typically understood as offering few constraints on the use of violence. It is in aspects of religious thinking related to this holy war tradition that we find the link between religion and terrorism.

The essence of holy war resides in the use of a religious framework for interpreting politics and conflict. By being characterized as good or evil in a religious sense, otherwise mundane issues, political or not, are given cosmic significance. For example, when a dispute over land or power is articulated in religious terms, its stakes are dramatically increased, and extreme measures (such as taking life) appear justified. This is the basis for violent action. Peaceful compromise is less likely to occur in such circumstances, since any accommodation will be seen as heresy and a violation of God's will. Moreover, when the religious community to which one belongs – however defined – is designated as uniquely deserving, then any action taken on its behalf is perceived as morally justified. This is the basis for the so-called "necessity defense," where a higher moral good is used to sanction otherwise reprehensible actions and justifies the abdication of personal moral responsibility. Any action, regardless of its immorality, is seen as justified in the name of a greater good.

Sidebar 15.1   Terrorism

Terrorism is commonly understood as violence carried out by "sub-state" actors against civilian populations, for political ends. The emphasis here is on the political nature of the violence and on the fact that it is carried out by groups other than states. This understanding of terrorism differentiates it from *crime* (indiscriminate violence against civilians) on the one hand, and from *war crimes* (state atrocities) on the other. The question remains, however, whether or not this definition is too narrow. Do states commit terrorism? What about state terror against the populations under their control? More to the point, is terrorism, as some have argued, simply violence carried out by others against us? These debates are complicated by the fact that terrorism (together with the threat of terrorism) has commonly been used by governments to justify repressive policies at home and aggressive policies abroad. This raises the following question: Is terrorism a *genuine* threat, or is it simply a tool that politicians use to create fear and acquiescence in a given population?

This understanding of the holy war tradition provides an insight into the militancy associated with groups such as al-Qaeda, Lashkar-e-Taiba, and others that emerged in the aftermath of the Afghan War in the 1980s (see below). The motivations for these militant organizations are complex; the latter are frequently driven by political considerations rather than by religious ones. Particular conflicts – such as those in Kashmir, Palestine, Chechnya, the Philippines (where the Abu Sayyaf group operates) – are fundamentally about issues of self-determination and are very much a reaction to military rule and the occupation of territories inhabited by Muslim populations. Nonetheless, the fact that their political goals are articulated in religious terms and their self-understanding is informed by a religious narrative gives these political organizations a religious dimension. And this religious framework – or worldview – also links these militant groups with other, non-violent organizations affiliated with the Salafi or Islamist movement writ large.

It should be noted from the outset that the transnational Islamist movement is not a monolithic whole but rather represents a variety of groups and activists with differing interests, agendas, and motivations. Distinctions can be made between Islamists who support a particular state (such as clerics in Saudi Arabia), and those who seek to overturn a particular social and political order. There are also sharp distinctions between Islamists as to whether or not violence is a legitimate – let alone useful – means of pursuing one's ends (see below). The primary emphasis of this chapter is on the ideology that informs a particular niche within this larger category: groups that have emerged from the 1980s Afghan War and have proved willing to use violence in order to challenge the existing patterns of economic and political power. The chapter does not give significant attention to groups whose motivations are tied to particular regional conflicts, such as Ḥamas or Ḥizbullah. Nor does it focus on the majority of Muslims, who clearly reject the use of violence for the promotion of religious goals. In this regard, the emphasis on terrorism and militancy that has preoccupied the West since 9/11 – and has prompted the writing of this chapter – is itself a distortion, since the perpetrators of those attacks distinctly represent a minority voice (and, many would argue, a misguided one) in the broader tradition.

The permission for militant action that al-Qaeda and related organizations advocate is drawn only selectively from the Islamic tradition. Although rooted in the Islamist movement, the transnational militant network of today has been significantly transformed in recent decades. Its ideological roots are based on the writings of Ibn Taymiya, the 13th-century jurist associated with the Hanbali School of Islamic jurisprudence discussed earlier on (see Chapter 4). Ibn Taymiya was writing in the context of the Mongol invasions, and he is known for two key theoretical contributions. First, he argued that it was legitimate to disobey – and even to rebel against – rulers who were Muslim in name only. This idea reflected the era in which he wrote – a time when the Mongol conquerors had converted to Islam nominally but did not rule in accordance with Islamic *sharia*. Fighting such rulers was not only legitimate but also necessary, since it was seen as a defensive action against outside invaders. Second, Ibn Taymiya argued that armed struggle against non-Muslims who threatened their society (or threatened fellow Muslims) was a duty. Again, his thought reflected historical circumstances – namely a period when the lands of Islam were overrun by external armies.

These themes have resonated with contemporary Islamists in part because many see the 20th century as analogous to that earlier period. This attitude is evident in the work of Rashid Rida, Hasan al-Banna, and Mawlana Mawdudi, all of whom lived under European colonial rule and emphasized the need to defend tradition from external influences and invaders. It is also evident in the later work of Sayyid Qutb, who would become closely linked to the issue of violence and rebellion. Qutb's seminal work, *Ma'ālim fī al-Ṭarīq* (*Signposts along the Road*), is notable for its revolutionary views and its lasting influence. At the heart of this book and of Qutb's vision lies the assumption that humanity is in a state of crisis, the essence of which is a loss of values. This is evident, according to Qutb, not only in the West, but also among the ruling circles of the Arab Middle East. *Signposts* is, thus, both an indictment of the modern world and a call for reform and action. Qutb is very much rooted in the Islamist tradition, particularly when he pleads for the creation of a just Islamic community here on earth. To achieve this goal, he looks to a "vanguard" of pious individuals destined to lead the community. The analogies with the first generation of Muslims are unmistakable.

Ironically, one of the defining features of Qutb's work is that the "enemy" he warns about was no longer the European powers, but rather the secular Arab nationalists. Although the Muslim Brotherhood in Egypt was initially supportive of Nasser and the Free Officers' Movement, Nasser's failure to embrace Islamic rule and to share power led to confrontation. The early struggle between the Islamists and the secular nationalists was particularly brutal, as Nasser imprisoned and tortured hundreds of Egypt's Muslim Brothers, including Qutb. The ill-treatment of Egypt's Islamist opposition at the hands of Nasser's security services radicalized Qutb, and this is reflected in the writings he produced in prison. His execution in 1966 – Qutb was hung and buried in an unmarked grave – only served to enhance his stature as a martyr. Although his untimely death left many questions about his work open to interpretation, subsequent writers stepped in to offer their reading of the tradition. It is the willingness of these latter activists to advocate violent action and to engage in it that has created the image of Islam as a religion prone to violence and hostile to the West.

A central feature in the work of Qutb and other writers – such as Mawlana Mawdudi, discussed in Chapter 7 – is the notion of *jāhilīya*, a Qur'anic term that designates the period of pre-Islamic ignorance. The concept refers to a particular state of contemporary society, not to a particular time period. Specifically, it describes a community at the whim of individual rulers who govern it, and not ruled in accordance with a divine mandate. The secular regimes of the mid-20th century were said to epitomize this state of affairs, because they placed the rule of man above the rule of God. Like the early Mongols, these secular leaders were seen as Muslim in name only, and thus they were a legitimate object of rebellion. These were radical claims, but they were based in part on the actions of the regimes themselves. In Egypt, for example, the willingness of state security forces to torture fellow Muslims was evidence of their unbelief. Similarly, the politics of the era was said to demonstrate the essence of *jāhilīya*. As Qutb argues, the idola-trization of Nasser during the 1950s and 1960s was yet another example of the state of Egyptian society. Instead of praising God, the community was worshipping false idols such as the president, the state, and the ruling party.

The Islamist response to this state of affairs was to call for a clean break with the old order and for its replacement with a form of government that would enforce God's laws. This was a common theme among Islamist writers from various parts of the world during the period. As noted in earlier chapters, however, claiming to know God's will in matters of politics is presumptuous at best; at worst, it is likely to result in manipulation and abuse. Nonetheless, individuals such as Qutb, Mawdudi, and others took it upon themselves to translate the Islamist call to action into concrete proposals. Political activism was thus an essential part of the religious project. In *Milestones*, for example, Qutb argued that the Islamic revolution needed a "Vanguard of the Ummah" to lead this movement, because he did not feel that mainstream Muslims were sufficiently aware or spiritually oriented. Thus Qutb saw two distinct phases to the Islamist revolution. The first was the spiritual maturation of the Vanguard; the second was the active confrontation with the forces of *jāhilīya*. Qutb's concept of jihad (struggle) encompassed both stages.

Perhaps the most contentious – and controversial – aspect of this trend is the question of violence. Although the call for an active defense of Islam was common among Islamist writers of the period, what this meant in practice was not clearly spelled out. Subsequent interpreters were more explicit in their call for violent action. This was evident in the work of M. ʿAbd al-Salam Farag's *The Neglected Duty*, an influential text that argues that it is not only legitimate to deploy violence against the state, but it is the duty of all good Muslims to do so. Farag's argument is based on the larger critique of secular nationalists and on the perception that modern society is in a state of crisis. Farag goes on to argue that government leaders such as Egyptian President Anwar Sadat were *kāfir*, "unbelievers," because of specific actions they took while they were in office. This argument was the basis for Farag's assertion that such leaders were legitimately killed. The declaration of unbelief – known as *takfir* – is drawn from the Khariji tradition discussed in Chapter 5, which viewed those who committed grave sins as having abandoned their faith. This line of thinking provided the basis for Sadat's assassination in 1981 and for the violence against different Muslim governments in the 1990s.

The act of *takfir* – declaring someone an unbeliever – is enormously controversial. The potential for abuse is great, since the initiative is taken in practice by self-appointed guardians of the tradition. Moreover, it is unclear whether the notion of *jāhilīya* sanctions violence against the state or against society as a whole. This last point was a major item of dispute among militant groups in Egypt in the 1980s and 1990s. The excesses associated with this philosophy were evident in the 1990s Civil War in Algeria. In that context, militant groups readily declared anyone who disagreed with them to be an unbeliever, and hence to be justifiably killed. This contributed to the brutality of the Civil War, which wracked the country throughout the 1990s. What made that conflict particularly gruesome was that neither the government nor the militant opposition made much of a distinction between civilians and combatants. The result was widespread massacre and atrocities; the death toll in this brutal civil war is estimated to be between 150,000 and 200,000 people. The use of *takfir* was also in evidence in Egypt during the 1990s: secular writers, scholars, and intellectuals were designated "unbelievers" and either forced into exile or assaulted. The writer and Nobel Laureate Naguib Mahfouz, for example, was targeted in this way.

Sidebar 15.2   The Algerian Civil War

In 1990 and 1991 the Algerian government held elections at both local and national level. These elections were a response to a series of popular uprisings against the government going back to 1988. In the elections, the population voted overwhelmingly for the opposition led by the Islamic Salvation Front (FIS), a coalition of Islamist groups and political parties. This outcome was not surprising, given the government's corruption and misrule during the previous 30 years. The military, however, fearing a loss of power, intervened in the political process, overturned the elections, and imprisoned the FIS leadership. They also established a military government. In response, the Islamist opposition split into a variety of factions – including some that sought to continue working within the political system and some that chose to pursue a path of violence. Many in this latter group had fought in the Afghan War of the 1980s and were eager to replicate in Algeria what the *mujihedin* had done in Afghanistan.

For the next ten years Algeria was wracked by a brutal civil war, which pitted a variety of Islamist militant groups against the military and security services. The Algerian population was caught in the middle. The government was responsible for numerous human rights violations – including the use of death squads to target pro-FIS villagers – while the Islamist militants were guilty of slaughtering anyone who supported the government. In the end the militants failed, in part because of infighting among the groups, but more importantly because the excessive violence undermined whatever support the groups once had among the population.

It is not surprising that liberal – or so-called "modernist" – interpreters of the Islamic tradition reject the intolerance and violence associated with the militants, their ideology, and the selective interpretation of Islam that supports it. Why, it is argued, do the militants, in their selective interpretation of the tradition, leave out those parts that argue in favor of peace and tolerance? Mainstream thinkers and jurists who challenge Islamic militancy offer an alternative reading of the same tradition, pointing to those verses of the Qur'an that call upon Muslims to be tolerant in matters of religion and to respect members of the Jewish and Christian communities.[1] As fellow believers – so-called "people of the book" – members of these other faiths are deserving of respect and tolerance. This perspective, moreover, is not a marginal view, but is well represented within the 1,400 years of Islamic thought and practice.

Significantly, the question of violence is a source of debate even within the Islamist movement itself. While any number of religious authorities (including the sheikh of Al-Azhar) disagreed with the militants on the use of violence, members of the Muslim Brotherhood similarly offered a dissenting opinion. Having rejected violence in the 1970s, members of the Brotherhood were appalled by the excesses of the 1980s and 1990s, which were carried out by both the government and by militant opposition groups. In one statement, a Muslim Brother offered a critique of the rampant use of *takfir* by militant groups, arguing that no one has the right to declare another an apostate or an unbeliever, since only God knows what lies within another's heart. More to the point, they argued that violence is not a legitimate means of spreading God's message. In the 1990s, members of al-Gamaa al-Islamiyya came to the same conclusion when they renounced the use of violence (see Sidebar 15.3), which they saw as both ineffective and, ultimately, counterproductive. There is also a continuing debate over the legitimacy of violent jihad given the lack of education and understanding of Islam both within society and among the young men who are potential recruits to the militant network.

The Afghan War and the Rise of Transnational Militancy

If there is so much debate over the use of violence within Islam, how did the militant tendency come to be so prominent in the public mind? Part of the answer can be found in recent history. As we saw in the Chapter 14, Western (and particularly American) governments supported Saudi Arabia and the other Gulf monarchies during the Cold War. The promotion of religion, particularly a Saudi-inspired understanding of Islam, was perceived at the time as a useful means of containing the socialist left and Soviet influence in the Middle East and in South Asia. Consequently the United States was supportive of Saudi efforts to promote a Salafist vision of Islam as a means of undermining popular support for communism and socialism in these regions. These policies came to fruition in the US support for the *mujahidin* in Afghanistan after the 1979 Soviet invasion of that country. The policy of supporting Islamist militants in Afghanistan was driven by a variety of strategic considerations, including a belief among Reagan Administration officials that a Saudi-inspired Sunni Islam could serve as a bulwark both against the influence of the Soviet Union and against the resurgent Shi'ism of the Iranian Revolution. In the context of the Cold War, the CIA's covert support of Islamic militants was seen as an asset for American interests and led President Reagan to extol the virtues of these fighters, describing the Afghan *mujahidin* as "the moral equivalent of American founding fathers."

A second set of issues that have given rise to Islamist militancy (and will be discussed below) is the continuing legacy of American intervention in the region and the security regime that has developed throughout the post-World War II period. The Middle East emerged as a strategically significant region in the mid-20th century

Sidebar 15.3   Former militants renounce violence

Al-Gamaa al-Islamiyya (the Islamic Group) was one of the two dominant militant organizations in Egypt that challenged the Mubarak regime in the 1980s and 1990s. Its members were responsible for violence against government officials, tourists, secular intellectuals, and Coptic Christians. During the late 1990s, however, there was a significant debate between different factions within the Gamaa over the utility – and religious legitimacy – of violence. Much of this debate occurred in prison, where many were being held and where former militants had time to reflect upon their course of action.

Many of these former militants felt that they had been manipulated and that violence was wrong. They also recognized how counterproductive the violence had been. Popular support for the group had fallen dramatically once the Gamaa moved away from political activism and embraced a path of violence. Most Egyptians simply did not see the killing of tourists, let alone that of fellow Egyptians, as consistent with the teachings of Islam.

The prison debates produced a startling result: the leadership of the Gamaa renounced its former actions, called for a ceasefire, and argued that violence was not a legitimate understanding of jihad. In a series of books and pamphlets, the leaders of al-Gamaa argued that violence was incapable of bringing people to Islam; on the contrary, it tarnished the image of Islam both at home and abroad. Violence, in short, was antithetical to their wider goals of creating a more just Islamic society. Consequently in 1999, two years before 9/11, al-Gamaa al-Islamiyya renounced violence, not just in Egypt but everywhere.

A similar renunciation was published in 2009 by Sayyid Imam Al-Sharif, a former leader of Egypt's al-Jihad militant organization and a founding member of al-Qaeda. In a book published in serial form, Imam critiqued the justification for violence that al-Qaeda had long relied upon and argued that the jihadist movement's embrace of violence did not have a sound basis in Islamic law (for references, see Wright 2008: 38).

(Continued)

Imam was also critical of his former colleague, Ayman al-Zawahiri, the man who took over the leadership of al-Qaeda after Osama Bin Laden's death in 2011. Not only did Zawahiri promote an erroneous understanding of Islam, according to Imam, but he – along with the other leaders of al-Qaeda – established a "deviant school of jurisprudence," with the sole intention of permitting "mass killing." Indiscriminate violence and the use of *takfīr* to justify such violence, Imam believed, were violations of *sharia*, which, rightly understood, prohibited precisely such actions. According to Imam, "there is nothing that invokes the anger of God and His wrath like the unwarranted spilling of blood and wrecking of property."

because of its large oil reserves. More than two thirds of the world's proven reserves of oil lie beneath five countries in this region: Iran, Iraq, Saudi Arabia, Kuwait, and the United Arab Emirates. Western reliance upon cheap oil to sustain the international capitalist order prompted the United States to do whatever was necessary to contain Soviet influence in the region and to ensure that governments favorable to Western interests remained in power. It is for this reason that the United States (and other Western powers) consistently intervened militarily in the region's politics. This strategy included the overthrow of Iran's democratically elected government in 1953 and the subsequent support for the shah and his security services. It also included direct military intervention – for example the American involvement in the 1990 and 2003 wars with Iraq, or US military support for Israel (such as in the 1973 war).

During the Afghan War of the 1980s, the United States – in conjunction with Pakistan and Saudi Arabia – provided financial and military support to the various groups and individuals associated with the *mujahidin* that were fighting the Soviet forces. American assistance is estimated to have been between $6 and $8 billion over the course of ten years – a figure that was matched dollar for dollar by Saudi Arabia. This aid was distributed by the Pakistan intelligence services, the Inter-Service Intelligence (ISI), which tended to support groups that were both anti-Soviet and anti-Western. The promotion of a Salafist interpretation of Islam by clerics from throughout the Arab world was a key part to this effort. So, too, were the establishment of an extensive fundraising network to augment the covert government aid and the recruitment of foreign fighters from around the Muslim world. A leading figure in the effort was ʿAbdallah Azzam, who differentiated between an offensive jihad, designed to expand Muslim influence – which, he argued, is a collective responsibility – and the "defensive jihad" intended to protect Muslim lands from invaders. This latter jihad, Azzam argued, is an individual duty that falls on all Muslims; and, defined this way, it constituted the basis for recruiting young men to fight in Afghanistan.

There were an estimated 30,000 to 40,000 foreign-born Muslims – the so-called "Afghan Arabs" – who came from a variety of countries to fight in the jihad. From their perspective, this was a clear example of Islamic lands being under attack. Hence they saw the war as part of a defensive jihad, and themselves as defenders of their religion and people from an external – and self-proclaimed atheistic – invader. Moreover, as one diplomat noted, fighting in Afghanistan was simply perceived at the time as "the patriotic thing to do" (cited in Weaver 1996: 28). Among these recruits there were fighters as well as organizational personnel who raised money, set up training camps, and coordinated the effort on the ground in Afghanistan. One of these young personnel members was Osama Bin Laden, whose office of special services provided the organizational basis to what would later come to be known as al-Qaeda. The larger effort also entailed the establishment of an infrastructure of training camps in Pakistan, Islamic schools, and an international fundraising network.

After the Soviet withdrawal from Afghanistan and the subsequent collapse of the USSR, a loosely affiliated network of militant groups emerged from the ashes of the conflict. This was one of the most significant among the unintended consequences of the 1980s war in Afghanistan. By supporting the *mujahidin*, the Reagan Administration helped to create an infrastructure for an international jihadist movement that would live on after the Soviet withdrawal. Another bitter consequence was the ten years of civil war in Afghanistan that followed the Soviet departure and pitted different factions of the *mujahidin* against one another. Many of the Afghan Arabs, however, left for other conflict regions – such as Kashmir, Chechnya, and Bosnia. This "nomadic jihad" was similarly justified by the notion of a defensive jihad, because of the oppression suffered by Muslim populations at the hands of local governments in those other areas. Such oppression was particularly evident in the genocidal policies of the Serbian government, which sought to eradicate Bosnian Muslims from the regions of the former Yugoslavia and invoked to this end their own Christian justifications for their religious militancy.

> ## Sidebar 15.4   The Afghan War: The 1980s
>
> In 1979 the Soviet Union invaded Afghanistan to support a collapsing allied regime. At the time, the American political establishment saw this as an aggressive move on the part of the Soviets toward the Persian Gulf. In an effort to raise the costs of the Soviet occupation – and, reportedly, to give the Soviets their "own Viet Nam" – the Central Intelligence Agency (CIA) began providing arms and money to a variety of Afghan militant groups that came to be known as the *mujahidin*. That many of these Islamist militants were vehemently opposed to Western ideals and influence was largely overlooked by Western policy-makers. Defeating the Soviet Union seemed at the time to justify any policy. In short, the ends justified the means.

Violent opposition groups also challenged the Egyptian and Algerian governments in the 1990s (as discussed above). Islamic militants who had fought in Afghanistan returned to their home countries seeking to replicate the Afghan experience and to overturn corrupt rule in their own countries. Both regimes were perceived to be puppets of the West, since they received financial and military support from Western governments. The close association of government leaders to Western interests – and their characterization as agents of Western imperialism – provided part of these militants' motivation for challenging them. The challenge also took on a religious hue, as the militant opposition characterized these governments as apostate (in other words, as governments that had abandoned their faith), and thus illegitimate.

The militant attack on the Algerian and Egyptian government failed, however, and was ruthlessly repressed by the military and security services of the two governments. Both of these conflicts were defined by brutality, particularly from the government forces. But these defeats contributed to a re-orientation of militant groups such as Egypt's Islamic Jihad, the remnants of which returned to Afghanistan to join Bin Laden's al-Qaeda. The target now shifted away from what was known as the "near enemy" (the Arab regimes) to the "far enemy" (the West) (see for example Gerges 2005). Since Western powers such as the United States, France, and England continued to support authoritarian regimes in the Middle East and South Asia, militants such as Ayman al-Zawahiri believed that they would be unable to change their local governments as long as these regimes continued to receive military and financial support from the West. Moreover, the American military had established a significant presence in Saudi Arabia during the 1990s. During the 1990–1991 Gulf War the United States had sent to Saudi Arabia 450,000 American soldiers to drive Iraqi forces from the oil-rich country of Kuwait. After the war, America retained a significant number of American troops in Saudi Arabia to protect American strategic interests in the region. This military presence was perceived by those in the region as a Western occupation of Muslim holy lands.

The focus of the "global jihad" that evolved at this time was consciously anti-imperialist. The transnational, though loosely connected, militant network that had emerged out of the Afghan War – and had spread to a variety of regions around the world – began to emphasize its opposition to the West, particularly to the United States. Its members saw themselves as global actors, who, in the absence of the Soviet Union, were the "only force willing to resist the absolute dominance of the United States" (Devji 2005: 28). This is one of the reasons why it is important to distinguish between the global movement – which includes al-Qaeda – and other groups, which are concerned with particular, regional conflicts. Ideologically as well, this new militant organization bore only a faint resemblance to the Islamist movement of the mid-20th century. It may have sprung from that earlier tradition, but its manifestation and its target were something quite new. This was a network that operated on the margins of political power, influencing the center from the periphery, and it threatened both the dominant states of the affected regions and their superpower patron.

The changing nature of this militant network was evident in the 1990s, which witnessed a steady increase in attacks on the manifestations of American military, economic, and political power. The goal of such attacks was to drive American forces away from the Arabian Peninsula, to end (or undermine) American support for regional autocrats, and to raise the costs of the unqualified support that the United States provided to Israel. The first such action came in 1993, when a handful of militants – including individuals from the Afghan conflict – set off a truck bomb in the underground parking facility of the World Trade Center. Two years later, in 1995, militant operatives detonated a bomb in a National Guard Training center in Riyad, Saudia Araba. There was a similar bombing of the Khobar Towers apartment complex in Dahrain, Saudi Arabia the following year (see Sidebar 15.5). The complex was targeted because it housed American military personnel in that country. Al-Qaeda, one central organization in the web of international militancy, was also involved in the bombing of two US Embassies in Africa in 1998. These attacks – in Dar Es Salaam, Tanzania and in Nairobi, Kenya – left more than 220 people dead and over 4,000 wounded victims (mostly Kenyans and Tanzanians). In 2000 an al-Qaeda cell in Yemen struck the USS Cole, an American destroyer harbored in the port of Aden. Finally, on September 11, 2001, 18 young Saudis and Egyptian militants hijacked four American airliners, two of which were crashed into the World Trade Center and one into the Pentagon. The events of this day sparked two wars – the invasions of Afghanistan and Iraq by American military forces – and opened a gulf of distrust between the West and the Muslim world.

Understanding the War on Terror

In the immediate aftermath of 9/11, a debate emerged about the meaning of the attack and how America ought to respond. At the heart of this debate was a question of motives. Why would the 9/11 hijackers carry out such wanton attacks on American citizens? Why, in other words, did they hate us? There were two answers that were offered at the time. The first was offered by President George W. Bush, who argued that they "hate our freedoms – our freedom of religion, our freedom of speech, our freedom to vote and assemble and disagree with one another."[2] The second was that they hate our policies. As Susan Sontag noted, this was not an attack upon the "free world," but rather a strike against "the world's self-proclaimed super-power, undertaken as a consequence of specific alliances and actions" (Sontag 2003: 215). But the debate was somewhat confused from the outset, since it was never clear whether those who asked the question were referring to the 9/11 hijackers or to the Arab and Muslim world as a whole.

Although this debate was over before it ever really began, the issues it raised are informative. The first perspective – they hate us for our freedoms – locates the source of conflict in the realm of ideology and in the hostility that Islamist groups and regimes supposedly

---

Sidebar 15.5   Terrorism 1995–1996

While there is a tendency to equate terrorism with Islam, the reality is that many different political groups resort to violence to achieve their ends. A quick look at the major terrorist attacks carried out in 1995–1996 reflects a much broader phenomenon and a diversity of ideological motivations. These attacks include the following:

- The most significant terrorist attack on American soil prior to 9/11 was the destruction of the Alfred P. Murrah Federal Building in Oklahoma City on April 19, 1995. The attack was carried out by right-wing extremist Timothy McVeigh, who packed explosive material into a truck that was then parked in front of the building. The resulting explosion killed 168 people, including 18 children, and damaged over 300 buildings within a 16-block radius. McVeigh and his accomplice Terry Nichols, along with two others, were subsequently arrested and convicted for the crime.

- The Irish Republican Army (IRA) carried out (or attempted to carry out) several attacks in England during 1996, including a bombing in London's Dockland's area on February 9, 1996 that killed two people. Several months later, on June 15, 1996, there was another, more serious bombing in Manchester, which wounded over 200 people and caused damage amounting to over $1 billion.

- On June 25, 1996, a car bomb was detonated outside of the Khobar Tower complex in Saudi Arabia, which was housing American service members. The blast inflicted a significant amount of damage on the two towers and killed 19 people. Blame, however, has never been definitively determined. Although Iran was initially suspected of being behind the bombing, the more likely suspect is al-Qaeda.

- On July 27, 1996, a bomb was exploded in the Olympic centennial park in Atlanta, Georgia, during the 1996 Olympic games, killing one person and injuring over 100 others. The perpetrator, Eric Robert Rudolph, was a right-wing Christian who carried out the attack to "embarrass the Washington government in the eyes of the world for its abominable sanctioning of abortion on demand" (posted on www.armyofgod.com and accessed September 20, 2012).

nourish toward Enlightenment values. This perspective is based on a Western interpretation of Islamist thinkers such as Qutb, Mawdudi, or al-Banna. As noted before, these theorists believed that the political decline of the Islamic world is rooted in the efforts of Muslim communities to emulate a secular West. The adoption of Western cultural norms at an individual level, as well as the acceptance of a non-religious (i.e. secular) vision of society by political leaders, were said to be the sources of ills in the Islamic world. From this perspective, the liberal emphasis on individual rights and the Enlightenment's belief that conscience is the ultimate arbiter of religious truth appear to be antithetical to a more literalist reading of religious tradition. Moreover, from the Islamist point of view, the political revitalization of society required a more central role for religion in public life and a state that was committed to enforcing a uniform Islamic law. While the Islamists saw this ideology as a more authentic reading of their tradition, many in the West perceived it as a cause of cultural conflict. The close connection between religion and political authority, it was argued, was simply a form of religious totalitarianism.

The second perspective on 9/11 argued that the attacks were a reaction (or "blowback") to American foreign policies in the Middle East and South Asia. As such, they had little to do with either religion or ideology, even if the political grievances emanating from these regions are commonly articulated in religious terms. Rather, this alternative interpretation locates the source of conflict squarely in the realm of politics. This view is derived, in part, from the various fatwa (religious edicts) and statements issued by Osama Bin Laden during the 1990s. Bin Laden's 1998 fatwa, for example, said nothing about American society, but it did supply a list of complaints against the US government. These included sharp criticisms around the points mentioned above: the continuing presence of US troops in Saudi Arabia, America's unqualified support for Israel, and the policy, adopted by successive US governments, of backing repressive Arab regimes.

This last point is of particular interest. On the one hand, it reflects the core challenges of the region: the absence of democracy, rampant corruption, and the mismanagement of the region's economic development. On the other hand, it highlights the connection between American foreign policy and the Islamist backlash: American support for the governments of Saudi Arabia, Algeria, and Egypt is what led the Islamists to conflate their opposition to local regimes (i.e. the "near enemy") and to the United States (the "far enemy"). Moreover, despite its rhetorical commitment to democracy and democratic change, the United States has consistently supported autocratic regimes in the Middle East and South Asia since the end of World War II as a means of furthering its economic and political interests (many of which revolve around ensuring reliable access to the region's oil reserves). American support for autocratic rule prompted Bin Laden to note: "our fight against these governments is not separate from our fight against you [the United States]."[3]

Those who argued that the 9/11 hijackers were motivated by an animus toward American values took exception to the view that American foreign policy was an issue at all. Conservative commentators such as Charles Krauthammer harshly criticized those who implied that American actions had somehow contributed to the 9/11 attacks. Krauthammer, as well as others, saw such criticism as patently unpatriotic in a time of crisis and as symptomatic of the moral relativism of the political left. More to the point, the belief that the attacks may have been brought on by American actions overseas was anathema to Krauthammer, who argued that the massacre of innocent civilians in the World Trade Center marked "an obvious moral truth" (Krauthammer 2001). These sentiments were echoed in the criticisms directed at Rev. Jeremiah Wright during the 2008 presidential campaign, after Wright, a former pastor of Barak Obama's Chicago church, characterized the 9/11 attacks as America's "chickens coming home to roost."

Invariably, the answer to the broader question – why do they hate us – was both a matter of values and a matter of policies. It was a matter of values insofar as Islamist militants themselves situate their opposition to the West in largely religious and moral terms. However, the animus of the Islamist groups is perhaps primarily a matter of policy. Islamist militants – as well as many mainstream Muslims – question the policies of successive American governments discussed above. More importantly, the despair and hopelessness common among the poor in these societies provide a fertile ground for anti-American sentiments. As numerous commentators have argued, the popular support for Islamist movements has little to do with religion; rather it reflects the lack of economic opportunities, affordable housing, and education (Tessler 1997). The anti-Western overtones, from this perspective, are due to the complicity of the West in perpetuating an inequitable status quo.

The official response to the events of 9/11, however, did not take into account these various issues. Rather, by viewing the matter in ideological – and often religious – terms, the

---

Sidebar 15.6   Bin Laden's 1998 fatwa

From Osama Bin Laden's *Jihad against Jews and crusaders*, World Islamic Front Statement, February 23, 1998:

Praise be to God, who revealed the Book, controls the clouds, defeats factionalism, and says in His Book: "But when the forbidden months are past, then fight and slay the pagans wherever ye find them, seize them, beleaguer them, and lie in wait for them in every stratagem (of war);" and peace be upon our Prophet, Muhammad Bin-'Abdallah, who said: I have been sent with the sword between my hands to ensure that no one but God is worshipped, God who put my livelihood under the shadow of my spear and who inflicts humiliation and scorn on those who disobey my orders.

The Arabian Peninsula has never – since God made it flat, created its desert, and encircled it with seas – been stormed by any forces like the crusader armies spreading in it like locusts, eating its riches and wiping out its plantations. All this is happening at a time in which nations are attacking Muslims like people fighting over a plate of food. In the light of the grave situation and the lack of support, we and you are obliged to discuss current events, and we should all agree on how to settle the matter.

No one argues today about three facts that are known to everyone; we will list them, in order to remind everyone:

First, for over seven years the United States has been occupying the lands of Islam in the holiest of places, the Arabian Peninsula, plundering its riches, dictating to its rulers, humiliating its people, terrorizing its neighbors, and turning its bases in the Peninsula into a spearhead through which to fight the neighboring Muslim peoples.

If some people have in the past argued about the fact of the occupation, all the people of the

(Continued)

Peninsula have now acknowledged it. The best proof of this is the Americans' continuing aggression against the Iraqi people using the Peninsula as a staging post, even though all its rulers are against their territories being used to that end, but they are helpless.

Second, despite the great devastation inflicted on the Iraqi people by the crusader–Zionist alliance, and despite the huge number of those killed, which has exceeded 1 million... despite all this, the Americans are once against trying to repeat the horrific massacres, as though they are not content with the protracted blockade imposed after the ferocious war or the fragmentation and devastation.

So here they come to annihilate what is left of this people and to humiliate their Muslim neighbors. Third, if the Americans' aims behind these wars are religious and economic, the aim is also to serve the Jews' petty state and divert attention from its occupation of Jerusalem and murder of Muslims there. The best proof of this is their eagerness to destroy Iraq, the strongest neighboring Arab state, and their endeavor to fragment all the states of the region such as Iraq, Saudi Arabia, Egypt, and Sudan into paper statelets and through their disunion and weakness to guarantee Israel's survival and the continuation of the brutal crusade occupation of the Peninsula.

All these crimes and sins committed by the Americans are a clear declaration of war on God, his messenger, and Muslims. And *ulamā* have throughout Islamic history unanimously agreed that the jihad is an individual duty if the enemy destroys the Muslim countries. This was revealed by Imam Bin-Qadamah in "Al-Mughni," Imam al-Kisa'i in "Al-Bada'i," al-Qurtubi in his interpretation, and the shaykh of al-Islam in his books, where he said: "As for the fighting to repulse [an enemy], it is aimed at defending sanctity and religion, and it is a duty as agreed [by the *ulamā*]. Nothing is more sacred than belief except repulsing an enemy who is attacking religion and life." On that basis, and in compliance with God's order, we issue the following fatwa to all Muslims:

(Continued)

Bush Administration and its allies overlooked the genuine sources of grievance that animate anti-American sentiment overseas. Consequently, there is little popular understanding of the context in which the Islamist movement emerged, and even less for the issues that continue to animate it. There has been little public discussion, for example, of the link between the Cold War support for the Afghan *mujahidin* and the rise of al-Qaeda. More to the point, there has been little public debate regarding central elements of American foreign policy, and whether the continued support of undemocratic regimes and of the Israeli occupation of Palestinian lands genuinely serves American national interest. On the contrary, the central goals and policies of the US government have remained largely unchanged, and American military intervention in the region has increased, not decreased, since 2001.

Terrorism, Islamophobia, and the Media

The events of 9/11 have left a legacy of fear and suspicion both in the West and in the Muslim world. In terms of the latter, the wars that followed this tragic event – the invasions of Iraq and Afghanistan – have reinforced negative perceptions of American foreign policy and have played into the Islamist argument that the West is at war with Islam. Within the United States, this legacy of fear and suspicion has manifested itself in a xenophobic and nativistic form of "Islamophobia." At the root of contemporary Islamophobia lies a belief that there is something intrinsically flawed within the religion itself, and that the values embodied in Muslim traditions are antithetical to those of Western civilization. Much of this is ascribed to the fact that Islam did not experience a "reformation" (as happened in Christianity), or that Muslim societies have not embraced the Enlightenment norms of individual rights, democracy, and freedom of conscience. As a result, the rise of Islamist militancy is *not* seen in the West as a reaction to the socio-economic conditions prevalent in the Middle East and South Asia (as described above), or to a history of unjust rulers and Western interventionism. Rather, the phenomenon of Islamist militancy is considered to be an intrinsic manifestation of the religious tradition. The source of conflict between East and West, then, is said to lie in the realm of values. In Huntington's prosaic words, this clash of civilizations "is not only real, it is basic."

Modern Islamophobia is also rooted in a monolithic vision of Islam. Not only is the tradition flawed from the perspective of writers/ activists such as Robert Spencer, Daniel Pipes, or Pam Geller (see Sidebar 15.8), but, they argue, all Muslims see the world through similar eyes. Consequently these Western political commentators do not see the 9/11 hijackers as part of a fringe movement – and marginal by the standard of what most Muslims believe – but rather as symptomatic of mainstream Muslim thinking. This is ironic, given the widespread revulsion that Muslims feel toward the 9/11 attacks. This lack of nuance is reflected in the discourse of "Islamo-fascism" promoted by David Horowitz (among others), which blurs the distinction between the Islamist ideology and the religion of Islam. At the heart of this discourse is the belief that America is at war with both militant Islam and the religion of Islam in general. In the foreign policy arena, the fear of Islamo-fascism has justified military action overseas, while domestically it has sanctioned intrusive surveillance and detention policies. The link to Islamophobia is evident in the provocative assertion that there is a secret plan for the "Islamization of America" and that this is part of the larger cultural conflict. In making such wild and unsubstantiated claims – a variation

The ruling to kill the Americans and their allies – civilians and military – is an individual duty for every Muslim who can do it in any country in which it is possible to do it, in order to liberate the al-Aqsa Mosque and the holy mosque [Mecca] from their grip, and in order for their armies to move out of all the lands of Islam, defeated and unable to threaten any Muslim. This is in accordance with the words of Almighty God, "and fight the pagans all together as they fight you all together," and "fight them until there is no more tumult or oppression, and there prevail justice and faith in God."

This is in addition to the words of Almighty God: "And why should ye not fight in the cause of God and of those who, being weak, are ill-treated (and oppressed)? – women and children, whose cry is: 'Our Lord, rescue us from this town, whose people are oppressors; and raise for us from thee one who will help!'"

We – with God's help – call on every Muslim who believes in God and wishes to be rewarded to comply with God's order to kill the Americans and plunder their money wherever and whenever they find it. We also call on Muslim *ulamā*, leaders, youths, and soldiers to launch the raid on Satan's US troops and the devil's supporters allying with them, and to displace those who are behind them so that they may learn a lesson.

Almighty God said: "O ye who believe, give your response to God and His Apostle, when He calleth you to that which will give you life. And know that God cometh between a man and his heart, and that it is He to whom ye shall all be gathered."

Almighty God also says: "O ye who believe, what is the matter with you, that when ye are asked to go forth in the cause of God, ye cling so heavily to the earth! Do ye prefer the life of this world to the hereafter? But little is the comfort of this life, as compared with the hereafter. Unless ye go forth, He will punish you with a grievous penalty, and put others in your place; but Him ye would not harm in the least. For God hath power over all things."

Almighty God also says: "So lose no heart, nor fall into despair. For ye must gain mastery if ye are true in faith."

Sidebar 15.7   Socio-economic basis of popular support for the Islamist movement

Interpreting the motivations for Islamist militancy – and the support for Islamist ideas more generally – has long been a source of debate. During the 1990s, Western policy sought to understand the sources of support for the Islamist movement. Was it driven primarily by ideology – in other words, was it a religious utopianism – or did popular support emerge from the endemic poverty, authoritarianism, and corruption that defined so much of the Middle East and South Asia? In short, was this a religious or political issue? The answer to this question was that both issues were relevant. Those who looked to the political basis of the trend focused on socio-economic issues: lack of housing, unemployment, social dislocation. Although these issues may be articulated in religious terms, the underlying problem, it was argued, was the lack of democracy and human rights and the low standards of living. As one commentator noted in the 1990s: "As long as Arab governments resist political participation and refuse to tolerate different political opinions, the strength of the Islamist movement as an alternative political ideology will continue to grow" (al-Suwaidi, cited in Tessler, p. 110).

of which is the belief in the existence of "stealth jihadists" within the government and society – conservative commentators such as Spencer and Geller conflate the peaceful practice of Islam with the militant ideology of Bin Laden or Farag. These commentators embody the same kind of unwarranted paranoia that characterized the 1950s' anti-communist hysteria.

This misunderstanding of the Islamic world was also evident in official characterizations of the war on terror during the Bush Administration. The official view of Islamic militancy during that period readily lumped together a broad swath of political actors in an undifferentiated manner: Sunni insurgents in Iraq, the Shiʿi government in Iran, al-Qaeda operatives in Afghanistan, the Palestinian Hamas, the Lebanese (and Shiʿi) political party Hizbullah, the Taliban (a former ally of Saudi Arabia and mortal enemy of Iran), and any number of other groups, with widely differing agendas and interests. From the perspective of the Bush Administration, however, all of these groups shared a tendency toward fanaticism (that is, irrationality) and an enduring hostility to Enlightenment values of individual freedom. Although some individual members of the Bush Administration differentiated between "extremist" and "mainstream Islam," others did not. Moreover, the willingness of Administration officials to invoke the rhetoric of "Islamo-fascism" helped to validate the view of their conservative supporters, who readily blurred such distinctions. By portraying Islamic extremists in such terms and, what is more, by linking the extremist ideologies of Osama Bin Laden to mainstream Muslims, conservative activists helped to shape public perceptions to the effect that America is at war not with a radical minority associated with al-Qaeda, but with Islam itself.

It is important to recognize that Islamophobia is not a new phenomenon, even if it has gained greater currency in the post-9/11 era. Moreover, Islamophobia did not emerge in a vacuum. On the contrary, the fear and hatred associated with this trend are – and have been – actively promoted by a variety of religious and political actors. These include, among others, activists such as the ones noted above (Geller, Spencer, and Horowitz); but they also include more mainstream political actors such as Newt Gingrich and numerous members of Congress, as well as Republican Party activists operating out of privately funded Washington think tanks. They also include right-wing political commentators such as Rush Limbaugh, Glenn Beck, and others. These individuals consciously fanned the flames of religious division for partisan gain. They were, in short, tapping into the fear and xenophobia latent within Western society – much of it produced by the social dislocation associated with economic change – in order to further a conservative political agenda. Fear of Islam thus serves as a divisive "wedge issue" in American electoral politics, the goal of which is to demonize liberal cosmopolitanism and to increase the salience of cultural – as opposed to economic – issues as a criterion for voting.

The politicization of the Park 51 Mosque during the summer of 2010 reflected precisely this type of political manipulation. The group that was seeking to build the community center was not a part of "militant Islam," though it was consistently characterized as such by Newt Gingrich, Geller, and a host of commentators on Fox Television News. Ironically, the man behind the Park 51 Mosque, Imam Faisal Abdul Rauf, is an adherent of Sufism, the mystical side of Islam that eschews violence and is commonly depicted as heretical by the more austere fundamentalism of the Wahhabi tradition. Rauf even served as an emissary of the Bush Administration to the Islamic world during the post-9/11 era, and he was previously portrayed by government officials as precisely the type of person that

Sidebar 15.8   Robert Spencer and Pam Geller

Robert Spencer is the founder of Jihad Watch, a program associated with the politically conservative Freedom Center. He is also the author of several books on Islam and Islamic militancy that are characterized by their selective – and often misleading – interpretation of the tradition. He has, nonetheless, become an influential polemicist and commentator in American right-wing circles. Many of his theories revolve around the fear of "stealth jihadists" who seek to subvert American society from within. Spencer, along with Pam Geller, were leading opponents of the Park 51 Mosque project. Geller, a single mother and blogger, has described herself as a "racist–Islamophobic–anti-Muslim bigot." Geller became a national figure for her involvement in the mosque controversy, though she has been writing an anti-Muslim blog for many years.

The concern that many commentators have raised – including commentators on the political right – is that the writings and public statements of both Geller and Spencer are consciously misleading, xenophobic, and factually inaccurate. Particularly in regard to Geller, the caustic and hateful rhetoric that she uses – and that has been picked up by politicians like Newt Gingrich and Sarah Palin – helps to spread the kind of bigotry and intolerance that characterized the anti-Semitic and anti-Catholic sentiments of earlier periods in American history. As a former colleague of Geller noted in an interview, "I think she's enabling a real bigotry – a lot of people are convinced by the propaganda she repeats like a mantra" (Charles Johnson, quoted in Barnard and Feuer 2010, p. 1B).

America should be supporting. Yet these facts were obscured by the effort to link the community center to the events of 9/11. The deliberate mischaracterization of the issue was evident in the common reference to the community center as a victory monument built on "conquered land" and in the depiction of Rauf as a radical extremist. Similarly, the proposed center was consistently portrayed as being located at ground zero (the point closest to detonation), when in fact it was planned to be built several blocks away, in a rundown building that used to be

Sidebar 15.9   Commentary on 9/11

Members of Egypt's Muslim Brotherhood, Palestinian Hamas, and Pakistan's Jamaat-e-Islami (along with others) signed the following statement shortly after 9/11:

> The undersigned, leaders of Islamic movements, are horrified by the events of Tuesday 11 September 2001 in the United States, which resulted in massive killing, destruction and attack on innocent lives. We express our deepest sympathies and sorrow. We condemn, in the strongest terms, the incidents, which are against all human and Islamic norms. This is grounded in the Noble Laws of Islam, which forbid all forms of attacks on innocents. God Almighty says in the Holy Quran: "No bearer of burdens can bear the burden of another" (Surah al-Isra 17: 15). (Cited in Devji 2005: 31)

Sayyid Imam al-Sharif, in a media interview:

> People hate America, and the Islamist movements feel their hatred and their impotence. Ramming America has become the shortest road to fame and leadership among the Arabs and Muslims. But what good is it if you destroy one of your enemy's buildings, and he destroys one of your countries? What good is it if you kill one of his people, and he kills a thousand of yours? [...] That, in short, is my evaluation of 9/11. (Quoted in Wright 2008, p. 49)

owned by the Burlington Coat Factory. Yet, as a result of describing the community center as a mosque and of representing it as being built on "ground zero," the issue acquired an emotional appeal that helped mobilize conservative voters in the lead up to the 2010 congressional elections.

Anti-Muslim sentiments and Islamophobia have also been on the rise in Europe. One of the more well-known political activists in Europe is Geert Wilders, a member of parliament from the Netherlands and head of the Party for Freedom. Wilders has consistently sent warnings about the Islamization of the Netherlands and, like Spencer and Geller, argues that Islam is a violent faith and that extremists are simply adhering to their tradition. These views are evident in the controversial film *Fitna*. This short documentary – produced by Wilders – highlights elements of the Qur'anic tradition that support or in some way sanction violence. The selective reading of the tradition, the sensationalist nature of this film, and the caricature it makes of the Islamic tradition have all proven enormously controversial and remarkably influential. Its central argument – that Islam sanctions violence and the ill-treatment of women among other things – sparked a backlash in Europe and resulted in death threats to Wilder. Another Dutch filmmaker, Theo Van Gogh, was killed for his role in producing a similar film, *Submission*, which sparked retaliatory violence against Dutch mosques.

Contemporary Islamophobia in the United States has been similarly promoted by conservative Christians such as Pat Robertson, Pastor John Hagee, and other elements of the so-called "religious right." Their access to money, television, and audiences has given them an enormous influence in the public realm. More to the point, their religious ideologies provide a theological basis to the kind of Islamophobia that has been common in recent years. This influence is evident in two aspects of the broader trend. First, the literalist reading of the Christian tradition and the conservative theology of Hagee and others have helped shape a popular view of the world as locked in a titanic struggle between good and evil. Like the Islamist militants, these conservative Christians interpret current political issues through a religious lens. Contemporary issues – such as the Israeli–Palestinian conflict – are infused with cosmic meaning when they are articulated in a religious vernacular and situated in the context of a larger conflict (what is often described as "World War IV"). Moreover, the hatred and stigma associated with Islamophobia are validated when influential ministers like Franklin Graham describe Islam as a "wicked religion" and disparage the Muslim faith.

Second, the Christian "dispensationalism" associated with many Christian fundamentalists posits a vision of the end times defined by a conflict between Christians and Muslims. By dispensationalism we mean the belief that the world is living through the so-called "end times," as described in the Book of Revelations. From this point of view, the return of the Messiah (Jesus Christ) is premised upon the unfolding of key events in time, and this return would be followed by the "Rapture" (which would include the removal of all true believers to Heaven), then by a period of war and famine, and finally by the battle of Armageddon. This type of "end times" scenario was popularized in the Left Behind book series (later made into a film) and is central to the ministry of Hagee and others. Significantly, the part of the "enemy" in this larger conflict is commonly played by radical Islamists, cosmopolitan Europeans, Arabs, and/or Russians. This illiberal theology readily contributes to enmity and hatred between peoples – not to mutual understanding or to a recognition of their shared humanity. Like the ideology of Bin Laden, this religious interpretation of contemporary politics – together with the Manichean worldview it perpetuates – has been used to sanction violence and the ongoing involvement of the US military in the Middle East and South Asia.

Finally, the coverage of these issues by the news media has contributed greatly to the popular misunderstanding that lies at the heart of Islamophobia. On the one hand, the simplistic coverage of issues such as the Park 51 Mosque feeds into a storyline that is readily comprehended but inaccurate. The characterization of the dispute in mainstream media – along with the unwillingness of news outlets to question basic assumptions behind it – has helped to validate many of the claims made by Islamophobes. While it is understandable that Fox News would pick up on the issue since it fits with the partisan orientation of the network, it is surprising – and troubling – that other national media outlets did so little to counter obvious disinformation. Perhaps they did not wish to appear unpatriotic; perhaps they did not understand (or care to explain) that a simplistic characterization of the issue served no one's interest. In any event, the willingness of major television networks to offer media platforms to Geller, Spencer, and other xenophobic commentators helped to frame the debate in a manner that reinforced anti-Muslim prejudice instead of dispelling it. Similarly, various media's coverage of the wars in Iraq and Afghanistan, the idolatrization of the events of 9/11, and the sensationalism associated with an amorphous terrorist threat have seared into the public mind the image of an external Other implacably hostile to the West.

Conclusion

To be sure, Islamophobia did not begin with 9/11. Much of the post-Cold War era was informed by a sense that the "green peril" of Islam had supplanted communism as the new enemy of Western powers. The roots, moreover, go back even further. Depictions of Muslims within the 19th-century orientalist discourse, the historical animosity between Western European nationalisms and Ottoman ambitions, and the colonial legacy all left a sense of antagonism between the so-called Western and Eastern civilizations. Moreover, the caricaturization (and vilification) of Arabs and Muslims through film, television, and news broadcasts has been common practice in American media for decades. The underlying tension and suspicion were activated by subsequent events during the Cold War, including the Iranian Revolution and acts of terrorism carried out by left-wing Palestinian groups during the 1970s and 1980s. This trend has only been exacerbated in the post-9/11 environment.

Still, the significance of Islamophobia for American society is deeper: it goes to the heart of the country's self-image and challenges the ideals for which America stands. The United States has historically been torn between two competing visions of national identity: is America a genuinely inclusive and tolerant society, or is there an ethnic and religious basis to American identity that precludes minorities from full membership? In other words, is America an open society rooted in Enlightenment values, or is it one with closed membership, reserved only for particular ethnic or religious groups? This tension is not new. On the contrary, it informed the anti-immigrant (and anti-Mexican) xenophobia of recent years, and it was manifest in the anti-Catholic and anti-Jewish sentiments of the early and mid-20th century. It also informed the hostility toward Germans, Irish, and Chinese during the 19th century and toward the Japanese during World War II. The anti-Muslim sentiment of the post-9/11 environment reflects this same conflict between inclusion and exclusion. By denigrating all Muslims and by linking them to the events of 9/11, those who fan the flames of Islamophobia have stigmatized an entire community on the basis of their identity, and not on the basis of their character (let alone content of their actual beliefs).

Ironically, the Enlightenment's norms, which are extolled as quintessentially Western – and which supposedly differentiate "the West from the rest" – argue for the kind of inclusive cosmopolitanism that is antithetical to the Islamophobia prevalent today. And yet those who promote hatred and fear consistently claim to be defending Western values. This highlights the central paradox at the heart of this narrative. Individuals such as Spencer and Geller condemn the intolerance and chauvinism of Muslim extremists, but they manipulate the beliefs of these militants in order to justify their own intolerance and chauvinistic extremism. This is evident in the politicization of the *sharia* and in the effort to make it a campaign issue in the 2010 election cycle. In other words, it is not freedom and tolerance that

Geller and Spencer are fighting for, but the repression of a religious minority and its exclusion from American public life.

A second paradox along this line of argument involves the exercise of American foreign policy overseas. While the denigration of Muslim minorities and the fact that suspicion is cast on individual Muslims are byproducts of 9/11, the demise of America's standing overseas has been underway for many years. Moreover, this demise is closely intertwined with the policies of successive American governments. The 9/11 hijackers may have been driven by an illiberal ideology, but the anti-Western sentiments that exist in Muslim and Arab society have little to do with America's values and everything to do with its policies. The legacy of Western intervention in Arab and Muslim lands, the willingness to support autocratic regimes in the Middle East and South Asia, and the discrimination evident in Western societies all contribute to the wave of anti-Western and anti-American sentiments. In short, it is not necessarily Western values that are at stake here; it is rather the failure to live up to those self-proclaimed values and the willingness to abandon the commitment to Enlightenment norms that fuel the vicious cycle of inter-communal hostility. This insight brings into question the larger issue: Are the Western policies adopted in the so-called war on terror making things better or worse? The events of 9/11 have justified an increased military presence in the regions involved and a continuation of the same foreign policies that have guided Western states for decades. Far from eradicating the scourge of terrorism, however, these measures appear to be only perpetuating the underlying conditions that give rise to extremism: poverty, authoritarianism, and hopelessness.

Notes

1   There are two verses of the Qur'an that are commonly invoked in this context. The first is, "there is no compulsion in matters of religion," and the second, "to you your religion and to me, my religion."

2   President George Bush, Address to a Joint Session of Congress, September 20, 2001.

3   Osama Bin Laden, Jihad against Jews and crusaders. World Islamic Front Statement, February 23, 1998, to be found at http://www.fas.org/irp/world/para/docs/980223-fatwa.htm. See also Osama Bin Laden, Declaration of war against the Americans occupying the land of the two Holy Places (Expel the infidels from the Arab Peninsula), August 23, 199, to be found at http://www.pbs.org/newshour/updates/military/july-dec96/fatwa_1996.html.

Discussion Questions

1   How real is the threat of terrorism?

2   Do states engage in terrorism?

3   What is a proper response?

4   Is violence ever justified in the pursuit of political goals? Of religious goals?

5   Should a free society tolerate intolerance? In other words, should free countries tolerate the intolerant ideas of Islamist extremists? Should such societies tolerate Islamophobia?

6   What are the similarities and differences between the worldviews of Islamic, Christian, and other religious activists?

Suggested Further Reading

Abu-Rabi, Ibrahim (1996). *Intellectual Origins of the Islamic Resurgence in the Modern Arab World*. Albany, NY: SUNY Press.

Appleby, R. Scott (2000). *The Ambivalence of the Sacred: Religion, Violence and Reconciliation*. New York, NY: Rowman & Littlefield.

Barnard, Anne and Alan Feuer (2010, October 10). Outraged, and outrageous. *New York Times*.

Chomsky, Noam (1991). International terrorism: Image and reality. In Alexander George (ed.), *Western State Terrorism*. New York, NY: Routledge.

Devji, Faisal (2005). *Landscapes of the Jihad: Militancy, Morality, Modernity*. Ithaca, NY: Cornell University Press.

Gerges, Fawaz (2005). *The Near Enemy and the Far Enemy: Why Jihad Went Global*. New York, NY: Cambridge University Press.

Habeck, Mary (2006). *Knowing the Enemy: Jihadist Ideology and the War on Terror*. New Haven, CT: Yale University Press.

Hibbard, Scott and David Little (1997). *Islamic Activism and US Foreign Policy*. Washington, DC: US Institute of Peace Press.

Hunting Bin Laden (n.d.). *Frontline*. (Documentary.) At http://www.pbs.org/wgbh/pages/frontline/shows/binladen/ (accessed September 14, 2012).

Kelsay, John (2009). *Arguing the Just War in Islam*. Cambridge, MA: Harvard University Press.

Kepel, Gilles (2001). *Jihad: On the Trail of Political Islam*. Cambridge, MA: Harvard University Press.

Kepel, Gilles and Jean-Pierre Milelli (eds.) (2010). *Al-Qaeda in Its Own Words*. Cambridge, MA: Harvard University Press.

Krauthammer, Charles (2001, September 21). Voices of moral obtuseness. In Micah Sifry and Christopher Gerf (eds.), *The Iraq War Reader: History, Documents, Opinions*. New York, NY: Simon & Schuster, pp. 217–218.

Power of Nightmares. BBC documentary series. At http://www.archive.org/details/ThePowerOfNightmares (accessed September 22, 2012).

Sontag, Susan (2003). Reflections on September 11th. In Micah Sifry and Christopher Gerf (eds.), *The Iraq War Reader: History, Documents, Opinions*. New York, NY: Simon & Schuster, pp. 215–216.

Stories from the aftermath of infamy. *Face to Face*. At http://archive.itvs.org/facetoface/intro.html (accessed September 15, 2012).

Tessler, Mark (1997). The origins of popular support for Islamist movements: A political economy analysis. In John Entelis (ed.), *Islam, Democracy and the State in North Africa*. Bloomington, IN: University of Indiana Press, pp. 93–126.

Weaver, Mary Anne (1996, May). Blowback. Atlantic Monthly, 28, pp. 24–36.

Wright, Lawrence (2008, June 2). The rebellion within: An al-Qaeda mastermind questions terrorism. *The New Yorker*, pp. 37–56.

Conclusion
Image and Reality Reconsidered

Aminah Beverly McCloud, Scott W. Hibbard, and Laith Saud

The goal of this volume has been to provide an overview of the Islamic tradition that captures its diversity, debates, and regional differences. To this end, the editors are pleased to present a view of Islam in the 21st century that will give a nuanced perspective on its tradition to those who are engaging this world system for the first time as well as to those who have, until now, only looked at one region or another. Previous scholarship has worked diligently to provide gateways to the world of Islam, albeit from a particular perspective, theological or other. The editors of the present volume believe that investigating this world system from the vantage point of a multidisciplinary approach is a more effective – and ultimately more accurate – means of presenting Islam to a Western audience.

As noted in the Introduction, Islam and Muslim communities have been commonly portrayed as static and defined through an unchanging set of beliefs, which are supposed to transcend time and place. This view has been reinforced both by Western scholarship and by those traditionalists (and Islamists) who find that a literal reading of Islam is applicable today just as it was 500 years ago. All these scholars tend to present Islamic thought and action either by using the classical terminology of the medieval era or by describing Islam as invariably hostile to the ideals and values associated with the European Enlightenment. This latter presentation also assumes that Islam has a unique proclivity toward violence. What the previous chapters have sought to illustrate, however, is quite the opposite. Islam is a varied tradition, characterized by a diversity of views and practices. Although all Islamic thought is rooted in the basic concepts of *tawhīd* and justice, how these are interpreted and applied in practice varies dramatically across time and place. Moreover, it is clear that the violent stereotypes common in the Western media are simply unfounded. Muslims all over the world live in concert with members of other faith traditions

An Introduction to Islam in the 21st Century, First Edition. Edited by Aminah Beverly McCloud, Scott W. Hibbard, and Laith Saud.

and are, alternately, proponents of and protesters against the vagaries of the modern world in the same proportion as members of these other faiths are.

Islamic Thought and Practice

At the center of this volume is a coherent and cohesive narrative regarding the spectrum of thought that has molded Islamic thinking for 1,500 years. The glue that holds the tradition and the people together is the transcendent belief in the "oneness of God" (*tawhīd*). Muslims have almost always – since the inception of historical Islam – struggled with understanding the Qur'an and its commandments, along with its ethical guidance for achieving a healthy society. Muslim thought has not taken the path of modern Western thought, which has divided itself into disciplines and thus fractured (and factionalized) knowledge. Rather, in the Islamic tradition, knowledge has always been understood as holistic and its aspects are intimately interconnected. But this approach to belief and knowledge has helped create an image of Islamic thought as unable to compete with the disparate disciplinary views developed in the West. Our review of Islamic thought has attempted to provide a necessary corrective to such assumptions and stereotypes.

The origins of the modern Western critique of Islam go back to the 19th century. At that time, orientalist claims of "backwardness" and "barbarity" contributed to justifying the atrocities of colonialism and were a precursor to the biases toward Islam that are evident in contemporary politics. It was also during this period of European colonial rule that Western scholars (and rulers) started to consider the absence of economic and political development to be a byproduct of religion. From this perspective, modernity was construed as requiring the elimination of Islam and its practices; their central role in public life had to be abolished. This belief created the basis for embracing secularism and secularization – which at the time was depicted as a phenomenon distinct from Westernization. It should be noted that this bias against religion was not limited to Islam or to the Muslim world; it affected other traditions as well, including Hinduism in India, and even Christianity in Western Europe and North America.

Our chapters dealing with this wide set of issues and societal responses gleaned several distinct topics that retain a high degree of contemporary relevance. In almost all of the societies examined, those who felt that Islam was marginalized in favor of a secular political order were pitted against those who felt that tradition continued to hold too much sway over people's lives. In other words, those who embraced the latter position believed that the social revolutions of the 1950s and 1960s had not gone far enough in breaking the hold of religion on society and that religion ought to be relegated to the realm of private affairs, while those who took the former position believed that these same revolutions had already gone way too far. From the Islamist or traditionalist point of view, the separation of religion and politics and the division of life into personal and public spheres were entirely arbitrary processes and the result of an encroachment of the West upon traditional

Islam. And, while in places such as Turkey, Egypt, Algeria, Iraq, and other countries the secular experiment was fraught with political repression, countries that pursued a more traditionalist path faced their own challenges. States such as Saudi Arabia, Iran, and Pakistan sought to cultivate political unity through an emphasis on religious uniformity, as we have shown, but unfortunately they found that state promotion of religion generated its own ills. These states are all characterized by sectarian division and poor human rights records, and the promised unity they sought remains elusive.

The prognosis is still uncertain as to which ideology will win the hearts and minds of the people in these various societies, but all the indications are that there is a push toward a synthetic middle ground that can bridge these two extremes. Whatever the outcome, these debates reflect the ongoing struggle to reinterpret the Islamic tradition for the contemporary era. That these debates are unresolved should not be surprising, since they are current in other traditions as well, and have been so for many decades. Just as American politics remains mired in a set of culture wars, countries around the world continue to struggle with religion and politics. In short, how to reconcile the religious tradition with an ever-changing modern (and postmodern) world remains an ongoing challenge everywhere.

Islam's Regional Differences

As with other traditions, it is difficult to separate the history of Islam as a religion from the political events that have helped shape Islamic civilization. In the past two centuries, such events have included wars, colonial exploitation, the evolution of the modern nation-state, and the emerging dominance of an international economic order defined by neoliberal (that is, free-market capitalist) economic policies. These global trends, and the politics associated with them, have greatly shaped the various regions, countries, and populations discussed in this book. These trends have also had an enormous impact upon Islam, Islamic societies, and Western perceptions of the Islamic tradition.

Muslims in parts of Africa, for example, have been subject to brutal dictatorships and tribal antagonisms in the aftermath of equally brutal colonial occupations. This, coupled with droughts and the lack of infrastructure and economic enterprise, has precluded development and the formation of healthy communities. The 21st century forecasts even greater turmoil. The lack of funding for education, for basic infrastructure, and for job creation (particularly in private enterprises designed to provide employment outside the government) is just one of the factors contributing to a bleak future in the near term. Elections in countries such as Senegal and Gambia suggest the myriad problems facing Muslim societies in Africa. In Senegal the opposition party has won, but it continues to face long-standing (and apparently intractable) problems such as illiteracy, poor infrastructures in all major cities, and an increasingly radicalized young adult population without education and employment opportunities. Gambia's citizens often took the road of re-electing a problematic president, which seems to ensure more of the same problems and more of the same despair.

Muslims living in former Soviet states have found their revitalization efforts to be challenging. The Soviet destruction of houses of worship and schools, along with the killing of almost all the intellectual elite and the cutting of ties with the rest of the Muslim world, stunted growth and development in Islamic learning and normal Muslim community cohesion. On the other hand, many possibilities are created as Muslims incorporate their rediscovered Islamic heritage into pre-existing patterns of societal order. In Malaysia and Indonesia Muslims have experienced the effects of waves of colonization, but their pluralist heritage has helped them cope with the various issues raised by the restructuring of political and social life after independence.

The role of Muslims in South and East Asia is particularly poignant for this volume. One the one hand, that is where the demographic weight of the world's Muslim community is to be found. As noted in Chapter 10, one third of the entire Muslim population resides in Pakistan, India, Bangladesh, and Sri Lanka. Add to this the populations of Indonesia and Malaysia, and a very different picture of Islam emerges from the one typically held in the West – which is that of a population centered in the Middle East. On the other hand, the South Asian influence on the Islamic tradition could not be more obvious. As argued in the earlier chapters, the sheer diversity of this population – ethnic, ideological, cultural, and political – has fostered a vibrant, inclusive, and varied tradition. Perhaps more to the point, the South Asian experience of Islam can offer an example to other countries in their efforts to cope with the challenges of diversity inherent in modern society.

Similarly, as noted in Chapter 11, Muslims in Malaysia and Indonesia have had to come to terms with multicultural and multi-religious communities, all the while cautiously engaging a globalized economy that is keen to exploit their natural resources. It was the region's abundance that first attracted the European powers there and provided the impetus for the development of the vast infrastructures needed to extract the region's raw materials and to transport them to other parts of the world. Post-independence governments were greatly influenced by the colonial legacy and have continued to integrate their economies into the international capitalist order. However, in regard to the social aspects of the post-independence period, both the Sukarno and Suharto regimes consciously sought to promote a more inclusive and tolerant interpretation of religion in public life. They subsequently engaged the educational and state organizations to achieve this end. Although recent climatic changes have increased the number and ferocity of tsunamis and earthquakes – and thus have created a new set of regional challenges – the religious health of these Southeast Asian countries is quite positive. As happened among all Muslims living in postcolonial societies, the attempts to relegate Islam to the margins of social life have resulted, ironically, in a revitalization of the religion and in conscious efforts to reconnect with the Islamic heritage, while each group acknowledges its own societal pecularities.

Muslims living in Latin and South America have a history that in some ways mimics that of early Muslim communities in Western nations. Initially there were migrants from the Iberian Peninsula, indentured Indian Muslims whom the British brought as workers, and Muslim migrants and refugees from the Arab countries of Palestine, Lebanon, and Syria. To this eclectic mix are added Latin American converts. Muslim populations in this part of the world are given even less attention than those of the former Soviet Republics. Our initial incursion has found that Islam played and continues to play a role there – albeit a small one – in defining the contours of society through civic practices, creole ideologies, and counter-terrorism politics. This region gives us an important lens through which to view the framing of Islamic world politics and the counter-terrorism logics that threaten to upend the politics of affected societies, as John Karam has demonstrated in Chapter 13. Despite their vast array of interactions and their clear engagement in all things modern all over the globe, Muslims in the West remain enigmatic and are stereotyped as hopelessly violent and unable to live in the modern world.

Finally, the challenges faced by Muslim minorities living in the United States and Europe reflect to some degree the challenges of any other minority community. To what extent can one integrate into the mainstream population, and to what extent ought one to do so? On the one hand, there is the understandable desire to retain one's own cultural identity. On the other hand, there will always be some resistance from members of the dominant population, who will limit the degree to which a minority group can be assimilated. Moreover, for Muslims living in the West, these challenges are complicated by history. As suggested in Chapter 8, some of the angst felt by Muslims and non-Muslims in the West stems from a series of antagonisms that go back over a millennium. Part of the problem resides in the refusal of some Western scholars to grasp the complexity of the Islamic experience, and in their determination to presume that Islam represents some kind of threat to Christian (and Western) hegemony. This presumption, many contemporary scholars assert, began before the first Crusade and continues into its present in the form of the war on terrorism. The most remarkable attributes of this anti-Islam discourse are its ignorance of the diversity of tradition and its unwillingness to move beyond misleading stereotypes.

Islam in the 21st Century

Any introduction to the study of Islam in the 21st century would be remiss if it omitted an insightful examination of the political and economic climate in which we all live today. The events surrounding 9/11, the 2003 invasion of Iraq, and America's long military involvement in Afghanistan and other countries in the region have all colored Western views of Islam (as well as Muslim views of the West). This is evident in the classroom and in the way Islam is taught in the post-9/11 period. It is also evident in the media and in political discourse. Our brief, yet thorough examination of this climate has sought to provide readers with an unflinching and provocative narrative of the various interpretations of the concerns surrounding secularization, modernity, and the politicization of religion. We found that, just as there are protests in the United States against the ill-effects of economic globalization and unresponsive government, there have been similar protests in Muslim societies against the tyranny of an unresponsive political order. While this trend emerged with an "Islamist face" in the 1990s, it was similarly evident in the events of the so-called "Arab Spring" of 2011.

Islamophobia, terrorism, the treatment of these issues in the Western media, and the ecology of relations between Muslims and their neighbors in the West are topics of pressing concern. While all of these relationships have come to be seen as problematic and even toxic, the final group of chapters in the volume are intent on reminding readers that many of these conflicts are artificial and obscure the common humanity that underlies our shared experiences on this planet. Of course, the Islamophobia of the past decade draws upon a long historical narrative, but we must remember that this is an artificially constructed and selectively interpreted history. Or, to use the prosaic words of Eric Hobsbawm (2000), this history reflects the conscious construction, or invention, of tradition – one that relies heavily upon the assistance of technology and media to further its cause. Moreover, as argued in Chapter 15, the problem has less to do with Islam than with the conscious distortion of the Islamic tradition for political gain. This distortion serves neither an educational nor a socially useful purpose, even if it serves narrow political interests. Our concern is that such parochialism is harmful to social relations both within the West and abroad.

It is the hope of the editors of this volume that the contributions offered here provide an accurate, comprehensive, and nuanced introduction to Islam for the 21st century. To this end, we have tried to dispel misleading stereotypes and to depoliticize the study of Islam. Religion, we believe, should unite peoples, not divide them. Moreover, the real challenge for the next generation will be, not foreign armies (let alone people of different faiths!), but the common ills of poverty, disease and ignorance, and the malice of extremism. Insofar as we have been able to elevate the discussion about Islam and to encourage students – even to a small extent – to reflect upon the complexity of this tradition side by side with their own, we can consider this project a success.

Suggested Further Reading

Hobsbawm, Eric and Terence Ranger (eds.) (2000). *The Invention of Tradition*. New York, NY: Cambridge University Press.

Index

Page locators in *italic* type indicate illustrations.

An Introduction to Islam in the 21st Century, First Edition. Edited by Aminah Beverly McCloud,
Scott W. Hibbard, and Laith Saud.
© 2013 Blackwell Publishing Ltd. Published 2013 by Blackwell Publishing Ltd.

CPSIA information can be obtained
at www.ICGtesting.com
Printed in the USA
JSHW011212140822
28879JS00003B/10

9 781405 193610